Choice in Language

Functional Linguistics
Series Editor: Robin Fawcett, Cardiff University

This series publishes monographs that seek to understand the nature of language by exploring one or other of various cognitive models or in terms of the communicative use of language. It concentrates on studies that are in, or on the borders of, various functional theories of language.

Published:

Functional Dimensions of Ape-Human Discourse
Edited by James D. Benson and William S. Greaves

System and Corpus: Exploring Connections
Edited by Geoff Thompson and Susan Hunston

Meaningful Arrangement: Exploring the Syntactic Description of Texts
Edward McDonald

Explorations in Stylistics
Andrew Goatly

From Language to Multimodality: New Developments in the Study of Ideational Meaning
Edited by Carys Jones and Eija Ventola

Text Type and Texture
Edited by Gail Forey and Geoff Thompson

An Introduction to the Grammar of Old English: A Systemic Functional Approach
Michael Cummings

Morphosyntactic Alternations in English: Functional and Cognitive Perspectives
Edited by Pilar Guerrero Medina

Reading Visual Narratives: Image Analysis of Children's Picture Books
Clare Painter, J. R. Martin and Len Unsworth

Systemic Functional Perspectives of Japanese: Descriptions and Applications
Edited by Elizabeth A. Thomson and William S. Armour

Choice in Language: Applications in Text Analysis
Edited by Gerard O'Grady, Tom Bartlett and Lise Fontaine

Choice in Language
Applications in Text Analysis

Edited by
Gerard O'Grady, Tom Bartlett and Lise Fontaine

SHEFFIELD UK   BRISTOL CT

Published by Equinox Publishing Ltd.

UK: Unit S3, Kelham House, 3 Lancaster Street, Sheffield S3 8AF
USA: ISD, 70 Enterprise Drive, Bristol, CT 06010

www.equinoxpub.com

First published 2013

ISBN-13   978 1 908049 54 4   (hardback)
          978 1 908049 55 1   (paperback)

British Library Cataloguing-in-Publication Data
A catalogue record for this book is available from the British Library.

Library of Congress Cataloging-in-Publication Data
Choice in language : applications in text analysis \ Edited By Gerard O'Grady, Tom Bartlett and Lise Fontaine.
    pages cm—(Functional Linguistics)
  Includes bibliographical references and index.
  ISBN 978-1-908049-54-4 (hb)—ISBN 978-1-908049-55-1 (pb)
  1. Applied linguistics—Methodology. 2. Functionalism (Linguistics) 3. Critical discourse analysis—Methodology. 4. Sociolinguistics—Methodology. I. O'Grady, Gerard, editor of compilation.
  P129.C53 2013
  410.1'8—dc23
                        2013000309

Typeset by S.J.I. Services, New Delhi
Printed and bound in Great Britain by Lightning Source UK Ltd, Milton Keynes, and in the US by Lightning Source Inc., La Vergne, TN

Contents

Introduction

Gerard O'Grady[a]

1   Introduction

Within systemic functional linguistics (SFL) the notion of choice provides a constant underlying theme to work, whether this is concerned with in-depth description of the system of lexicogrammatical choices available within specific languages, or with the analysis of the semiotic and/or social implications of the choices taken within specific texts. This chapter aims to contextualize the following chapters by sketching the relationship between SFL and choice (in §2). §3 provides a quick sketch of the revolutionary idea underpinning SFL, namely that once language is modelled with paradigmatic primacy three independent clusters of interdependent meanings emerge (Halliday, 1967a, 1968; Halliday and Matthiessen, 2004). The three parameters of context – Field, Tenor and Mode – will be described and their relationship with the three metafunctions outlined. §3 also contains a brief introduction to Appraisal theory. Readers who are familiar with the basics of SFL theory are invited to skip this section. §4 sketches the strength of SFL as a theory of applicable linguistics (Halliday, 1985; Mahboob and Knight, 2010). Finally §5 shows how and why the present volume is organized as it is.

2   Systemic functional linguistics and choice

Systemic functional linguistics according to Halliday (2009: 63) is 'a variety of system – structure theory'. Unlike generative approaches to language it

---

a   Gerard O'Grady lectures at the Centre for Language and Communication Research in Cardiff University. His chief research interests are critical discourse analysis, SFL – especially in investigating connections between intonation and the lexicogrammar, examining differences between language as process and product, and examining how spoken discourse unfolds and creates meaning in real time. He is the author of *A Grammar of Spoken English Discourse* and *Key Concepts in Phonetics and Phonology*.

describes language in terms which de Saussure (1959) labelled syntagmatic, and associative or paradigmatic relations. Since the inception of the theory, SFL has been a theory of choice, with paradigmatic choices having primacy over syntagmatic ones. Most grammatical theories, as Halliday (2009: 63) noted, have tended to downgrade or ignore the paradigmatic axis; for such theories the notion of choice is redundant. In SFL the system or paradigmatic axis is given priority in the sense that system is considered to be more abstract than structure. Systemic choices are realized in terms of structure.

SFL views language as a dynamic social semiotic which, like other semiotic systems, serves as a systemic resource for making and exchanging meanings (Webster, 2009). The system represents the overall meaning potential found within language. Figure 1 illustrates this using a simplified network representation of the English MOOD system.

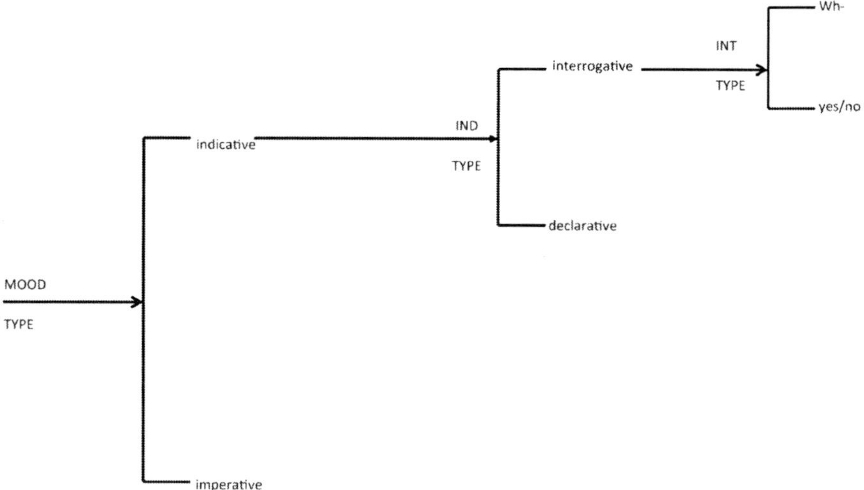

Figure 1 The English MOOD system.

In a system network such as that represented in Figure 1, the speaker enters the network on the left-hand side at the level of primary delicacy. Each subsequent systemic choice represents a more delicate meaning. A speaker wishing to produce a wh- question has a choice at the primary level of delicacy between indicative and imperative. At the secondary level of delicacy the speaker has the choice between the indicative types interrogative and declarative. At the tertiary level of delicacy the speaker has the choice between the interrogative types wh- and yes/no. In the

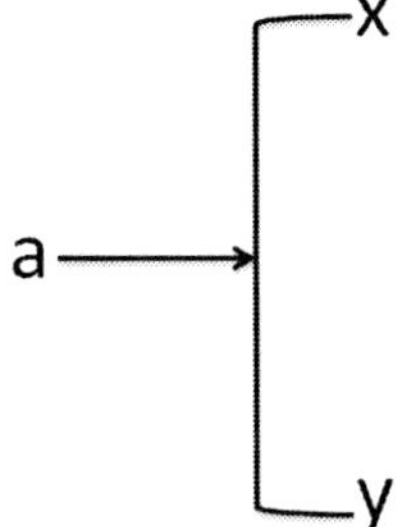

Figure 2 Either/or choice.

example above the system network has been presented as a series of either/or choices notated as shown in Figure 2.

With entry condition 'a' the speaker has the choice of either x or y. Yet not all choices in the network are either/or. The use of curly brackets represents a simultaneous choice.

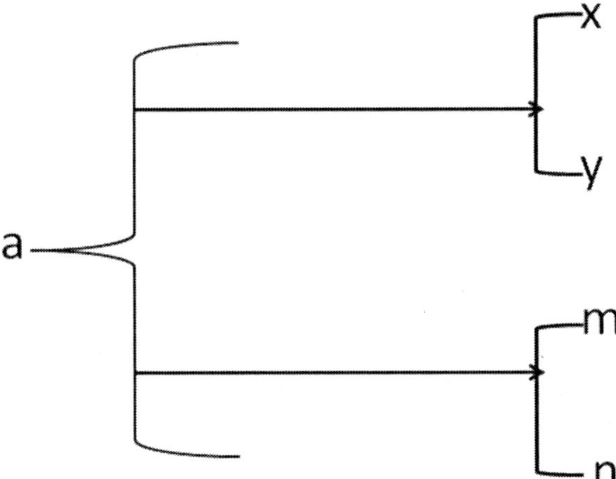

Figure 3 Simultaneous choice.

Figure 3 is read as follows: there are two systems, one containing the features x/y and the other m/n, which both have the same entry condition. In other words once a is chosen the speaker must simultaneously choose either x or y and m or n. Figure 4 presents a simplified version of a system network with a clause as point of entry.

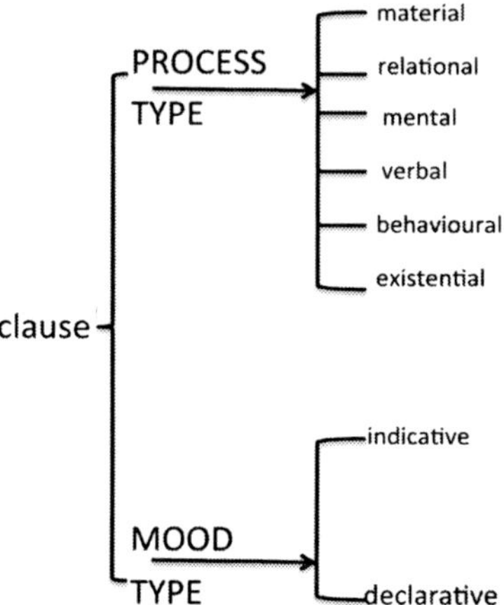

Figure 4 Process types.

Once a speaker chooses to produce a clause he/she must simultaneously choose both a MOOD and a PROCESS TYPE. The MOOD and PROCESS TYPES represent independent choices and the speaker may produce a clause containing any combination of PROCESS and MOOD TYPE. Yet, in practice, this is somewhat of a simplification as both contextual factors and more primary choices may influence (or even constrain) more delicate choices. Choices earlier in the network increase or decrease the probabilities of choices later in the network. For instance Matthiessen (1995: 151–2) notes that the three primary choices within the system of expansion are not 'equi-probable'. Tucker (2006: 98–100), recognizing that large scale corpus-driven studies have shown that lexical and grammatical patterning is 'far from what might be expected with unrestricted selection', postulates what he describes as 'a pre-selected path' through the systems network. In other words certain options are frequently adopted in the realizing of certain meanings and the more frequently the options are realized, the more probable it is that they will be realized in the future. Thus, Tucker represents a system network, as in Figure 5, with the particular set of choices most frequently taken being the particular set of choices which are most likely to be taken. While speakers, in principle, are able to avail themselves of all of the choices set out in Figure 5, in practice, their choices will be influenced by the particular set of choices which are most commonly realized within the language. The higher the frequency in which a particular set of choices has occurred, the higher the probability that it will reoccur. The pathway notated in bold in Figure 5 represents the most probable particular set of choices taken by speakers.

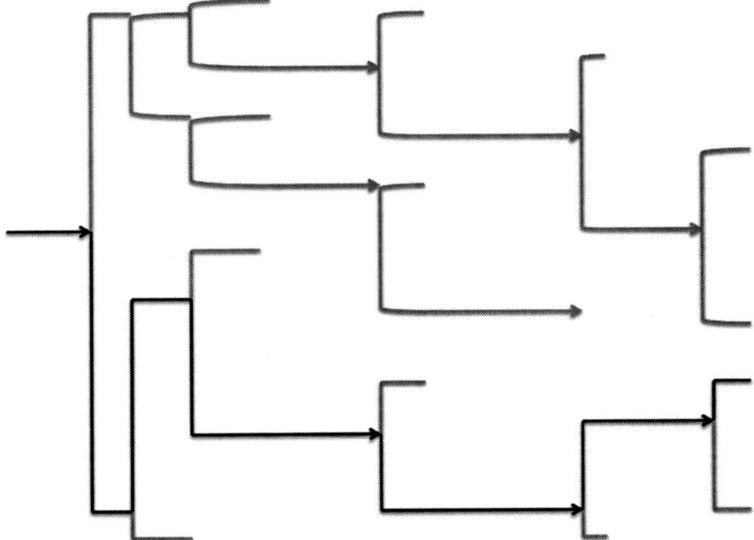

Figure 5 A pre-selected path through a network.

3   What is systemic functional linguistics?

Language according to the SFL view is organized as a series of hierarchically organized strata: which from top to bottom are lexicogrammar, phonology (or in written language graphology) and phonetics. Context is a higher order semiotic system which is above the linguistic system. SFL recognizes three parameters of context namely Field, Tenor and Mode. Halliday (1978: 62) and Halliday and Hasan (1989: 12) define the terms as follows. Field refers to the ongoing activity which is happening, and the particular purposes that the use of language is serving within the context of the activity. Tenor refers to the nature of the interrelations occurring between the participants in terms of their status and their roles. Mode refers to the part which language is playing which includes the symbolic organization of the text and whether or not the language is primarily spoken or written. Halliday and Hasan (*ibid.*: 45–6) note that text and the context of situation are interrelated – with Field realized through the Ideational metafunction, Tenor realized through the Interpersonal metafunction and Mode realized through the Textual metafunction.

Contextual choices are realized by semantic choices which are themselves realized by choices in the lexicogrammar. Lexicogrammar choices are realized by choices in the phonology which are themselves realized by choices in phonetics. Each stratum is itself organized in terms of rank and axis. Elements of a higher rank are composed of units of a lower rank, clauses are composed of groups which are composed of words which are composed of morphemes. In the phonological stratum the rank scale is tone unit (or group) foot, syllable and phoneme. Clauses are realized in the phonological stratum as tone units, though there is not necessarily a one-to-one correspondence between clauses and tone units. Yet, as well as being organized stratally, language is simultaneously organized axially with paradigmatic choices realized as syntagmatic patterns. As noted in §1 paradigmatic choices result in three relatively independent metafunctions: Ideational, Interpersonal and Textual. Matthiessen, Teruya and Lam (2010: 173) note that outside of SFL Ideational meaning is often treated as semantics while Interpersonal and Textual meanings are often treated as pragmatics.

3.1   The Ideational metafunction

The Ideational metafunction contains two types of meaning: logical and experiential. Logical meaning refers to the relationship between units contained within a larger complex. For instance, the clauses within clause complexes may have equal status (be in a paratactic relationship) as in (1) or have an unequal status (be in a hypotactic relationship) as in (2):

(1)   Mary is going to the bank and || John is going to the shop
          1   2

(2)   If Mary goes to the bank || John can go to the shop
          β   α

In (1) the two clauses within the clause complex would have realized independent clauses had they not been joined by the linker *and*. In (2) the first clause (notated by β) is subordinate to the second clause (notated by α).[1] In SFL notation paratactic sequences are numbered while hypotactic ones are notated by the use of the Greek alphabet. As paratactic clauses are coordinate, the numbering (1, 2, etc.) simply refers to the order in which the clauses were produced. In the notation of hypotactic clause sequences, however, α indicates a clause which could have stood on its own. It is the clause which functions as the head of the complex. Clause complexes may enter into two types of relationship; namely that of projection and that of expansion. Figure 6 diagrams the system of clause complex relations.

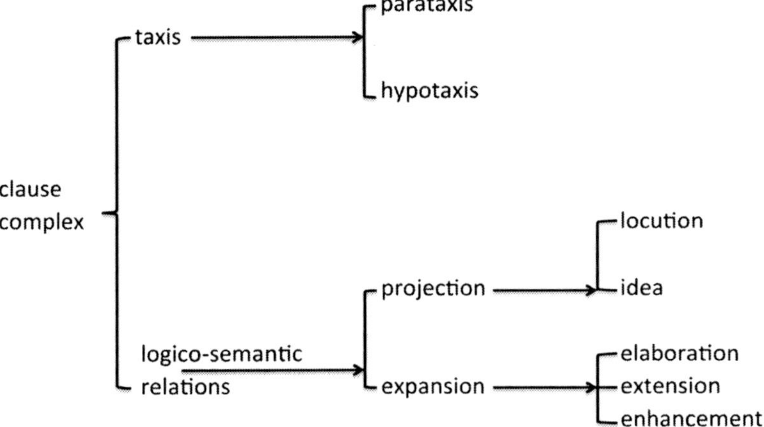

Figure 6 System of clause complex relations.

Speakers simultaneously choose from two systems, the first taxis, the second logico-semantic relations; with any combination from the two systems possible. The system of projection consists of two further choices, idea (notated by ') and locution (notated by "), which are illustrated in examples (3) and (4).

(3a)   I believe || John died yesterday
       α   'β

(3b)   Who died yesterday || I wondered
      '1   2

(4a)   She said || that John had died the previous day
      α   "β

(4b)   "John died yesterday" || she said
     "1   2

The system of expansion consists of three further choices. The first of which is elaboration (notated by =) which is a relation of equivalence or restatement:

(5a)   She would complete her painting || by framing it
      α   =β

(5b)   She would complete her painting; || she would frame it
     1   =2

The second choice is extension (notated by +) which is a relation of addition:

(6a)   As well as going to the bank || Mary went to the shop
         $^{+}\beta$ α

(6b)   Mary went to the bank || and to the shop
         1                              $^{+}2$

The final choice is enhancement (notated by ^{x}) which is a relation of development:

(7a)   If John goes to the bank || Mary will go to the shop
         $^{x}\beta$ α

(7b)   Mary was due to go to the shop || so John went to the bank
         1 $^{x}2$

Readers who are interested in a fuller description of the logico-semantic metafunction are invited to refer to Eggins (2004: ch. 9) and Halliday and Matthiessen (2004: ch. 7).

The other strand of meaning within the Ideational metafunction is the experiential metafunction which is the resource people use to construe the world around them. It operates at clause level. Clauses represent the world as figures of happening, doing, sensing, saying, being or having. Halliday and Matthiessen (2004: 169) note that experientially a clause construes a quantum of change as a configuration of a process, attendant participants and optional circumstantial elements. Processes are typically realized by verbal groups, the participants by a nominal group and the circumstances by an adverbial group or a prepositional phrase. Table 1 presents some illustrative examples while Figure 7, adapted from Halliday and Matthiessen (2004: 173, Fig. 5-3), diagrams the systemic possibilities. The numbers cross-referenced between Table 1 and Figure 7 refer to the example clauses in Table 1 and the systemic choices in Figure 7. Processes are italicized, participants underlined and circumstantial elements presented in small capitals.

Halliday (2003: 21–2) uses the term grammatical metaphor to label instances where a meaning which is typically construed by one kind

Table 1 Examples of the six English process types.

1.	<u>A hunter</u> *is chasing* <u>a lion</u> ACROSS THE MOUNTAIN.
2.	<u>The boss</u> *recognizes* <u>the issue</u>.
3a.	<u>Mary</u> *is* <u>an intelligent woman</u>.
3b.	<u>John</u> *is* <u>the best footballer</u> IN HIS YEAR.
4.	*Did* <u>they</u> *tell* <u>you</u> <u>a story</u>?
5.	<u>He</u> *is dancing* BEAUTIFULLY.
6.	THERE *is* <u>a new shop</u> ON THE CORNER.

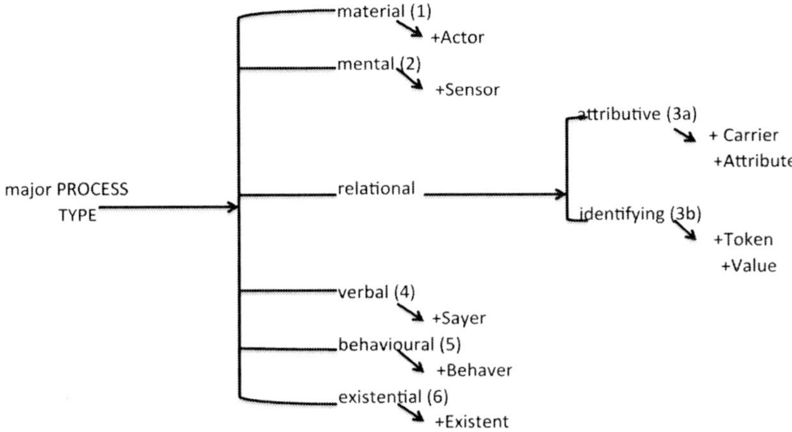

Figure 7 TRANSITIVITY represented as systems network.

of wording is instead realized by another. He notes that grammatical metaphor is common in the language of scientific discourse (Halliday and Martin, 1993: ch. 4; Halliday, 2004: ch. 7), though as example (8) illustrates grammatical metaphor is not confined to scientific discourse.

(8)   He *played* BADLY | they *lost* the match → His bad play *lost* them the match

The Material process 'play' has been reconstrued as a thing in a nominal group which functions as the Actor participant in a Material process. The adverb 'badly' which functioned as a quality has been reconstrued by the adjective 'bad' which functions as the epithet of the nominal group. The pronoun 'he', which functioned as an Actor in a Material process, has been reconstrued as a deictic within the nominal group. The meaning has shifted from two paratactic clauses encoding a sequence of events: (a) something happened and (b) this something resulted in something else, to a single clause which encodes a relationship between two things. Readers interested in fuller details of the grammatical metaphor and how it construes meaning should refer to Halliday and Matthiessen (1999: ch. 6).

3.2   The Interpersonal metafunction

The Interpersonal metafunction organizes language as a resource for enacting meaning between interlocutors. It is the grammatical resource for enacting social relations. The clause functions as a unit of exchange within an interaction. The system of MOOD, diagrammed above in Figure 1, is the grammatical resource for realizing an interactive move in discourse. Table 2 illustrates some examples of MOOD choices in English.

Table 2 Examples of MOOD choices in English.

Example	*MOOD*
The politician kissed the baby	indicative: declarative
Who did the politician kiss? Who kissed the baby?	indicative: interrogative/Wh
Did the politician kiss the baby?	indicative: interrogative/yes-no
Kiss the baby!	Imperative.

As dialogue is an interactive activity in which people give and demand things from their interlocutors SFL recognizes that the most fundamental type of speech roles are (a) giving and (b) demanding. These notions are more complex than the terms indicate and include the notions 'inviting to receive' and 'inviting to give'. The thing which can be given or demanded can be either a physical commodity or information. Figure 8 diagrams the systemic possibilities.

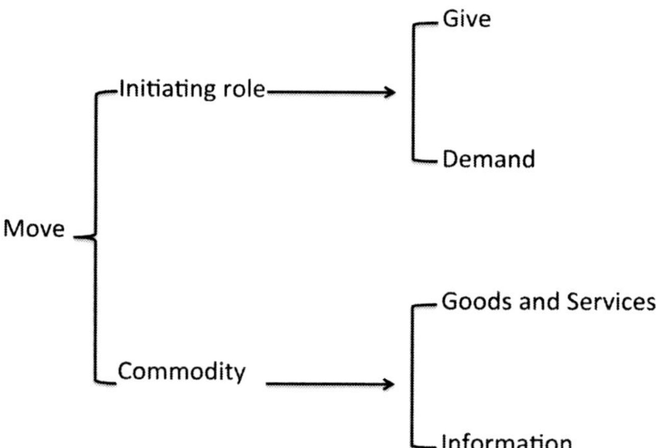

Figure 8 The system of speech function.

Table 3 Illustrative examples of initiating Giving and Demanding moves.

	Good and Services (i)	*Information (ii)*
Give	I will pass you the newspaper (offer – proposal) Shall I pass you the newspaper (offer – proposal)	He is passing her the newspaper (statement – proposition)
Demand	Could you pass me the newspaper? (command – proposal) Pass me the newspaper! (command – proposal)	Is he passing her the newspaper? (Question/yes-no – proposition) What is he passing her? (Question/wh – proposition)

Initiating speakers can grade their proposition on a cline between positive (it is 100 per cent so) and negative (it isn't so, or it is 0 per cent so) through their choices from the system of modality which represents the intermediate choices encoded in the language between yes and no. In a proposal there are two types of intermediate possibilities: degrees of probability and degrees of usuality. These are collectively known as Modalization. In a proposition the type of intermediate possibility is dependent on the speech role. In a command the intermediate possibilities represent degrees of obligation while in an offer they represent degrees of inclination. These are collectively known as Modulation (Halliday and Matthiessen, 2004: 147). Figure 9 diagrams the systemic possibilities.

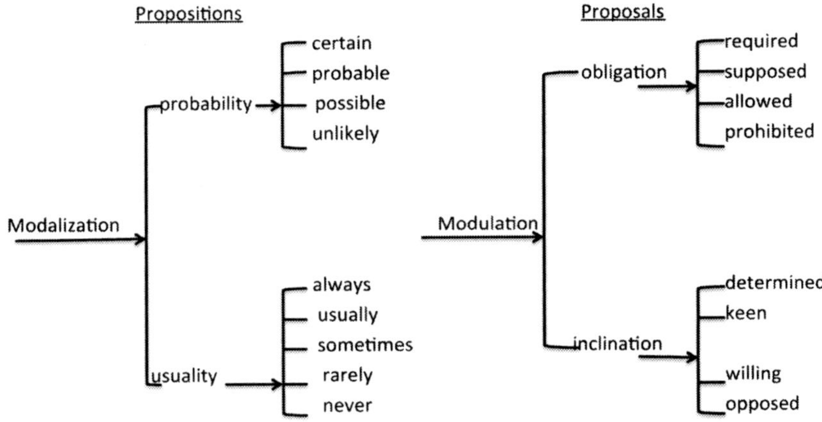

Figure 9 The systems of Modality.

Modulation and Modalization as Table 4 illustrates are typically realized within the clause by Mood adjuncts.

Table 4 Some illustrative examples of Modulation and Modalization.

MODALIZATION	*MODULATION*
Probability	Obligation
That must be so/That's certainly so.	He must do it.
That will be so/That's probably so.	He will do it.
That may be so/That's possibly so.	He may do it.
That might be so.	He might do it.
Usuality	Inclination
He always does it.	He is determined to go.
He usually does it.	He is keen to go.
He sometimes does it.	He is willing to go.
He rarely does it.	He won't go.
He never does it.	

Speakers may incongruently realize Modalization and Modulation outside the clause by choosing either an explicit or implicit source. Examples (9) to (12) illustrate incongruent realizations of high probability, high usuality, high obligation and high inclination respectively. Readers who are interested in a full account should consult Halliday and Matthiessen (2004: 616–25).

(9)   I am sure that it is so (explicit).
(10)   He will do it (implicit).
(11)   It is expected that he does it (explicit). He is supposed to do it (implicit).
(12)   He promises that he will go (explicit).

SFL uniquely incorporates intonation within the grammar. Interpersonally the combination of MOOD and tone choice realizes a speech function. For instance the co-occurrence of declarative mood and falling tone signals a neutral statement while the co-occurrence of declarative mood and rising tone signals a querying statement. More delicate options are realized by the co-occurrence of secondary tones and MOOD. For instance the co-occurrence of declarative MOOD with a wide fall signals strong commitment while a narrow fall signals mild commitment. Halliday (1967b), Halliday and Greaves (2008) and Tench (1996) provide detailed accounts of how intonation functions as an Interpersonal resource.

3.2.1 Appraisal theory

Since the 1990s much work has been carried out within SFL on explicating the subjective presence of speakers within texts. It has focused on how they adopt stances towards the messages which they are communicating and towards the people with whom they are communicating. This work is collectively known as Appraisal theory and the key publications which the following paragraphs draw from are Eggins and Slade (1997), Martin and Rose (2003) and Martin and White (2005). Figure 10, which is based on Martin and White (2005: 38), diagrams the primary appraisal options.

Three systems are entered simultaneously. The first system which will be sketched here is that of engagement, which Martin and White (2005: 92) state 'is concerned with the linguistic resources by which speakers/ writers adopt a stance towards the value positions being referenced by the text and with respect to those they address'. Figure 11 diagrams the Engagement system. Speakers/writers encode their value position as one that can be presupposed or challenged by a particular audience.

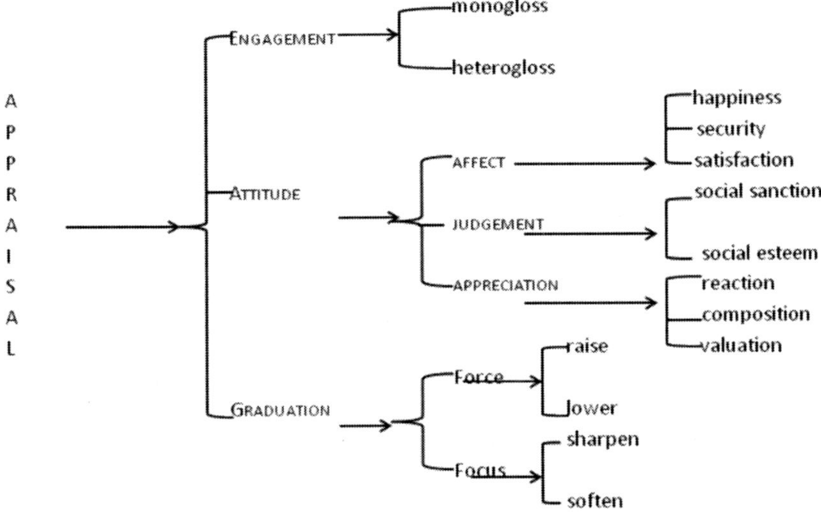

Figure 10 The systems of Appraisal.

Monoglossic contributions close discussion by failing to recognize any notional diaglostic alternatives. Hetroglossic contributions notionally allow for other diaglostic alternatives. The presupposed nature of **monogloss** is illustrated by the following example: *John's stupidity lost us the match.* The speaker presents it as taken for granted that John was stupid and that without John's stupidity the match would not have been lost. By contrast, hetroglossic utterances make room for diaglostic alternatives by either contracting or expanding the dialogue. **Contract** allows for two further choices: **proclaim** and **disclaim**. There are three choices within proclaim, the first of these is **endorse** which refers to wordings sourced to external sources which are construed by the speaker as 'correct, valid, undeniable or otherwise maximally warrantable', (Martin and White, 2005: 126). Wordings such as *show, illustrate, demonstrate, prove, confirm* and *substantiate* align the speaker/writer with an external voice. An example is: *The report shows that John's stupidity lost us the match.* The second choice is **pronounce** which involves speaker emphasis or an active speaker intervention into the discourse (*ibid.*: 127). For instance: *It is my considered opinion that John's stupidity lost us the match.* The final choice is **concur** which involves wordings which 'overtly announce the addresser as agreeing with, or having the same knowledge' as the hearer. An example is: *As you know John's stupidity lost us the match.* While dialogic contraction notionally allows for other diaglostic alternatives it functions like **monogloss** to close discussion down.

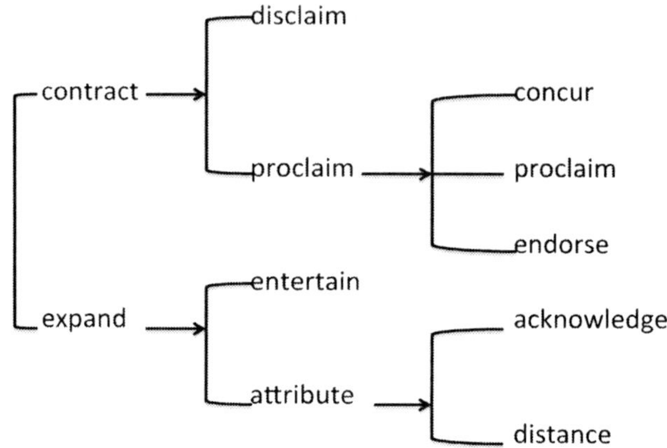

Figure 11 Engagement abridged.

Dialogic expansion by contrast functions to open up the discussion. Speakers have the option of choosing **entertain** or **attribute** (*ibid.*: 117). The term entertain refers to instances where speakers choose a wording which indicates that their position is one of a number of possible positions, e.g. *John's stupidity possibly lost us the match.* Attribute refers to speakers opening up the dialogic space by making space for alternate positions in their evaluation of a proposition. Attribution may be realized by verbal or mental projection and the source of the attribution is an external voice. For instance, *The chairman said/thinks that John's stupidity lost us the match.* Within Attribute there are two further choices **acknowledge** and **distance**. Acknowledge refers to wordings where there is no overt indication as to where the speaker stands as regards the proposition, e.g. *The chairman says that John's stupidity lost us the match.* Distance refers to wordings where speakers explicitly distance themselves from the proposition expressed by the external voice. It is most frequently realized by means of the reporting verb *claim*, e.g. *The chairman claims that John's stupidity lost us the match.* The hearer must explore the co-text in order to understand whether the speaker is aligned with the quoted source (*ibid.*: 112–13).

The second system to be sketched here is that of Attitude which codes tokens as positive or negative. It involves 'three semantic regions involving what is traditionally referred to as emotions, ethics and aesthetics' (*ibid.*: 42). Affect, Judgement and Appreciation are generally lexicogrammatically distinctive but there will be instances where the differences between the three types of Attitude are underspecified. Martin and White (*ibid.*: 45) state that Affect is the heart of the Attitude systems with Judgement and Appreciation representing 'institutionalized feelings'. Judgement recasts feelings as rules and regulations in a system administered by a sanctioning body. Appreciation recasts feelings as propositions about values in a system of socially sanctioned awards. Attitudes are distributed prosodically throughout a text and are gradable. Attitudes may be inscribed by the speakers' lexicogrammatical choices or invoked by the build up of prosody across the discourse. This necessarily not only introduces a measure of subjectivity into the analysis but also allows for the double coding of some items. For instance in the example *John's stupidity lost us the match* the clause is coded simultaneously as negative Affect and negative Judgement.

The Affect system is concerned with registering positive and negative feelings and it groups feelings into three clusters of meaning. The first type of meaning is un/happiness which involves the moods of feelings and is realized by wordings such as *misery, whimper, miserable, cheerful, chuckle* and *jubilant*. The second is in/security which involves the emotions concerned with peace and anxiety in relation to the eco-social environment and is realized by wordings such as *anxious, uneasy, assured, comfortable* and *startled*. The final type of meaning is dis/satisfaction which involves the emotions concerned with the achievement of goals and is realized by wordings such as *frustration, satisfied, scold, praise* and *impressed*.

The Judgement system is concerned with attitudes towards behaviour in terms of social esteem or social sanction. Judgements related to social esteem refer to the normality, tenacity and capacity of an action. Martin and White (2005: 53) state that these categories of meaning are probed by the following questions respectively: How special is the person? How dependable is the person? How capable is the person? Social sanction refers to more serious judgements[2] which refer to veracity and propriety. These meanings are probed by the following questions: How honest or truthful is the person? How far beyond reproach is the person?

The Appreciation system is concerned with meanings which evaluate phenomena aesthetically either in subjective or objective terms. It is classified into three subtypes: reaction, composition and valuation. These three subtypes are probed by the following questions respectively (*ibid.*: 56). Did the phenomena grab me or did I like it? Did the phenomena hang together or was it coherent for me? Was the phenomenon worthwhile for me? These different types of Appreciation, as shown in Table 5, may be realized either by a group or a relational or mental clause.

Table 5 Appreciation realized as group and clause.

	CLAUSE
Reaction	His guitar playing is impressive. (Relational)
	I like his guitar playing. (Mental)
Composition	The writing was lucid. (Relational)
Valuation	That was an exceptional goal. (Relational)
	GROUP
Reaction	His impressive guitar playing ...
Composition	Her lucid writing ...
Valuation	That exceptional goal ...

The final Appraisal system is Graduation which is the resource for up-scaling or down-scaling an evaluation. Evaluations are scaled across two axes. The first, labelled Force, refers to intensity or amount; the second, labelled Focus, refers to the prototypicality of the evaluation (*ibid.*: 136). Table 6 illustrates this.

Table 6 Some examples of Graduation.

Force

John's <u>complete and utter</u> stupidity lost them the contract. (Up-scale)

It was <u>sort of</u> stupid of John to lose them the contract. (Down-scale)

The writing was <u>highly</u> lucid. (Up-scale)

The writing was <u>kind of</u> lucid. (Down-scale)

It was <u>terribly</u> funny. (Up-scale)

It was a <u>little</u> funny. (Down-scale)

Her rationale was <u>crystal</u> clear. (Up-scale)

Her rationale was <u>partly</u> clear. (Down-scale)

Focus

It was a <u>genuine</u> antique. (Up-scale)

It was <u>sort of</u> an antique. (Down-scale)

The lad is a <u>real</u> talent. (Up-scale)

The lad is <u>a bit of</u> a talent. (Down-scale)

He's is a <u>complete</u> miser. (Up-scale)

He's <u>a kind of</u> a miser. (Down-scale)

Force interacts with Attitude to turn up or reduce the volume of an evaluation. Up-scaling construes the speaker as being maximally committed to the evaluation while down-scaling construes the speaker as being only partly affiliated to the evaluation (*ibid.*: 153). An up-scaled focus indicates the maximal investment by the speaker/writer in the value position and attempts to strongly align the hearer/reader with the value position being expressed. A down-scaled focus on a negative value is a conciliatory solidarity maintaining gesture towards those who hold opposing views.

A down-scaled focus on a positive value represents a softening of an assessment which is construed as being in some way problematic for the hearer/reader (*ibid.*: 139–40).

3.3   The Textual metafunction

The third metafunction in SFL is the Textual metafunction, which enables the presentation of Ideational and Interpersonal meanings as a flow of information unfolding within a contextually bound text. There are two systems within the Textual metafunction: Theme, which organizes the clause as a message; and Information, which is concerned with the assignment of Given and New information within the information unit. Martin and Rose (2003: 177–9) note that discourse creates expectations which flag what is to come and consolidates them by summarizing what has been relayed. This results in discourse having a wave like form with peaks of greater informational prominence separated by troughs of lesser informational prominence. Within a clause there are two peaks of prominence: one at the beginning and one at the end. The Textual prominence at the beginning of the clause is the Theme, the point of departure in the process of interpreting the clause. The Rheme is the portion of the clause which is not Theme. In English according to Halliday (1967a, 1968) the Theme is completed by the Topical Theme which is the first element of transitivity, i.e. participant, circumstance or process.[3] In addition there may be optional Textual and Interpersonal Themes preceding the Topical one. Examples (13) to (15) illustrate this:

(13)

But	Mary maybe	he	will come after all
Textual	Interpersonal	Topical	
Theme			Rheme

(14)

Oh baby	don't cry	for the good old days
Interpersonal	Topical	
Theme		Rheme

(15)

On the other hand	perhaps	their new Spanish signing	will score a lot of goals
Textual	Interpersonal	Topical	
Theme			Rheme

Themes are classed as unmarked or marked. In declarative clauses marked Themes are those in which the first element of Transitivity is not the Subject. In the following example the Circumstance as the point of departure for the clause is given greater prominence while the Subject is given less prominence. Marked Themes are of significance in that they represent motivated choices which often signal significant transitions within the discourse, for example:

(16)

But	possibly	on Wednesday	he will come
Textual	Interpersonal	Topical	
Theme			Rheme

The system of Theme while primarily a system of the clause also operates within other domains of the grammar. Halliday and Matthiessen (2004: 392–3) note that in hypotactic clause nexuses the initial clause is the Theme for the entire nexus. Example (7a) is represented as (17). The Theme/Rheme structure has been analysed both at clause and clause nexus level with clause level Theme notated as 1 and clause nexus level Theme notated as 2.

(17)

If $^x\beta$	John	goes to the bank	Mary α	will go to the shop
Textual	Topical	Rheme1	Topical	Rheme1
Theme1			Theme1	
Theme2			Rheme2	

Martin (1992: 437–9) has shown that the system of Theme operates above the clause at the level of semantics. Thus, texts and paragraphs as well as clauses have Themes. A hyper-Theme is a sentence or set of sentences which function to predict the speaker's Thematic choices at clause nexus and clause level. To illustrate, the opening sentence of this paragraph is its hyper-Theme. Texts have macro-Themes which Martin defines as a group of sentences which predicts a set of hyper-Themes. In this chapter, §1 functions as the macro-Theme for the chapter and the chapter itself, or possibly only §5, functions as the macro-Theme of the entire book.

At clause level the other peak of informational prominence is New which is concerned with the information which the speaker has expanded upon as the text unfolds. Fries (1995) has coined the term N-Rheme to refer to the last constituent in the clause, which is the unmarked location for New information. It is the newsworthy part of the clause which the speaker wishes the reader to notice. In spoken language New information is signalled by the placement of the tonic syllable. The tonic syllable is the sole obligatory component of the tone unit and it is realized through a combination of amplitude and duration and, most significantly, by being the locus of the major pitch movement within the tone unit (Halliday and Greaves 2008: 54; Tench 1996: 53, 54). Halliday (1967b: 20) noted that a tone unit (or as he then labelled it, a tone group) realizes an information unit which, in the unmarked case, is coterminous with a clause. Within the tone unit the unmarked position for tonic prominence is the final lexical item of the tone unit; any other tonic placement realizes marked Tonicity. The tonic syllable represents the focal element in the tone unit. Any elements found after the tonic syllable realize Given information in the sense that the speaker projects the information as recoverable from the context or prior co-text. While the tonic syllable represents the culmination of New information, the informational status of elements prior to the tonic is potentially ambiguous. However, if the elements in the pretonic are within a salient foot and not recoverable, they are projected as New. Examples (18a–c) originally from O'Grady (2013) illustrate. In the examples, the tonic syllable, which is the focus of the utterance, is capitalized. Foot boundaries, unless tone unit initial, are notated by a backslash /. English as a language has descending feet and so commences with a beat at the beginning of the foot. This beat may be realized either by a salient syllable which phonetically is realized as louder, longer and on a higher pitch than the surrounding syllables or by a silent beat notated by a caret ^ (Abercrombie, 1967: 97–8; Halliday, 1970: 1–2).

(18a) *What happened?*

|| mary /went to the /BANK ||
New

(18b) *What happened to Mary?*

|| mary	/went to the /BANK ||
Given	New

(18c) *What happened?*

|| ^ she	/went to the /BANK ||
Given	New

In all three examples the tonic syllable *bank* is the focus of the utterance and it is projected as unambiguously New. In addition to the tonic syllable, examples (18a) and (18b) contain two salient syllables *Ma* and *went*. As *Mary* is recoverable from the previous co-text in (18b) it is Given while in (18a) it was not previously mentioned and is consequently New. In

(18c) the initial foot does not contain a salient syllable and is Given. These examples suggest that in many cases, though not all, the Theme maps onto Given and New information is located in the Rheme. The N-Rheme tends to map onto the tonic syllable and hence equates with the focus. But this is by no means always the case as speakers are free to manipulate their placement of tonic prominence.

4   Choice – SFL as an appliable theory

Halliday (2003: 1) commented that in his own work he was unable to distinguish working on SFL theory and using SFL to work on something else. SFL as a theory has been chosen by scholars committed to an ideologically committed form of social action who are interested in mapping out how language helps to create social meaning across different contexts. SFL is thus simultaneously a theory of action and a theory of reflection. SFL has long been the choice of scholars focused on language education (e.g. Halliday, 2007) and academic literacy (e.g. Martin and Rose, 2008). Earlier work in this field tended to focus on how novice first and second language writers choose from the system of Theme to develop their argument while more recent work has used the Interpersonal system of Appraisal to explicate evaluation in academic and scientific writing. Scholars working within the discipline of Stylistics have used SFL to provide comprehensive and detailed accounts of the choices authors have made in creating verbal art (e.g. Halliday, 1973: 103–40; Hasan, 1985; Miller and Turci, 2007). The advent of new technology has led to multi-modal texts and SFL in conjunction with Kress and Van Leeuwen's theory of social semiotics, itself a theory influenced by SFL, for example Kress and Van Leeuwen (2006) has led to the development of innovative multimodal analyses. The fusion of SFL and social semiotic theory has resulted in the careful analysis of meaning-making potential in art (e.g. Chen, 2010) and in the classroom (e.g. Caldwell, 2010).

In recent years technology has led to a major re-evaluation of norms in language use and SFL is the theory chosen by numerous scholars to make sense of the noise which emerges from the study of large corpora, for example Thompson and Hunston (2006). SFL has been and remains the theory used by CDA practitioners interested in exploring how language use is used to reproduce power and dominance. While early SFL inspired work focused largely on the Field of discourse (e.g. Fowler, 1991; Fairclough, 1989), more recent CDA work has also focused on the

Mode and Tenor of discourse (e.g. Lukin, 2010). Martin (2004) recasts CDA as positive discourse analysis and opens up space for the knowledge gleaned by theoretical investigation to be used in ensuring the smoother maintenance of discourse in problematic sites such as youth counselling interviews (e.g. Zappavigna *et al.*, 2010).

SFL as a theory focuses on how language has evolved to fit the communicative niches its speakers operate within. As such it has provided rich insights into how language and other semiotic meaning systems develop, and how pre-school children communicate with others in their environment (Halliday, 2004; Hasan, 2009). Matthiessen's work on the Nigel grammar (Matthiessen, 1985: 96–118) and Fawcett's work on the COMMUNAL project (e.g. Fawcett, 1990), have both demonstrated that SFL can be used to generate English with clear applications for those interested in all types of machine text interactions. Benson and Greaves (2005) have even managed to demonstrate the utility of SFL in helping us make sense of inter species semiotic interactions. To conclude, SFL, as a social semiotic theory, is a powerful, comprehensive and theoretically rigorous account of language, and one which is eminently suitable for investigating the practical problems faced by numerous groups of people who are engaged in one form or other with language.

5   Organization of the book

To date little has been published exploring how choice underpins the practice of SFL as a theory of appliable linguistics across various contexts. This book addresses this gap in the literature by presenting a selection of writings that develop the analytical perspective of choice across wide-ranging contexts. The book has been organized into four parts which illustrate the appliability of SFL as a tool for investigating language in the world. The first part, Interpersonal Choice and the Construction of Author Identity, consists of three chapters. It illustrates how choices, chiefly in the Interpersonal system of Appraisal, individualize highly constrained and conventionalized texts. The opening chapter by Ralph Adendorff and Kiran Pienaar reports on their combined Transitivity and Appraisal analysis of a corpus of South African sex worker classified ads. Their transitivity analysis reveals a discourse-world where the actions promised by the sex workers are packaged as asexual ones which become sexual only after the potential clients take action. Their Appraisal analysis shows that the writers' choices of tokens invoke sexual meaning. Within the sex worker corpus tokens from the Appreciation sub-system were statistically the most frequent, a patterning which results in the self-commodification of the sex workers as aesthetic objects. The double coding of tokens was frequent and Adendorff and Pienaar suggest that this allowed the sex workers to 'exploit maximally the linguistic resources in response to the demands of a complicated context'. Indeed, as they convincingly demonstrate, it is precisely because sexual meaning is not inscribed but invoked that the sex workers were able to promote illegal commercial sex without explicitly referring to the nature of the activities offered.

Elizabeth Swain's contribution is an extension of Appraisal theory. She employs a corpus taken from fourteen Italian language newspapers using the framework of evaluative key in order to investigate whether it is possible to identify reporter voice, commentator voice and correspondent voice as present in Italian press discourse. Her careful analysis shows that the three voices recognized in English journalistic discourse are not fully present in its Italian counterpart. Rather the Italian journalistic discourse seems to pattern into a broad two part typology which contrasts reporter voice with writer voice. Writer voice tends to choose more tokens of social esteem, social sanction and authorial appreciation than does reporter voice. Swain notes that the partisanship of the Italian media coupled with the extreme individualistic nature of Italian journalistic practice may not allow the labelling of voice along probabilistic lines. Swain's chapter illustrates that registers are not simply transferable from language to language and that the functioning of a language must be investigated *de novo* within the socio-cultural environment within which it operates.

Norma Barletta, Jorge Mizuno and Gillian Moss report on how Columbian novice postgraduate students assume the identity of experienced second language teacher/researchers in the construction of their individual neophyte professional identities. They analysed monographs written in English as a requirement for graduation. They found that at a macro-level the postgraduate students uncritically adopted the global organization of renowned theorists within the field of second language education. At the micro-level the postgraduate students' constructed discoursal selves which aligned them with a stance of scientificity. Notably they produced a high proportion of monoglossic utterances. Their hetroglossic utterances tended to contain modals signalling their own high investment in their propositions. These choices aligned the students uncritically with the tenets of a positivist scientific discourse. This may have been, as the authors note, because of their desire to enter the community of experts or because as neophytes they were not (yet) comfortable with aligning themselves as dissidents. In any case it seems that the assumption of a more expert status resulted in the uncritical reproduction of the assumed scientific knowledge of the discipline they wished to join.

The second part, Choice in Political Speech: Tension Between the Need to Inform and Project Solidarity, contains two chapters. Political rhetoric is a mixture of identity projection and informative content (Dickson and Scheve, 2006). Political actors attempt to gain or maintain support by simultaneously informing and maintaining solidarity. David Banks's contribution examines the genre of political tracts, unique to French culture. Political tracts are single-sided A4 sheets of paper which are handed out to passers-by at street demonstrations. Banks shows that a salient feature of these tracts is the high incidence of grammatical metaphor, especially nominalized processes. Previous studies have demonstrated that in English nominalization plays a role in discourse construction primarily by repackaging earlier Rhematic elements as Theme. Banks illustrates that in his French data the nominalizations are presupposed items which develop in-group solidarity while simultaneously closing down the space for dissent. Thus, a strategy which is used to inform in English is used to foster solidarity in French.

Gerard O'Grady examines how intonational choices help structure spoken text by guiding the hearer along a favoured listening path. He contrasts the spoken texture of eleven readings of a political text with the original rendition. His examination of the relationship between spoken paragraphs (paratones), orthographic paragraphs and phases of the text found that while all the speakers' intonational choices demonstrated their cognisance of the unfolding of the stages of the text, their choices were not constrained by the formal arrangement of the text. The intonational choices of the original political speaker differed in a manner which allowed him alone to foreground a particular meaning potential which invoked solidarity with his audience. Within paratones O'Grady found that the speakers' tone selections did not simply reflect the tactic relations established by the lexico-grammar but instead primarily functioned to manage discourse expectations created by the prior co-text.

Part C, The Effects of Choice in Text-type, contains five chapters, four of which report on computational investigations of corpora. The remaining chapter is a manual corpus analysis. Inas Mahfouz argues that the advent of computers has made it possible for analysts to conduct large-scale computational studies explicating the connection between sense and domain in polysemous verbs. Her chapter studies the fifty most frequent verbs found in the BNC Baby corpus in order to examine the role of domain in disambiguating polysemous verbs. She found that as a domain activates or suppresses certain senses it is crucial for the disambiguation of polysemous meanings. She concludes by arguing that prior to conducting transitivity analyses it is necessary to consider the domain in which the item occurred in order for its sense to be disambiguated.

Julia Lavid, Jorge Arús and Lara Moratón's contribution is a corpus based study which, unlike Mahfouz, approaches the data from a pre-determined theoretical standpoint. They illustrate how the investigation of thematic choices in their corpus was used to create a semi-automatized annotation scheme, itself a significant step towards the creation of algorithms which can automatically code Theme. Their work is of significance to the SFL and NLP communities in that it details how theoretically-informed methodological choices resulted in the final coding scheme. Furthermore production of an automatic coder for Theme will be of enormous benefit to the SFL community.

Akila Sellami-Baklouti employs Mick O'Donnell's UAM CorpusTool to investigate the probability of tactic relations occurring in Research Abstract articles from two disciplines, linguistics and medicine. She finds that there is a higher probability of clause simplexes and parataxis occurring in the medical sub-corpus and a higher probability of hypotaxis occurring in the linguistic abstracts. This she attributes to differing research methodologies inherent in the two research disciplines. Her findings provide further evidence that contextual factors affect the probabilities of systemic choices and that micro-registers are to be identified through the proportion of instantiated choices. Sellami-Baklouti's work indicates that teachers of academic writing need to pay attention to the local contexts of individual disciplines, and that learners will need to learn how to make appropriate choices in order to integrate themselves into their chosen disciplines.

Margaret Berry reports on part of a long-term study into academic writing. Her study aims to help teachers of English develop the academic literacies of English native school children by exploring the appropriacy of different thematic options in both registers. She finds that contentlight Subject Themes are most prevalent in her spoken English data while in written data contentful Subject Themes are the norm. Thus she argues that in the teaching of academic literacy learners need to be helped to recalibrate their Thematic choices from contentlight to contentful.

Ben Clarke's examination of the context-metafunction hook-up hypothesis (CMHH) closes the section. In an investigation of a corpus consisting of four subcorpora controlled to vary only in the Mode of discourse, he used the type and frequency of occurrence of ellipsis to test the CMHH. While his results are not entirely clear-cut he finds that the more ancillary a text is, the higher the frequency of occurrence of all types of ellipsis is. He further finds that the proportion of textual ellipsis correlates inversely with the ancillary nature of a text. Clarke wisely notes that his prior decision to assign a Field and Tenor value to an entire text may have inadvertently weakened his overall findings and that stronger support for the CMHH might have been obtained had he examined his corpora on a clause by clause basis. Regardless, Clarke's work is the only study which provides empirical support for the CMHH.

The final part of the book, The Interplay of Choice across Different Modalities, consists of two chapters. In the first Arsenio Jesús Moya Guijarro illustrates how the interplay of textual and visual features is used to construct textual and compositional meanings in a corpus of hotel brochures. In a typical double page ad the hotel name is presented as part of the Theme on the left, while the hotel's exclusive attributes are presented as Rhematic on the right-hand side. Despite the pictorial images in the brochures not entirely conforming with Kress and Van Leeuwen's account of the information pattern of Ideal and Real, the visual component of the brochures interacts with the verbal to create a reading path which guides the prospective client towards 'a world of luxury and exclusivity' and uncritically reproduces an ideology of exclusion. Moya's work, like O'Grady's, illustrates that, where appropriate, the meaning potential of texts must be analysed multimodally in order to explicate the authorial choices designed to glean perlocutionary effects.

The final chapter in the book, by Ann Montemayor-Borsinger, Eija Ventola and Célia Magalhães, reinforces the notion that while the core concept within SFL is choice, choice is not restricted to verbal texts. Their study is a multi-modal analysis of the covers of the first three editions of Halliday's *Introduction to Functional Grammar* (*IFG*). *IFG* as a text is unusual in that the covers themselves represent important aspects of SFL theory. The evolution of SFL as a theory can to some extent be tracked by changes in the cover design of the three editions of *IFG*. The first edition used an image from Henry Moore to represent SFL's tripartite and dynamic view of language. The second, largely unrevised edition had a cover design based on the colour wheel which foregrounded one particular aspect of SFL, the experiential metafunction which at the time of publication was most prominent in SFL studies. The third edition, which is a substantial reworking of the earlier editions, has as cover design a diagram which not only provides a more rounded representation of SFL theory, but one which captures the developments within the theory since the publication of the first edition. The cover of the third edition presents the metafunctions as equal and illustrates how language is organized stratally, while at the same time representing how the potential of the system is instantiated as text. Indeed so clever is the pictorial representation that, according to the authors, it alone could be used as a teaching tool modelling the SFL view of language. This chapter is an appropriate end to a book which, itself, illustrates that current studies in SFL no longer focus narrowly on SFG as represented by the cover of *IFG* 2.

Notes

1. The term hypotaxis as used in SFL is restricted only to clauses which are not rankshifted and does not include embedded clauses such as: *the man << who is sitting on the steps>> is bald.*
2. Martin and White (2005: 53) label a shift from social esteem to social sanction as analogous to that from venal to mortal sins.
3. It is worth noting that not all scholars working within SFL accept that the Topical Theme culminates with the first element of transitivity (see Chapters 7 and 9, this volume).

References

Abercombie, D. (1967) *Elements of General Phonetics.* Edinburgh: Edinburgh University Press.

Benson, J. D. and Greaves W. S. (2005) *Functional Dimensions of Ape-Human Discourse.* London: Equinox.

Caldwell, D. (2010) Making many meanings in popular rap music. In A. Mahboob and N. K. Knight (eds) *Appliable Linguistics* 234–50. London: Continuum.

Chen, Y. (2010) Contestable reality: A multi-level view on modality in multimodal pedagogic context. In A. Mahboob and N. K. Knight (eds) *Appliable Linguistics* 221–33. London: Continuum.

de Saussure, F. (1959) *Course in General Linguistics.* New York: McGraw-Hill.

Dickson, E. S. and Scheve, K. (2006) Social identity, political speech and electoral completion. *The Journal of Theoretical Politics* 18(1): 5–39.

Eggins, S. (2004) *An Introduction to Systemic Functional Linguistics,* 2nd edn. London: Continuum.

Eggins, S. and Slade, D. (1997) *Analysing Casual Conversation.* London: Equinox.

Fairclough, N. (1989) *Language and Power.* London: Longman.

Fawcett, R. P. (1990) The computer generation of speech with semantically and discoursally motivated intonation. In *Proceedings of 5th International Workshop on Natural Language Generation* 164–73. Pittsburgh.

Fowler, R. (1991) *Language in the News.* London: Routledge.

Fries, P. H. (1995) Themes, development and text. In R. Hasan and P. H. Fries (eds) *On Subject and Theme* 317–60. Amsterdam: John Benjamins.

Halliday, M. A. K. (1967a) Notes on transitivity and theme: Part 1. *Journal of Linguistics* 3(1): 37–82.

Halliday, M. A. K. (1967b) *Intonation and Grammar in British English.* The Hague: Mouton.

Halliday, M. A. K. (1968) Notes on transitivity and theme in English: Part III. *Journal of Linguistics* 4(2): 179–215.

Halliday, M. A. K. (1970) *A Course in Spoken English: Intonation.* Oxford: Oxford University Press.

Halliday, M. A. K. (1973) *Explorations in the Functions of Language.* London: Edward Arnold.

Halliday, M. A. K. (1978) *Language as Social Semiotic.* London: Edward Arnold.

Halliday, M. A. K. (1985) Systemic background. In J. D . Benson and W. S. Greaves (eds) *Systemic Perspectives on Discourse,* vol 1, 1–15. Norwood, NJ: Ablex.

Halliday, M. A. K. (2003) On the 'architecture' of human language. In J. J. Webster (ed.) *On Language and Linguistics, The Collected Works of Michael Halliday,* vol 3, 1–29. London: Continuum.

Halliday, M. A. K. (2004) The language of early childhood. In J. J. Webster (ed.) *On Language and Linguistics, The Collected Works of Michael Halliday,* vol. 4. London: Continuum.

Halliday, M. A. K. (2007) Language and education. In J. J. Webster (ed.) *On Language and Linguistics, The Collected Works of Michael Halliday,* vol. 9. London: Continuum.

Halliday, M. A. K. (2009) Methods – techniques – problems. In M. A. K. Halliday (ed.) *Continuum Companion to Systemic Functional Linguistics* 59–86. London: Continuum.

Halliday, M. A. K. and Greaves, W. S. (2008) *Intonation in the Grammar of English.* London: Equinox.

Halliday, M. A. K. and Hasan, R. (1989) *Language, Context, and Text: Aspects of Language in a Social-semiotic Perspective,* 2nd edn. Oxford: Oxford University Press.

Halliday, M. A. K. and Martin, J. R. (1993) *Writing Science: Literacy and Discursive Power.* London: The Falmer Press.

Halliday, M. A. K. and Matthiessen, C. M. I. M. (1999) *Construing Experience Through Meaning.* London: Continuum.

Halliday, M. A. K. and Matthiessen, C. M. I. M. (2004) *An Introduction to Functional Grammar,* 3rd edn. London: Edward Arnold.

Hasan, R. (1985) *Linguistics: Language and Verbal Art.* Geelong, Vic: Deakin University Press.

Hasan, R. and Cloran, C. (2009) A sociolinguistic interpretation of everyday talk between mothers and children. In J. J. Webster (ed.) *Semantic Variation: Meaning in Society, The Collected Works of Ruqaiya Hasan,* vol. 2. London: Equinox.

Kress, G. and van Leeuwen, T. (2006) *Reading Images: The Grammar of Visual Design*, 2nd edn. London: Routledge.

Lukin, A. (2010) 'News' and 'register': A preliminary investigation. In A. Mahboob and N. K. Knight (eds) *Appliable Linguistics* 92–113. London: Continuum.

Mahboob, A. and Knight, N. K. (2010) *Appliable Linguistics*. London: Continuum.

Martin, J, R. (1992) *English Text*. Amsterdam: John Benjamins.

Martin, J. R. (2004) Positive discourse analysis: Power solidarity and change. *Revista Canaria de Estudios Ingeleses* 49: 172–202.

Martin, J. R. and Rose, D. (2003) *Working with Discourse*. London: Continuum.

Martin, J. R. and Rose, D. (2008) *Genre Relations: Mapping Culture*. London: Equinox.

Martin, J. R. and White, P. R. R. (2005) *The Language of Evaluation*. London: Palgrave.

Matthiessen, C. M. I. M. (1985) The systemic framework in text generation: Nigel. In J. D. Benson and W. S. Greaves (eds.) *Systemic Perspectives on Discourse*, vol. 1, 96–118. Norwood, NJ: Ablex.

Matthiessen, C. M. I. M. (1995) *Lexicogrammatical Cartography*. Tokyo: International Science Publishers.

Matthiessen, C. M. I. M., Teruya, K. and Lam, M. (2010) *Key Terms in Systemic Functional Linguistics*. London: Continuum.

Miller, D. R. and Turci, M. (2007) *Language and Verbal Art Revisited*. London: Equinox.

O'Grady, G. (2013) An investigation of how intonation helps to signal information structure. In W. L. Bowcher and B. A. Smith (eds) *Systemic Phonology: Recent Studies in English* 27–52. London: Equinox.

Tench, P. (1996) *The Intonation Systems of English*. London: Cassell.

Thompson, G. and Hunston, S. (2006) *System and Corpus: Exploring Connections*. London: Equinox.

Tucker. G. (2006) Systemic incorporation: On the relationship between corpus and systemic functional grammar. In G. Thompson and S. Hunston (eds) *System and Corpus: Exploring Connections* 81–102. London: Equinox.

Webster, J. J. (2009) Introduction. In M. A. K. Halliday (ed.) *Continuum Companion to Systemic Functional Linguistics* 1–11. London: Continuum.

Zappavinga, M., Cleirigh, C., Dwyer, P. and Martin, J. R. (2010) Visualizing appraisal prosody. In A. Mahboob and N. K. Knight (eds) *Appliable Linguistics* 150–67. London: Continuum.

Part A

Interpersonal choice and the construction of author identity

1

'Busty babes and passionate pleasures': A systemic functional linguistic analysis of sex worker discourse in a South African city

Ralph Adendorff[a] and Kiran Pienaar[b]

1.1 Introduction

This chapter draws on a corpus of one month's newspaper advertisements for commercial sex published in the 'Social' column of *The Herald*, a provincial, South African, English-language daily newspaper with a (relatively) liberal reputation, and a reader base of over 245,000 (Peel, 2008). It reports on the way sex workers construct their identities and the services they offer (as part of touting for clients) in these entries. It also considers the inferencing work that readers must do to interpret the entries. The Social column is tableau-like, 60 to 80 sex workers silently displaying their wares in their own metaphorical windows as might sex workers in cities around the world. Indeed, the tableau is not unlike the traditional scene of Dutch sex workers sitting in the window of a brothel enticing passers-by inside by posing suggestively. The entries have a 3-part structure: (1) identification, (2) self-promotion and (3) contact detail provision; but this ordering is not rigid. Part 2, with its epithetical function, constitutes the core of the entry. Examples are:

---

a   Ralph Adendorff is Professor and Head of the Department of English Language and Linguistics at Rhodes University in Grahamstown, South Africa. He received his MA in Linguistics from Indiana University, Bloomington, USA, and his PhD from the University of Natal, Durban, South Africa. He is a member of the Academy of Science of South Africa and has published in the areas of pidgin and creole linguistics, code-switching, critical ethnography, the New Literacy Studies and APPRAISAL.

b   Kiran Pienaar is based in the School of Political and Social Inquiry at Monash University, Melbourne, Australia. Her research interests include the cultural construction of sexuality, HIV, ontologies of disease and the role of politics in shaping disease epidemics.

(1)   Kaysha [1]. New, well-built coloured lady to please you [2]. 083-520-0650 [3];
(2)   Pretty young blond with an exceptional figure. Model lookalike. Ready to play. Awaits your call. Travel also [2]. Nicole [1]. 078-237-2449 Humewood [3].

We use the tools of systemic functional linguistics (SFL), including a transitivity analysis and an analysis using the APPRAISAL system to highlight the considerable contextual constraints on the linguistic choices sex workers make in these entries. The analysis seeks to identify and interpret patterns in these choices in terms of how they construct an aged, raced and sexualized identity of the sex workers. Given that the sexual nature of the services is only alluded to in the entries, we are also interested in the inferences that readers must make to decode the *sexual* subtext created by the euphemisms, innuendo, hyperbole and metaphoric usage on the surface of the text. In discourse analytic terms, we suggest that, to interpret the entries, intended readers (the potential clients) draw on their Members' Resources (MR; Fairclough, 1992, 2001), that is, their knowledge of relevant social structures, norms and discourse conventions. The analysis considers inferences that readers must make to reveal the latent sexual meaning of the advertisements, as well as the textual cues which guide their interpretation. In particular, we address the following research questions:

1.   What 'discourse world' do the entries evoke (Caldas-Coulthard and Moon, 2010: 101)?
2.   What inferences are readers called on to make in order to understand the underlying sexual content of the entries?
3.   How do the entries bear the impress of the context and help to shape aspects of this context?

An important shift in the recent literature and debates on commercial sex has been the inclusion of sex workers' firsthand experiences and perspectives (Rickard and Storr, 2001) and we see our study as contributing to this literature by focusing on the discourses sex workers themselves use to promote sex work.

1.2   Method

The analysis is based on 30 extracts from the Social column of *The Herald* newspaper, collected on weekdays over the months of April and May 2008. We chose entries during these months because they represent fairly unremarkable months where there was no big event happening in the city (e.g. sports match, music festival) which might have influenced the content of the entries. These newspaper advertisements are available in the public domain and therefore present accessible data. We used a custom-made concordancing programme to delete duplicate entries as they would have skewed the quantitative analysis of particular tokens. Punctuation was treated as insignificant since its presence appeared to be random. What interested us was lexical variation. We omitted advertisements for escort agencies and massage parlours because we were interested in how individual sex workers promote their services in order to attract clients. Also omitted were entries advertising 'live phone chats' which we believe offer a different kind of service to the face-to-face service offered by the bulk of entries. Once we had deleted entries that did not match the selection criteria described above, we were left with a total of 410 unique entries.

We chose systemic functional linguistics (SFL) as our interpretive framework because it sees in the linguistic choices of a writer both the impress of the context and the creation of the context. Such a perspective seemed especially suitable given the goals of our research to consider how the sex workers' linguistic choices respond to the demands of a complicated context and help to (re)inscribe this context. The transitivity analysis that follows focuses on the participants, processes and circumstances in the data. It profited from the insights of Ravelli (2000) and Martin (2000b) but is necessarily selective and less detailed than these accounts. The starting point of our analysis was the frequency distribution lists and other concordance information acquired from the computer programme mentioned above, used in conjunction with Wordsmith. The purpose of the analysis was to capture the ideational features of the world in which the sex workers operate.

The APPRAISAL analysis, with its interpersonal orientation, relies on the procedures recommended by Martin and White (2005) for carrying out this form of analysis. According to the theory of APPRAISAL, there are three systems or semantic domains through which speakers/writers express evaluative meaning:

1. Attitude, which concerns the resources for 'expressing emotion, judging character and valuing the worth of things' (Martin and Rose, 2003: 24).
2. Engagement, which pertains to the resources for positioning the speaker/writer's voice in relation to other viewpoints (i.e. intersubjective positioning).
3. Graduation, which considers how speakers/writers amplify the force of attitudinal values and graduate (sharpen/blur) their focus.

Due to space constraints and the detailed account of interpersonal meaning afforded by an analysis in terms of the Attitude subsystem, we focused attention only on the expression of Attitude in the data. However, we acknowledge that an analysis of the manifestation of Graduation would yield additional insights in terms of how the Attitude resources are amplified to promote each sex worker's services as distinct from and better than those of their co-workers. This would be a fruitful avenue for further research but is outside the remit of this chapter. After identifying all expressions of Attitude in the entries, we coded each expression according to the broad type of Attitude it represents, for example Affect, Judgement or Appreciation, and, within each of these categorizations, according to the relevant subsystem/s which each instance of evaluative meaning expresses, for example Security, Capacity, Valuation, and so on. We identified whether each expression was inscribed (expressed explicitly) or evoked (expressed implicitly), whether it required double/triple coding, and whether it was positive or negative. We recorded all of this information in tabular form – in addition to recording the line number of each instantiation, the instantiation itself and indicating who/what the appraiser and appraised were in each case. This provided a synoptic display of the choices that, in conjunction with sensitivity to the co-text in each case, allowed us to trace the patterned nature of the APPRAISAL choices. In turn, this allowed us to explore how, through making such choices, the sex workers attempt to encourage their readers to enter into a collusive alignment that will culminate in sexual engagement.

1.3   Analysis of ideational meaning

The analysis begins with a brief account of the words in the corpus with the highest frequencies as these suggest what is fundamental in the sex workers' construal of the ideational world in which they operate and what is deemed permissible in light of the constraints within which sex workers operate in South Africa. Hereafter, we report on the transitivity analysis, i.e. the relations between elements in a clause, namely the processes ('goings-on' or 'happenings'), the participants (the entities involved in the processes) and the circumstances (details of how, when and/or where the processes took place) (Halliday, 1994). We start by providing an account of the principal participants in the data, namely the sex workers, focusing on how their identities are constructed – in keeping with our first research question. We then report on the processes that are employed in the entries and, in particular, make various inferences as to the kinds of services that are on offer and what it would take to activate them. The inferencing work required is a concern central to the second question underlying our research. Both here and in relation to the participants and their identities, we draw attention to silences and forms of indirectness in the data, attributable to the constraints which operate on sex work as an industry in South Africa. The last part of the transitivity analysis addresses briefly the circumstances which form part of the newspaper entries. We then turn to an account of how interpersonal meaning is conveyed in the entries, particularly in the form of modifiers of different kinds within nominal expressions. This is revealed through an APPRAISAL analysis.

1.3.1   Frequency analysis

Table 1.1 shows, in rank order of their frequency, the words with a frequency of 30 or more in our corpus. The most frequently used lexical

Table 1.1 Words with a frequency of >30.

Rank order	Word	Frequency
1	and	96
2	to	93
3	lady	90
4	a	80
5	beachfront	78
6	travel	75
7	new	70
8	with	68
9	private	67
10	in	64
11	body	63
12	African	60
13	you	59
14	for	56
15	babe, massage	47
16	Cape, tall	42
17	busty, call, Coloured	40
18	alone	39
19	blond(e)	36
20	Road, the, town	34
21	your	33
22	also	32
23	of, slender	31
24	choose	30

items ostensibly indicate the central features and preoccupations of the sex workers. Conversely, those which are infrequent or indeed absent signal what is less significant.

As the table shows, *lady, babe, body, you, massage* and *blond* are the most frequently occurring nominal entities. The frequency of *blond* derives from it being both a nominal (e.g. *a pretty petite blond*) and a modifier (*a blond busty dancer*). *Beachfront* and *road* (always in the expression *Cape Road*) specify prominent locales for commercial sex, while *town* owes its frequency to the fact that it occurs in the expressions *new in town, back in town* and *best in town*. Only three processes have a frequency of 30 or more: *travel* (as in the clandestine *travel to hotels* and *travel only*), *call* (as in *call* and *call me* followed by a cell phone number) and *choose* (in injunctions such as: *Two entertaining friends for fun. Choose one*). Modifiers are well-represented. Those with high frequencies are *new, African* and *Coloured*; *private* and *alone*; and *tall, busty* and *slender*.

Grammatical/function words make up the rest of the listed items: articles, *a* (80 occurrences) and *the* (34); and the prepositions, *to* (93), *with* (68), *in* (64), *for* (56) and *of* (31) are all high frequency. *With* usually appears in nominal expressions that list the sex worker's attributes (*seductive coloured lady with stunning body*) (42) or services (*massage with nice ending*) (20) or else is used to instrumentalize the sex worker (*ready to assist you with my exotic body*) (2). *In* specifies place (*alone in Humewood*) (12), manner (*satisfy you in many ways*) (8), 'configuration' (*beauty in a perfect frame*) (12) and occurs in such fixed expressions as *new in town* (14), perhaps suggesting innocence or purity; *back in town* (6), experience?; and *the best in town* (3), signifying high quality. *To* in infinitive constructions appears 72 times (*lady to pamper you*), and as a preposition, 21 times. As such it indicates place (*Cape Road next to Five Ways*) (8), destination (*SMS FUN to 363938*) (3), extent (*from root to tip*) (5) or manner (*male to male*) (4). The preposition *of* links nominal expressions headed by a participant (*queen of all*) (16) or by an epithet (*lots of TLC*) (13) or else it is used in a predicate structure (*tired of being disappointed?*) (2). Lastly, *for* introduces a purpose (*discreet refined hostess for the selective discerning gentleman*)/reason (*everything goes for your pleasure*) (50) or else figures in fixed expressions (*body to die for*) (6). We consider the significance of a selection of the high frequency items in what follows.

1.3.2 Participants in the data: the entities on offer

Reference to the sex workers takes various forms in the data. We notice that certain sex workers use alter egos, that is the same sex worker promotes him/herself differently in different entries, for example by changing the description of their services, their physical attributes, age and name. We identified this phenomenon by checking entries with the same phone number (which we presume means that they were written by the same individual) and discovered that, in approximately 20 per cent of the cases, the individuals adopt different personae. A good example is *Pamela/Zaza/Wendy/Linda* – the tip-toned African lady:

(1)   073-119-0524. Cape Road near Five Ways. New 20 year Pamela Anderson look-alike. Busty, curvy, tall African to tease from root to tip. Everything goes. Pam 24/7. Pensioners welcome.

(2)   073-119-0524. A centrefold, busty, broadminded African for an Oriental treat, eager to please and tease. Beachfront. Zaza. 24/7. Safe.

(3)   073-119-0524. Cape Road next to Five Ways. New tiptoned 19 year African babe to spoil. A no tease. Busty, tall in private. Wendy. 24/7.

(4)   073-119-0524. A new tip-toned busty, tall African babe to tease, everything goes. Linda.

Here the writer relexicalizes certain items and introduces new components into the entry. We read this relexicalization as a refashioning of the sex worker's identity and, in some cases, the description of her services, to attract clients. To extend the analogy of a tableau, the sex workers are changing their outfits and striking new poses to create an apparently new tableau. The changes to names, attributes and services indicate in addition that novelty value is important, which may be a function of the competitive market in which sex workers operate. This is corroborated by the frequency of references to *new* in the entries, with *new* appearing a total of 70 times and ranking as the seventh most frequent item in the corpus. Here is an example: *ANNELIEN. <u>New</u> broadminded lady. Lots of specials, no rush. Private venue, Cape Rd. 078-501-8753. Travel also.* The frequency of the attribute 'new' may also allude to the sex worker's newness to the profession and thus could imply that she is less likely to have a sexually transmitted infection (STI). In this sense, relative newness could be read as symbolically associated with a kind of sexual–physical purity ('untouched by disease' and 'sexually innocent').

By far the most frequent form of identification that the sex workers employ in reference to themselves is a nominal expression in which the head acts as subject or direct object and is third person. The lexical item that occurs with the highest frequency in the corpus, *lady/ladies* is such a case. From a semantic point of view one possible justification for the use of *lady* is that it suggests gentility and upmarketness. In addition to *lady*, *babe* (47), *blond(e)* (18), *goddess* (14), *beauty* (11), *model* (8) and *queen* (14) also occur as the third person head of (sometimes extensive) nominal constructions identifying sex workers in the data. What is significant about the third person reference is that it objectifies the sex workers but also results in associated effects which are byproducts of the context in which sex work operates. Exoticization is one such effect, achieved through the choice of such nominal classifiers as *goddess, queen, Naomi, JLo* and *Pamela Anderson* – the last three are intertextual references to Naomi Campbell, Jennifer Lopez and Pamela Anderson, all three contemporary celebrities who are often presented in the media as sexually attractive. Racialization (coupled with exoticization) is a further effect brought into being through the use of the following words (whether as the head of a nominal expression or as classifiers within nominal groups): *African* (60), *Coloured* (40) *White* (28), *Black* (16), *Chinese* (14), *Sotho*[1] (11), and so on.

Such racialization and exoticization is in many ways an Apartheid legacy, stemming from legislation which prohibited sexual relations between people of different races (The Immorality Act, 1927), and which today arguably still makes the idea of sexual contact across racial lines almost transgressive. We argue that, in making implicit appeals to 'the exotic' and 'the transgressive', the sex workers evoke a world of sexual possibilities, where clients can play out their fantasies unchecked.

A further byproduct of the sex workers representing themselves as third person entities is their commodification as objects of desire. Examples are:

(1)   Tall natural blonde.
(2)   beautifully packaged in a slim body.
(3)   Brand new.

Newness also helps to construe the sex worker as a product akin to others within Western consumer capitalism, further contributing to their commodification in the data. Thus, structures such as *new curvy college lady* and *new African goddess* (New (+ epithet) + classifier + thing) are common, as are *new from London* and *new in town*, which wrap the newness in other-worldliness.

The image of the sex worker as an object of desire is also reflected in the way in which the ideal body is referenced in the data. Table 1.2 shows the body parts that are foregrounded in the advertisements, working from the top of the body, down.

Table 1.2 Frequency of references to body parts in the data.

Body part	*Frequency*
Hair	4
blond(e)	36
brunette	5
Eyes	3
blue	8
brown	3
Busty	40
Legs	4
leggy	10
legged	3
Heels (as in high heels)	4

The epithet *long* appears 7 times and applies both to *hair* and to *legs*. In other words, the most prominent bodily profile proffered, is a long-haired, blond, blue-eyed, busty woman, with long legs: a Barbie, in other words. The Barbie aesthetic is reinforced by the descriptors used for body shapes in the data: *tall* (42), *busty*, (40), *slender* (31), *slim* (23), *curvy* (24), *model-like* (21) and *leggy* (10). In addition, suggestive of the ideal body shape are: *babe, goddess, queen, Naomi look-alike, JLo* and *surfer*. As for features that are *not* described, we note that facial features are hardly ever mentioned – face, ears, nose, mouth, lips, teeth (though *complexion* as in *light complexion* is mentioned twice). Since the face conveys emotion and is arguably the most distinct marker of subjectivity, its absence in the entries could be read as bound up with the objectification of the sex workers: they are produced in the data as aesthetic objects, rather than as thinking, feeling individuals. It is also noteworthy that neither sexual organs nor erotic zones are mentioned (other than in the epithet *busty* as a reference to breasts).We read the absence of references to nudity and sexual/erotic organs as further evidence of the context bearing down on the discourse, circumscribing the linguistic choices available to the writers for promoting their services. However, in terms of sexual activities there are many indirect references, such as *tease* and *please*. We consider these references next in our analysis of the processes in the data.

1.3.3 Processes in the data: The services offered

While nominal expressions in the entries convey much of their semantic content, the *processes* in the data also play an important semantic role.

We need first to note that the entries rely on very elliptical forms of expression as seen, for example, in the following selection:

(1)   BRITNEY. Slim curvy figured African model. Long hair, brown eyes and lovely legs in high heels. 072-736-3584.
(2)   VERONICA (24). White lady. New in town. Beachfront. Wearing mini skirts. 100% Safe. Private, also travel. 076-043-6137.
(3)   AMBER. Radiant beauty. True lady for the gent that prefers the finest touch. 072-657-5250.

Viewed from a reader's point of view there seems to be an implicit, underlying structure to the second part of the entry, the self-promotion element. This structure takes two forms, with two implicit kinds of verbal element:

1.   I am (a) ...
2.   This entry introduces (a) (someone) ...

The purpose of the entries is for the sex workers to introduce themselves to the reader and say something about themselves which the reader will find enticing. The first of these putative underlying forms is more personal, and more direct, and construes a first person addresser: [I am] *Kendra. You are the moth, I am the flame.* [I am] *A stunning beauty in a perfect frame.* By contrast, the second form, which is more evident in our data, designates a third person addresser: [This entry introduces a] *Beautiful broadminded, slim, petite, Chinese. Meet the girl of your dreams, to tease and please you.* Admittedly, the distinction between the two underlying forms is slight, and there are overlaps between them in the data.

The second part of the entries, the promotional element, is where the verbal forms appear – if indeed a verbal form is used at all. Example (1) above (for Britney) is a verbless entry. Finite verbs also occur in the data, such as *travel* in (2). A further feature of the verbal dimension of the data is the use of verbs in the imperative form. This is illustrated in entries like: *Spoil yourself. REALISE your fantasies!* and *Take time out. Come and relax.* It is worth noting that the reference to *fantasies* can be read in this context as the nominalization of a sexual act, if implicit. The data is richly sprinkled too with non-finite verbal forms, which are introduced by *to* in 77 per cent of the instances of *to* in the data. Such non-finite constructions take the form:

(1)   come to my door to find out more.
(2)   [Nominal group, e.g. Sotho model] to rock your world.

They also appear in constructions of the following sort where there is a greater sense of desire on the sex workers' part to offer their services:

(1)   ready to entertain you.
(2)   eager to please and tease.
(3)   willing to satisfy you in many delicious ways.

The significance of these non-finite expressions lies in the fact that, because they are not tensed, they are not arguable. Moreover, they denote potentiality, imply a state of limbo and are future-looking. The sex workers are construed in each case merely as propositioning their addressees; it is their readers (clients) who have to initiate any action. Therefore, the power to actualize any encounter is vested in the addressee. The tableau remains a silent display, full of possibilities, but inert unless/until a reader decides to activate it by enlisting the services of a sex worker who is part of the tableau. Notable too is an emphasis on indulgence, encoded in the lexical set: *indulge, tease from root to tip, spoil, satisfy every desire.* Such linguistic choices seek to transport the reader to a fairytale world of desire, where reality is suspended. Some of these choices infantilize the addressee by promising such things as *TLC* (tender loving care), *pampering* and *spoiling.*

Turning now to the finite material processes, *travel* is the highest frequency process in the data, which sometimes occurs in combination with the modals *can* (12) and *will* (2). It only ever refers to a service option that sex workers offer. *Spoil* (with a frequency of 16) is different, in that, in addition to patterning with *to* (8), it appears in constructions such as the following, the first of which is an assertion or promise, the second an exhortation, the third an offer and the fourth an instruction or injunction:

(1)   I spoil you
(2)   You deserve to spoil yourself
(3)   Let us spoil you
(4)   Spoil yourself

The injunction *spoil*, along with material processes like *call/phone, sms, choose and come* (as in *come visit my world*), forms a lexical set of actions which the reader must perform to access the service. The agency for establishing initial contact thus again lies with the reader.

1.3.4   Circumstances in the data: Place, time and manner

Turning now to the analysis of circumstances in the data, Table 1.3 shows a selection of examples of circumstances of place, time/duration and manner:

Table 1.3 Examples of circumstances in the data.

Type of circumstance	Place	Time/ Duration	Manner
Example	next to five ways	24/7	male to male
	come to my door to find out more	travel til late	to tease from root to tip
	beachfront	24 hours	to satisfy you in many ways
	travel to hotels		everything goes for your pleasure

The kinds of circumstances evident in the data are restricted in their reference to time (in the sense of 'unlimited time'), place and manner. There are a limited number of adverbials, largely, we suggest, because of the restricted number of processes in the data. Consequently, the reader gets very little sense of *how* the sex workers will render their services. It is not clear, for instance, what *to satisfy you in many ways* means in practice. The details of the services offered, on the strength of the data available, are essentially vague, at best gently suggestive. Consequently, the detail is largely in the mind of the reader – evoked, that is, through recourse to the relevant interpretive schemas. Linked to this point, we note that there is no mention of sex. The reader is only able to infer that sex work is really what is on offer by decoding such euphemisms as *friendly lady; will travel to hotels; any desire, any need; massage with a happy ending.* S/he does so, too, by filling in what is left unsaid. The schemas or MRs we draw on are products of our socialization, related, in the instance under consideration, *inter alia,* to cultural taboos associated with sex and, stemming from them, cultural treatments of and modes of talking and writing about sex and sexual activity – acquired in the home, at church, in the classroom and school playground, via jokes and cartoons and from exposure, for example, to commercial advertising in the media where, for instance, sexual innuendo is a common ingredient of advertising strategy.

1.4   APPRAISAL analysis

The focus in APPRAISAL analysis is essentially on the expression of the directive and interpersonal functions – seeking to get someone to do what one desires by aligning them with one's preferred course of action/

community of feeling/set of value positions. In our data, the sex workers aim to entice their readers into co-constructing a fantasy world of sensual delights as a means of encouraging them to engage a specific sex worker's services and so actualizing a commercial undertaking between them. The preferred reader, as the analysis reported on below shows, is someone who reads the brief, cryptic *Herald* entries congruently. By this we mean that the ideal reader draws on such Members' Resources as enables them to transcend the cryptic character of the entries (reflected in the prominence of evoked linguistic choices, rather than inscribed ones), and decide which sex worker's services to enlist.

Of the three major APPRAISAL systems (Attitude, Graduation and Engagement), we draw only on the Attitude system, in the interests of space. We have further narrowed our account by restricting our analysis to 200 entries in the corpus. This translates into 930 instantiations, requiring 1208 codings, of which 278 involve double or triple codings. The overall profile of Attitude choices is shown in Table 1.4.

Table 1.4 Frequency of APPRAISAL choices in terms of each subsystem.

Attitude subsystem	Affect	Judgement	Appreciation
Frequency	187	174	847

Of note is, on one hand, the roughly even distribution of Affect resources (187: used to evaluate feelings/emotion) and Judgement resources (174: used to evaluate people's behaviour/ethics) and, on the other, the far greater statistical prominence of Appreciation choices (847: used to evaluate things/aesthetics).

What is significant about the Appreciation resources is the fact that the sex workers use them, somewhat unusually, to positively evaluate their own attributes: biographical (age, newness, experience), demographic (racial, ethnic, national) and physical (physique), in the process commodifying, sexualizing and exoticizing themselves as objects, artwork-like, to be admired and engaged.

The breakdown of the Appreciation choices in the data is as shown in Table 1.5.

Table 1.5 Frequency of Appreciation subsystems.

Appreciation subsystem	Valuation	Composition	Reaction
Frequency	470	182	195

Valuation choices reflect how useful, worthy or significant something is considered to be (Martin, 2000a). In doing so they reproduce fundamental subcultural assumptions about what is valued and marketable in the world of sex work. Accordingly, we coded the following, for example, as instances of [+ Valuation]:

(1)   twenty year old, 25, very young, college lad, mature signorita, new, experienced
(2)   African, blond, White, Coloured, Sotho, Chinese, Cape Malay
(3)   Greek goddess, African queen, Swazi princess
(4)   attractive, lovely, special, pretty

The first set of instantiations foregrounds (and sexualizes) youthfulness and newness (possibly connoting sexual purity) on the one hand, and experience and maturity on the other. On the whole, youth is more prestigious than age, though age itself can be construed in terms of experience and projected as a reassuring attribute. The second set exoticizes ethnic/racial difference (especially in the South African context, as discussed in the section on participants above), as do the instantiations in (3), the difference being that the nominal heads in (3) carry evaluative meaning in addition to the classifiers that modify them. The choices in the fourth set are positive forms of valuation which, when coupled with their collocates, often signal sexual allure.

Composition, the second of three subsystems of Appreciation, ordinarily evaluates how coherent, logical and balanced something is (Martin and Rose, 2007). In the situational context of our data, it is the compositional characteristics of sex workers' bodies, that is, their physical attributes, which are aestheticized. Hence the prevalence of instantiations such as the following, which foreground and eroticize the compositional features of their referents: *curvy, slender, busty, lovely legs in heels, petite.*

Reaction, the remaining Appreciation subsystem, measures how much we like something (quality) or how emotionally captivating it is (impact). While it is acknowledged (Martin and White, 2005: 45) that Affect is the core of the Attitude sub-system, they point out that Judgement and Appreciation are institutionalized affect (feelings within a specific subcultural context). Since we are indeed dealing here with a form of institutionalized discourse, it precludes the expression of the sex workers' feelings. Instead, the sex workers evaluate their value to the reader in aesthetic terms, in order to evoke suitable affect on the reader's part. In our data, the statistical presence of each form of Reaction is as shown in Table 1.6.

Table 1.6 Frequency of Reaction choices.

Reaction subsystem	*Quality*	*Impact*
Frequency	63	132

We coded choices such as the following as [+Reaction/Quality]: *broadminded, superior, caring*. The choices listed next we coded as [+Reaction/Impact]: *bubbly, gorgeous, sophisticated, model-looking, bombshell, beach babe* – the last two of which are things, not classifiers or epithets. We double-coded every instance of Reaction (Quality or Impact) with [+Valuation], since we see the above as functioning to nuance the pervading positive valuation of the sex workers' physical attributes, again evoking their sexualization.

Fully illustrative examples of the concurrent presence of all three forms of Appreciation are found in the following:

(1) An African [+Valuation], petite [+Valuation +Reaction/Quality +Composition], sassy [+Valuation +Reaction/Impact] and sophisti-cated [+Valuation +Reaction/Impact] upmarket [+Normality +Valuation +Reaction/Impact] babe [+Valuation +Composition +Reaction/Impact].

(2) A tall [+Composition], busty [+Composition], curvy [+Composition] African [+Valuation] bombshell [+Composition +Valuation +Reaction/Impact] to tease [+Satisfaction], with a body to die for [Valuation +Reaction/Impact].

(3) Beachfront, loveable [+Valuation +Reaction/Quality], experienced [+Valuation], Malaysian originated [+Valuation]. Queen of all [+Valuation +Reaction/Impact].

Turning now to the contribution of choices made in our data from within the Affect subsystem, the second of the Attitude subsystems, we report as shown in Table 1.7.

Table 1.7 Frequency of Affect choices.

Affect subsystem	*Happiness*	*Security*	*Satisfaction*
Frequency	0	85	102

As one of three systems of resources for construing emotions, we note first that manifestations of Happiness are totally absent, perhaps because this emotional response is considered to be naïve or irrelevant within the realm of transactional sex, where the focus is arguably on the satisfaction of physical/sexual desires, as opposed to, or at least secondary to, fostering an emotional connection. This reading of our findings corresponds with Plumridge *et al*'s account of male patrons' justification for pursuing commercial sex. The authors note that: 'The exchange of money for sex was taken by the patron to absolve him of any obligations outside the sexual exchange itself' (Plumridge *et al.*, 1997: 172). The perceived freedom from emotional and social obligations, along with the patrons' assumptions about sexual mutuality (despite evidence to the contrary), allowed them to experience unadulterated sexual pleasure (*ibid.*). In our study, the absence of tokens for construing emotions of happiness/unhappiness supports and, indeed, reproduces this conventional view of commercial sex as being about physical and sexual exchange, rather than about forming an emotional attachment. By contrast, Security choices have a reasonably strong presence and are a reminder of one of a number of contextual constraints that impact on the sex work industry. Instantiations of Security include *private, safe, home alone, discreet venue, won't let you down*. The largely formulaic references to safety, privacy and discretion are ambiguous and can be construed as referring to the safety of the venues mentioned in the entries and/or to the dangers of exposure, given the taboo nature of transactional sex, or, in the case specifically of safety, of reassurances that clients are not in danger of contracting an STD. Another security dimension in the data – though present relatively weakly – relates to the sex workers themselves and is encoded in terminology relating to their cleanliness (and presumably to associated risk of disease): *clean, clean in everything*, and so on.

The third and last subsystem of resources for conveying emotions, Satisfaction, has the greatest prominence in our Affect data. Choices of this kind pertain to emotions associated with (or, here, *anticipate*) feelings of achievement – *sexual* achievement in our case. In the data such accomplishment is strongly vicarious and evoked, its realization (i.e. true satisfaction) possible only if the reader moves beyond the realm of fantasy and acquiesces to the sex workers' temptations.

Illustrations which incorporate the abovementioned forms of Affect (Security and Satisfaction) follow:

(1) New, sweet and curvy 20-year-old Sotho College girl to satisfy you in many ways [+Satisfaction]. Alone [+Security] 24/7.

(2) 20 year Pamela Anderson lookalike. Busty, curvy African to tease from root to tip [+Satisfaction]. Everything goes [+Satisfaction]. Alone [+Security], safe [+Security].

(3) Pretty young Blond with an exceptional figure, model lookalike. Home alone [+Security]. And ready to play [+Satisfaction]. Awaits your call [+Satisfaction].

Judgement is the third Attitude system evident in our data. Overall, such resources are employed when evaluating the behaviour of others and can be done both according to legal norms (Social Sanction) and to value-based norms (Social Esteem). Significantly, the first of these categories of choices is almost completely absent in our data. None of the entries evaluates the sex workers' (or anyone else's) ethical stance on any matter and only one pertains to honesty, it being: *BRITNEY. Sweet elegant African beaut, slim body. <u>I'm no lie</u> ...*

Given the pattern of APPRAISAL choices in our data, specifically the absence of 'Veracity' instantiations, we chose to code it [+Valuation] and [+Satisfaction], double-coding it with [+Satisfaction] because it implies that Britney is not falsifying her attributes and therefore will satisfy her client.

The absence of references to ethical matters is clearly significant. A consequence of the illegality of sex work in South Africa, it is also an indicator of a pervading paradox, namely that, while the profession as a whole is illegal, the entries are nevertheless permitted, albeit much more cryptically than they would be were sex work permitted. Such a paradox helps to tinge every entry with a degree of daring transgression which is interpersonally significant, since it helps construct the reader and writer as collusive and mutually vulnerable and therefore already aligned to a degree.

Judgement, as it relates to value-based norms (i.e. Social Esteem), manifests in the data in Table 1.8.

Table 1.8 Frequency of Social Esteem choices.

Social Esteem subsystem	*Capacity*	*Normality*	*Tenacity*
Frequency	139	33	2

Capacity has to do with 'capability', that is, whether someone has the ability to do something (Martin, 2000a). We see evidence of this in the context of our data in examples such as:

(1)   everything goes
(2)   you name it, I do it
(3)   massage with nice ending
(4)   all private adult needs

The tokens of Capacity in these examples are suggestive of the kind, range and extent of the services that the sex workers offer – but without being specific, since such specificity, presumably, would expose the services for what they are.

Normality construes someone (or what they offer) as special, or better than average, in a way that others (here, rival sex workers) would aspire to emulate. This category of choice within Judgement/Social Esteem manifests in formulations such as the following:

(1)   A centerfold, busty, broadminded African <u>for an Oriental treat</u>, eager to please and tease ... 24/7. Safe.
(2)   JUAN-MARI. White lady. <u>Exotic show</u>, broadminded, spoil yourself.
(3)   BRANDY. <u>The dark chocolate.</u>

These choices could arguably be double-coded as [+Normality] and [+Valuation] on account of the constraints of the context and how 'hard' the linguistic tokens have to work to advertise the sex workers' services (without specifying them).

Finally, Tenacity, the last Social Esteem subsystem, relates to 'reliability' and 'resolve' (Martin, 2000a) – how one acts on one's traits. As indicated in Table 1.8, this has a very weak presence in the data, evident only in two instantiations:

(1)   20 Coloured stunning body 24/7 work alone ... <u>never tired</u>.
(2)   A all-in-one, A–Z, <u>do it all hour</u>, expert.

Both these examples characterize the sex workers as indefatigable, an attribute which relates to their ability to satisfy a potential client.

Moving beyond the detailed findings per APPRAISAL subsystem, we now summarize the findings of the APPRAISAL analysis more generally. The predominance of Appreciation choices in our data (with a frequency of 70 per cent of the total APPRAISAL choices) helps to present the sex workers as objects of sexual desire. Of the Appreciation tokens, 55 per cent are tokens of positive Valuation, emphasizing youthfulness, exoticism and, implicitly, sexual allure. The focus on physical attributes is particularly evident in the Appreciation choices, reinforcing the image of the sex workers as aesthetic objects. Finally, a significant feature of the APPRAISAL analysis is the frequency of Security tokens, which support our claim that the entries reflect a context of risk (associated both with the illicit status of commercial sex and with the risk of contracting a sexually transmitted disease). The instantiations of Security (85 in total) function as a reassurance to prospective clients that either a particular venue is discreet (presumably to mitigate the risk of exposure) or that the services offered are safe, which we read in the context of disease as 'healthy'. We discuss further the relevance of frequent references to safety and security in the next section, where we consider the contextual constraints shaping the entries.

1.5   A discourse of compromise: Working the contextual constraints

The SFL analysis of the data bears out our initial impression that the entries are shaped by an overarching discourse of compromise. By this we mean that the macro context boxes the writers in and limits the linguistic choices available to them. In this mode, they have to rely on their attributes and on linguistic innovation to entice the reader. We consider briefly the confluence of legal, practical and social factors that impact on the language the sex workers use to promote their services.

In terms of the legal constraints on the commercial sex industry, sex work is illegal in South Africa, according to the Sexual Offences Act No. 23 of 1957. Despite the recommendations of the 1999 Commission on Gender Equality (CGE) to decriminalize prostitution, it remains illegal (Wojcicki, 1999). One of the factors influencing the legal status of sex work in South Africa is public opinion and the stigma surrounding the industry. Wojcicki (1999) reports on a number of surveys commissioned by independent local research agencies (for example, the Human Sciences Research Council, Market Research Africa and Research Surveys' OmniCheck) which consistently show negative public opinion of sex workers and rejection of the proposal that sex work be decriminalized. In this regard, Port Elizabeth, the harbour city where *The Herald* newspaper is based, is no exception. Two petitions to the mayor of the city, which were published in *The Herald*, describe sex workers as needing 'to be placed on the straight and narrow road by our moral example' (Hill, 2009) and as 'bringing in sexually transmitted diseases, crime and devaluation' to otherwise good neighbourhoods (Kohler, 2004). The predominance of conservative attitudes towards sex work and its illicit status underscores why sex workers advertising their services in *The Herald* newspaper are forced to do so discreetly, relying on evoked APPRAISAL tokens, euphemisms, elliptical language and a focus on their physical attributes, rather than on the sexual services they offer. Additionally, the coy euphemistic references to a *massage* in the entries, the use of aliases and the use of cell phone numbers which cannot easily be traced to a street address (unlike landline numbers) are attributable to this moralistic dimension of the context.

In terms of the practical constraints on the data, the entries are short and concise as they appear in the Classified section of the newspaper, where the specified word limits per advertisement result in a telegraphic style typical of the 'small ad' genre (Coupland, 1996; Shalom, 1997). The high number of entries (each newspaper issue contained an average of 50) means that the sex workers have to be innovative in their linguistic choices in order to attract potential clients. This is achieved through, among other things, euphemism, deploying resources in the Appreciation subsystem to positively code their physical attributes, and relexicalization.

A significant social factor influencing our data is the tension between discourses of eroticism and those of disease transmission. Since transactional sex carries an attendant risk of contracting a sexually transmitted infection and given the high HIV/AIDS prevalence rates in South Africa, it is notable that the entries in our corpus do not contain explicit references to safe sex. However, the word *safe* appears 115 times, most frequently in the context of describing the safety of the locales in which the sex workers operate, for example, *private and safe venue.* The denotation of safe in such entries is ambiguous as it could equally refer to the clients' protection from molestation or to the safety of their property (e.g. car and other personal effects). A less frequent usage of *safe* is in examples like *Do everything. 100% safe.* We read this as an indirect reference to protection against STDs, including HIV/AIDS. It is significant that references to safety, while frequent in our data, are deliberately vague, providing a general reassurance to the potential client without confronting them with the risks against which 'safe' is defined. In an analysis of the language used to discuss safe sex amongst a sample of South African women, Hoosen and Collins (2004: 489) describe how the initiation of condom usage 'is experienced as a rude interruption of the fantasies of mutual trust that are an important part of intimate relationships'. The notion of interrupting a fantasy may apply to commercial sex in that overt references to health risks and disease transmission would jar with the discourse of sexual fantasy realized in the advertisements. This observation is supported by Peng (2007) who notes that the appeal of commercial sex is not about *buying* sex, it is about the transgressive nature of the sexual encounter. In this client-oriented study of sex work, reasons clients cited for the appeal of commercial sex include:

- the choice of sexual acts available and the capacity to specify a sexual act;
- the 'ability to seek out women with different attributes or images' (*ibid.*: 322);
- the opportunity to have sex with different people (outside the boundaries of a monogamous relationship).

Our data suggest that sex workers exploit these appealing aspects of commercial sex when they advertise their services; they evoke a world of sexual possibilities, where the client can play out their fantasies unchecked.

1.6   Conclusion

The analysis reveals that a discourse of compromise prevails in the entries, a discourse which allows the sex workers to navigate a narrowly circumscribed context. As mentioned above, salient features of this context include the illegality of sex work in South Africa, strong moral resistance to it (Keeton, 2009), the challenge of reconciling commercial sex with the attendant risk of HIV transmission, the fact that the entries are in competition with one another and that they appear in the classified section of the newspaper and so must be short. In relation to our first question about the 'discourse-world' evoked by the entries, the findings of our transitivity analysis show that the ideational world of the entries is restricted (and, seemingly, asexual). This is supported by our account of the circumstances which prevail in the entries, circumstances of manner being noteworthy for their vagueness. The analysis of the processes in the data reveals a high frequency of non-finite processes which express potentiality and a sense of futurity, for example, *ready to play and tease*. As a result, the entries conjure up a world of possibilities and of waiting, but not of action. The ability to 'make the entries come to life' by engaging the services of a particular sex worker lies with the reader (as prospective client). To access the meaning generated in this way and infer the underlying sexual content of the discourse, readers are required to draw on their Members' Resources, the social, cultural and linguistic resources needed to interpret a given text (Fairclough, 2001). Alongside the reader's MR, texts contain traces of the production process which serve as a set of cues to guide the interpretation process (*ibid.*). Our second research question pertains to the kinds of inferences readers need to make in order to decode the entries. These inferences are based on the available textual cues and information from the situational, intertextual, legal and social contexts. They can be categorized as follows:

1.   Extralinguistic inferences – the legal and social sanctions placed on commercial sex mean that, in a public domain like a newspaper, it has to be advertised implicitly.
2.   Linguistic inferences for ideational meaning
     i.   *Social* as in 'Social column' is a euphemism for commercial sex.
     ii.   High frequency linguistic tokens like *massage, passionate* and *sensual* carry sexual connotations, which in light of the surrounding text, is suggestive of the nature of the services on offer.

   iii.   Readers need to recognize that, in this context, terms like those above (and others such as *pleasure, tease, ultimate satisfaction*) are euphemistic and rely on indirectness. Readers must move beyond a purely literal, denotative interpretation of these terms to access their sexual subtext.

   iv.   The emphasis on physical features (as opposed to personality traits) is another important clue as to the sexual subtext of the entries.

3.   Meta-textual inferences – the textual pattern of the entries, with their shared semantic and structural features (in the form of contact details, a promotional part, and an identification part) cues readers to the underlying sexual content.

4.   Intertextual inferences – knowledge of similar texts within the intertextual context (e.g. dating advertisements, advertisements seeking friendship) also helps to distinguish the entries as advertisements for commercial sex.

In terms of the APPRAISAL analysis, we found that the APPRAISAL choices in the entries – principally epithets but, also, interestingly, classifiers and things – are often evoked rather than inscribed. To arrive at the sexual meaning generated through evoked tokens, readers are required to draw inferences from their knowledge of the sociocultural, linguistic and legal contexts in which the entries are located. By doing so, the reader engages with the sexual subtext that is created by the euphemisms, innuendo, hyperbole and metaphoric usage on the surface of the texts. Of the three Attitude subsystems, Appreciation tokens were statistically prominent in our data, constituting 70 per cent of the Attitude tokens. We argue that the frequent occurrence of Appreciation tokens helps to commodify the sex workers and the services they offer. Lastly, the APPRAISAL analysis found that the expressions of Attitude were frequently double- or triple-coded in the data. We suggest that these instances of multiple coding enable the writers to exploit maximally the linguistic resources in response to the demands of a complicated context. It is this facet of the analysis that enabled us to reveal the sex workers' agency and ingenuity in their entries.

In relation to our third question pertaining to the ways in which the entries are shaped by and shape the context, we showed essentially that the sex workers' discourse not only bears the impress of the context in which it is formulated, but helps create aspects of that context – as such it reflects and reinforces the ambiguous social status of sex work in South Africa. The bulk of the chapter reported on the 'wiggle room' that the sex workers exploit in their entries, identifying the linguistic devices used to promote commercial sex without explicitly referring to it. We argue that the sex workers are not engaging in a subversive discourse, nor are they seeking to revise the context in any radical kind of way. Rather, they are pushing back at the contextual constraints in a small but ingenious way – one, essentially, which will enable them to connect with a clientele. In the absence of pictures and other advertising media, the sex workers must embellish language and exploit its power of suggestivity to create a strobe-light of desire which entices the reader into a clandestine world of erotic fantasy, excess and indulgence. By means of linguistic devices such as euphemistic language, intertextual references to attractive celebrities and the APPRAISAL choices drawn largely from Appreciation, the writers, in effect, illuminate the tableau windows to which we referred at the beginning of this chapter.

Note

1. Sotho refers to the linguistic and ethnic group of people residing in Lesotho and the Limpopo and Gauteng provinces of South Africa.

References

Caldas-Coulthard, C. R. and Moon, R. (2010) 'Curvy, hunky, kinky': Using corpora as tools for critical analysis. *Discourse & Society* 21(2): 99–133.

Coupland, J. (1996) Dating advertisements: Discourses of the commodified self. *Discourse & Society* 7(2): 187–207.

Fairclough, N. (1992) *Discourse and Social Change*. Malden, MA: Blackwell.

Fairclough, N. (2001) *Language and Power*, 2nd edn. Harlow: Longman.

Halliday, M. A. K. (1994) *An Introduction to Functional Grammar*, 2nd edn. London: Edward Arnold.

Hill, R. (2009) Prostitutes need moral example. *The Herald*, 8 June, www.epherald.co.za/opinion/article.aspx?id=429831 (accessed 21 June 2009).

Hoosen, S. and Collins, A. (2004) Sex, sexuality and sickness: Discourses of gender and HIV/AIDS among KwaZulu-Natal women. *Psychological Society of South Africa* 34(3): 487–505.

Keeton, C. (2009) Sex work: Legalise or don't legalise. *Sunday Times*, 4 June, www.thetimes.co.za/News/Article.aspx?id=1011711 (accessed 21 June 2009).

Kohler, D. (2004) Move brothels/strip clubs/adult entertainment facilities out of residential areas in Port Elizabeth, www.gopetition.com/petitions/move-brothels-strip-clubs-adult-entertainment-facilities-out-of-residential-areas-in-port-elizabeth.html (accessed 21 June 2009).

Martin, J. R. (2000a) Beyond exchange: Appraisal systems in English. In S. Hunston and G. Thomson (eds) *Evaluation in Texts: Authorial Stance and the Construction of Discourse* 142–75. Oxford: Oxford University Press.

Martin, J. R. (2000b) Close reading: Functional linguistics as a tool for critical discourse analysis of texts. In L. Unsworth (ed.) *Researching Language in Schools and Communities: Functional Linguistic Perspectives* 275–302. London: Cassell.

Martin, J. R. and Rose, D. (2003) *Working with Discourse: Meaning Beyond the Clause,* 1st edn. London: Continuum.

Martin, J. R. and Rose, D. (2007) *Working with Discourse: Meaning Beyond the Clause,* 2nd edn. London: Continuum.

Martin, J. R. and White, P. R. R. (2005) *The Language of Evaluation: Appraisal in English*. London/New York: Palgrave Macmillan.

Peel, J. (2008) Marketing information. *The Herald,* www.epherald.co.za/aboutus/default.aspx (accessed 21 June 2009).

Peng, Y. (2007) Buying sex: Domination and difference in the discourses of Taiwanese Piao-ke. *Men and Masculinities* 9(3): 315–36.

Plumridge E. W., Chetwynd, J. S., Reed A. and Gifford S. J. (1997) Discourses of emotionality in commercial sex: The missing client voice. *Feminism & Psychology* 7(2): 165–81.

Ravelli, L. (2000) Getting started with functional analysis of texts. In L. Unsworth (ed.) *Researching Language in Schools and Communities: Functional Linguistic Perspectives* 27–64. London: Cassell.

Rickard, W. and Storr, M. (2001) Editorial: Sex work reassessed. *Feminist Review* 67: 1–4.

Shalom, C. (1997) The real supermarket of desire: Attributes of the desired other in personal advertisements. In K. Harvey and C. Shalom (eds) *Language and Desire: Encoding Sex, Romance and Intimacy* 186–203. London: Routledge.

Wojcicki, J. (1999) Race, class and sex: The politics of the decriminalisation of sex work. *Agenda* 42: 94–103.

2

Choice in a 'partly free' press: Evaluative key in Italian journalistic discourse

Elizabeth Swain[a]

Il quotidiano italiano. Circolare privata di gruppi di potere, strumento di occultazione delle informazioni troppo scomode, date ma date in modo che nessuno possa realizzarne il potenziale politico tranne i casi in cui servono al discorso a puntate. Macchine per una selezione classista del proprio pubblico.

The Italian newspaper. A private circular of power groups, a means for concealing inconvenient information, provided, but in a serial format, so that no one understands its political potential, save when the paper's interests are served. Machines for a class-based selection of their readership.

Umberto Eco

2.1 Introduction

This chapter is concerned with linguistic indicators of subjectivity in the Italian press, or, put more specifically, with those lexicogrammatical outcomes of choice in the interpersonal discourse semantics, which cumulatively define *evaluative key*. Drawing on the framework for describing evaluative key presented in Martin and White's account of appraisal (2005), the paper reports an exploration of the extent to which Italian journalistic discourse can be said to distinguish between the two broad categories of 'fact' and 'opinion' articles which are traditionally recognized in English

---

a   Elizabeth Swain is an applied linguist employed as a researcher and lecturer in English and translation at Trieste University, Italy, where she teaches postgraduate students of international relations. Her research interests lie in applications of linguistic theory to English language teaching and to discourse analysis. She has published articles on academic writing, language and humour, literary translation, foreign policy making discourse and, more recently, the multimodal discourse of political cartoons. A book on diplomatic discourse is in preparation.

and other language journalistic discourse, and which have each been found to correspond broadly to regular patternings of interpersonal meanings implicated in evaluative key. The investigation also seeks to establish whether, and to what extent, the three types of evaluative key found to exist in the English language press – reporter voice, correspondent voice and commentator voice (Martin and White, 2005; White, 1998; Iedema *et al.*, 1994) – can be said to be present in Italian journalistic discourse. The results from the analysis of a small corpus of Italian press articles are compared with, and discussed in relation to the afore-mentioned studies of the UK and Australian press and media, and to a recent analysis of Italian news reporting (Pounds, 2010). They are also considered in the light of sociocultural factors.

The chapter is organized as follows. §2.2–2.4 provide some contextual background information to, and a brief overview of linguistic studies of the Italian press, and a description of the corpus. §2.5 explains in more detail the concept of evaluative key and the kinds of appraisal meanings implicated in descriptions thereof. §2.6 and 2.7 describe the analysis and its results. §2.8 discusses the findings and §2.9 concludes by offering an interpretation of them in relation to the sociocultural and political context of Italian journalism.

2.2   The Italian press: Sociocultural considerations

Statistics from the *Accertamenti Diffusione Stampa* (ADS) and Italian National Institute of Statistics (ISTAT)[1] suggest that a large part of the population of Italy does not read newspapers, either in paper form (104 copies sold per 1,000 citizens) or online (about one fifth of the population regularly used the internet in 2010), and that about 80 per cent depends on the television for news. In accordance with Italy's regional history and character, most national newspapers have local as well as national editions: *Il Mattino* (719,000), the highest circulation newspaper, is classified as a regional paper, with 7 local editions as well as a national edition.

The most widely read national daily is the Milan-based *Corriere della Sera* with a circulation of about 620,000; this is followed by the Rome-based *Repubblica* on 580,000, the financial daily *Il Sole 24 Ore*, with about 344,000, the Turin-based *La Stampa*, 310,000, and the Milan-based *Il Giornale*, about 210,000, owned by the Berlusconi family.[2] Recently, public complaints about Italy's press have become more vociferous. The complaints are against government funding of newspapers and their consequent political bias, and against the close relationship of newspapers with interest groups (emblematized by Silvio Berlusconi's conflict of interest between his political career and media ownership). This public protest has given impetus to the emergence of new publications such as the Rome-based *Fatto Quotidiano* (circulation estimated around 110,000) and an online paper *Linkiesta*, founded respectively in 2009 and 2011. A full list of the national papers used for this study, together with their circulation figures, is provided in Appendix 1.

The 2009 world survey of press freedom by the NGO Freedom House ranks as 'free' the presses of all west European nations except Italy, whose press is ranked 'partly free'.[3] The parameter on which Italy scores highest is political interference, confirming the view of Umberto Eco cited at the start of this chapter. It seems likely that the political pressures to which the Italian press is subject affect not only ideational choices concerning what 'content' is reported in newspapers but also textual choices, concerning news discourse organization, and interpersonal choices concerned with the evaluation of things, events and people and with reader/author positioning. Political pressures, though not the focus of this chapter, are a significant feature of the sociocultural environment of the Italian press, and their possible connection with appraisal choices will figure in the discussion.

2.3   Studies of the language of the Italian press

Descriptions in Italy of language in the Italian press (e.g. Bonomi, 2002; Antelmi, 2006; Gualdo, undated) often reflect a prescriptive orientation and are situated in the context of the normative debate (ongoing since the Italian unification process began) about national standard versus regional varieties of Italian, and about 'standards' of Italian language use. Hence, these studies may also evaluate 'quality' in line with purist and language standardization principles (e.g. denouncing the widespread use of foreign – especially English – words and of 'regionalisms'). Dardano (1986), Bonomi (2002) and Antelmi (2006) also report stylistic analyses of lexis and syntax, and offer various classifications of text types within Italian journalistic discourse. Few studies of the language of the Italian press appear however to be concerned with matters of subjectivity/objectivity, although both Dardano (1986) and Bonomi (2002: 222) note a tendency to mix news and comment in the same articles. One exception in this scenario is a recent, contrastive study by Pounds (2010).

Pounds' investigation draws, like mine, on the appraisal framework and on Martin and White's concept of evaluative key (Martin and White, 2005, henceforth M&W). Her study may be located in the context of recent work (as in Thomson and White, 2008; Thomson *et al.*, 2008), exploring to what extent 'reporter voice' – a perceivably impersonal style described in §2.5 below – can be identified in journalistic writing in languages other than English.[4]

Pounds' study differs from mine however in several respects. First, like the multilingual case studies in Thomson and White (2008), it is concerned only with news reporting, and not with editorial/analysis/comment type articles. Second, as mentioned, it is a comparative study which investigates a smaller number of articles – seven from each of a smaller range of newspapers, two Italian (*Corriere della Sera* and *Repubblica*) and two British (the *Guardian* and the *Times*) – though in more detail. This greater detail entails a further difference with my study. Pounds introduces some adaptations to Martin and White's framework. She makes a more detailed classification of attributed and non-attributed material, taking into account the status of sources of attributed evaluation, and the evaluative implications of reporting verbs. Pounds also considers intensification via non-core vocabulary (the domain of the graduation system in appraisal). Another difference is her choice to interpret markers of modality and evidentiality as indicators of attitude (doubt, certainty) rather than as heteroglossic items from the engagement system. Further, she includes the parameters of 'narrative detail', of colloquial expression, and tense choice for reporting events (see Dardano, 1986: 253–61; Bonomi, 2002: 321–42 and Antelmi, 2006: 30–39 on the spoken, informal register of Italian journalistic discourse). Overall Pounds finds considerable differences in hard news reporting between the British and Italian newspapers (2010: 115–20). The Italian reporting tends to use more infusion, more 'evaluative reference',[5] more appreciation of the 'reaction' type, more dramatization (through narrative detail, present tense), more use of direct quotation, less quotation of experts, and greater use of mediated, first person affect. Pounds also finds some differences between the two Italian papers, whereas the British papers show more uniformity.

'Reporter' voice has been primarily defined in terms of appraisal features it does *not* have – principally, the absence or extremely rare use of unmediated judgements of behaviour – as compared to the two 'writer' voice styles (see §2.5 below). In this respect, Pounds' comparative investigation of reporter voice in English and Italian hard news reporting is innovative, bringing in new categories to consider in the description.

2.4   Choosing the corpus

My study, like M&W (2005) and earlier investigations using appraisal (Iedema *et al.*, 1994; White, 1998), is concerned not only with news reporting but also with evaluative styles of journalistic discourse typically found in comment/analysis/editorial type articles. The chosen corpus thus seeks to be broadly representative of a variety of styles, as well as of the full spectrum of political alignments. It consists of 40 articles taken from 14 national daily newspapers, whose political affiliation ranges from the left (*Unità, Liberazione, Il Manifesto*) to the stance of the Catholic Church (*L'Avvenire*) and the *Confindustria* or Confederation of Italian Industry (*Il Sole 24 Ore*), to the centre-left (*Repubblica*), the pro-Berlusconi (*Il Giornale*) and secessionist Northern League (*Libero*). (See Appendix 1 for the full list of papers used; Appendix 2 lists all the articles considered, together with their provenance, date and author where given.)

Matching the articles to conventional journalistic text categories, however, was not always possible. In English-language journalistic writing, conventional textual categories are traditionally signposted with bylines, section and page headings: 'news', 'comment', 'analysis', 'editorial', 'opinion' 'special feature' etc. Thus, in sourcing their material M&W (2005: 116) use conventional textual (as well as experiential content) categories: 60 articles were 'news page' items; 10 were from 'analysis' sections or with other 'evaluative' bylines, and 15 were from the comment/editorial/opinion pages. Knowing this provenance of their material *a priori* they were able to link the findings of their analyses to these explicitly named textual categories, and to report a fair degree of correspondence between them and their three-part typology of evaluative key.

Most Italian newspapers, by contrast, though recognizing in principle a 'factual' versus an 'opinion' category of writing, do not always apply any corresponding category headings systematically (see Bonomi, 2002).[6] The indexes below the nameplate on the front pages variously use pairs of terms such as *cronache*[7] – *opinioni; attualità* – *opinioni; notizie* – *commenti e inchieste; news* – *editoriali*. However, the inside pages and links to articles in both print and online versions often dispense with such labels and use more rarely than their English-language counterparts 'textual' bylines or section and page headings. Of the 40 Italian articles considered for this study, only 15 carried a textual byline or appeared in a section of the newspaper bearing a specific textual label. Italian newspapers appear to prefer experiential labels or headings, for example, *immigrazione* ('immigration') over textual ones. These experiential headings are often in the form of subheadings for smaller, 'satellite' pieces on a bigger story, for example, *'Il personaggio'* or 'character' (in a story); *'la polemica'* or 'the quarrel' between personalities about some controversial subject. This fits with the convention of placing adjacently on the same page both 'news' type accounts of, and comments on the same story (also noted by Pounds, 2010: 121). The parsimonious use of textual labelling in the Italian press meant that any representative selection of articles based on conventionally recognized textual categories was necessarily largely intuitive and impressionistic, relying on features such as text length, subject matter, headline/title and organization.

I did not choose articles provided by international press agencies (Reuters, AFP, APA, etc.), which are translated into Italian, rather than indigenous to the Italian press culture. However, I did use two articles from the Italian press agencies, ANSA and APCOM (since 2010, TM News).

The main period from which the articles are taken was summer 2009, and the stories they cover are concerned with contemporary topics such as the European parliamentary elections and the Berlusconi–Mills court case, which saw the then Italian prime minister accused of bribery, corruption and perverting the course of justice. Political coverage also included controversial issues of immigration, educational reform, the financial crisis, bioethics, the environment and nuclear power. The topics of news type articles in the corpus include war reporting and crime (arrests of mafia and child pornography suspects, murders and violent attacks).

2.5 Evaluative key

Also referred to as 'voice' and 'interpersonal style', evaluative key corresponds to a typical configuration of linguistically disparate appraisal resources realizing attitude, intensity and focus, and is responsible also for positioning authors and readers intertextually and dialogistically with regard to thematic content and the views of other authors and readers. As an abstract category, evaluative key can be described in terms of probabilities of occurrence of these types of resources.

The results of analysis for evaluative key in English language journalistic discourse have shown the presence of two main types: **reporter voice** and **writer voice**. These are found to correspond largely to the traditional division of newspaper articles into 'hard news' (popularly considered objective) and 'comment' (acknowledged to be subjective). Within the more subjective 'writer' voice category a further distinction is made between '**correspondent**' and '**commentator**' voice, with both inclined to make authorial evaluations of human behaviour, but the latter particularly inclined to make authorial evaluations of the moral sanctioning kind.

An account of evaluative key entails familiarity with appraisal, the theoretical framework on which it is based. The framework will be briefly outlined below, and illustrated with a preview of Italian language examples from the corpus used for this study.

Developed in the mid-1990s in the context of language in education, and out of studies of media discourse (Iedema *et al.*, 1994; White, 1998), and grounded in systemic functional linguistics, the appraisal framework provides a new set of tools for investigating evaluative meaning in verbal (and, more recently, visual; e.g. Economou, 2008, 2009) discourse. Previously, since the 1980s, evaluative meaning in the press had been largely the domain of critical discourse analysis (CDA). Applying adapted versions of systemic functional grammar, CDA 'interprets' grammatical features in terms of power and bias in its concern with uncovering racist, sexist, capitalist and other ideologically objectionable discourses in the press (e.g. Van Leeuwen, 1987; Van Dijk, 1988; Fowler, 1991; Fairclough, 1995), often tacitly subscribing to the view that unbiased and objective reporting is possible. Appraisal theory, by contrast, has no explicitly declared moral or political agenda but provides a rich and elaborate framework for describing lexicogrammatical choices in terms of what they contribute to attitudinal meaning, its intensity, and how these choices affect and effect intertextual and dialogistic positioning. The regular deployment of certain types of resources in association builds up a 'prosody' or evaluative configuration characterizing individual texts and the registers to which they belong. Readers unfamiliar with the appraisal framework and with the configurations of appraisal resources defining evaluative key might like to refer to Table 2.1 at the end of this section, while reading the following paragraphs. Based on M&W (2005), the table seeks to show, broadly, the characteristic presence or absence of different types of appraisal values implicated in the three evaluative keys found in English language journalistic discourse: reporter voice, and, within writer voice, correspondent and commentator voice.

Of the three appraisal systems – attitude, graduation and engagement – attitude has proven primary in distinguishing types of evaluative key and in accounting for perceptions of degrees of subjectivity of texts. The attitude system consists of three subcategories: affect, referring to emotional dispositions; judgement, concerned with moral and ethical judgements of human behaviour, and appreciation, which has to do with aesthetic evaluations of things, and also with assessments of their social value.

The degree to which different types of attitude are present in texts is, however, in itself insufficient to determine key. The source of the attitude, namely whether it is authorial (unmediated), or external (mediated, or attributed), is also crucial. If the attitude in a text is authorial, the impression of subjectivity is high; if attributed to some external source, an impression of impartiality can be maintained. Thus, the attribution category of the engagement system, which as its name suggests has the function of ascribing/mediating external viewpoints, is also important in describing evaluative key, and particularly in the first 'cut' between 'objective' reporter voice texts and 'subjective' writer voice texts. Within the judgement category of the attitude system, the distinction between social esteem and social sanction type evaluations, that is, between evaluations of people's normality, capacity and tenacity on the one hand (social esteem), and of their honesty and moral propriety on the other (social sanction), is also key to differentiating between the different voice styles: authorial social sanction is characteristic of commentator voice texts but not of reporter or correspondent voice texts; authorial social esteem is found in correspondent voice but rarely in reporter voice texts.

A further element implicated in the description of evaluative key is the presence of authorial directives, or exhortations to take some kind of action perceived as necessary and right, for example, *The government should take measures to cut public spending*. These are characteristic of commentator voice, but not of correspondent or reporter voice. I report below, by way of illustration, some Italian language examples of authorial and attributed attitude from my corpus. The provenance of each excerpt is provided after the English translation beneath. The attitude values are highlighted in bold throughout. In the examples of attributed judgement and appreciation and of observed affect, the source of the attitude or the emoter is also highlighted in bold, and underlined.

(1)   **Authorial affect**

       Oggi queste due forze di sinistra sconfitte ma non arrese   + security
       *(di questo siamo ben **convinti**) dovrebbero avviare una serie*
       di incontri ...
       Today these two forces of the left, who though defeated have
       not surrendered (of this we are quite **convinced**) should start
       a series of meetings ...   *Il Manifesto*

(2)   **Observed affect**
      *Nelle ultime ore non è cambiata **la posizione Britannica,***   - security
      ***preoccupata** che il nuovo assetto della supervisione*
      finanziaria in Europa indebolisca oltre misura i poteri
      nazionali di vigilanza e la finanza Britannica.
      In the last hours there has been no change in **the position
      of the British, concerned** that the new direction of financial
      supervision in Europe may excessively weaken British national
      sovereignty and finance.   *Il Sole 24 Ore*

(3)   **Authorial appreciation**
      *Lo stato di salute un po' **precario** del settore elettrico in Italia*   - social
      – causa non secondaria del black-out di ieri – affonda le sue   valuation
      radici nella tormentata storia del settore dal dopoguerra ai
      giorni nostri.
      The somewhat **precarious** state of the health of the electricity
      sector in Italy – no secondary cause of yesterday's blackout –
      is rooted in the tormented history of the sector from the end
      of the war to the present day.   *La Repubblica*

      Quattordici arresti in flagranza di reato nei confronti di   - reaction
      *persone trovate in possesso di migliaia di video **molto cruenti***
      di pornografia infantile
      Fourteen cautionary arrests of people found in possession of
      thousands of **shockingly crude** videos of child pornography.
      L'Avvenire

(4)   **Attributed appreciation**
      'Il respingimento deve essere certificato da un documento e
      non può essere rivolto a minorenni e donne incinte' ricorda
      *ancora una volta Laura Boldrini. **Boldrini reputa** positiva*   + social
      la proposta di Maroni di migliorare lo stato di protezione   valuation
      *dei rifugiati in Libia, finora **penosa***   - social
      'Refused entry has to be certified by a document and cannot   valuation
      be applied in the case of minors and pregnant women' Laura
      Boldrini recalls once again. **Boldrini considers** positive
      Maroni's proposal to improve the level of protection given to
      refugees in Libya, which has so far been **pitiful**.   *Liberazione*

(5)   **Authorial judgement: social esteem**
      Ma certo, Makiguchi! Sappiamo tutti chi è: pensatore e   + normality
      *pedagogista **celeberrimo,** teorizzatore della ormai diffusissima*
      (anche troppo!) 'educazione creativa'.
      But of course, Makiguchi! We all know who he is: an
      acclaimed thinker and educationalist, theorist of the now
      (excessively!) widespread 'creative education'.
      Corriere della Sera (byline: Immigration)

*Un paese **così ipnotizzato** dalle mitologie internazional-
mondialiste da credere ormai che la propria storia e la
propria identità non vogliano dire più nulla per nessuno, non
abbiano più alcun valore.*   - capacity

A country **so hypnotized** by international-globalizing
mythologies [ ] that it believes its own history and identity
no longer mean anything to anyone, or have any value.
Corriere della Sera (byline: Immigration)

***L'inossidabile** Mastella e **l'highlander** De Mita. I*   (ironical)
parlamentari europei se li troveranno a Strasburgo.   + tenacity
The **all-weather-proof** Mastella and **Highlander** De Mita.   + tenacity
Euro MPs will find them in Strasbourg.   *L'Unità*

(6)   **Attributed judgement: social esteem**
Con una certa astuzia, e sempre allo scopo di mettere paura a   - tenacity
*quelli che <u>**definisce 'fannulloni'** il Ministro della Pubblica</u>*   (-propriety)
<u>*Amministrazione*</u> *non ha fatto altro che dedicare l'intero
articolo 55-quinquies del decreto alle 'false attestazioni e
certificazioni'*
Somewhat cunningly, and with the aim of frightening those
he defines as '**loafers**', the Minister of Public Administration
has done no more than dedicate the whole of article 55 of
the decree to 'false declarations and certifications'   *La Stampa*

*'L'Arma – <u>**ha dichiarato il ministro della Difesa Ignazio**</u>*   + capacity
<u>*La Russa*</u> *- con l'operazione di oggi ha confermato l'eccellenza
della propria capacità investigativa e l'elevato livello di
professionalità del proprio personale'*
'The Military Police' – **<u>declared the Defence Minister</u>**
<u>Ignazio La Russa</u> – 'with today's operation has confirmed its
excellent investigative capabilities and **the high level of**
professionalism of its personnel'   *Il Sole 24 Ore*

(7)   **Authorial judgement: social sanction**
*Dal canto suo Berlusconi **fa lo smargiasso**: 'Spazzatura, solo*   - veracity
spazzatura. La spazzerò via come ho fatto a Napoli'
For his part, Berlusconi **plays the braggart**: 'Rubbish, pure
rubbish. I'll sweep it away like I did in Naples'   *Liberazione*

*Il nostro premier è, per l'ennesima volta, **un corruttore**, per*   - propriety
giunta impunito per legge.
Our Prime Minister is, for the umpteenth time, **a corrupter**,
and what's more, unpunished by the law.   *L'Unità*

(8)   **Authorial directive**   In Italian, as in English, directives may be expressed in
various ways but typically use forms of the verb *dovere* as here:
> *Come **le banche devono tornare ad essere più vicine alle imprese**, così i
> mercati devono tornare a funzionare nell'interesse degli investitori finali.*

Just as the banks must go back to being closer to businesses, so the markets must go back to functioning in the interest of final investors. *Il Sole 24 Ore*

(9)   **Attributed judgement: social sanction**
    Insegnanti, genitori e studenti, però, non possono contestarla   - propriety
    [Gelmini, Ministro Istruzione], altrimenti diventano
    '_fascisti rossi_'[8]
    Teachers, parents and students, however, cannot contest her
    [Gelmini, the Education Minister], otherwise they become
    'red fascists' *Il Manifesto*

    Il Ministro [Gelmini] ha commentato: '*Impedire, in un paese*   + veracity
    democratico, che si svolga la presentazione di un libro dà il
    senso dell'intolleranza e della prepotenza di chi vuole lasciare
    la scuola così com'è opponendosi al cambiamento. Il libro di
    Giordano **_contiene scomode verità_** *su una scuola diventata*
    un ammortizzatore sociale ...'
    The [education] Minister commented: 'In a democratic country, to prevent the presentation of a book gives an idea of the intolerance and bullying nature of those who want to leave the school system as it is, opposing change. Giordano's book contains **inconvenient truths** about a school system which has become a welfare system ...' *La Repubblica*

M&W (2005: 164–84) publish some of the results of the frequency counts (occurrences per 500 words) of their corpus study of English language journalistic voice or key, which, they write, largely confirm the findings of previous investigations by Iedema *et al.* (1994) and White (1998). Their 2005 study also refers to values for the different categories of the engagement and graduation systems (2005: 181–4), though the description does not provide the exact frequency rates for all categories. For ease of reference I provide a diagrammatic representation of the three evaluative keys in English language journalistic discourse, showing, as far as it was possible to establish, both the presence and absence of each type of attitude feature in each key. It should be emphasized that this is necessarily an approximation, first because, as the authors note, the presence of a feature across the range of keys is in most cases a matter of cline rather than of discrete categories, and second because M&W, due to lack of space, provide a selective prose description and not the complete statistical results of their study. The presence of a tick in Table 2.1 means that the corresponding feature is reported as a significant presence in the description of key; two or more ticks indicate that the feature is reported as particularly frequent, and no tick means that the feature is either not present or not mentioned as a significant presence in M&W's account.

Table 2.1 Evaluative key in English language journalistic discourse: rough diagrammatic representation of typically occurring attitude features (based on Martin and White, 2005: 164–84).

		Reporter voice	Writer voice	
			Correspondent voice	*Commentator voice*
Attitude	Authorial social sanction			✓✓✓
features	Authorial social esteem		✓✓✓	✓✓✓
	Authorial appreciation		✓	✓
	Authorial affect			✓
	Attributed social sanction	✓	✓	
	Attributed social esteem	✓	✓	
	Attributed appreciation	✓		✓✓✓
	Observed affect	✓	✓	✓
Directives				✓

Thus, applying the above profile specifications for evaluative key to the Italian language examples (1)–(7), we might expect examples (1), (7), (5) and (8) to come from a writer voice type text, typically associated with editorial type articles in English-language journalistic discourse, and not from a reporter voice type text, typically associated with news reporting articles.

2.6   Analysis

I analysed each of the 40 newspaper articles closely for values of authorial and non-authorial affect, judgement and appreciation, and for authorial directives. I calculated the frequencies of each category per 500 words in order to build up an attitudinal profile for each text. I then looked for any patterns that emerged when the attitudinal profiles for the individual texts were compared, and sought to operate a classification into groupings based on these.

2.7   Findings and discussion

As mentioned earlier, a table of the complete results of the analysis is provided in Appendix 2 (hereafter A2), it being too large and too detailed to include here. The table reports the frequencies per 500 words for all the nine attitude features listed in Table 2.1 above, in each one of the 40 articles analysed.

The texts in A2 are already arranged in two broad groupings of 20 texts each: texts A–T, and texts U–NN. Texts A–T all have authorial attitude, in most cases of at least two or three types; almost half have directives. Texts U–NN by contrast mostly have no authorial attitude and no directives, but they do have attributed attitude. I included eight texts with some authorial attitude in this latter grouping because they purport to be '*cronache*', i.e. news reporting, which suggests they belong with texts with no authorial attitude. To see how the evaluative key categories are distributed within each individual article, it is necessary to turn to A2.

The frequencies, frequency ranges and patterns of co-occurrence discussed below refer to the complete table of results in A2. As a prelude to the discussion and to grouping the texts on the basis of patterns of occurrence, two further tables are provided in this section to provide an overview of some key results referred to the corpus overall. Table 2.2 summarizes for each attitude feature, the number of texts in which it is present. Table 2.3 shows the range of the frequencies per 500 words for each evaluative key category across the corpus as a whole. Table 2.4, in §2.7.1 below, proposes a broad specification of the features of two voice styles which appear distinguishable in the Italian language corpus.

Table 2.2 shows how widely or narrowly represented each attitude feature is across the corpus as a whole. It reports the number of texts (out of 40) in which each feature – attributed and authorial affect, two types of judgement, appreciation, and authorial directives – is present.

Table 2.2 Number of texts (out of 40) in which each attitude feature is present.

	Attributed context	*Authorial*
Affect	30	3
Judgement: social esteem	17	21
Judgement: social sanction	11	17
Appreciation	23	15
Directives	0	9

It can be seen that the most widely represented feature is affect in attributed contexts (30 texts), followed at some distance by attributed appreciation and authorial social esteem (23 and 21 respectively), authorial social sanction and attributed social esteem (each present in 17 texts), authorial appreciation (15), attributed social sanction and authorial directives (11 and 9 respectively). The least represented category is authorial affect (3).

If we consider the category frequencies per 500 words as calculated for each individual text, considerable variation among the texts emerges. Table 2.3 shows the frequency range for each attitude feature.

Table 2.3 Range of frequency per 500 words of each attitude feature in the corpus overall.

	Attributed context	*Authorial*
Affect	1–12	0.9–1
Judgement: social esteem	1–3.3	0.5–16
Judgement: social sanction	0.4–16.7	0.5–10.4
Appreciation	0.5–11.9	1–13.2
Directives		0.4–4

From these figures it can be seen that the widest range is shown by attributed social sanction. This is followed by authorial social esteem, attributed appreciation and affect, and authorial social sanction, all with similarly wide ranges. The narrowest ranges are for authorial directives, attributed social esteem, and lastly, authorial affect. The only frequency for attitude categories which M&W report is authorial appreciation – a complete range from 0.9–11.3 – so no other comparisons can be made with the results reported here.

Some observations can be made however concerning associations between the different categories within the individual texts. If related to the patterns reported by M&W for evaluative key in English language journalistic discourse (see Table 2.1 above), some consistencies and disparities emerge.

Authorial affect is absent from all but 3 of the 40 texts. As can be seen from A2, in these 3 texts it is present at the low frequencies of 0.9 and 1, and co-occurs with **unmediated social esteem and sanction**. M&W's profile for English commentator voice would predict such a co-occurrence. The rarity and low frequency of authorial affect throughout the Italian corpus also corresponds with their findings (2005: 177).

Affect in attributed contexts by contrast is present in 30 texts, with a frequency ranging from 1–12. It is the most widely represented category in the corpus. In M&W's study, it occurs in all three types of evaluative key (2005: 178).

As shown in A2, 27 texts have some form of **authorial attitude**, which, if present in significant amounts, would assign them to the English writer voice category. Only 13 texts have no **authorial attitude** at all. Of the 13 texts within this authorial attitude-free category, 7 have varying amounts of attributed appreciation, 3 have only observed affect, and 4 have neither. These 13 authorial attitude-free texts would seem to correspond variously to English reporter voice profile.

Tables 2.2 and 2.3 above show that **authorial social sanction** occurs in 17 texts, at frequencies between 0.5 and 10.4. **Authorial social esteem** is present in 21 texts, at frequencies between 1–12.9. Looking again at the full list of profiles for individual texts in A2, **authorial social esteem** and **authorial social sanction** can be seen to co-occur in 13 texts. 8 texts have both **authorial social sanction** and **authorial appreciation**. 4 of the texts with authorial social sanction, esteem and appreciation also have **authorial directives**. Texts with authorial social sanction and these patterns of features would correspond to the English language commentator voice profile reported in M&W. The 7 texts without authorial social sanction and only **authorial social esteem** and **authorial appreciation,** would correspond to the correspondent voice profile (2005: 178) outlined in Table 2.1 above.

From Tables 2.2 and 2.3 it can be seen that **authorial directives** are present in 9 texts, in frequencies ranging from 0.4 to 4. A2 shows that in the majority of cases – 6 – they co-occur with **authorial social sanction.** In 3 cases, however, 2 of which are higher frequency ones (frequencies of 4 and 3), authorial directives do not co-occur with authorial social sanction. This is different to M&W's English language corpus data (2005: 179), in which authorial directives were present only with authorial social sanction, the hallmark of commentator voice texts. In the two Italian texts with high-frequency directives but no authorial social sanction – one about educational reform in *Corriere della Sera*, the other about financial regulation in *Il Sole 24 Ore* – the directives did co-occur however with **authorial social esteem**. The findings for directives are discussed in §2.7.1 below.

Referring again to A2, it can be seen that 27 texts – almost three quarters of the corpus – have **authorial attitude** of some kind or other, in various combinations. Of these, 22 (over half the corpus) have **authorial judgement** and 5 have **only authorial appreciation**. Two of the three low frequency cases of authorial affect appear in texts with authorial social sanction; the other occurs with authorial social esteem.

14 of the 27 texts with **authorial attitude** have no or very low frequencies of **mediated judgement or appreciation**. Of the 13 texts with **no authorial attitude**, only 7 deploy attributed attitude of these types, and 5 of these 7 texts have observed affect too.

Attributed social sanction is less common than authorial, occurring in only 11 (against 17) texts, with a frequency range of 0.4–16.7. It co-occurs with the authorial kind in just over half of the cases (6). In 2 of the remaining 5, it co-occurs with authorial social esteem and/or appreciation. In 3 of these 5, it is present with observed affect and/or mediated judgement and appreciation.

Authorial social esteem is present in 21 texts, just over half the corpus. It appears in 14 texts with, and in 7 texts without, **authorial social sanction**. In the latter 7, it occurs with **authorial appreciation**. This configuration – authorial social esteem and appreciation – would appear to correspond to the English language correspondent voice profile, outlined in Table 2.1 above.

2.7.1   Grouping the articles for evaluative key

Grouping the texts into 'voice' categories on the basis of these findings was not a straightforward matter. As anticipated by the broad division of the texts into two groups, a first, broad distinction between more 'reporter voice' and more 'writer voice' texts was mostly operable following criteria adopted for M&W's English language corpus of journalistic texts. Table 2.4, based on the individual text profiles in A2, suggests which attitude features are more or less likely to figure in each voice style (one tick means possible, three ticks means very probable). There are some differences with the voice styles in English language journalistic discourse, represented in Table 2.1 above.

Distinguishing within writer voice, between correspondent and commentator voice was even less straightforward. Within writer voice

Table 2.4 Proposal for evaluative key in Italian language journalistic discourse: rough diagrammatic representation of attitude features (based on Appendix 2).

		Reporter voice	*Writer voice*
Attitude	Attributed appreciation	✓✓	✓✓
features	Authorial appreciation	✓	✓✓✓
	Observed affect	✓✓✓	✓✓✓
	Authorial affect		✓
	Attributed social esteem	✓	✓✓
	Authorial social esteem	✓	✓✓✓
	Attributed social sanction	✓	✓✓
	Authorial social sanction	✓	✓✓✓
Directives			✓✓

profiles, there is a wide range of frequencies for unattributed judgement and appreciation. Overall, there were some differences of patterning in the Italian texts with respect to the patterns reported for English, so that the Italian voice profiles did not fit neatly into the English voice categories. I mentioned earlier the presence of directives in 4 texts with no authorial social sanction, for example. These texts, using the 'English' criteria, would fall within the correspondent voice category, though they are hortatory and thus more suited perhaps to a commentator voice label. In an article (text F in A2) where the author gives his opinion about cuts in government funding for universities with no authorial social sanction, there is a frequency of 4 per 500 words for authorial directives. Here is an excerpt:

> *Io sono d'accordo, perché l'università di fatto gratuita è un trasferimento dai poveri ai ricchi, ma se questa è la strada occorre il coraggio di dirlo. Ciò che non si può fare è aspettare senza far nulla, e lasciare che a novembre le università chiudano.*
>
> I agree [with raising university tuition fees and giving grants to the less well off], because universities which are free are a transfer from the poor to the rich, but if this is the way, then we have to have the courage to say it. What we can't do is wait and do nothing, allowing the universities to close in November.

Text F also carries a hortatory byline: *comportamenti da cambiare* ('behaviours which need changing') and has one instance of authorial affect: *Io sono d'accordo* ('I agree').

Text O, a comment on the losses taken by the Italian left in the European elections, similarly has no authorial sanction but uses directives. It also appears with a *'commento'* byline in the newspaper, assigning it to the traditional text category of comment:

> *Noi del Manifesto, nella modestia della nostra forza e delle nostre capacità, siamo in edicola (è il nostro campo) per questo. Compito arduo, ma necessario, indilazionabile.*
>
> We at the *Manifesto*, in the modesty of our strength and capacities, are available at the newsstands (our battleground) for this. It's a hard task [to defeat the threat of Berlusconi-ism], but it's necessary, and cannot be put off.

Text J – a comment piece from *Il Foglio* supporting the denial of global warming, with the byline *Per gli americani il global warming non è un problema* ('For the Americans, global warming is not a problem') – has no authorial judgement at all, only authorial appreciation, but opens with a directive:

> *La prima annotazione da fare è sottolineare come rispetto a poco tempo fa certo atteggiamento catastrofista sia passato di moda, faccia meno notizia ...*
> The first thing we have to do, is emphasize how, compared to not so long ago, a certain catastrophist attitude has gone out of fashion, and is less newsworthy ...

The fourth text P from *Il Sole 24 Ore* argues for regulation of the financial and banking sector. An instance of directives from this text appears in example (8) in §2.5 above.

Similar cases of hortatory prose without authorial social sanction were not reported by M&W. The fact that one tenth of my texts had authorial directives without authorial social sanction suggests the difficulty of applying the probabilities for English commentator voice to Italian journalistic discourse, which includes patterns of **authorial social esteem + directives**.

Another striking aspect which emerged was that the category groupings operated on this basis did not always correspond to the conventionally recognized Italian journalistic text categories (in the 14 cases where these were indicated, or where their provenance as either '*cronaca*' or correspondent/editorial type reporting was recognizable). By contrast, in English language journalistic discourse, reporter voice was found to correspond to 'news' reporting, and 'correspondent' and 'commentator' voice to comment/analysis/editorial type articles. There is also one case of a text (political analysis) in the conventional '*editoriale*' category, assigned to 'correspondent' voice owing to its lack of authorial sanctioning. This non-correspondence with conventional journalistic text types was particularly the case with articles labelled 'news' or '*cronaca*', however. Texts from 'news' and '*cronaca*' sections did not always correspond to the English language 'reporter voice' profile, but corresponded to the correspondent and even commentator voice profile in a couple of cases.

As an example, text CC, entitled *Caserta, 'arancia meccanica' a Lusciano: seviziato e violentato per ore* (Caserta, 'clockwork orange' in Lusciano: tortured and raped for hours), from *Il Mattino* newspaper, includes two instances of authorial social sanction (the protagonists are *delinquenti incalliti*; *avevano continuato a delinquere*), and one of authorial appreciation (the story is macabre), though it is clearly in the style of the *cronaca nera*, or crime reporting category:

> *La storia, **macabra**, è quella di **due delinquenti incalliti** di 31 e 26 anni di origini tunisini, già noti alle forze dell'ordine, arrivati in Italia circa dieci anni fa dove **avevano continuato a delinquere**.*
> The **macabre** story is one of two **hardened criminals** aged 31 and 26, of Tunisian origin, already known to the law, who arrived about 10 years ago in Italy, where they **continued to commit crimes**.

Similarly, a piece mainly concerned with factually reporting the results of the European elections (text S) opens with sarcastic comments about two 'life-long' politicians of dubious reputation who were elected (see the second example of (5) in §2.5, of ironically positive authorial social esteem), and about another candidate – the aristocrat Emanuele di Savoia – who failed. Like text CC above, this article mixes comment with reporting. Another instance is an apparent 'news' item in *Liberazione* (text EE) which reports, in inverted commas by way of a title, media and political reactions to an escort scandal involving the then prime minister Berlusconi; its function appears to be to introduce more detailed accounts of the story appearing on later pages. This article however – though it is in the style of Italian 'news' reporting – deploys authorial social sanction to judge Berlusconi's behaviour (negative veracity, see example (7) in §2.5 above). There are two other examples from the corpus of a mismatch between conventional and the assigned 'English voice style' categories. Text NN is an account of the ceasing of hostilities in Ireland and Iraq, and text N is an account of the post-war history of electric power in Italy. Both text NN from *Il Foglio*, which has the idiosyncratic *'cronachette'* ('little chronicles') byline, and text N from *la Repubblica*, which also carries a *'cronaca'* byline, have authorial social esteem and appreciation at frequencies between 3 and 5 occurrences per 500 words yet are assigned to a supposedly factual type of reporting by the respective newspaper. This excerpt, which follows an account of two episodes of 'terrorist' violence in Iraq and in Northern Ireland, is from article NN:

> *Ma non è rimasto molto altro. Fatta eccezione per **<u>questi sprazzi di ferocia</u>**, entrambi i gruppi sono **<u>'deadenders', bande al capolinea</u>**. I superstiti di **<u>terribili</u>** guerriglie che un tempo hanno prima dichiarato guerra e poi l'hanno sostenuta per anni contro interi eserciti, ma **<u>ora sono guerriglie moribonde, abbandonate dai loro stessi membri</u>**.*
> But there's not much of that left. Apart from these **<u>gushes of ferocity</u>**, both groups are **<u>dead-enders, at the end of the line</u>**. Survivors of **<u>terrible</u>** guerrilla groups, who once declared war and then carried it on for years against whole armies, but who are **<u>now moribund, abandoned even by their own members</u>**.

Overall, then, there are some similarities with English language journalistic discourse as documented by M&W. The most obvious ones are the overall rarity of authorial affect, and the presence throughout the corpus of observed affect. Also, there does seem to be a 'cut-off point' in the corpus (from text U on, in A2) where authorial attitude ceases to be present and where attitude is mediated, if it is present at all. Concerning the differences with English, there would seem to be rather more variation between the individual text patterns, and less conformity to a particular voice style 'standard' in the Italian corpus (confirming the findings of Pounds, 2010). This situation is evident in the combination of authorial directives with authorial social esteem or appreciation but without social sanction. It is also apparent in the varied profiles which correspond to the conventional Italian journalistic textual categories, where these are signalled. This is particularly the case for news reporting in Italian, which, unlike in English, seems to allow for authorial attitude, even occasionally judgement of the sanctioning kind.[9]

2.7.2   Other features implicated in evaluative key in the Italian press

Pounds's (2010) analysis of Italian news reporting led her to suggest some additional categories of analysis (outlined in §2.3 above) for Italian reporter voice. My analysis of a wider range of text types including comment and analysis-type articles suggests that there are further, more or less prominent features contributing to interpersonal meaning, which are more or less strongly implicated in evaluative key in Italian journalistic discourse. Due to lack of space, I have not covered them here, but they warrant a brief mention. One concerns the considerable use of irony and sarcasm, where positive attitude is meant to be read as negative, as in the *Repubblica* excerpt reported in §2.8. below. The irony here is both intertextually recoverable and textually cued. The explicitly positive evaluation of Berlusoni's propaganda initiative appears in a newspaper well known for its strong opposition to the man and his party, and cannot be taken literally. This reading is reinforced by the ideational description of Berlusconi's unawareness of a prostitute next to him in bed. Irony might be seen as a reader-positioning mechanism akin to the 'concur' category within the engagement system, whereby the reader is positioned as complicit and so concurring with the author's intended evaluation. Another feature is the frequent use of both expository and rhetorical questions, again resources which come under the engagement system (respectively entertain and concur) in the appraisal framework. And yet another is the frequent use, in articles deploying attitude, of scare quotes (noted, for example, by Antelmi, 2006). This usage is evident in article headings and subheadings, where they are often used to attribute evaluative positions to external sources, often in the form of a paraphrase. This heading from a front page article in *Liberazione* anticipating further coverage of a political scandal, illustrates the practice:

> *'Avvenire': Il Premier chiarisca. Voto anticipato? PD in ansia. Berlusconi: 'spazzatura'. Fini: 'a rischio la politica'*
> *'Avvenire'* [a Catholic national daily]: The Prime Minister must clarify. Will there be an early vote? The Democratic Party is anxious. Berlusconi: 'rubbish'. Fini: 'politics at risk'

Scare quotes are also used for purposes of authorial distancing, but particularly for indicating a non-literal (often evaluative) meaning of the term thus marked off, which the reader is positioned to share. These engagement features of Italian journalistic discourse do appear to be quite distinctive and would merit investigation in any further categorization of evaluative key, as would, of course, values for the graduation system concerned with intensity and focus and found to be particularly relevant in English language reporter voice (White, 2011).[10]

2.8 The role of evaluative key in a 'partly free' press

Before closing, the title of my contribution to this volume imposes some reference to the political interference at the basis of the distinctive categorization by Freedom House of the Italian press.

Political, economic and legal constraints on a 'partly free' press may mean certain kinds of information may be withheld or manipulated (censorship), or even fabricated (lies, propaganda). Investigating the manner in which a party or government line is maintained in journalistic discourse probably implies investigating patterns of deployment of engagement and graduation as well as attitude resources. Whether, and if so how, the 'partly free' classification could be linked to the deployment of attitude resources which I have described, can only be here a matter of speculation.

About one half of my corpus articles were concerned with topics that were politically sensitive at home in Italy (education, immigration, corruption scandals, energy, environment, the justice system) and may therefore have been more or less heavily influenced by the political affiliation of the paper in which they appeared. Almost all of them are assigned to the writer voice category, and were forms of analysis or comment on the topic covered. What emerges from the articles is that, rather than attitudinal reticence of the authorial voice, there seems to be an emphasis on authorial attitude. This may be to plug an ideational gap imposed by the paper (censorship of information), or alternatively, it may work to bolster the partisan position of papers with persuasive ammunition of the moral kind. The very different coverage of the Berlusconi–Mills scandal and the Naomi 'Papì' scandal respectively in *Il Giornale* (text E) and the *Repubblica* (text I) illustrates well this type of rhetorical behaviour. Each paper deploys authorial attitude to savage its opponents. These are respectively Antonio Di Pietro[11] and the Italian left for calling for new elections in the wake of the scandals, and Berlusconi for trying to convince the electorate through a media initiative to believe that his family situation is a model for all:

> *Per fare concorrenza a uno come Di Pietro bisogna necessariamente mettersi **alla sua misura, ovvero scendere molto in basso. Bisogna toccare il fondo.** Subito raggiunto, prendendo a pretesto una faccenda personale, una vicenda privata per inscenare **una isterica e ipocrita questione di credibilità politica.** (from Il Giornale)
> To compete with someone like Di Pietro you have to necessarily put yourself **on his level, which means going very low. You have to touch the bottom,** which is quickly reached, using a personal matter, a private affair, as a pretext to create **a hysterical and hypocritical issue of political credibility.**

> *In un'atmosfera da caminetto, il premier ricompone **la solita scena patinata da fotoromanzo a cui non crede più nessuno, neppure nel suo campo.** La tavolozza del colore è sempre quella: una famiglia unita nel ricordo sempre vivo di mamma Rosa e nell'affetto dei figli; l'amore per Veronica ferito – certo – ma impossibile da cancellare; [] **una vita irreprensibile che non impone discolpa; l'ingenuità di un uomo generoso e accogliente che non si è accorto della presenza accanto a lui, una notte, di uno 'squillo' di cui naturalmente non ha bisogno e non ha pagato perché da macho latino conserva ancora il 'piacere della conquista'.** (from La Repubblica)
> In a fireside atmosphere, the prime minister reconstructs **the usual shiny photo romance scene that nobody believes in any more, not even in**

his own camp. The palette is always the same: a family united in the living memory of Rosa his mother and in the love of the children; the love for Veronica [his now estranged wife] is wounded – of course – but impossible to extinguish; **an irreprehensible life, which needs no exoneration from blame; the ingenuousness of a generous, welcoming man who didn't notice there was a prostitute next to him, one night, who of course he didn't need and never paid because as a macho Latin, he maintains the love of conquest.**

In my corpus the majority of texts on international news are in the 'reporter voice' category, with no authorial attitude. It would be interesting to compare Italian language comment type articles on international news – which is arguably a little less subject to domestic political pressures – to see whether they deploy authorial attitude of the same types found in the articles on domestic news, and at similarly high frequencies.

2.9   Conclusion

The analysis suggests that a broad, two-part typology of the reporter voice and writer voice kind may be applicable to Italian journalistic discourse, though the distinction is perhaps less clear-cut. However, the variety and non-conformity which emerged from the study suggest that a three-part typology of key similar to that for English language journalistic discourse may not be applicable: Italian journalistic discourse may accommodate too great a level of individualism on the part of journalists to permit labelling for voice styles on the same probabilistic lines. This lower level of conformity to conventional text types is partly institutionalized in the unsystematic use of conventional text categories in the newspapers, and the frequent preference for experiential type headings and subheadings over textual ones. The apparently less clear distinction between 'factual reporting' and 'comment' articles may be variously interpreted in the light of sociocultural factors. It may reflect a common impulse to fill ideational gaps constrained by forms of censorship with interpersonal meaning, or, particularly in domestic political reporting, it may respond to the perceived need to bolster the political allegiances of newspapers through moral suasion techniques entailing deployment of authorial attitude. It may also reflect a traditional feature of the Italian journalistic culture which encourages journalists to be *opinionisti,* and to acquire professional prestige and social status through their comments and opinions on politics and society. And, although to say so is to perpetuate cultural stereotyping, it may have something to do with the greater role, also observed in this context by Pounds (2010), played by spontaneity and emotionality in Italian culture generally.

In summary, the analysis for appraisal resources of attitude has shown some advantages over the largely syntagmatic (and normative) descriptions of the Italian press reported early in this chapter. The focus on choices in the three attitude categories of appraisal, and their patterned expression in Italian language journalistic texts has enabled a meaningful comparison and contrast with voice styles found applying the appraisal framework to the English-language press. The results of the appraisal analysis shed light on the mixing of news reporting and commentary in Italian press articles observed by some authors, and provide a basis from which to inquire into the relationship between these choices in interpersonal meaning and the contextual environment in which they are made.

Notes

1. Accertamenti Diffusione Stampa (Italian audit bureau of newspaper circulation) 2008: www.adsnotizie.it/; ISTAT www.istat.it/en/ from the Annuario ISTAT 2010.
2. It is noteworthy that these circulation figures are not markedly different from those for the quality press in the UK, a country with a comparable population size. Large swathes of the UK press audience read the daily tabloids *The Sun* and *The Daily Mail*. However, it might be argued that Italian publications with predominantly similar content (e.g. human interest and celebrity stories, which are covered in publications like *Oggi*, *Gente* and *Chi*) do not enjoy the status of newspapers in Italy.
3. At the time of writing, the Freedom House report for press freedom in 2009 is unavailable online. The 2011 report – in which Italy's press is still classified as 'partly free' – can be accessed here: http://www.freedomhouse.org/sites/ default/files/FOTP%202011%20Tables%20and%20Graphs_0.pdf Assessment criteria applied include 'the legal environment in which the media operate; the degree of political control over the news media; economic pressures on content; and violations of press freedom ranging from the murder of journalists to other extra-legal abuse'.
4. These studies have shown that Japanese, French, Indonesian, Thai and Chinese hard-news reporting achieve a degree of impersonalization similar to that found in English reporting.
5. By 'evaluative reference' Pounds means use of attitudinally-charged names to refer to represented participants, e.g. 'bullies'. As assessments of behavioural

dispositions, such choices are classifiable within the judgement category of the attitude system, and when authorial, they contribute to an impression of subjectivity typical of the writer voice style.

6. Bonomi (2002: 222–8) lists nine conventionally recognized text types, which are becoming less distinct from one another; Dardano (1986) refers only to the *cronaca, pastone politico* (a commentary on domestic politics by a correspondent) and *intervista* (interview).

7. The *'cronaca'* category is broadly similar to 'news' reporting in terms of the field values of purpose (reporting information) and subject matter (crimes, scandals, misdemeanours, war and politics). However, it is not systematically used within newspapers to designate a category of reporting. There are also different, 'colour-coded' categories of *'cronaca': cronaca rosa* (celebrity gossip and human interest; *cronaca nera* (crime, scandals); *cronaca bianca* (local news) (Online version of Treccani encyclopaedia www.treccani.it/vocabolario/cronaca/, accessed 11 March 2013).

8. Here the attribution is typographically expressed through quotation marks, a practice widely used in Italian journalistic discourse.

9. This convention is hinted at in the idiosyncratic and original label of *'cronachette'* used in the *Foglio* newspaper: the diminutive *-ette* hints at self-indulgence, as well as at the 'de-dramatizing' pose the paper sometimes likes to adopt.

10. White (2011) analysed the use of graduation in reporter voice articles to convey attitude in a seemingly objective fashion, a process he termed 'tarnishing and burnishing'.

11. Founder and leader (1998–2013) of the *Italia dei Valori* ('Italy of Values') party, which stands against corruption, Di Pietro became famous for his role as public prosecutor during the 'Clean Hands' scandal in the early 1990s. He resigned as party leader after the party's poor performance in the 2013 elections.

References

Antelmi, D. (2006) *Il discorso dei media.* Rome: Carocci.

Bonomi, I. (2002) *L'Italiano giornalistico.* Florence: Cesati.

Dardano, M. (1986) *Il linguaggio dei giornali italiani.* Bari: Laterza.

Economou, D. (2008) Pulling readers in: News photos in Greek and Australian broadsheets. In P. R. R. White and E. Thomson (eds) *Communicating Conflict: Multilingual Case Studies of the News Media* 253–80. London: Continuum.

Economou, D. (2009) Photos in the news: Appraisal analysis of visual semiosis and verbal-visual intersemiosis. Unpublished PhD dissertation, University of Sydney.

Fairclough, N. (1995) *Media Discourse.* London: Edward Arnold.

Fowler, R. (1991) *Language in the News.* London: Routledge.

Gualdo, R. (undated) La Lingua dei Giornali Italiani, www.treccani.it/Portale/sito/lingua_italiana/speciali/giornale/gualdo.html (accessed 11 February 2013).

Iedema, R., Feez, S. and White, P. R. R. (1994) *Media Literacy.* Sydney: Disadvantaged Schools Programme, NSW Dept. of School Education.

Martin, J. R. and White, Peter R. R. (2005) *The Language of Evaluation: Appraisal in English.* London: Palgrave Macmillan.

Pounds, G. (2010) Attitude and subjectivity in Italian and British hard-news reporting: The construction of a culture-specific 'reporter' voice. *Discourse Studies* 12: 106–37.

Thomson, E. and White, P. R. R. (2008) *Communicating Conflict: Multilingual Case Studies of the News Media.* London: Continuum.

Thomson, E., White, P. R. R. and Kitley, P. (2008) 'Objectivity' and 'hard news' reporting across cultures. *Journalism Studies* 9: 212–28.

Van Dijk, T. (1988) *News as Discourse.* Hillsdale, NJ: Erlbaum.

Van Leeuwen, T. (1987) Generic strategies in press journalism. *Australian Review of Applied Linguistics* 10(2): 199–220.

White, P. R. R. (1998) Telling media tales: The news story as rhetoric. Unpublished PhD dissertation, University of Sydney.

White, P. R. R. (2011) English language hard-news style as a strategic stance: Understanding the rhetorical potential of the 'objective' news report. Contribution to the panel 'The entextualisation of journalistic stance: cross-linguistic and cross-media insights', 12th International Pragmatics Conference, Manchester, UK, 3–8 July.

Appendix 1: The Italian national dailies and press agencies from which the articles for this study were taken, with circulation figures where available

National dailies

	URL	Circulation[*]
Avvenire	www.avvenire.it/	103,203
Corriere della Sera	www.corriere.it/	620,605
Il Foglio	www.ilfoglio.it/	20,000
Il Giornale	www.ilgiornale.it/	214,052
Il Manifesto	www.ilmanifesto.it/	29,008
Il Mattino	www.ilmattino.it/	719,000
Il Riformista	www.ilriformista.it/	17,000
L'Unità	www.unita.it/	61,492
La Stampa	www.lastampa.it/	309,150
Liberazione	www.liberazione.it/	NA
Libero	www.libero-news.it/	126,549
Opinione	www.opinione.it/	NA
Repubblica	www.repubblica.it/	556,433
Sole 24 Ore	www.ilsole24ore.com/	343,855

[*] Source: http://wapedia.mobi/it/ as declared to *Accertamenti Diffusione Stampa*: http://www.adsnotizie.it/

Italian press agencies

ANSA	www.ansa.it/
APCOM	www.apcom.net/

Appendix 2: Frequencies of attitude features per 500 words in individual articles

	A	B	C	D	E	F	G	H	I	J	K	L	M	N	O	P	Q	R	S	T
Authorial																				
social sanction	–	6.7	1.7	1.9	5	–	10.4	4.2	9.6	–	2.8	1.4	7.5	–	3	–	9.8	–	2.5	1.9
social esteem	5	5	–	10	16	7.1	2.2	5	12.5	–	12.9	–	1.2	3.5	8.2	4.8	5.3	–	2.5	1.9
appreciation	2.5	–	13.2	5.9	1	4	3.2	2.5	5.7	5.2	2	2.1	2.5	5	–	13	–	4.7	–	1.9
Attributed																				
social sanction	–	16.7	–	–	–	1	–	0.4	4.3	0.7	–	1.4	–	–	–	–	1.7	–	–	–
social esteem	3.3	3.3	1.7	–	–	–	–	–	2.4	0.7	1.2	–	–	–	3	–	1.7	0.9	–	1.9
appreciation	–	1.7	–	0.9	–	–	–	–	0.5	–	–	–	4.2	–	8.2	0.7	–	2.8	–	0.6
Observed																				
affect	2.8	8.3	2.5	2.9	4	–	–	4.5	5.3	3.7	4.5	–	3.3	5	3	1.4	0.9	3.8	–	3
Authorial																				
affect	–	–	–	0.9	–	1	–	–	–	–	–	–	–	–	1	–	–	–	–	–
Auth.directive	–	–	1.7	0.9	–	4	1.5	0.4	0.5	0.7	–	–	–	–	3	3	–	–	–	–

A   La Parabola del Prodismo. *Corriere della Sera.* Angelo Panebianco, 26.01.2008, online, editorial.
B   Contestato il Ministro Gelmini. *Il Manifesto.* 16.06.2009.
C   'Scomodità' che fa crescere. Questo sono gli immigrati per noi. *Avvenire.* Pio Cerocchi, 20.05.2009.
D   L'integrazione non si fa così. *Corriere della Sera.* Ernesto Galli della Loggia, 20.05.2009.
E   Il Richiamo giustizialista. *Il Giornale.* Paolo Granzotto, 20.05.2009.
F   Prova di verità per gli Atenei. *Corriere della Sera.* Francesco Giavazzi, 24.06.2009.
G   La Mafia ringrazia. *Il Manifesto.* Giuseppe Di Lello, 11.06.2009.
H   Ventun anni per fare giustizia. *Opinione.* Biagio Marzo, 8.06.2009.
I   La Verità che non può dire. *La Repubblica.* Giuseppe D'Avanzo, 24.06.2009.
J   A Siracusa inizia il G8 sull'ambiente e i ghiacci dell'Antartide crescono. *Il Foglio.* Piero Vetti, 22.04.2009.
K   L'Europa premia i partiti conservatori. Grecia e Scandinavia in controtendenza. *La Repubblica.* Anonymous, 8.06.2009, online, politica (politics).
L   Aeri ed elicotteri Fininvest diventano voli di Stato. *l'Unità.* Claudia Fusani, 05.06.2009.
M   Falsi certificati, carcere per i medici. Dipendenti imbroglioni e dottori compiacenti potranno essere condannati fino a 5 anni. *La Stampa.* Roberto Giovannini, 20.05.2009, online edition under heading 'il caso' (the case) + paper edition with no additional byline.
N   Dal nucleare al grande buio quarant'anni di sfide perdute. *La Repubblica.* Ettore Livini, 29.09.2003, online, cronaca.
O   E' il momento di ripartire. *Il Manifesto.* Valentino Parlato, 8.06.2009, online, comment.
P   Le regole? Sono il pettine per sciogliere i nodi. *Sole 24 Ore.* Marco Onado, 20.05.2009, online and inside cover, no byline
Q   Le leggi 'à la carte' e il libro paga del grande corruttore. *l'Unità.* Marco Travaglio, 08.06.2009, online, analysis.
R   Via libera alle nuove lauree nel segno della flessibilità. *la Repubblica.* Monica Ellena, 19.06.2004, online, Università.
S   Ecco la lista degli eletti in Europa. *L'Unità.* Anonymous, 8.06.2009, online, 'speciale europee' (European elections special).
T   Maroni: 'Avanti coi respingimenti'. Per Berlusconi 'i centri sono lager'. *Liberazione.* Laura Eduati, 20.05.2009, online + print version.

Table of frequencies continued:

	U	V	W	X	Y	Z	A	B	C	D	E	F	G	H	I	J	K	L	M	N
							A	B	C	D	E	F	G	H	I	J	K	L	M	N
Authorial																				
social sanction	0.5	–	–	–	–	–	–	–	2.7	–	2.3	–	–	–	–	–	–	–	–	–
social esteem	0.5	5.8	–	–	–	–	–	–	2.7	–	–	–	1	–	–	–	–	–	–	3
appreciation	–	8	–	–	–	–	–	–	2.7	–	–	–	1	–	–	–	–	3	3	4.6
Attributed																				
social sanction	3.9	–	1.8	–	–	–	–	–	–	–	–	–	–	–	–	6	0.68	–	–	–
social esteem	1	–	2.5	1	9	1	–	–	–	–	–	–	–	–	–	–	–	1.6	–	1.5
appreciation	–	3.5	1.5	5.9	3.6	5.5	–	0.8	–	–	11.9	–	–	–	–	–	0.68	–	–	–
Observed																				
affect	2.1	3.5	2.5	2	–	1	8.5	–	–	2	9.5	–	5	–	–	12	2.72	6.4	3	9.1
Authorial																				
affect	–	–	–	–	–	–	–	–	–	–	–	–	–	–	–	–	–	–	–	–
Auth.directive	–	–	–	–	–	–	–	–	–	–	–	–	–	–	–	–	–	–	–	–

U	Scontri Berlusconi-Giudici Le Mills e una Notte. *Il Riformista*. Fabrizio d'Esposito, 20.05.2009, online & print.

V	Ancora Barroso: Degno campione di un'Europa malata di liberismo. *Liberazione*. Bruno Steri, 20.06.2009, online

W	Berlusconi, inchiesta Bari: altre 3 ragazze parlano di denaro ricevuto. Polemica su tg. *Il Mattino*. 18.06.2009, online, news.

X	Studenti italiani tra i più scarsi dell'area OSCE. *Il Mattino*. 22.06.2009.

Y	Alitajani. *Il Foglio*. David Carretta, 10.03.2009, 'cronachette'.

Z	Arrestato a Caracas il superlattitante Salvatore Miceli. Anonymous *Il Sole 24 Ore*. 21.06.2009.

AA	Referendum o astensione La Mappa dell'incertezza. *Avvenire*. Giovanni Grasso, 20.06.2009.

BB	Pedofilia, maxi-operazione: arresti e indagati in tutt'Italia. *Avvenire*. 20.06.2009, 'indagine' (inquiry).

CC	Caserta, 'arancia meccanica' a Lusciano seviziato e violentato per ore. *Il Mattino*. 22.06.2009, online.

DD	In Somalia ucciso in un attentato il ministro della Sicurezza. *Il Sole 24 ore*. 18.06.2009, online 'notizie mondo' (world news).

EE	'Avvenire': Il Premier chiarisca. Voto anticipato? Pd in ansia. Berlusconi 'spazzatura' Fini: 'a rischio la politica'. *Liberazione*. 20.06.2009, online.

FF	Napoli, madre e figlia arrestate al Vomero mantenevano una casa di appuntamenti. *Il Mattino*. 18.06.2009, online.

GG	Al vertice UE intesa vicina per Barroso e sfuma l'ipotesi Mauro. *Il Sole 24 ore*. 18.06.2009, online.

HH	Afghanistan: 7 poliziotti uccisi. *ANSA*. 6.07.2009.

II	Afghanistan; Esplosione uccide 2 soldati Usa, totale sale a 6. *APCOM*. 6.07.2009.

JJ	Aldrovandi: Condannati 4 poliziotti. *ANSA*. 6.07.2009.

KK	Cina, protesta uiguri. Donne in piazza. Riparte la protesta. *Il Giornale*. 7.07.2009 (from *APCOM*).

LL	Viterbo, neonato gettato dal balcone. Arrestata la cugina: 'Era gelosa'. *La Repubblica*. 30.05.2009, cronaca.

MM	Arrivano i primi 'schiaffi' alla politica bioetica di Obama. *Il Foglio*. Valentina Fizzotti, 27.03.2009, online, 'cronachette'.

NN	Guerra finita in Irlanda e in Iraq, i terroristi attaccano il 'powersharing'. *Il Foglio*. 11.03.2009, online, 'cronachette'.

3

The use of appraisal resources in the construction of second language teacher-researcher identity

Norma Barletta,[a] Jorge Mizuno[b] and Gillian Moss[c]

3.1 Introduction

In the theory and practice of systemic functional linguistics (SFL), the notion of choice is of central importance. The systems which represent the meaning potential of the language are made up of paradigmatic contrasts, sets of alternatives available to writers and speakers of the language as they go about making meaning. As Halliday (2004: 23) put it, 'A text is the product of ongoing selection in a very large network of systems – a **system network** … a language is a resource for making meaning, and meaning resides in systemic patterns of choice' (original emphasis). In analysing text from a systemic functional perspective then, a large part of the analyst's task is to interpret the meanings chosen in the text in contrast to other possible meanings which could have been chosen in the context but were not.

In this chapter, we set out to interpret the meanings of choices from the appraisal system (Martin, 2000; Martin and White, 2005) made by a

---

a   Norma Barletta is Associate Professor at Universidad del Norte in Barranquilla, Colombia. She works closely with Jorge Mizuno and Gillian Moss. Their research interests include discourse analysis, especially of educational texts; relations between discourse, learning and citizenship; teacher development; and second language teaching and learning. Among their publications are the books *El texto escolar y el aprendizaje: Enredos y desenredos* (Textbooks and learning: Entanglements and disentanglements) and *Urdimbre del texto escolar: ¿Porquéresultandifícilesalgunostextos?* (The tapestry of the textbook: Why are some textbooks difficult?). They are also interested in applying SFL to the description of Spanish.

b   Jorge Mizuno is an Emeritus Professor at Universidad del Norte in Barranquilla, Colombia.

c   Gillian Moss is an Emeritus Professor at Universidad del Norte in Barranquilla, Colombia.

group of Colombian postgraduate students. In particular, we focus on how these choices are used by these writers in the process of constructing for themselves a new identity as teacher-researchers. We consider appraisal resources, more specifically the resources of attitude and engagement, to be of particular relevance in this process of identity construction. The expression of certain attitudes, especially when invoked or implicit, may often be a defining characteristic of participants in specific discourse communities. Novice writers, therefore, are likely to make language choices which associate them with the community's values and goals and thus help to gain them recognition as members. Similarly, the use of engagement resources to revoice or quote experts in the field in order to lend authority to their own work and to do so in ways which are generally acceptable and recognized within the community is an important stepping-stone towards fully-fledged membership. We will see how the appraisal choices made by these teacher-writers in the construction of their new identity as teacher-researchers vary in their similarity to choices made by more experienced writers in the field.

The study presented in this chapter was carried out at the Universidad del Norte in Barranquilla, Colombia with students of a postgraduate diploma in the teaching of English. All the students are in-service teachers of English, non-native English speakers. The texts analysed are the monographs written by the students as a requisite for graduation. The structure of these monographs will be described in detail in §3.3.

In the first section of the chapter, we present some theoretical viewpoints on the question of identity and its relation to discourse and knowledge. We then describe in more detail the study: context, participants, texts; and the methodology used for the analysis, before going on to describe findings as regards the use of attitudinal resources and engagement resources in the monographs analysed. Finally, we attempt to draw some conclusions as to the characteristics of the identity the writers construct for themselves through these choices, their success in this endeavour and possible pedagogical implications of these conclusions.

3.2 Identity, discourse and knowledge

Identity, in simple terms, means 'being recognized as a certain "kind of person"' (Gee, 2000–2001: 99). Ochs (1993: 288) defines it as 'a range of social personae, including social statuses, roles, positions, relationships, and institutional and other relevant community identities one may attempt to claim or assign in the course of social life'. Individuals can not only have different affiliations, roles and positions, but they can also create new identities depending on context, situation, purpose, and so on.

The process of identity construction is a semiotic process that can involve many forms of representation, such as clothing, gestures, and art. Language is a major system for social and individual representation and a privileged resource for identity construction. 'Identities [...] are discursively, by means of language and other semiotic systems, produced, reproduced, transformed and destructed' (De Cillia *et al.*, 1999: 153). Following Ivanič (1998), discourse is 'the mediating mechanism in the social construction of identity', that is, 'the way in which people take on particular identities is by reproducing and receiving culturally recognized, ideologically shaped representations of reality' (17).

An individual is recognized as a certain type of person because of how other people interact with him or her, or through the discourse of other people about him or her (Gee 2000–2001). What is at work is a process of recognition, or of interpretation of the identity of the individual based on certain behaviours in a particular environment. A reader can deduce or ascribe a certain type of identity to a writer based on an interpretation of the linguistic choices of the text and the type of interaction accomplished in the reading process which, in turn, is propitiated by the choices in the discourse of the writer.

Wenger (1998), however, argues that who we are is not so much who we say we are or what others say we are, though these can be part of what we are, but identity 'is produced as a lived experience of participation in specific communities' (*ibid.*: 151). For Wenger, the construction of identities is profoundly connected to the participation of individuals in the practices of social communities and becoming a member of a community of practice is a form of competence. A similar idea, but one specifically focused on the use of language, has been developed around the notion of discourse community, though it has not often been addressed in terms of identity construction. Swales (1990) referred to the notion of discourse community to emphasize academic communities' sharing of linguistic forms and rules and the use of the more stable and further-reaching written medium rather than the oral one.

In describing the characteristic features of a discourse community, Swales (1990) highlights the fact that it agrees on a set of common goals, develops mechanisms of intercommunication among members, creates mechanisms for participation and sharing information and feedback, possesses one or more genres to pursue its goals, uses a specific set of lexical choices, and has mechanisms and conventions to control newcomers on the margins of or outside the group. Belonging to a certain discourse community requires training to achieve a suitable level of relevant content and discourse expertise in the given genres, that is, a certain competence. Not surprisingly then, there are expert and novice members. Experts, according to Duszak (1997: 25–6), are prototypical members in that they are assumed to combine high field expertise with high language skills.

The discourse we discuss in this paper is that of a group of teachers who aspire to be recognized as members of the discourse community of applied linguists. The method to achieve this recognition is by using the written language in ways they believe are shared by the members of that community, specifically the conventions of the institutionalized genre of a monograph, which bears resemblance to the Research Article (RA). The use of references and citations, the subsectioning of the text, the use of nontextual material such as tables, all of which have characterized the development of RAs in ELT/Applied Linguistics (Swales 1990), are part of the conventions adopted by the group of novices. A significant move towards their construction as community members is the recognition of the ideas and contributions of visible and older members and the status of the new piece of research in relation to the existing knowledge.

Individuals do not construct their utterances by themselves but use the words of others in a complex and conflictual process. In Bakhtin's words:

> Our speech, that is, all our utterances (including creative works), is filled with others' words, varying degrees of otherness or varying degrees of 'our-own-ness', varying degrees of awareness and detachment. These words of others carry with them their own expression, their own evaluative tone, which we assimilate, rework, and reaccentuate. (Bakhtin, 1999: 130)

It can be said, then, that part of the academic task of novices consists of precisely this borrowing, appropriation, re-elaboration of others' voices, usually those of authorities and experts, in order to be accepted as part of a specific community and to formally establish a new identity.

Writer identity, according to Ivanič (1998) entails four aspects or four ways of conceiving it: *autobiographical self, discoursal self, self as author,* and *possibilities for self-hood.* The *autobiographical self* is associated with how the experiences, background and life history make writers write in the way they do. We do not have an individual biographical portrait of each of the writers whose works we analysed, but we do know the following:

- that they all are non-native English teachers who had obtained an undergraduate degree in Colombia;
- they had not taken formal courses in academic writing;

- they share a common profession and the daily experience of teaching English to students in a classroom;
- they also share a desire to obtain postgraduate education, a common coursework and a number of preparatory readings prior to submitting their final monograph.

The *discoursal self* 'is the impression – often multiple, sometimes contradictory – which they consciously or unconsciously convey of themselves in a particular written text' (*ibid.*: 25). This is the identity that is constructed through the particular choices in their writing, specifically in this paper, through the choices within the appraisal system, in terms of attitude and engagement resources. The discoursal self thus constructed must be interpreted by analysing the linguistic features of the monographs against the context of production and consumption of their texts: they are the final requirement for graduation; these are artefacts that can be considered as a synthesis of what the teachers are left with, or what they choose to represent as their gains in knowledge, growth and development as teachers and researchers after a great effort towards professional and personal development. Each monograph should reflect an awareness of a problematic situation and describe needs that are unmet, as well as make an attempt to provide a solution based on a personal understanding of the knowledge that has been made accessible to them through a postgraduate diploma course.

The third category, *self as author*, focuses on the degree of authority the author claims with respect to the content in a piece of writing. This angle of identity can be conveyed through the representation of objectivity of the content of the writing or the responsibility taken for the assertions made. Hyland (2002) argues that academic writers do not all stick to impersonal, faceless discourse and that even in this apparently dry genre there is room for negotiation of academic identities. According to Ventola (1997: 176), 'academic texts are not more objective than other texts; they are simply more effective at hiding subjectivity linguistically'. This aspect of identity is explored here through the analysis of the engagement resources described below.

Regarding the fourth meaning of identity, *possibilities for self-hood*, these are the options that the socio-cultural and institutional context make available for writers. In this particular case, the set of alternatives is rather limited. The monograph must be written within the conventions of the community of applied linguists, perhaps not the rigid and demanding standards of the Centre (Canagarajah, 2002), but certainly local and institutional ones. Centre is a term used by Canagarajah (1999) to refer to the industrially and economically advanced English-speaking communities (mainly North America, Britain, Australia and New Zealand). Periphery, in turn refers to the usually less developed societies which are historically more recent users of English. According to Duszak (1997) local and institutional standards are less rigid and mostly concerned with successful message exchange.

Canagarajah (2002) establishes a clear-cut difference between two opposite traditions of knowledge construction. The tradition of scientific positivism, a paradigm inherited from the Enlightenment, although not as powerful today as it used to be in the middle of the last century, has been dominant for a long time. From this perspective knowledge is universal, stable, decontextualized and value-free. A post-modernist perspective on knowledge, on the other hand, will conceive it as discursively shaped, constantly negotiated and collectively constructed through the collaboration of different human agents. It changes and is reconstructed periodically under contextual influences and also under the influence of values and beliefs, which necessarily render it subjective. From a critical perspective, the domination of empirical and positivist science is the result of the multifaceted expansion of the worldview of the West in complicity with the colonial enterprise, a product of 'a Judeo-Christian worldview based on individualism, detachment from and control over nature, a teleological view of time, and the celebration of reason' (Merton, 1970, cited in Canagarajah, 2002: 58) which complements the political, cultural and economic agenda of the Centre. A post-Enlightenment view of knowledge recognizes a dynamic relation between text and knowledge and questions the role of publications in legitimizing knowledge produced in the Centre. In constructing identity, then, writers situate themselves with regard to the perspective on knowledge to which they subscribe.

On the matter of the legitimation of knowledge, Bernstein (2000: 157) distinguishes between *horizontal discourse* which is segmentally organized and differentiated according to the way 'the culture segments and specialises activities and practices', and *vertical discourse* which has a systematically principled structure. Horizontal discourse is typical of 'common sense' knowledge and is therefore potentially accessible to all, while vertical discourse is typical of academic disciplines in both science and humanities and has 'strong distributive rules' which regulate access to it (*ibid.*). Within vertical discourse, Bernstein further distinguishes between hierarchical and horizontal knowledge structures. A hierarchical knowledge structure, typical of the natural sciences, 'attempts to create very general propositions and theories, which integrate knowledge at lower levels, and in this way shows underlying uniformities across an expanding range of apparently different phenomena', (*ibid.*: 161). In contrast, horizontal knowledge structures, typical of the social sciences and humanities, 'consist of a series of specialised languages with specialised modes of interrogation and criteria for the construction and circulation of texts' (*ibid.*).

Elaborating on Bernstein's theory, Maton (2007: 97) proposes a topology of legitimation codes of specialization for different disciplines. The notion of legitimation codes refers to the ways in which writers in different disciplines strive to give their texts authority and status and to ensure that they are recognized and respected within the academic community in question. Maton's topology differentiates between knowledge-oriented legitimation codes and knower-oriented legitimation codes. Knowledge-oriented legitimation codes emphasize the possession of knowledge (procedures, skills, techniques) and require the writer to appeal to these factors in establishing the authority of his/her text. These codes are generally related to hierarchical knowledge structures. Knower-oriented legitimation codes emphasize the disposition or 'gaze' of knowers and require the writer to stress the legitimacy of his/her identity, or that of the informants consulted, as knower(s) in the particular context under study. These are likely to be related to horizontal knowledge structures. Maton also posits the existence of relativist codes which require neither the possession of knowledge nor the gaze of knowers for legitimation and elite codes which require both. In this study, we will be making reference to knowledge-oriented legitimation codes which are typical of applied linguistics and knower-oriented codes which are important in the context of recent ethnographic research in which participants in the situation under study have a say in the analysis of their experience (Hood, 2007).

3.3 The study

The present study focuses on the written production of a group of in-service teachers from the Caribbean coast of Colombia who took a postgraduate diploma course in English Language Teaching over one year at a private university in the region. The course leads to the degree of 'Specialist in the Teaching of English'. It also counts as the first year towards a Master's degree in English Language Teaching offered by the same institution.

The teachers come from large and small towns and villages in the region; they teach at schools (pre-school, primary and secondary), universities and language centres in the region. Classes take place on Fridays and

Saturdays every other week. For some teachers, attending the sessions necessitates travelling two to six hours from their towns to the university and sometimes paying for overnight lodging, though some find accommodation with relatives. They all feel they need to study to become better teachers and serve their students and institutions better.

During the diploma course the teachers take classes in History and Theory of ESP (English for Specific Purposes), Learning Processes, Language as Discourse, English Teaching Methodology, Materials Evaluation, Materials Design, Course Design, and Evaluation and Assessment. Simultaneously they carry out a needs analysis in the institutions where they work and, based on the results, they design a course and materials for their target groups. In this process they have the support of a tutor during research tutorial sessions in small groups every weekend that they have classes. The readings for the courses, usually book chapters and articles in the field of applied linguistics, are made available for the participants and are, with very few exceptions, in English. The tutorial sessions are held in the language chosen by the participants. Some groups decide to use Spanish all the time, others start in English and switch to Spanish at certain points, and others stick to English throughout. At the end of the first semester the teacher-writers submit a first report on their research process. It contains a description of the context and methodology of the research, and the results and pedagogical implications of their needs analysis. On completion of the diploma course six months or so later, they submit the whole research work as a monograph. These monographs are read and graded by the tutor but also by another evaluator, usually a faculty member in the programme.

The first part of the monographs contains the following chapters: Introduction, Rationale, Research Methodology, Results of Needs Analysis, and Pedagogical Implications. The second part is the description of the English course they design to meet the needs identified in their research. This part includes: Approach to Education, Approach to Learning, Approach to Language, Goals and Objectives of the Course, Syllabus Design, Content of the Course, Teaching Methodology, Learning Evaluation and Course Evaluation.

The corpus consists of a set of twenty examples of monographs from the postgraduate diploma course described above. The monographs chosen were those which were available in digital form at the time the corpus was first collected (Barletta, 2007). An initial reading of these texts allowed us to identify two fairly distinct registers in use in virtually all cases: a reporting register in which the teacher-writer describes the context of their study, records actions taken in the research process and describes the data collected and the results of analysis of these data; and an expository register used by the teacher-writer to justify the type of study undertaken and decisions made about methodology and data collection instruments and to discuss pedagogical implications of the results and decisions about approaches to course design made on the basis of such implications. It is typically in this second, expository register that teacher-writers attempt to construct their identity as researchers and to align themselves with points of view expressed by course tutors and by authors recommended in course bibliographies. For the purposes of the detailed analysis to be presented in what follows, we have concentrated on those sections of the monographs in which the expository register is principally used: Rationale, Methodology, Pedagogical Implications, Approaches to Course Design and Conclusions. In analysing appraisal choices made by the teacher-writers in these sections of the monographs, we focus on the interpersonal metafunction, in seeing the stance they construct towards the content they present as structuring their identity in relation to the presumed reader-evaluator; however, we also relate these choices to the ideational meanings which are at stake.

The system of appraisal is one of the principal resources for the realization of interpersonal meanings. Through its subsystems of *attitude*, *engagement* and *graduation*, it provides resources for writers or speakers to position themselves in relation to phenomena which they are describing and also in relation to views expressed by other writers or speakers. Attitudinal resources relate to feelings and values attributed to people, objects, phenomena or ideas; graduation addresses the degree of force assigned to such feelings and values, while engagement relates to the manipulation of different voices in the text and the writers' or speakers' degree of commitment to them. Our analysis of these writers' choices of appraisal resources is based principally on the theory of appraisal as presented by Martin (2000) and Martin and White (2005). We have, however, adapted the network presented by Martin and White (2005: 38, 104, 134, 154) and White (personal communication, July 26, 2011) in accordance with the aims of the study and the nature of the data. First, we decided to focus our analysis on the subsystems of attitude and engagement since we consider that the analysis of attitudinal resources allows us to perceive ways in which our teacher-writers make choices of evaluative lexis which they hope will associate them with the values and goals of the programme and therefore of the tutors who will evaluate the monographs. Similarly, we are interested in analysing the way students make use of engagement resources both to quote experts in the field in order to lend authority to their own work and to express the degree of certainty they feel with regard to the results of their research. It should be pointed out, however, that some features, particularly of modalization, which Hood (2010) deals with under the category of graduation, we have dealt with in the analysis of engagement. For example, Hood considers modal verbs such as 'should', 'have to' and 'must' in terms of *graduation: force* (*ibid.*: 93) since they indicate varying degrees of force of obligation. We have taken these as contrasting with the monoglossic, unmodalized simple present or past tense forms and therefore as indications of heterogloss, with varying degrees of investment (White, pers. comm. 2011).

Furthermore, within the subsystem of *attitude, affect* is very infrequent and we have therefore included no further levels of delicacy; *affect*, then, is analysed simply as positive or negative, and invoked or inscribed. *Appreciation*, which is the resource of *attitude* most frequently chosen by our teacher-writers (cf. Hood, 2010: 82), and *judgement* are taken to two further levels of delicacy, as shown in Figure 3.1.

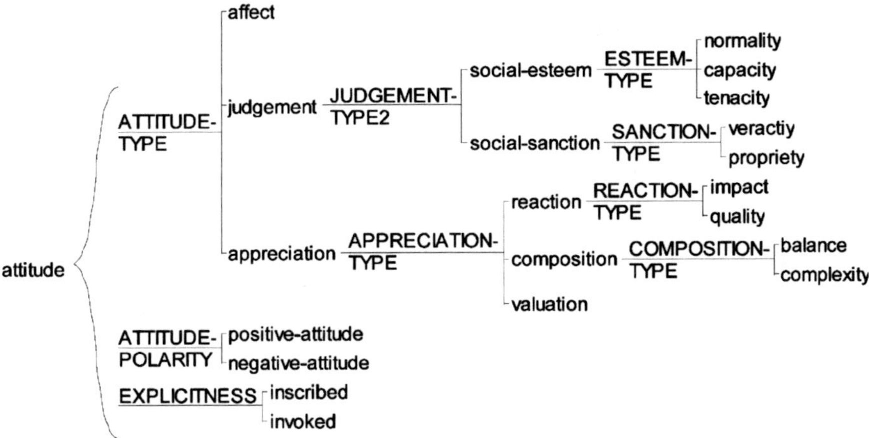

Figure 3.1 System network for attitude.

As regards the subsystem of *engagement*, it was not possible to differentiate clearly in the data between subcategories of *monogloss* using either Martin and White's (2005: 100) categories of *taken-for-granted* and *at-issue*, or White's (pers. comm. 2011) categories of *presume* and *assert*. *Monogloss* has therefore not been further subdivided in this study. By contrast, in the subsystem of *heterogloss*, the data suggested some further levels of delicacy. In cases of *denial*, there appeared to be a purposeful choice between *absolute* and *attenuated denial*; these have therefore been included in our system network. For example, in (1), the writer is *absolute* in her *denial* of the possibility of removing help, whereas, in (2), the *denial* is *attenuated* by the use of **completely**:[1]

(1)   The provision of such help **cannot be removed** and must not be seen in isolation.

(2)   A lesson report **is not a completely accurate** report of what happened during a lesson.

In the case of *heterogloss: contract: proclaim,* we have found it useful to include White's (*ibid.*) expansion of the network to include the category *justify.* The teacher-writers in our study have considerable recourse to this option in order to justify their decisions, as exemplified in (3):

(3)   With respect to methodology, this must be based on both inductive and deductive **because** the emphasis of the course will be speaking and also **because of** the grammar rules the students must learn in order to be better speakers of the target language in the target situation.

In the category of *entertain,* we have considered it useful to differentiate between levels of writer *investment* in the proposition: *high, median* and *low* (*ibid.*). Teacher-writers in the study frequently make use of *high investment* in propositions through the choice of modality such as **must** and **should**, as, for example, in (4) and (5):

(4)   (...) the approach to language **should be** skills-based which is going to help learners to arise strategy awareness (...).

(5)   You **must have** a theory of the strategies you will investigate in your research.

Finally, we have included in the subcategories of *expansion,* one that we have called *L2 use,* where we feel that the teacher-writer's choice of engagement resource has been limited by his/her repertoire as a non-native writer of English. Examples of this are presented in (6) and (7):

(6)   **It is advocated** to satisfy the students' needs through input that is meaningful and useful for their lives.

(7)   **Mackay (1978) confirms my decision** when he says: They are two formal ways of gathering information by questionnaires to be complemented by the learner or teacher or by means of a structured interview (MacKay, 1978: 21)

The network used in our analysis of engagement is presented in Figure 3.2.

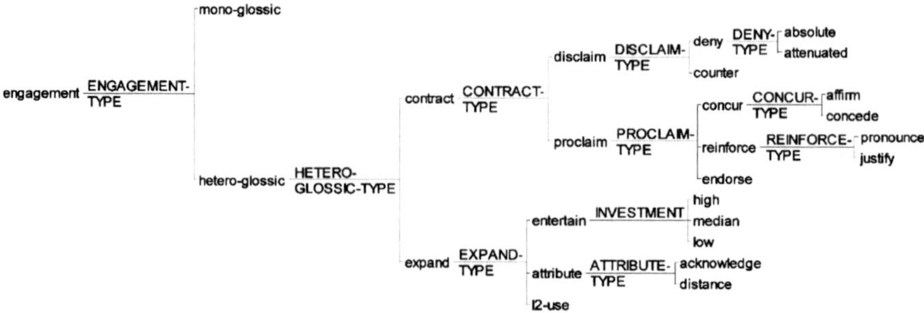

Figure 3.2 System network for engagement.

In addition to the resources chosen by these writers in constructing their texts, we were interested in identifying in each case, the appraiser or source of the evaluation and the evaluated entities. Identifying the appraiser allows us to see how the teacher-writers are attempting to align themselves with certain authors, to construct a voice of authority for themselves by endorsing or acknowledging generally recognized authorities in the field. The identification of evaluated entities allows us to map relations in these texts between interpersonal and ideational meanings. Figures 3.3 and 3.4 present the networks used for identifying appraisers (APPRAISAL-LAYER) and evaluated entities (APPRAISAL-OBJECT) respectively.

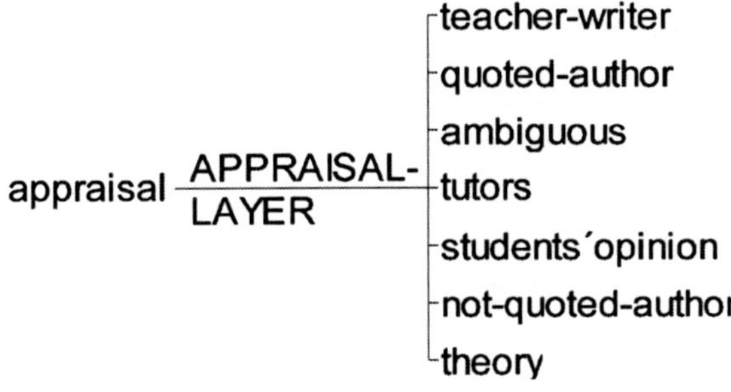

Figure 3.3 System network for appraisal-layer.

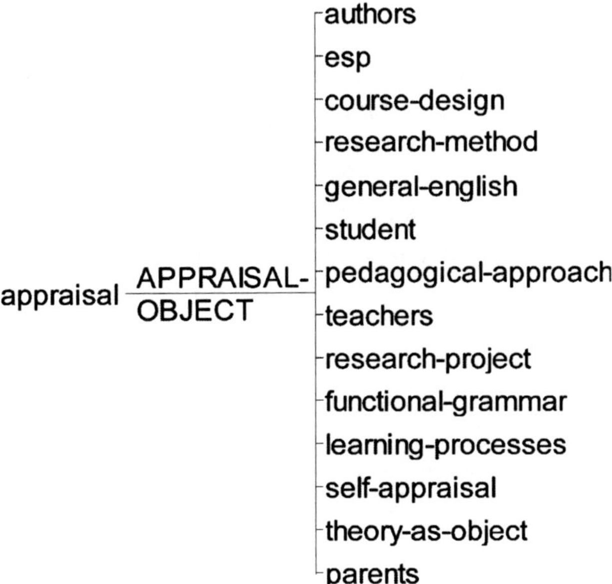

Figure 3.4 System network for appraisal-object.

These networks were drawn and the analysis carried out using UAM CorpusTool (O'Donnell, 2008) which facilitates the combination of qualitative and quantitative analysis. In this chapter we focus on the qualitative analysis but the quantitative analysis has been useful in pointing up which are the most frequently used resources in order to concentrate the qualitative analysis on these.

3.4   Use of attitudinal resources

As mentioned above, the most frequently used attitudinal resource in this corpus is that of *appreciation*, typically *positive valuation* and, more often than not, *inscribed,* as in (8) and (10). This resource is used by writers to describe characteristics of courses or pedagogical approaches which they wish to identify as positively meeting students' needs. The appraiser is typically the teacher-writer as in (8) or the quoted author as in (9). (10) shows an example of what we have called 'ambiguous' in terms of appraisal layer as it is difficult to determine whether the source of the evaluation is the teacher-writer him/herself or the quoted author. There is no immediate reference to an author but the sentence comes immediately after a quote from Candlin and the wording suggests to us that it is a quotation.

(8)   They will **help** the researcher design **proper** materials, activities, **appropriate** learning goals, approach to education, syllabus and skills to develop.

(9)   Yalden (1987a: 132) expresses that a classroom observation is an approach that **requires little explanation** if a checklist or set of notes is at hand.

(10)   Understanding students' needs are **crucial** to the **successful** design or redesign of any course of learning activity.

Also frequently appraised through use of this resource are research methods which are considered by the writers to 'guarantee' reliable and unambiguous results, as in (11) and (12), examples whose appraisal layer is quoted-author and teacher-writer, respectively.

(11)   According to Mackay (1978) the **main advantage** of the structured interview is its **completeness of coverage** and the **opportunity to clarify and extend** because of the physical presence of the analyst.

(12)   [Needs analysis] **will help to get a wide scope** about the process itself and how it can take place.

In their selection of the resource of *appreciation: valuation* for appraising course design characteristics and research methods as well as in their emphasis on the central importance of skills and procedures, these writers are aligning themselves in these examples with a knowledge-oriented legitimation code. They validate their claims with reference to authorising sources (Hood, 2010: 190), as in example (11), and also construct their identity as course designers and knowledge producers by including statements in which they themselves are appraisers and their actions are positively appraised, as in example (12).

Another interesting use of attitudinal resources is a double-layering of *judgement* and *appreciation* (Martin and White, 2005: 67–8) which these writers use, with some frequency, for appraising characteristics of course design and/or pedagogical approaches. In (13), for example, we have interpreted the expression in bold as invoked positive *judgement* (*social sanction: propriety*) of the students' behaviour and, at the same time, inscribed positive *appreciation: valuation* of the pedagogical approach which facilitates this behaviour.

(13)   This approach stresses that English is not just an object of academic interest neither merely a key to passing an examination; instead, English becomes **a real means of interaction and sharing among people**.

In (14), we find fairly complex inscribed positive *judgement* of students' or future professionals' behaviour, firstly in terms of *social sanction: propriety* ('to face problems, have values: accept and respect others'), then in terms of *social sanction: veracity* ('honesty') and finally in terms of *social esteem: capacity* ('be able to work cooperatively and have knowledge of the English language'), thus building up a very positive invoked *appreciation* of the pedagogical approach which makes all this possible.

(14)   It means **to face problems, have values: accept and respect others, honesty, be able to work cooperatively and have knowledge of the English language**.

This double layering of attitude, at the same time depersonalized as *appreciation* of skills and procedures and personalized as *judgement* of the behaviour of people directly involved in the object of study, permits the writers to locate themselves simultaneously in knowledge-oriented and knower-oriented legitimation codes and thus to identify themselves simultaneously as knowers and as knowledge producers.

3.5   Use of engagement resources

In terms of engagement, the teacher-writers in this study use what seems to be an unusually high proportion of monoglossic propositions: rather more than a third of the total number of propositions is monoglossic in nature, recognizing neither the presence of other voices nor the possibility of other points of view, 'no dialogistic alternatives which need to be recognised, or engaged with in the current communicative context' (Martin and White, 2005: 99). (15) to (18) are examples of this tendency.

(15)   [Needs analysis] **is essential** for the configuration of the course design, **it allows** researchers, teachers and/or anyone involved in the designing process **to determine** through questionnaires, interviews and other instruments **all the issues** which **best suit** the students in a given situation with the English language.

(16)   This approach **allows** teachers to track students' progress in multiple skills at the same time. Integrating the language skills also **promotes** the learning of real content.

(17)   Students who enter this field will undoubtedly be faced with foreigners and it **is** absolutely **necessary** to be able to speak in the international language in order to communicate with them.

(18)   It **is** important for them to realize the importance of practising English outside the classroom.

In these four examples, the use of unmodalized simple present tense indicates *monogloss* which is reinforced by lexical choices such as **determine** and **necessary** and the use of *graduation* resources such as **essential, all, undoubtedly, absolutely** and **best**.

Among those propositions which are heteroglossic, that is to say which recognize a 'backdrop of prior utterances, alternative viewpoints and anticipated responses' (Martin and White, 2005: 97), those which tend to close down or contract the dialogic space (*contract*) are slightly less frequent than those which, in contrast, are open to interaction with other voices and points of view (*expand*). Within *contraction*, we have found examples of both *proclaim* and *disclaim*. *Proclaim* is most frequently of the *reinforce: justify* type which the writers use to justify their decisions and actions and to fend off suggestions that there could be equally valid alternatives, as, for example in (19) and (20).

(19)   From what I have been taught, questionnaires must have 50% target questions and 50% learning questions, **so they can be balanced in their approach**.

(20)   I consider classroom research must be conducted by teachers **because they are the ones guiding the learning process, they know the weaknesses of the process, so they must know where and how to look for answers to solve and improve certain situations**.

Disclaim resources are fairly evenly divided between *deny* and *counter*; however, *deny: absolute* is almost twice as frequent as *deny: attenuated*. Since *deny: absolute* is closer to *monogloss* than *deny: attenuated*, this tendency would seem to be another characteristic of these writers' propensity to express certainty with regard to their findings. The following examples show cases of *deny: absolute* (21, 22), *deny: attenuated* (23) and *counter* (24).

(21) Once the questionnaire is administered, **is impossible** to rectify it.
(22) It is so important to live in harmony and that is one of the aspects, as I said before, that was forgotten and **not taken into account**.
(23) **Generally**, teachers **do not like** to be observed.
(24) Through needs analysis, teachers may have the opportunity to discover each learner's general necessities in the acquisition of a foreign language, **although** several criticisms have arisen.

Within *expansion*, the situation is rather different. While it is true to say that these teacher-writers use *expansion* slightly more frequently than they do *contraction*, the *expansion* resource most frequently used is that of *entertain* with *high investment*. That is to say that even when apparently opening up the dialogic space, they are in fact heavily committed to the position which they are putting forward, as may be appreciated in the following examples:

(25) Also, the environment of this process **must be analyzed**, the actual situation of the process and the state of art of it.
(26) A reading comprehension of specialized texts English course **must be designed** according to their field of study.
(27) This mixture **will allow** students the improvement of their skills.
(28) Using material related to other subjects in the program **will make** the ESP course meaningful and consequently the learners **can be** successful.
(29) A suitable course **has been** the final outcome.

The category of *entertain* with *median* or *low investment*, using, for example, modal verbs such as 'may' and 'might', is less frequently found in these texts. The reason for this may be a desire to express profound commitment; however, it may also be due to a lack of experience in using differing degrees of modalization.

In referencing authorizing sources as validation for their claims, our teacher-writers make use of both *proclaim: endorse* and *attribute: acknowledge*, the latter being the more frequent of the two. (30) and (31) exemplify these resources.

(30) **According to** Dudley-Evans (1997), ESP has some typical characteristics.
(31) In the first place, **Porcher (1983) writes** (...). In the second place, **Richterich and Chancerel (1987) point out** (...). In the third place we may mention **Brookfield (1988) who defines** (...) while **Brindley (1989)** and **Robinson (1991) consider** (...).

It is not always easy to differentiate between acknowledgement and endorsement in the data. We have in general assigned the category *proclaim: endorse* in those cases where a piece of text makes reference to just one source, seeming to suggest that this source is, if not the only valid one, then at least sufficient support for the point of view being expressed. We have assigned *attribute: acknowledge* in cases where a number of sources are cited with regard to the same topic, suggesting that several voices are equally valid. It is of note, however, that in these cases the various sources cited virtually all support the same point of view and that we have found only one clear case of *attribute: distance* (32); dissenting voices are not considered in any of the other texts.

(32) **It appears that Carter is implying** that the end purpose of both EAP and EOP are one in the same [sic]: employment. However, despite the end purpose being identical, the means taken to achieve the end is very different indeed. I contend that EAP and EOP are different in terms of focus in Cummins' (1979) notions of cognitive academic proficiency versus basic interpersonal skills.

The use of *attribute: distance* in this example is successfully complemented by *proclaim: concur* (despite...), *disclaim: counter* (the means...) and *proclaim: reinforce: pronounce* (I contend...) in the following clauses to complete the expression of a point of view which differs from that of the cited source.

We have also found cases in which teacher-writers apparently attempt to construct themselves as authorities by incorporating into their text the ideas of authors they have consulted without supplying the reference. This kind of 'transgressive intertextuality' (Chandrasoma *et al.*, 2004) we have categorized as not-quoted author. An example of this is presented in (33) where the reference is clearly to van Lier (1996) but the author is not mentioned.

(33) Out of these five principles or approaches to the teaching of English, three of them are foundational principles: **Awareness, autonomy and authenticity**, or AAA for short.

This frequent choice of varying degrees of dialogic contraction through the use of *monogloss, heterogloss: contract* and *entertain: high*, particularly with regard to research methods and pedagogical approaches might be construed as indicative of a lack of sophistication, a somewhat ingenuous belief in the efficacy of certain research procedures and the results they produce. Almost all of these writers, in their desire to construct an authoritative identity, present their chosen methods and techniques as virtually infallible (25) and the data they have obtained from them as complete and leading to unambiguous pedagogical implications (26). This, in its turn, permits them to design courses which will unquestionably achieve their aims (27, 28, 29). As Hood (2010: 158) suggests, 'academic writers frequently choose to be less bold, and less dichotomising'. Furthermore, these writers reveal their novice status by omitting to consider and argue against points of view which differ from their own, as is traditional in the texts of more experienced writers in the field. It will be a matter for further research to discover whether the boldness of these novice writers is due to a lack of resources in their repertoire as second language writers which would allow them a greater range of heteroglossic possibilities, a lack of confidence to question or criticize established authors, a tendency to imitate the 'bold' style of some of the authors they most frequently cite or (most probably) a combination of these factors.

3.6   Teacher-writers' identity construction

Unlike *the autobiographical self* and the *possibilities for self-hood,* whose evolution can barely be traced in the writing of the monographs, though they almost certainly influence a considerable share of the end product, the *discoursal self* and the *self as author* are reconstructed choice after choice.

A number of features in their monographs convey the *discoursal self* the teacher-writers aim at: the global organization follows the moves of research articles, namely, review of the literature, methodology and results sections; there are plenty of references to external sources and citations of previous work in the area; there is ample use of accepted terminology in the field, of extended nominal groups and nominalizations; writers usually adopt an impersonal stance.

Thus the discourse they construct in many ways resembles that of the community of practice to which they aspire (Lave and Wenger, 1991), that of specialists in the teaching of English. In particular, they wish to identify with the ESP, needs-analysis-based approach to the teaching of English which is endorsed in the postgraduate programme in which they are enrolled. They therefore wish to align themselves with prominent writers in the field of ESP, such as Hutchinson and Waters, Richards and Rogers, Nunan, Holmes, Kennedy and Bolitho and Dudley-Evans, to mention the most frequently cited. They also, perhaps strategically and predicting the reading stance of their evaluators, wish to align themselves with points of view expressed by course tutors, for example, Moss (2008).

In order to gain acceptability in this community, it is necessary to move on from being a classroom teacher to being a teacher-researcher; that is to say from being a consumer of knowledge produced by others to being a producer of knowledge. This is clearly expressed by one of the teacher-writers in (34):

(34) I will be a designer of my own courses. I will stop being a consumer of other people's syllabuses.

At the micro level, the *discoursal self* can be interpreted from the combination of choices made within the appraisal system, from what the writers choose to appraise and who they decide to represent as appraiser. Choices from the attitudinal system, mainly *appreciation: valuation: positive*, usually inscribed, referring to the characteristics of the courses they have designed, the theoretical foundation, and the scholars they cite in order to support their decisions, construct them positively as well-informed about the tendencies in the field of language teaching, and at the same time as successful designers and teachers.

In this process of transition, of apprenticeship into the community of teacher-researchers, the carrying out of a research project and the writing of the monograph to report it are seen as key activities. It is therefore of great importance to these writers that their texts establish their credentials as researchers, albeit novice researchers. To this end, as well as reporting on the work carried out, they apparently believe that it is necessary to construct stances of scientificity (Barletta, 2007).

Scientificity is a key element in the construction of the researcher identity. At the macro level it is represented in the fact that teacher-writers follow the norm regarding research methodology: they specify a lack of knowledge through questions or objectives, then they specify an approach or methods to address the questions and attempt to fill the gap by presenting the results. At a micro level, the linguistic choices represent an ideological view of the researcher in control of the object of study through almost perfect instruments which can yield unambiguous and complete data that speak for themselves. Part of this scientificity in their *discoursal self* is achieved through the construction of the *authorial self*, which we were able to trace by examining *engagement* choices. The teacher-writers resort to a high number of monoglossic assertions, as well as a considerable number of heteroglossic contractive statements; additionally, within the *entertain* category, which would open up the possibilities for dialogic space, the frequent use of high investment through the choice of modals such as 'must' and 'should', considerably constrains these possibilities. Through the use of these resources they position themselves as confident authorities who can recommend solutions and methodologies, ignoring perhaps that the opposite stance, that is, one that includes uncertainty, questioning about own results, distance from renowned scholars, can also convey a different kind of authority, one which is more reflective and self-aware of the relativity, incompleteness and transitory nature of knowledge.

Some of these writers, in their conclusions, make use of self-appraisal in order to express the ways in which they feel they have grown, matured or changed as a result of carrying out their research projects. This seems to indicate a conviction that they have indeed assumed a new identity as researchers. This is exemplified in (35):

(35) As a researcher, I must be engaged with a continuous work, concerning the pedagogical process, the new trends on education and my own context of research.

Of the twenty monographs included in the corpus for this study, none makes explicit reference to the status of Applied Linguistics as a science (or not) but comparison of the appraisal choices their writers make with Maton's ideas regarding knowledge-knower structures and the legitimation codes of specialization which they construct for different disciplines is interesting (Maton, 2007: 93). Appraisal choices made by the teacher-writers in this study suggest that they consciously or unconsciously locate Applied Linguistics as a knowledge-oriented code emphasizing epistemic relations with specialized skills and procedures. This resonates with Hood's (2007) comparison of argumentation in Applied Linguistics and Cultural Studies in which she finds Applied Linguistics to be more knowledge-oriented and Cultural Studies more knower-oriented. Examples of the kinds of choices made by writers in our study and which we consider indicative of this interpretation of the discipline's legitimation code include the following:

- most inscribed attitude in these texts is of the type *appreciation: valuation*, that is to say, it is not personalized;
- other voices cited are largely academic researchers (cf. Hood, 2007: 188);
- teacher-writers place great emphasis on specialized skills and procedures and a great deal of the *appreciation* used is related to these aspects;
- *appreciation* of the value of specific procedures is sometimes authorized by multiple sources thus representing knowledge of the object of study as 'generalized and abstracted from instances' (Hood, 2007: 198).

However, some of the choices frequently in evidence in these monographs move away from this pattern and seem somehow to 'slip out of' the knowledge code stance:

- teacher-writers depend, in many cases, on a single authorizing source for the validation of a technique, procedure or point of view, thus making the knowledge appear more particular and personalized;
- in nearly all cases, 'all referenced theoretical voices are represented as in alignment with the writer', a feature which Hood found to be more typical of a knower-oriented legitimation code (2007: 190);
- both positive and negative appreciation of procedures may be presented but from the same point of view; dissenting voices are almost never presented.

These apparently incongruous choices may indicate incomplete grasp of the legitimation code, inexperience, limitations of the writers' competence in written English, lack of confidence in their own knowledge, or a combination of these factors.

Additionally, the teacher-writers sometimes project voices of participants in the domain of the object of study, particularly students. These projections are used to legitimate knowledge claims through valuing the viewpoint of those directly involved in the teaching and learning situations under study, a more knower-oriented code (Maton, 2007; Hood, 2010). These insider voices make up an important part of the needs-analysis-based approach to course design endorsed in the monographs, particularly the reporting of findings from ethnographic research techniques such as interviews, surveys and observations. In this sense, these teacher-writers make appraisal choices which more or less successfully combine the knowledge-oriented legitimation code of theoretical approaches to language, language learning and research methodology with the more knower-oriented legitimation code of reporting on ethnographic research. This combination of knowledge-oriented and knower-oriented codes is also evident in the double-layering of judgement and appreciation mentioned above and exemplified in (13) and (14). The more personalized judgement layer, evaluating the behaviour of students or future professionals, would relate to a knower orientation and the more impersonal appreciation code, evaluating course design or pedagogical approaches, to the knowledge orientation.

With regard to conceptions of knowledge, these teacher-writers, in their quest for scientificity, seem to align themselves more with a positivist approach than with a postmodern one. This may also be related to the fact that the authors they consult in the preparation of their monographs are almost exclusively based in the Centre (Canagarajah, 2002) and therefore have been influenced by the positivist tradition of Western science. Novice writers, aspiring to enter the discourse community of applied linguists, tend to accept unquestioningly the views of 'experts' in the field, attempt to imitate their writing style and rarely dare to dissent.

Finally, we consider that this type of study may be of practical use for the process of tutoring postgraduate students. Understanding the ways in which appraisal resources contribute to the construction of identity could help us, as tutors, to guide students towards more appropriate choices in their writing; at the same time, our new awareness of the great complexity of these resources and their impact should make us more understanding of the difficulties students face in attempting to become research writers.

Note

1. The examples have been transcribed as in the original and have not been edited.

References

Bakhtin, M. M. (1999) The problem of speech genre. In A. Jaworki and N. Coupland (eds) *The Discourse Reader* 121–32. London: Routledge.

Barletta, N. (2007) English teachers in Colombia: Ideologies and identities in academic writing. Unpublished doctoral dissertation, University of Arizona.

Bernstein, B. (2000) *Pedagogy, Symbolic Control and Identity: Theory, Research, Critique,* rev. edn. Lanham, MD: Rowman and Littlefield Publishers.

Canagarajah, S. (1999) Interrogating the 'native speaker fallacy': Non-linguistic roots, non-pedagogical results. In G. Braine (ed.) *Non-native Educators in English Language Teaching* 77–92. Mahwah, NJ: Lawrence Erlbaum.

Canagarajah, S. (2002) *A Geopolitics of Academic Writing.* Pittsburgh, PA: University of Pittsburgh.

Chandrasoma, R., Thompson, C. and Pennycook, A. (2004) Beyond plagiarism: Transgressive and nontransgressive intertextuality. *Journal of Language, Identity, and Education* 3(3): 171–93.

De Cillia, R., Reisigl, M. and Wodak, R. (1999) The discursive construction of national identities. *Discourse & Society* 10(2): 149–73.

Duszak, A. (1997) Cross-cultural academic communication: A discourse community view. In A. Duszak (ed.) *Culture and Styles of Academic Discourse* 11–41. Berlin/New York: Mouton de Gruyter.

Gee, J. P. (2000–2001) Identity as an analytic lens for research in education. *Review of Research in Education* 25: 99–125.

Halliday, M. A. K (2004) *An Introduction to Functional Grammar*, 3rd edn, revised by C. M. I. M. Matthiessen. London: Edward Arnold.

Hood, S. (2007) Arguing in and across disciplinary boundaries: Legitimizing strategies in applied linguistics and cultural studies. In R. Whittaker, M. O'Donnell and A. McCabe (eds) *Advances in Language Education* 185–200. London: Continuum.

Hood, S. (2010) *Appraising Research: Evaluation in Academic Writing*. London: Palgrave Macmillan.

Hyland, K. (2002) Authority and invisibility: Authorial identity in academic writing. *Journal of Pragmatics* 34: 1091–112.

Ivanič, R. (1998) *Writing and Identity: The Discoursal Construction of Identity in Academic Writing*. Amsterdam: John Benjamins.

Lave, J. and Wenger, E. (1991) *Situated Learning: Legitimate Peripheral Participation*. Cambridge: Cambridge University Press.

Martin, J. R. (2000) Beyond Exchange: APPRAISAL Systems in English. In S. Hunston and G. Thompson (eds) *Evaluation in Text: Authorial Stance and the Construction of Discourse*, 142–75. Oxford: Oxford University Press.

Martin, J. R. and White, P. R. R. (2005) *The Language of Evaluation: Appraisal in English*. Basingstoke: Palgrave Macmillan.

Maton, K. (2007) Knowledge-knower structures in intellectual and educational fields. In F. Christie and J. R. Martin (eds) *Language, Knowledge and Pedagogy: Functional Linguistic and Sociological Perspectives* 87–108. London: Continuum.

Moss, G. (2008) Making sandwiches: A combined approach to course design. Unpublished course materials. Barranquilla: Universidad del Norte.

Ochs, E. (1993) Constructing social identity: A language socialization perspective. *Research on Language and Social Interaction* 26(3): 287–306.

O'Donnell, M. (2008) Demonstration of the UAM Corpus Tool for text and image annotation. In *Proceedings of the ACL-08: HLT Demo Session (Companion Volume), Columbus, Ohio, June 2008*, 13–16. Stroudsburg, PA: Association for Computational Linguistics.

Swales, J. (1990) *Genre Analysis: English in Academic and Research Settings*. Cambridge: Cambridge University Press.

van Lier, L. (1996) *Interaction in the Language Curriculum: Awareness, Autonomy and Authenticity*. London: Longman.

Ventola, E. (1997) Modalization: Probability – an exploration into its role in academic writing. In A. Duszak (ed.) *Culture and Styles of Academic Discourse* 157–80. Berlin/New York: Mouton de Gruyter.

Wenger, E. (1998) *Communities of Practice: Learning, Meaning, and Identity*. Cambridge: Cambridge University Press.

Part B

Choice in political speech: Tension between the need to inform and project solidarity

<table><tr><td>4</td></tr></table>

The use of grammatical metaphor in French political tracts

David Banks[a]

4.1   Introduction

Grammatical metaphor is a phenomenon which has been widely studied in Systemic Functional Linguistics. It is usually conceived of as the use of a non-congruent type of grammatical encoding (Halliday, 2004a; Banks, 2005). For example, a process is usually encoded in language as a verb; this is its congruent form. It may however sometimes be encoded as a noun, for example, the noun *assistance* rather than the verb *assist*, in which case it is a nominalized process. A quality is usually encoded as an adjective, but sometimes it may have the form of a noun, for example, the noun *beauty*, rather than the adjective *beautiful*, in which case it would constitute a nominalized quality. These are both examples of grammatical metaphor. The congruent method of encoding possibility is by using a modal auxiliary, like *may*, but it can also be encoded by the noun *possibility*, or the adjective *possible*, in which case these too would be grammatical metaphors. Previous studies (e.g. Ravelli, 1988; Simon-Vandenbergen *et al.*, 2003) have dealt with this question mainly from an English standpoint. In this chapter[1] I would like to look at the use of this phenomenon in another language, French, and more precisely to consider how it is used in the peculiarly French genre of the political tract.

The type of grammatical metaphor which has most frequently been considered is that of nominalized processes:

---

a   David Banks is Emeritus Professor at the Université de Bretagne Occidentale in France. He is Director of ERLA (*Equipe de Recherche en Linguistique Appliquée*) and Chairman of AFLSF (*Association Française de la Linguistique Systémique Fonctionnelle*). His recent publication *The Development of Scientific English, Linguistic Features and Historical Context* (Equinox) won the ESSE Language and Linguistics book award 2010.

(1)   Formally, Russia has offered to help Obama in his **attempts** to deal with the deteriorating **situation** in Pakistan and Afghanistan, and last month it agreed the **shipment** of non-lethal supplies destined for Kabul across Russian territory. Informally, however, Russia has moved to reassert its **influence** in central Asia, a region it still regards as its backyard. (*Guardian Weekly*, 3–9 April 2009)[2]

In (1) the nouns *attempts, shipment* and *influence* are fairly obvious examples of processes encoded in nominal form; and if *situation* is interpreted as a set of relationships rather than an entity, then it might be considered an example (albeit marginal) of a nominalized relational process. This interpretation is saying that what is deteriorating is the way things relate to each other in Pakistan and Afghanistan. These examples do not necessarily exhaust the incidence of grammatical metaphor in this extract, but they are the most obvious ones.

Grammatical metaphor has not been studied as such in French. However the phenomenon of nominalization has. For example, as long ago as 1969, Dubois, in a generatively inspired grammar of French said,

> La nominalisation comporte dans tous les cas l'effacement de la copule être ; elle implique donc l'effacement des marques attachées au verbe et, en particulier, des auxiliaires de temps et d'aspect. (Dubois, 1969: 57) [Nominalization, in all cases, involves the removal of the copular verb être; it thus implies the removal of the markers attached to the verb and, in particular, the auxiliaries of tense and aspect.][3]

And more recently, in what is probably the best of contemporary French grammars, Riegel *et al.* (1998) say:

> … il existe de nombreuses correspondances entre la catégorie nominale et les autres parties du discours. La plus connue relève de la **nominalisation** qui convertit en noms les adjectifs (*fier>la fierté*) et des verbes (*fermer>la fermeture*). Mais une forme nominale peut également dénoter ce qu'expriment une préposition (*après* ↔ *la postériorité*), un conjonction (*parce que* ↔ *la cause, la causalité*) ou encore un morphème grammatical (p. ex. la *pluralité* des formes plurielles de déterminants). (Riegel *et al.*, 1998: 169)
> [… there are numerous relationships between the nominal category and the other parts of speech. The best known are those of **nominalization** which form nouns from adjectives (*fier>la fierté*) and verbs (*fermer>la fermeture*). But a nominal form can also express what is meant by a preposition (*après* ↔ *la postériorité*), a conjunction (*parce que* ↔ *la cause, la causalité*), or even a grammatical morpheme (e.g. the *pluralité* of the plural forms of determiners).]

4.2   Grammatical metaphor in French

Probably all the types of grammatical metaphor that have been found in English have a parallel in French. The following, which in no way attempts to be exhaustive, gives some examples. These were all found on pages 1 and 2 of a single issue of *Le Monde*, that for 15–16 June 2008.

(2)   La fin de la guerre froide et de la **division** de l'Europe l'a placée face à un dilemme : elle se montre incapable d'adapter son **fonctionnement** aux élargissements successifs, alors que l'**accroissement** du nombre de pays membres rend de plus en plus indispensable la **reforme** des institutions. (*Le Monde*, 15–16 June 2008)
[The end of the cold war and a divided Europe has placed it in a dilemma: it has shown itself incapable of adapting the way it functions to successive enlargements, while the increase in the number of member countries makes reform of the institutions increasingly necessary.]

In (2) there are five examples of nominalized material processes: *division, fonctionnement*, élargissements, *accroissement* and *reforme* (i.e. the processes of dividing, functioning, enlarging, increasing and reforming).

(3)   D'après une enquête du Pew Research Center réalisée dans vingt-quatre pays et publiée le 12 juin, la candidature de Barack Obama à la présidentielle américaine suscite non seulement des grands **espoirs**, mais améliore l'image des Etats-Unis dans le monde. (*Le Monde*, 15–16 June 2008)
[According to a study by the Pew Research Center carried out in twenty-four countries and published on 12 June, Barack Obama's candidacy for the American Presidency has not only raised great hopes, but has improved the image of the United States in the world.]

In (3) there is an example of a nominalized mental process in the word *espoirs* (the process of hoping).

(4)   Le fait que l'Irlande soit le pays qui a le plus bénéficié de son **appartenance** à l'Union européenne n'a pas pesé. (*Le Monde*, 15–16 June 2008)
[The fact that Ireland is the country that has most benefited from its membership of the European Union did not carry any weight.]

In (4), *appartenance* supplies an example of a nominalized relational process (the process of belonging to).

(5)   La réaction franco-allemande, à l'**annonce** des résultats, vendredi 13 juin, pointait dans cette direction. (*Le Monde*, 15–16 June 2008)
[The Franco-German reaction on the announcement of the results on Friday 13 June, pointed in this direction.]

In (5), *annonce* is an example of a nominalized verbal process (the process of announcing).

(6)   Les Sans-Rien, façon sans-culottes, ont entamé, lundi 9 juin à Bordeaux, un "tour de France" d'une douzaine de grandes villes pour sensibiliser à une chose simple : leur **existence**. (*Le Monde*, 15–16 June 2008)
[The Have-Nots, like the *sans-culottes*, started a 'tour of France' of a dozen major cities, on Monday 9 June at Bordeaux, to create awareness of a simple fact: their existence.]

In (6) there is an example of nominalized existential process in *existence* (the process of existing).

(7)   Il s'agit bien d'un **camouflet** pour l'Europe de Bruxelles, exactement trois ans après le refus du traité constitutionnel par les français, puis par les Néerlandais. (*Le Monde*, 15–16 June 2008)
[It's a real slap in the face for the Europe of Brussels, exactly three years after the rejection of the constitutional treaty by the French, and then the Dutch.]

In (7) we find an interesting example. In (2) to (6), all of the nominalized processes were also deverbal, in the sense that they have cognate lexical verbs. In (7) we have an example, *camouflet*, where there is no related lexical verb, at least not with the same meaning, in contemporary French. The verb *camoufler* does exist, but with the meaning of *hide, mask, camouflage*. There was a now obsolete verb (or perhaps the same verb whose meaning has altered over time), *camoufler*, which had the meaning of *humiliate by blowing smoke in someone's face*, hence the meaning of the modern noun *camouflet – humiliation*, or a metaphorical *slap in the face*.

(8)   Ils sont donc une "*tribu*", énonce leur site Internet (www.sansrien.net) où s'accrochent une rage certaine et leur revendications : être reconnu comme citoyen, respecté dans sa **dignité**, refuser d'être infantilisés et humiliés. (*Le Monde*, 15–16 June 2008)
[So they are a '*tribe*', declares their website (www.sansrien.net) where a distinct anger and their demands are displayed: to be recognized as a citizen, respected in his dignity, a refusal to be treated like children and humiliated.]

In *dignité*, (8) has an example of a nominalized quality.

(9)   Des individus "*par défaut*", dirait le sociologue Robert Castel, à qui il manque les outils pour accéder à un minimum d'**indépendance**, d'**autonomie**, de reconnaissance sociale – les attributs positifs que l'on reconnaît généralement aux individus dans les sociétés contemporaines. (*Le Monde*, 15–16 June 2008)

[Individuals '*by default*', as the sociologist Robert Castel would say, who lack the means of acquiring a minimum of independence, autonomy and social recognition – the positive features that are generally attributed to individuals in contemporary society.]

More examples of nominalized quality are found in (9): *independence* and *autonomie*.

(10)   Pour sortir de ce cercle vicieux, il n'y a qu'une **possibilité** : créer, à côté de l'union européenne actuelle, une avant-garde composée de pays prêts à accepter la règle de la majorité qualifiée pour approfondir l'intégration. (*Le Monde*, 15–16 June 2008)
[To get out of this vicious circle, there is only one possibility: to create, in parallel with the present European Union, a vanguard made up of countries willing to accept the rule of qualified majority to strengthen integration.]

Finally in (10) there is an example, *possibilité*, of nominalized modality.

I do not wish to imply that the occurrences I have indicated exhaust the incidence of grammatical metaphor in these examples. In (2), *guerre*, and perhaps *dilemme*, are candidates for the status of grammatical metaphor; in (3), the same might be said of *enquête* and *candidature*, and so on for the other examples. The point here is simply to show something of the range of grammatical metaphor in French.

In general, I think it would be true to say that English and French function largely in the same way. By that I mean that at the level of the major metafunctions, ideational, interpersonal, and textual, the two languages function in parallel. There are numerous differences but these operate at a more delicate level.

4.3   The French political tract

The French political tract constitutes a specific genre, and one which may be peculiar to French culture. These tracts, usually a single side of a sheet of A4 paper, less usually A5, are handed out to passers-by during strikes, at street demonstrations, and so on. The street demonstration is virtually part of the French way of life, and is much more frequent than in English-speaking cultures, for example. Redundancies and factory closures, cost of living, general or specific government policies, are examples of the many grievances which can trigger street demonstrations. In the university sector, demonstrations, often accompanied by blockades of university premises, seem to occur at a rhythm of about once every two years. In the town where my university is situated, a major street demonstration, even on university questions, can attract up to 15,000 demonstrators – in a town with a population of only 150,000!

The following is the first paragraph of a tract I was handed in the town of Rennes in 2005. The main nominalized processes and qualities have been highlighted.

(11)   Les **affrontements** qui se déroulent dans différents quartiers populaire depuis plus d'une semaine, faisant vivre aux populations et aux salaries de ces quartiers des moments extrêmement difficiles, sont révélateurs de la **crise** sociale qui s'est développée : **pauvreté, chômage, précarisation** sociale généralisée, mais aussi **discriminations** et **relégation** sociale. Le **démantèlement** des **services** publics, l'**asphyxie** financière et le **mépris** des associations de terrain, l'**abandon** des politiques de **prévention** : tout cela est au cœur du **désarroi** qui s'exprime aujourd'hui. Quel avenir pour ces populations et leurs enfants ? Ces **violences** sont aussi les signes de l'échec des politiques répressives conçues comme seule **réponse** aux **questions** sociales. (Rennes tract, 2005)
[The confrontations which have been taking place in various working-class districts over the last week, making the inhabitants and workers of these districts live through some extremely difficult times, are symptomatic of the social crisis which is developing: poverty, unemployment, generalized social instability, as well as discrimination and downward social movement. The demolition of public services, economic suffocation and contempt for groups on the ground, abandoning a policy of prevention: all that is at the heart of the disorientation that is being expressed today. What future for the people who live here and their children? This violence is also the symbol of the failure of the policy of repression conceived of as the only reply to social questions.]

It is immediately evident that the incidence of grammatical metaphor is relatively high. The extract has 105 words, and there are 17 highlighted examples, that is 16.2 per cent of the text. Most of my remarks will be based on this text, but in an attempt to show that this is not an isolated example, I will give two others. The first of these is a tract whose authors are university staff. It is reasonable to suppose therefore that this is, by normal standards, well written.

(12)   Nous, enseignants-chercheurs, chercheurs et membres du personnel de l'université, affirmons notre **opposition** catégorique à la loi dite LRU (loi de **réforme** de l'université), notre **soutien** plein et entier à la **mobilisation** étudiante et notre **participation** à ce **mouvement.**
Sous couvert "d'**autonomie**" (de **gestion**, mais ni intellectuelle ou scientifique) et afin notamment de favoriser la **constitution** de "pôles d'**excellence**" susceptibles d'améliorer la **place** des universités françaises dans le dérisoire

"palmarès de Shanghai" (ou dans la **course** pour attirer les meilleurs "cerveaux"), cette **réforme**, d'**inspiration** managériale, vise à amplifier la **concurrence** entre établissements du **service** public d'éducation et de **recherche**, laquelle risque à terme de transformer la majorité d'entre eux en "collèges" universitaires limités au niveau licence, ainsi qu'à déléguer à ces établissements le **soin** de gérer le **désengagement** croissant de l'Etat concernant leur **financement**. (University of Paris tract, 2008)

[We, lecturer-researchers, researchers, and non-teaching members of university staff, declare our categoric opposition to the so-called LRU bill [University Reform Bill], our full and entire support for the student movement, and our participation in that movement.

Under cover of 'autonomy' (of management, but not intellectual or scientific) and in particular to encourage the creation of 'poles of excellence' likely to improve the position of French universities in the laughable 'Shanghai rankings' (or in the race to attract the best 'brains'), this reform, of managerial inspiration, aims to increase competition between public service institutions of education and research, which risks ultimately turning most of them into university 'centres' limited to first degree level, as well as delegating to these institutions the task of managing the increasing withdrawal of the state from their funding.]

This extract of 133 words, has 21 examples of grammatical metaphor, which therefore constitute 15.8 per cent of the text, a similar rate to the Rennes 2005 extract.

Finally the following example emanates from a student union.

(13)   Face à la **pression** sociale qui s'est organisée ces dernières semaines, le gouvernement à été contraint de faire des **gestes** en direction du **movement** social. Suite à la forte **mobilisation** du 29 janvier, Nicolas Sarkozy a annoncé des premières **mesures** en direction des salariés, encore insuffisantes. Dans les universités, face à la forte **mobilisation** des étudiants et des personnels, le gouvernement a été contraint de concéder des premiers éléments de **réponse**.

François Fillon a annoncé que le gouvernement renonçait aux **suppressions** de postes dans l'**enseignement** supérieur en 2010 et 2011, et que le décret modifiant le statut des enseignants-chercheurs devait être entièrement réécrit. Ces premiers **reculs** du gouvernement sont des **acquis** de la forte **mobilisation** des ces dernières semaines. (Student union tract, 2009)

[Faced with the social pressure which has been organized in the last few weeks, the government has been forced to make some gestures towards the social movement. Following the strong mobilization of 20 January, Nicolas Sarkozy announced the first, but still insufficient, measures for wage-earners. In the universities, faced with the strong mobilization of students and staff, the government has been forced to concede the first elements of a reply.

> François Fillon announced that the government had renounced the reduction in posts in higher education in 2010 and 2011, and that the decree altering the status of lecturer-researchers would have to be completely rewritten. This first retreat by the government is the achievement of the strong mobilization of the last few weeks.]

The example is distinctly not well written; the repetition of *la forte mobilisation* three times in eight lines of text would be considered bad style in French. However, this extract of 119 words has 12 examples of nominalized processes, that is, 10.1 per cent of the text; to this might be added the expression *en direction de*, which occurs twice, and which is a nominalized preposition (roughly *towards*). This again produces a very heavy style, particularly in view of the fact that French has a perfectly reasonable preposition, *envers*, with the same meaning.

4.4   The effects of nominalized processes

The fact that a process is encoded in nominal form means that it no longer requires a subject, or, in the case of bivalent verbs, a complement. These can be expressed in the form, for example, of possessive modifiers, or postmodifying (qualifying) phrases, but these are not necessary and probably occur in only a minority of cases. On the other hand the nominalized form can have its own, sometimes numerous, modifiers and qualifiers, thus concentrating the information within a single nominal group.

It has also been shown that nominalized processes play a role in logogenesis, or discourse construction. This occurs when the unpacked, or non-metaphorical form (Halliday, 2004b; Ventola, 1996) occurs in a rheme, and the metaphorical form occurs in a following theme (Halliday, 1988, 1998; Ormrod, 2001, 2004). Once again, as a phenomenon, this has been noted by Riegel *et al.* (1998), though not in terms of grammatical metaphor.

> Dans **l'anaphore conceptuelle** … [l]a reprise prend souvent la forme d'une **nominalisation**. Le groupe nominal anaphorique contient un nom formé à partir d'un verbe ou d'un adjectif, qui ne figurent pas nécessairement dans le contexte antérieur … Le group anaphorique … résume globalement le contenu de la phrase précédente, sans que le verbe … y figure. (Riegel *et al.*, 1998: 614–15)
>
> [In **conceptual anaphora** … the repetition often takes the form of **nominalization**. The anaphoric nominal group contains a noun formed from a verb

> or an adjective which is not necessarily present in the previous context ... The anaphoric group ... summarizes in general the contents of the previous sentence, even though the verb ... is not present.]

I pointed out an example of this in Banks (2008); the extract comes from a 1900 article in the *Philosophical Transactions*.

(14)　In these, the seedlings **were steamed** in a water bath for ten to fifteen minutes, in order to kill the roots.
After **cooling,** I infected the roots with drops of water containing nitragin, and then kept the tubes in the dark.
In about ten days, a good growth **was obvious** along the radicles,
and upon **examination** the organism present appeared to be the one for which I was seeking.
I consequently **tried** to separate it in a pure state by means of plate cultures, but all my **attempts** failed owing to a rapid liquefying of the gelatine solution.

In the sixth clause, *attempts*, which occurs in the theme is obviously a nominalized form of *tried*, which occurs in the rheme of the fifth clause. The other cases are perhaps less immediate, but it seems reasonable to claim that *cooling* in the theme of the second clause is derived from *were steamed* in the rheme of the first. If something is steamed, then it is presumably cooled down again subsequently. Similarly, *examination* in the theme if the fourth clause is derived from *was obvious* in the rheme of the third. If things are obvious they must have been previously observed, though here the author is talking about further examination.

Finally, it needs to be pointed out that encoding a process in nominal form gives it some of the semantic 'feel' of nouns. That is, it seems more objective and 'solid' than its verbal counterpart. This comes about because the prototypical noun refers to a physical object: it is solid and relatively permanent. A typical process, on the other hand is an action or event: it takes place, and so is fleeting. Once it is over it no longer exists, it belongs to the past. Hence expressing a process in nominal form is to give it some of the permanence and solidity of the typical noun.

4.5　Nominalization in the Rennes 2005 text

In the extract from the Rennes 2005 text, the first nominalization is *affrontements*. This is a bivalent material process, but who is confronting whom? There are no putative subjects or complements encoded. We can guess that the putative participants are rioters and police. But are the rioters confronting the police, or the police confronting the rioters? Although this might be considered a reciprocal process, the two options don't mean quite the same thing, and which of them is to be understood is left vague. Similar, in that the text supplies no subjects or complements in the form of modifiers or qualifiers, are *précarisation, discrimination, relegation, asphyxie, prévention,* and *violences.* On the basis of the text, we do not know who is making who or what poor, who is discriminating against whom; we know that the relegation is in the social sphere, but no more than that, just as we know that the suffocation is in the economic sphere; nor do we know who is preventing what, or who is acting violently. There is one case where there is a possible subject: *services public,* thus it is the public authorities who provide these services. There are also two cases where a complement is provided: *démantèlement des services public* and *abandon des politiques de prevention,* but neither of these has a potential subject.

There are two examples of nominalized mental processes: *mépris* and *désarroi.* In the case of *mépris,* we know that it is a question of *mépris des associations de terrain;* but *associations de terrain* could function as either a potential subject or a potential complement. The text does not provide us with any evidence for selecting one rather than the other. No subject or complement is provided for *désarroi.*

There are two nominalized verbal processes, *réponse* and *questions.* Neither has a subject or complement.

There are two monovalent material processes, which like their bilvalent counterparts have no subject; these are *crise* and *chômage.*

Finally there is a nominalized quality, *pauvreté,* but; of course, the text does not tell us who is poor.

In fact, of course, we do know the answers to many of these questions, but not on the basis of what the text says; we know because of our external knowledge of the situation; we are familiar with the problems which have given rise to the strike or demonstration; we know, more or less, the position and attitudes of those who have written the text. So we can fill in the missing information, but it remains significant that this is left vague, and sometimes ambiguous, in the way the text is encoded. Since we know that the general attitude of those who write this type of tract is against authority and on the side of the demonstrators, the ambiguity of the text allows public authorities to be stigmatized, and demonstrators to be exonerated, without this being explicitly stated. Disambiguating the text would have involved naming names, and for those directly involved this would probably seem like stating the obvious.

It was also pointed out above that nominalized processes frequently form the heads of complex nominal groups, thus providing a concentration of information. It can be seen that this is far from the case here. The vast majority of the nominalizations here have very little, or even nothing at all, in the way of modification and qualification. The only concentration we find here is that of the nominalizations themselves. Their capacity to provide a hub for complex noun groups is not used by the writers of this text.

If we compare this with the text below, which is an extract from a leader article in *Le Monde* (part of which was used as example (2)), it will be evident that the situation is different.

(15) Le **non** irlandais au traité de Lisbonnne a replongé l'Union européenne dans la **crise** institutionnelle qui la mine depuis une dizaine d'années. La **fin** de la **guerre** froide et de la **division** de l'Europe l'a placée face à un dilemme : elle se montre incapable d'adapter son **fonctionnement** aux élargissements successifs, alors que l'**accroissement** du nombre de pays membres rend de plus en plus indispensable la **réforme** des institutions. (*Le Monde*, 15–16 June 2008)
[The Irish 'no' to the Lisbon Treaty has plunged the European Union once again into the institutional crisis that has been undermining it for the last ten years or so. The end of the cold war and of the separation of Europe has placed it in a dilemma: it is showing itself incapable of adapting the way it functions to repeated enlargement, while the increasing number of member countries makes reform of the institutions more and more necessary.]

This extract of 69 words has 9 examples of nominalized processes, that is 13.0 per cent of the text, slightly less, but comparable with the rate in Rennes 2005. The *non* is a *non irlandais*, so we know that it is the Irish who are saying 'no'. The *fin* is the *fin de la guerre froide*, so it is the Cold War that is ending. The nominalized process *division* does not have an encoded subject, but we know that it is a question of the *division de l'Europe*, so someone or something was separating Europe. The nominalized process *fonctionnement* has a possessive determiner, *son*, which is anaphorically linked to *Europe*, so it is Europe that is functioning. The *accroissement* is that of the *nombre de pays membres*, so the number of member states is increasing. The *réforme* is that of *des institutions*, so someone or something is reforming (or should be) the institutions. The only nominalization which does not have a subject or complement directly derivable from the text is *élargissement*. So in this extract even though readers of the newspaper will be familiar with the situation and would be able to fill in a great deal of implicit information, the subjects and complements of the nominalized processes are to a large extent recoverable from the text. This seems to suggest that the relative absence of such recoverability in the Rennes 2005 text is genre specific.

The final point I would like to consider is that of the use of nominalized processes in discourse construction. There are no cases in the Rennes 2005 extract where the grammatical metaphor constitutes a theme, and follows a rheme containing its non-metaphorical version. On the contrary, each of the nominalizations is posed, almost object like, thus taking on some of the objective nature proper to nominal status. This object-like presentation of these nominalized processes gives them the status of presuppositions: they are posed but also presupposed. The reader is presumed to know what they are, to know what they refer to, and so to accept that their existence is not in question. This is grammatically reinforced by the presence of definite articles with a large number of them: *les affrontements, la crise, le démantèlement, l'asphixie, le mépris, l'abandon, du désarroi.* It is difficult to disagree with a presupposition, which means that here no argument is possible. The argument, such as it is, is frozen in a set of presuppositions. Whereas in scientific texts grammatical metaphor is used as a way of building up the argument structure of the text, here we have a situation which seems to be almost the opposite: the grammatical metaphor is being used as a way of impeding argument, of fixing it in terms of the presuppositions which have been laid down. Thus the message is hammered out, and hammered home.

However, a final word must be said which relates to the context, or more specifically the tenor of this type of text. To whom are the texts actually addressed? Although they are handed out in relatively large numbers to people in the street, the number who actually read them is probably infinitesimal. Hence at best they may be preaching to the converted, and at worst they may be read only by those who actually wrote them in the first place. Hence the need to provide an argument structure fades into the ideological distance, and since those who wrote the document obviously agree with themselves, they only need to state their position.

4.6   Concluding remarks

The political tract is a genre which is specific to French culture. One of its features is the large number of grammatical metaphors, particularly in the form of nominalized processes. Unlike the use of nominalized process in other types of text, those used here usually do not have putative subjects or complements which can be recovered from the text; nor do they constitute the heads of complex nominal groups. Finally, they do not play a part in building up the argumentation through the thematic structure. They appear to be posed as presupposed items and, as such, to demand adherence and to impede further argument.

Notes

1. Some of the ideas broached here were originally discussed in meetings of the Association Française de la Linguistique Systémique Fonctionnelle, and with various groups of students. An earlier version of this chapter was presented at the 21st European Systemic Functional Linguistics Conference and Workshop, 8–10 July 2009, Cardiff. I would like to thank all those who took part in these different events, as well as the editors of this volume. Their comments, criticisms and suggestions have helped formulate the ideas presented here, though only I am responsible for any remaining deficiencies.
2. The highlighting in examples (but not in quotes) is mine throughout.
3. English glosses of French quotes and examples are mine throughout.

References

Banks, D. (2005) *Introduction à la linguistique systémique fonctionnelle de l'anglais.* Paris: L'Harmattan.

Banks, D. (2008) The significance of thematic structure in the scientific journal article, 1700-1980. In N. Nørgard (ed.) *Systemic Functional Linguistics in Use, Odense Working Papers in Language and Communications* 29 http://static.sdu. dk/mediafiles/Files/Om_SDU/Institutter/ISK/Forskningspublikationer/OWPLC/ Nr29/David%20Banks.pdf.

Dubois, J. (1969) *Grammaire structurale du français: la phrase et les transforma-tions.* Paris: Larousse.

Halliday, M. A. K. (1988) On the language of physical science. In M. Ghadessy (ed.) *Registers of Written English: Situational factors and Linguistic Features,* 162–78. London: Pinter. [Reprinted in Halliday & Martin, 1993: 54–68; Halliday, 2004b: 140–58].

Halliday, M. A. K. (1998) Things and relations: Regrammaticizing experience as technical knowledge. In J. R. Martin and R. Veel (eds) *Reading Science, Critical and Functional Perspectives in Discourses of Science* 185–235. London: Routledge. [Reprinted in Halliday, 2004b, 49–101].

Halliday, M. A. K. (2004a): *An Introduction to Functional Grammar*, 3rd edn, revised by C. M. I. M. Matthiessen. London: Edward Arnold.

Halliday, M. A. K. (2004b) *The Language of Science: Collected Works*, vol. 5, J. J. Webster (ed.). London: Continuum.

Halliday, M. A. K. and Martin, J. R. (eds) (1993) *Writing Science, Literacy and Discursive Power*. London: Falmer Press.

Ormrod, J. (2001) Construction discursive des noms composés dans des textes scientifiques anglais. In D. Banks (ed.) *Le groupe nominal dans le texte spécialisé* 9–23. Paris: L'Harmattan.

Ormrod, J. (2004) Creation and subsequent usage of terms for discourse purposes in the scientific research article. In *Actes de GLAT-Barcelona 2004 "La production des textes spécialisés: Structure et enseignement"*, 51–60. Barcelona: Groupe des Ecoles des Télécommunications.

Ravelli, L. J. (1988) Grammatical metaphor, an initial analysis. In E. H. Steiner and R. Veltman (eds) *Pragmatics, Discourse and Text: Some Systemically-inspired Approaches* 187–234. London: Pinter.

Riegel, M., Pellat, J.-C. and Rioul, R. (1998) *Grammaire méthodique du français*, 4th edn. Paris: Presses Universitaires de France.

Simon-Vandenbergen, A.-M., Taverniers, M. and Ravelli, L. (eds) (2003) *Grammatical Metaphor: Views From Systemic Functional Linguistics*. Amsterdam: John Benjamins.

Ventola, E. (1996) Packing and unpacking of information in academic texts. In E. Ventola and A. Mauranen (eds) *Academic Writing, Intercultural and Textual Issues*, 153–94. Amsterdam: John Benjamins.

5

Choices in Tony's talk: Phonological paragraphing, information unit nexuses and the presentation of tone units

Gerard O'Grady[a]

5.1 Introduction

This chapter aims to examine the neglected role intonation plays in projecting the texture of a spoken text.[1] By texture I refer to the way a text is given unity within the particular context in which it is produced (Halliday and Hasan, 1976: 2). Much has been written on the devices writers use to give texture to their texts, for example the choice of Theme, lexical repetition, anaphora, deixis, elision, substitution, expansion and projection. Much has also been written about the effects of these choices, and how they not only give unity to texts but also orientate the reader along a favoured pathway. Outside the SFL tradition, scholars such as Nation (1984), have noted that paragraphing not only projects tactic relations between clauses and clause complexes, but also indicates which clause complexes are given more weight, or, in other words, are more central to the achievement of the text producer's message. The paragraph structure of a text helps to guide the reader along a reading pathway. Within SFL, scholars such as Martin (1992), Martin and Rose (2003) and Hood (2009) noted the repeated patterning of stages within texts, which operate within the same field.

Far less has been written on the texturing of spoken texts, and less again on the effects of the devices speakers choose to make their texts 'texts'.

a Gerard O'Grady lectures at the Centre for Language and Communication Research in Cardiff University. His chief research interests are critical discourse analysis, SFL – especially in investigating connections between intonation and the lexicogrammar, examining differences between language as process and product, and examining how spoken discourse unfolds and creates meaning in real time. He is the author of *A Grammar of Spoken English Discourse* and *Key Concepts in Phonetics and Phonology*.

Any text is open to multiple readings, some of which may potentially be resistant though speakers, as text producers, may attempt to constrain their hearers' 'readings' by organizing a text in a manner which foregrounds certain 'interpretative' pathways over others. I am using the term 'interpretative' pathway in a manner analogous to 'reading pathway' (see, e.g., Coffin and Derewianka, 2008). Speakers' intonation choices project an organization on their texts, which they use to guide their hearers' interpretative choices. Speakers make tonality choices to segment the stream of speech into information units. Within the information units their tonicity selections project the focus of information and demarcate the extent of the New. Their tone selections project the tactic relationships between adjoining tone units, and their choice of high or low pitch level may project a spoken paragraph or paratone structure.

Much has been written on the roles of tonality and tonicity in segmenting the stream of speech into information units and in dividing the information unit into Given and New elements (e.g. Halliday, 1967, 1970; Halliday and Greaves, 2008; Tench, 1990, 1996). Yet, other than studies such as Brown *et al.* (1980), Brazil (1997), Tench (1996) and especially Wichmann (2000), little has been written about how intonation choices operating above the tone unit organize the speaker's instantiation of his/her spoken text into spoken paragraphs or paratones, and how the paratone structure creates texture by signalling which tone units are united within the same paratone and which are separated by being placed in separate paratones.

Almost nothing, with the exception of a brief outline in Halliday (2005), Halliday and Greaves (2008: 130–32) and Smith (2008: 123–5), has been written regarding how tone choices project the logico-semantic flow of information construed within the clauses which in speech are instantiated as tone units. To my knowledge, with the exception of Wichmann (2000), no previous work has explored the relationship between written paragraphs and paratones, and the relationship between paratones and phases of text. I am unaware of any previous work, which has employed a corpus to investigate how speakers use tone to project logico-semantic meaning and to explore how different speaker choices create different interpretative pathways. This chapter aims to contribute to existing knowledge by shedding some light on the following three questions.

- What is the relationship between paratones and written paragraphs?
- What is the relationship between paratones and stages of the text?
- Within clause nexuses, how do speakers use intonation to project logio-semantic meaning?

5.2 The text and the readers

The text chosen for analysis is the short statement made by the then UK prime minister Blair to the television cameras from the G8 conference at Gleneagles, expressing his first reaction to the London underground bombings of 7 July 2005. The authorship of the text is not clear, but it is a prepared speech which Blair delivered in his name. While not necessarily the physical producer or creator of the text, Blair, as the person who assumes ethical responsibility for the speech, can be considered its author. In Goffman's terms he assumes the role of the author as 'someone whose position is established by the words that are spoken, someone whose beliefs have been told, someone who is committed to what the words say' (Goffman, 1981: 146).

The text was subsequently published on the official UK government website, www.direct.gov.uk, and the written version published there is the text used here in the clause analysis. The text is presented in Appendix 1 with the orthographic paragraphs notated by capital letters from A to F. In his subsequent autobiography Blair stated that the purpose of the statement was 'about defining the feeling so that the reaction can be shaped and the consequences managed' (Blair, 2010: 566). A way of ensuring that the audience was presented with the desired message was to project the relations between the happenings and doings construed within the clauses in a manner which best suited Blair's goal of managing the audience's response.

In order to investigate how speakers perform texture I recruited eleven readers, all native English speaking university students at Cardiff University, ranging from final year undergraduates, to MA and PhD students. I recorded their reading of Blair's statement in one of the university's sound studios. These readings are compared with Blair's original reading in this paper. To ensure that the punctuation and orthographic layout of Blair's statement did not unduly influence the eleven readers I removed all punctuation marks, capital letters, except where they denoted proper nouns or the personal pronoun *I*, and set out the text without any indentation or spacing between paragraphs. The readers were given the script two days prior to recording and asked to fill out a short questionnaire concerning their views on the war on terror and the UK government. This was done to ensure that the readers thought about the meaning potential realized by the lexicogrammatical choices within the text. It was noticeable that many of the readers brought their own marked-up copies of the speech to the recording which they used as an aid to their readings.

Table 5.1 illustrates that within the confines of the meaning potential allowed by the text the speakers realized differing Tonality choices, with all eleven readers segmenting the text into fewer tone units than Blair did. Example (1) illustrates how the speakers, including Blair, presented the circumstantial elements *at the moment* which closed off the first orthographic paragraph. Speakers, depending on their perception of the speech's meaning potential could potentially place the circumstantial elements into its own tone unit, into the tail of the preceding tone unit or into the pre-head or head of the following tone unit.

Table 5.1 Speaker and speech data.

Name of speaker	*Gender*	*Duration of speech (seconds)*	*Number of tone units*
Tony Blair	male	198.13	95
CB1	male	135.67	92
SB2	male	120.94	92
CD3	female	136.53	89
MD4	female	164.01	79
ME5	female	118.75	84
CG6	male	118.37	86
TJ7	male	138.31	81
HM8	male	106.76	75
FR9	female	115.61	67
NS10	female	116.04	80
RT11	female	122.87	78

(1)   CONTEXT: and I will simply try and tell you the information as best I can **at the moment**. It is reasonably clear that there have been a series of terrorist attacks in London.

Tonic independent tone unit[2]
|| at the \\<u>MO</u>ment || *MD4*
|| at the \\/<u>Mo</u>ment|| *ME5*
||at the \\<u>Mo</u>ment|| *CG6*
||at the \\↓<u>Mo</u>ment|| *TJ7*
|| at the \\↓<u>Mo</u>ment|| *HM8*
||at the /↑<u>Mo</u>ment|| *NS10*
||at the \\/↓<u>MO</u>Ment|| *TR11*

Tonic with preceding material
||as ... as BEST i can at the \\↓<u>Mo</u>ment|| *FR9*

Non tonic in tail
|| as BEST i \\<u>CAN</u> at the moment || *CB1*
|| as ... BEST i\\↓<u>CAN</u> at the moment || *Blair*

Non tonic in onset/prehead
|| at the ↑MOment its REASonably \\<u>CLEAR</u>|| *SB2*
||at the moment its ↑REAsonably \\<u>CLEAR</u>|| *CD3*

Seven out of the eleven readers, excluding Blair, articulated the circumstantial element as an independent tone unit, and thus as an independent unit of information (Halliday, 1967). They represented the meaning potential of the text as consisting of numerous units of information linked together in various ways and for them *at the moment* was of sufficient interest to be one of these foci of information. One speaker, FR9, realized a choice where the circumstantial element was the information focus in a larger tone unit, while CB1, and Blair himself, projected that the information realized by the circumstantial was recoverable, and so placed the items in the tail of a larger tone unit. By so doing they downgraded its information status to Given. Two speakers, SB2 and CD3, choose to place the circumstantial element in the following tone unit. SB2 placed it in the onset, and therefore as part of the New, while CD3 placed it in the prehead and projected it as Given. CD3, along with SB2, projected the adverbial as part of the second orthographic paragraph while CB1 and Blair projected it as part of the first paragraph. Of the seven speakers who placed the circumstantial into an independent tone unit, one, NS10, projected it as tone unit initial in the second orthographic paragraph.

5.3   Paratones

It is well recognized that speakers in pre-planned or pre-scripted genres such as news reading, audio book reading, anecdotes and bible reading, may mark the beginning of a new topic by resetting the pitch level of the initial onset syllable, (Tench, 1996: 28; Wichmann, 2000: 29). Onset syllables may be pitched as High, Mid or Low. The paragraph is closed by a fall on the final tone unit, which is the lowest reached in the entire paratone. Finally there is likely to be a longer than usual pause until the commencement of the following tone unit (Brazil, 1997; Brown *et al.*, 1980; Esser, 1988; Tench, 1996; Wichmann, 2000).

After the closure of a paratone speakers have three options: they can reset their onset pitch level to high to signal maximum disjunction; reset it to mid to signal less disjunction or they can produce a following tone unit with a low onset. The options are outlined in Figure 5.1.

The choice of a high onset projects the introduction of a topic, which is contrary to the previously created discourse expectations. A mid onset signals the introduction of a topic which adds to the previously created discourse expectations, while a low onset projects that the following topic

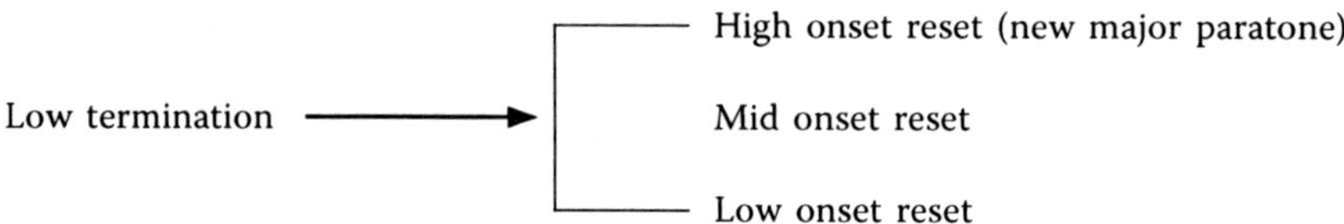

Figure 5.1 Choices available after the closure of a paratone.

is equivalent to the previously created discourse expectations (O'Grady, 2010: 28). Mid and low onsets immediately following a low termination and a significant pause project the introduction of dependent minor paratones which expand the prior paratone in a manner analogous to the relationship between an independent clause followed by a dependent clause.

Speakers may also choose to reset their pitch level following a pause to high or low after a previous mid termination or maintain their pitch level as mid (Figure 5.2).

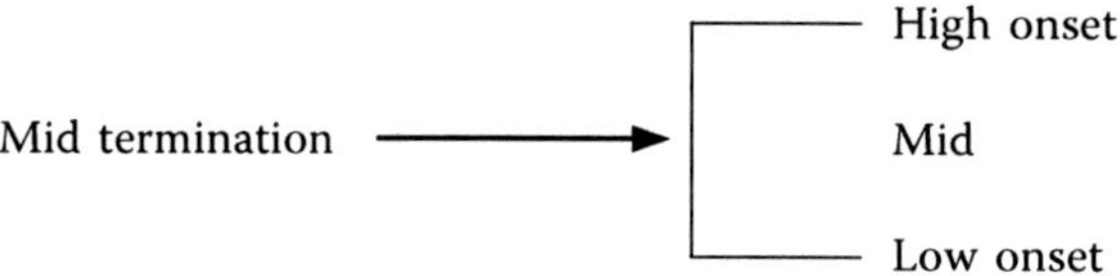

Figure 5.2 Choices available within a paratone.

If a speaker maintains the mid pitch setting they project that they are adding information to the previously created contextual expectations. However, if they choose either a high onset or a low onset they disrupt the previously created contextual expectations by signalling that the following meaning is either unexpected or equivalent. A high or low onset immediately following a mid termination and a longer than expected pause signals the boundary between two minor paratones which together form into a major paratone: for a slightly different view, see Tench (1990: 296–7).

Appendix 2 presents the correspondence between the speakers' projected paratone structure and the orthographic paragraph structure. None of the speakers, including Blair himself, projected a paratone structure which corresponded identically with the orthographic paragraph structure. All of the speakers produced major paratones coterminous with text which belonged to more than one written paragraph. Five of the speakers, not including Blair himself, produced minor paratones which contained text from more than one written paragraph. Example (2) illustrates how Blair's third paratone ran across two written paragraphs with the start of minor paratone {3.2} coinciding with the beginning of orthographic paragraph (C).

(2) || {3} there are obvi–↑OUSly || ca\SUALties || both \PEOple || that have /DIED || and people SEriously \INJURED || <pause> {3.1} and our ↓THOUGHTS and PRAYers of \COURSE are with || the \↑VICtims || and their \FAMilies || <pause> {3.2} its my in\TENTion to || LEAVE the g\EIGHT || within the next COUPle of \HOURS || and go DOWN to \LONdon || ....

Esser (1988: 26, 29) cautions that those who make their living through oral renditions of scripted material are more sensitive to the communicative value produced by high onsets and low terminations. Accordingly he argues that practised speakers may be far more successful at articulating the paragraph structure of a written text. There is some partial support for this view in Table 5.2. In Table 5.2 major paratones are notated by

Table 5.2 Written versus spoken paragraph structure.

Para	Clause	Blair	CB 1	SB 2	CD 3	MD 4	ME 5	CG 6	TJ 7	HM 8	FR 9	NS 10	RT 11
A	1	1.1 & 1.2	1.1, 1.2 ...	1.2 & 3	1 to 2.3	1 to 2.2	1.1 to 1.3 ...	1.1 to 1.3 ...	1.1 & 1.2	1.1 to 1.3	1 to 2.2	1.1 to 2.1 ...	1 to 2.2
B	2 & 3	2 to 3.1 ...	... 1.2 1.3 & 2.1 ...	4 & 5.1, 5.2	2.4 to 4	2.3 & 2.4	... 1.3 & 2	... 1.3 to 1.6	2 to 4	2	3 to 4.2	... 2.1 ...	3 & 4
C	4	3.2	2.2 & 2.3	6.1 ...	5.1 & 5.2	3.1 to 3.4 ...	3.1 ...	2.1 ...	5.1 to 5.4 ...	3.1 to 3.2 ...	5 to 6.1 ...	... 2.1 to 2.2 ...	5.1 ...
D	5 & 6	4, 5.1 & 5.2	3 to 4.2 ...	6.2 & 7.1 to 7.4 ...	6.1, 6.2 & 7 to 8.2	3.5 to 4.3 ...	... 3.1 to 4.2 ...	2.2 to 3	5.5 & 6.1 to 6.3 ...	4.1 to 5.2	6.2 to 6.5 ...	... 2.2 to 2.5 ...	5.2 to 6.1 ...
E	7, 8 & 9	6 & 7	4.3 ...	7.5 to 9 ...	9.1 to 9.3 ...	4.4 to 5.1 ...	... 4.2 to 4.6 ...	4.1 to 4.3	... 6.3	6.1 to 7.1 ...	... 6.5 to 7.1 ...	2.6 to 2.7 ...	6.2 to 6.4 ...
F	10 & 11	8 & 9	4.4 & 4.5	... 9 & 10	9.4	5.2 & 6	... 4.6 & 5	4.4	7	... 7.1 to 7.2	... 7.1 to 7.2	... 2.7 to 2.8	... 6.4 & 7

integers, for example 1, minor paratones by decimal points, for example, 1.1. (The numbers in Tables 5.2 to 5.4 refer to the clause structure of the text – see Appendix 3. Appendix 2 presents the text marked up in stages.) The notation '…' indicates that a major paratone continued across an orthographic paragraph boundary.

Blair proved to be more sensitive to orthographic paragraphs than the other readers. He produced five high keys to signal the commencement of a new written paragraph. He only failed to mark the opening of paragraph C through a sequencing of low termination, significant pause and high onset reset. The average for the other readers was 3.27 high keys, indicating that they marked half of the orthographic paragraph commencements by projecting the beginning of a major paratone. One reader, HM8, however, – see Table 5.2 – proved to be as sensitive as Blair in marking the beginning of new orthographic paragraphs. He projected a major paratone boundary to signal all orthographic paragraph openings except that of paragraph F.

All the speakers, however, projected a paratone structure, which, with two exceptions, ME5 and NS10, illustrated their recognition of the change in topic signalled in writing by paragraph structure. All readers predictably marked the opening of the text with a high onset. Only three of the eleven readers, CB1, ME5 and NS10, did not mark the beginning of paragraph B with a major or minor paratone boundary. Only NS10 did not mark the beginning of paragraph C with a major or minor paratone boundary. Two readers, ME5 and NS10, did not mark the beginning of paragraph D with a major or minor paratone boundary. ME5 and FR9 did not mark the beginning of paragraph E with a major or minor paratone boundary. In comparison seven of the readers did not mark the beginning of paragraph F with a major or minor paratone boundary. A possible reason for this will be advanced below. In conclusion it can be seen that readers faced with an unpunctuated and non-lineated text were for the most part capable of projecting a texture where topic shifts were projected as either new paratones or new minor paratones.

Blair's statement was designed to manage the expectations of the TV audience and control their reaction to the bombing. His statement clearly belongs to the field of politics but it is far more difficult to know which genre[3] it belongs to. It seems to combine elements of a report stating what happened, a justification explaining why it happened and a hortation proclaiming what must happen. Indeed it is not entirely clear that Blair's statement fits into any recognizable genre. However, as Table 5.3 indicates, the statement is formed out of recognizable stages though ones that are somewhat ad hoc.

It is immediately noticeable that the written paragraph structure, presented in Table 5.3, is not entirely in accord with the stages contained in the text. Paragraph A realizes the abstract in clause 1.1 by setting the scene for the speech. It prefigures what the statement will be about. Clauses 1.2 to 1.4 move the narrative along by orientating the hearer. These clauses inform the audience of the setting for the speech: Blair is unable to provide full details of what occurred and seeks the audience's recognition of this fact. Paragraph B realizes the incident: the audience is informed of what happened, namely the bombing in London, and then informed again of the consequences of the bombing, namely the fatalities and casualties. Paragraph C realizes a repercussion of the incident, the forced change to Blair's plans. Paragraph D realizes not only an interpretation of the repercussion by emphasizing that Blair's absence will not impact upon the working of the G8 but also subsequently an orientation to the stance of his fellow leaders. Paragraph E contains four separate stages of the text structure. There is an initial evaluation of the consequences of the act. This is followed by a restating of the incident, which appears to function as the basis for the immediately following thesis that the G8 was the target for the bombing. The text, however immediately defers consideration of the thesis until an unspecified later date.[4] Paragraph F realizes the argument that terrorism is futile in two stages. First it realizes the grounds– namely that the terrorists must be made aware of 'our determination to protect our values', and second it realizes the conclusion that because of 'our determination' the terrorists will never succeed.

Table 5.3 Text phases and orthographic paragraphs.

Paragraph	Text phases
A	Abstract (1.1), 1st orientation (1.2) – (1.4)
B	Incident (2) & (3)
C	Repercussions (4)
D	Interpretation (5), orientation (6)
E	Evaluation (7), incident repeat (8.1), thesis (8.2), deferral (9)
F	Argument/grounds (10), argument/conclusions (11)

Tables 5.2 and 5.4 illustrate that if minor paratones are considered to project discrete stages, then all of the readers and Blair produced more paratones than there were orthographic paragraphs. This indicates that they projected a texture richer than a string of six related unfolding topics. Table 5.4 sets out the correlation between the text stages and the speakers' projected paratone structure.

Table 5.4 Text stages and paratone structure.

Stages	Clause	Blair	CB 1	SB 2	CD 3	MD 4	ME 5	CG 6	TJ 7	HM 8	FR 9	NS 10	RT 11
Abstract	1.1	1.1 ...	1.1 ...	1	1	1	1.1 ...	1.1 ...	1.1 ...	1.1 ...	1	1.1 ...	1
Orientation 1	1.2 to 1.4	1.2	... 1.1 & 1.2 ...	2, 3 & 4	2.1 to 2.3 ...	2.1 to 2.2 ...	1.2 to 1.3 ...	1.2 to 1.3	1.2	1.2 to 1.3	2.1 to 2.2	1.2 to 1.3	2.1 to 2.3
Incident	2 & 3	2 & 3.1 ...	1.3, 1.4 & 2.1 ...	5.1 to 5.2	2.4, 3 & 4	2.3	1.4 & 2	1.4 to 1.6	2 to 4	2	3 & 4.1 to 4.2	2.1 ...	3 & 4
Repercussions	4	... 3.1 3.2	2.2 2.3	6.1 ...	5.1 5.2	3.1 to 3.3 ...	3.1 ...	2.1 ...	5.1 to 5.2	3.1 3.2 ...	5 & 6.1 ...	2.2 ...	5.1 ...
Interpretation	5	4	3	6.2 & 7.1 7.2 ...	6.1 6.2 7	3.4 & 4.1 ...	... 3.1 3.2	... 2.1 2.2	5.3 ...	4.1 4.2	... 6.1 to 6.3 ...	2.3 ...	5.2 ...
Orientation 2	6	5.1 5.2	4.1 to 4.2	7.3 7.4 ...	8.1 8.2	4.2 4.3 ...	4.1 4.2 ...	3	5.4 ...	5.1 5.2	6.4 ...	2.4 ...	5.2 ...
Evaluation	7	6	4.3 ...	7.5 7.6	9.1 ...	4.4 ...	4.3 4.4 ...	4.1 ...	5.5	6.1	6.5	2.5	... 5.2 & 6.1 ...
Incident repeat	8.1	7 ...	... 4.3 ...	8.1 ...	9.2 ...	4.5 ...	4.5 ...	4.2 ...	6.1 ...	6.2 ...	7.1 ...	2.6 ...	6.2 ...
Thesis	8.2	... 7 ...	... 4.3 ...	8.2	... 9.2 ...	... 4.5	... 4.5	... 4.2 ...	6.2 ...	... 6.2 ...	... 7.1 ...	... 2.6 ...	6.3 ...
Deferral	9	... 7	... 4.3 ...	9 ...	9.3 ...	5.1 ...	4.6 ...	4.3 ...	6.3 ...	7.1 ...	... 7.1 ...	... 2.6 ...	6.4 ...
Argument/grounds	10	8	4.4 ...	... 9	9.4 ...	5.2 ...	... 4.6	... 4.3 4.4	... 6.3	... 7.1	... 7.1	2.7	... 6.4
Argument/conclusions	11	9	4.5	10	9.5	6	5	... 4.4	7	7.2	7.2	2.8	7

Table 5.4 illustrates that none of the speakers projected a paratone structure which directly corresponded with the stages of the text. However, the readers' projected paratone structure indicated their awareness of how the various stages of the text contributed to the unfolding of their narrative. All the speakers with the exception of CB1, signalled the end of the abstract and the beginning of the orientation 1 phase by projecting a paratone or minor paratone boundary between the two stages of the text. Blair, along with five of the other readers, notated the transition between the abstract, which prefigured what was to come, and the Orientation 1 which grounded the narrative in the context in which it was to be told with a minor paratone boundary indicating that, while separate, the two stages were projected as being linked together. They represented two discrete stages of the text which were themselves separate from the telling which commenced with the incident stage.

All of the readers marked the transition from orientation to incident by projecting a paratone boundary. Blair, along with four other readers, projected a major paratone boundary signalling maximum disjunction from what has gone before. The paratone boundary signalled to the audience to pay attention to the transition from one stage of the text to another.[5] It is of interest that Blair alone did not project a major or minor paratone boundary between the incident phase and the repercussion phase. In other words, he signalled to the audience that the incident and the repercussions were to be treated by the audience as a single stage in the text. The repercussions, notably the disruption to the working of the G8, were according to Blair an entirely predictable consequence of the terrorist attack.

Only TR11 did not explicitly signal the transition from the factual report realized by the incident and repercussions stages to the interpretation. CB1 and TR11 were the only two readers who did not explicitly mark the shift to the following stage orientation 2. The readers, thus far, appeared to have few difficulties in identifying the stages of the text and in projecting the transitions. Paragraph E however contained four stages, the evaluation, the incident repeat, the thesis and the deferral. Neither Blair nor any of the other speakers projected all these stages as independent paratones. Blair, himself, projected a paratone structure where the evaluation alone was signalled as a discrete event. None of the other speakers signalled a paratone structure where the evaluation was projected as a major paratone. The effect of Blair's choice was to focus his audience's attention on the timing of the terrorist attack. This choice coupled with his earlier choice not to project the repercussions as a discrete stage in the text projected a meaning subtly different from that of the other readers. Blair uniquely signalled to his audience a focus on the G8 as the ultimate target of the attack.

All of the readers signalled their recognition that the incident repeat signalled a new stage in the unfolding text by the projection of a minor paratone boundary. However, only three of them, not including Blair, projected the incident repeat as a discrete stage in the text. The others projected that the incident repeat was linked to the thesis. It was the background upon which the thesis was advanced. Blair, unlike the majority of the other speakers projected a paratone structure where the deferral was part of the same textual stage as the thesis and the incident repeat. For him, alone, the thesis was informationally foregrounded.

I noted earlier that many of the readers did not explicitly signal the beginning of paragraph F by projecting a major or minor paratone boundary. This appears to have resulted from these readers' difficulties in incorporating the deferral stage into the structure of the text. Most recognized it as a different stage from the preceding thesis but seemed unsure as to what function it realized in the unfolding of the narrative. Hence, they tended to project it as part of the following stage, argument/ grounds. All of the speakers, including Blair, realized the final two stages, arguments/grounds and argument/conclusions, as either two major or minor paratones.

To conclude, it is clear that the speakers' projection of paratone structure showed that they were cognisant of the stages of the text when articulating the text. However, we have seen that Blair's projection of paratone structure differed in three significant ways. First he projected a context where the repercussions automatically followed from the bombing, a fact we can infer he believed that that the bombers were aware of. Second, Blair projected the evaluation as a discrete textual event. By so doing he focused attention on disrupting the G8 as the ultimate target of the terrorists. Finally, by projecting the incident repeat, thesis and deferral stages in a single major paratone he foregrounded his view that the G8 was the terrorist's target.

In short we can see that paratone structure reflects both the formal orthographic paragraph layout of presenting single topics in discrete units and the stages of the text. However, while the relationship is close it is not identical. Speakers are free to project paratone structures which foreground a meaning potential which may not be a meaning potential foregrounded by either the orthographic layout or the lexicogrammar.

5.4   Spoken taxis

Prior to an extended discussion of how speakers use intonation to project logico-semantic meaning it is first necessary to briefly sketch how clausal tactic relations are signalled by the lexicogrammar. Clause and clause like elements may be linked together in the following ways. First there may be no tactic relation signalled by the lexicogrammar as between clause 9 and clause complex 10 (see Appendix 3). Secondly potentially independent clauses may be linked paratactically: each clause or clause-like element has the same status, for example, clauses 1.1, 1.2, 1.3 and 1.4. Alternatively the clause or clause-like elements may be linked hypotactically with the clauses being projected as having an unequal status, as in clause complex 7 where the α clause is projected as the head of the clause complex. The other elements are dependent on the clause, which operates as the head of the clause complex.

Clauses which are linked together enter into two types of semantic relations: expansion and projection. The system of expansion develops the experiential meaning of a clause through Elaboration (signified by $=$) which is a relation of restatement; Extension (signified by $+$) which is a relation of addition and Enhancement (signified by $\times$) which is a relation of modification of time, space, means, cause condition and so on, (see Eggins, 2004: 278–9). The system of Projection is in Eggins's words 'the logio-semantics of quoting and reporting speech or thoughts' (*ibid.*: 271). In the statement the sole example of projection is found in Clause 1.2.

The statement itself comprises nine clause complexes and two clause simplexes. Including embedded clauses there are 52 clauses in all. Blair added the minor clause *thank you* to the statement and this element was included in the version given to the eleven other speakers to read. It is immediately noticeable that many of the clauses are quite long, as is to be expected from pre-planned discourse, and hence not likely to be produced in single tone units. Unsurprisingly all of the speakers produced far more than 53 tone units with Blair himself producing 96 (see Table 5.1). The logico-semantic relations within the first clause complex are detailed below following Eggins (2004) and Halliday and Matthiessen (2004).

Clause complex 1 consists of four paratactic clauses. All of the clauses are independent pieces of information which in the absence of the conjunction *and* could have stood on their own. Yet the text instantiates a meaning where clauses 1.2, 1.3 and 1.4 extend the meaning realized within clause 1.1. Clause 1.2, itself, consists of a projecting clause which consists of two clausal elements (see Halliday and Matthiessen, 2004: 444).

The projected idea *you understand* ... is an enhancement of the *hope*: it qualifies it first by reference to a condition and secondly by reference to a specific time. It is worth noting that there are four rankshifted clauses, found within the first clause complex which themselves modify nominal, verbal and adverbial elements operating within the clauses. In Clause 1.1 the rankshifted clause elaborates the previous nominal element *events* by clarifying exactly where the event occurred.

The orthographic version of the text subsequently published on the government website was broken down into six written paragraphs. Table 5.5 shows the relationship between the clause structure and the paratone structure.

Table 5.5 The relation between paragraphs and clause complexes/simplexes.

Paragraphs	*Clause complexes/simplexes*
A	1
B	2+3
C	4
D	5+6
E	7+8+9
F	10X11

It can be seen that paragraphs B, D and E are formed out of two or more independent and equal clause complexes which exist in a logico-semantic relationship of extension. Speakers though, as we have seen above, project the topical and episode character of the narrative they are telling not in paragraphs or clauses but in paratones and tone units. As noted, to date little work has been done exploring how tone choice projects logico-semantic meaning with the exception of Halliday and Matthiessen (2004: 482–5), Halliday (2005: 291–2) and Halliday and Greaves (2008: 130–35) who propose the following unmarked relationship between tone sequencing and taxis.

(3)	**Tactic relations**	**Tone sequencing**
	Two unrelated clauses	Tone sequence Fall ^ Fall
	One paratactic clause complex	Tone Sequence Rise ^ Fall
	One hypotactic clause complex	a ^ b = Fall ^ Fall-Rise or
		b ^ a = Fall-Rise ^ Fall
	One independent clause	Fall
	Tone Concord expansion	Tone repetition
	Elements identical in kind	e.g. Fall ^ Fall
	Projection (idea)	A single unit

Thus, if all things proved to be equal we would expect to find the end of a major clausal unit marked by a fall signalling the closure of a discrete unit. Within a clause complex the boundary between paratactic clauses should be signalled by a rise while the boundary at the end of the entire unit should coincide with a fall. However, if the paratactic clauses are elaborations we would expect tone repetition. In a two clause paratactic complex the sequence is predicted to be a rise followed by a fall while in a three or more clause paratactic complex the sequence is predicted to be a series of rises followed by a final fall. The boundary between a dependent clause and a following independent clause is noted by a fall-rise while if the hypotactic clause complex culminates in a dependent clause it is similarly notated by a fall-rise. Smith (2008: 124) notes that rises have the logical function of parataxis while fall-rises have the logical function of hypotaxis.

Other scholars who focus on the relationship between tone selection and the status of information, such as Tench (1990: 219–24, 1996: 80–86), and Crystal (1969: 244ff.), argue that the status of information projected by tone selection is as follows:

(4)   **Tone sequence**   **Informational value**

Tone sequence	Informational value
Fall ^ Fall	Two pieces of major information
Rise ^ Fall	Incomplete (major) ^ Major information
Fall ^ Rise	Major ^ Minor information
Fall-rise ^ Fall	Theme highlighting ^ Major information
Any tone ^ Fall-rise	Major information ^ Implication

Tench notes that rises either indicating major incomplete information or minor information co-occur on circumstantial elements which function to suggest a limitation on the information projected by the main clause (see also Cruttenden, 1997: 95). Thus, if a clause containing a final circumstantial element was realized by more than one tone unit, the tone which projects dependency across clauses is not the final rise but the tone which corresponds to the major information within the clause. If the final tone is a fall it completes the information. My constructed example (5a–5c) illustrates.

(5a) || it is my intention to leave the \G8 || within the next couple of /<u>HOURS</u> ||
           Major information   Minor information   pause

(5b) || it is my intention to leave the /G8 || within the next couple of \<u>HOURS</u> ||
           Major incomplete information   Major complete information   pause

(5c) || it is my intention to leave the /G8 || within the next couple of /<u>HOURS</u> ||
           Major incomplete information   Minor information   pause

The pause at the end of the examples projects disjunction and signals the start of a new unit. The combination of pause and tone selection projects (5a) and (5b) as independent units. They are not projected as being dependent on any following unit. (5c), however projects a context where the unit is projected intonationally as being dependent on a following unit. The proposition contained within the clause can only be evaluated in the light of following information (see Pierrehumbert and Hirschberg, 1990; Ladd, 2008). Thus, we could predict that if the projection of information is congruent with the tactic relations established by the lexicogrammar, an independent clause must contain a falling tone though the falling tone may not necessarily be clause final. Dependent clauses are predicted to contain non-falling tones indicating their informational incompleteness.

Table 5.6 shows the percentage of tone chosen by all the speakers. For all speakers the fall was the most common choice, ranging from 47.61 per cent to 79.01 per cent of all tones. For some speakers the rise is the second most common tone choice, ranging from 7.69 per cent to 21.73 per cent, but for others the fall-rise is the second most common choice, ranging from 2.46 per cent to 25.3 per cent. The level and the rise-fall are the least common choices. In short it is clear that the speakers choose different tone compositions while articulating the same text.

The tone composition chosen by Blair differed from that of the other speakers in three ways. Unlike the other readers, with the exception of RT11, he did not select any rise-fall tones. He produced the highest number of level tones and, with the sole exception of TJ7, produced the fewest number of fall-rise tones. A rise-fall tone signals the strength of a speaker's commitment to what he/she is saying. Brazil (1997: 97) describes it as projecting that the speaker has at the moment of speaking registered the significance of his utterance. It is clear why this would not be a meaning which Blair, who very much needed to appear to be in charge of the situation, would have wanted to convey in a response to a terrorist bombing.

Level tone projects speaker disengagement from the communicative context. Speakers may disengage because of momentary processing problems in assembling their message or because the words they are

Table 5.6 The readers' selections of tones in percentages.

Tone unit	Blair	CB1	SB2	CD3	MD4	ME5	CG6	TJ7	HM8	FR9	NS10	RT11
\	67.36	59.78	67.39	65.16	58.22	47.61	70.93	79.01	64	59.7	63.75	71.79
/	14.73	21.73	14.13	14.6	11.39	21.42	10.46	13.58	13.33	8.95	11.25	7.69
–	9.47	1.08	1.08	2.24	2.53	7.14	2.32	2.46	2.66	5.97	1.25	6.42
\/	8.42	15.21	16.30	14.6	25.31	21.42	13.95	2.46	18.66	23.88	20	14.10
/\	0	2.1	1.08	3.37	2.53	2.38	2.32	2.46	1.33	1.49	3.75	0

uttering are so routine that they do not need to take account of their informational status (Brazil, 1997; Tench, 1997). For present purposes it is sufficient to note that a level tone does not project that the speaker has articulated a piece of major information; the choice of level tone signals dependence and not independence (Crystal, 1975: 35). The paucity of fall-rise tones in Blair's articulation is of interest in that we would expect more fall-rises, all things being equal, to be present in a text which contains hypotactic clauses. This is a point, which will be revisited in the following section.

Prior to examining tone sequences in the actual data, however, it is necessary to establish that the sequencing of tones was different from what we could expect were the tones sequenced solely on the basis of chance, or, in other words, if we assumed that there was no meaning projected by the position of a tone in an utterance (see O'Grady, 2010 and, for a contrasting view, Brazil, 1997). El Menoufy (1969: 426 ff.), in an investigation or around 3000 tone units, found that there is a tendency for pairs of tones to co-occur more or less frequently than chance, or, in other words, tone sequencing was motivated in her data. Table 5.7 illustrates the tone sequencing found within the 14 minor paratones in Blair's articulation of the text. The bracketed numbers represent the number of tones which we would expect to find had the sequencing of tones been no more than an epiphenomenal effect. The * diacritic is used to indicate a paired sequence of tones which is much more or much less than chance.

Table 5.7 The sequencing of tones in Blair's speech.

First tone unit	Following tone unit						Total
	\	/	—	\/	/\	#	
#	10 (9.42)	1* (2.06)	2 (1.32)	1 (1.18)	0 (0)		14 (13.98)[6]
\	36 (37.57)	8 (8.22)	3* (5.28)	5 (4.69)	0 (0)	12* (8.22)	64 (63.98)
/	12* (8.19)	0 (1.79)	2* (1.15)	0 (1.02)	0 (0)	2 (1.79)	14 (13.94)
—	5 (5.31)	1 (1.16)	1 (0.75)	2* (0.66)	0 (0)	0 (1.16)	9 (9.04)
\/	4 (4.67)	3* (1.02)	0* (0.66)	1* (0.58)	0 (0)	0* (1.02)	8 (7.95)
/\	0 (0)	0 (0)	0 (0)	0 (0)	0 (0)	0 (0)	0 (0)

The first column # illustrates that the number of falling tones following silence (notated by #) is slightly more than chance. There are only half the number of rises following silence than a chance distribution would have predicted. While the number of falls, rises and fall-rises following falls is very similar to a chance distribution, the number of level tones and silences following falls differs from a chance distribution. The number of falling tones immediately followed by silence in Blair's articulation is 50 per cent more than a chance distribution and seems to be motivated by Blair's decision to choose final falling tones to signal completion. There are more falls following rises and fewer rises following rises than would be expected. No levels followed by silence were found in Blair's articulation. The number of fall-rises following levels is three times more than expected. The distribution of tones following fall-rises differs from what chance would lead us to expect. There are around three times as many rises following fall-rises than we would expect. Blair did not produce any final fall-rises contrary to expectations. We can conclude by saying that not only are Blair's tone selections motivated but the sequence of tones is similarly motivated.

5.5 Tone sequences

This section examines the information flow within the text. It chiefly focuses on clause complex 1 (see example (6)) as it is both the opening of the text and the longest clause complex found in the text. It is formed out of four paratactic nexuses, each of which contains an embedded clause. The lexicogrammar construes the following logico-semantic relationships: the initial clause construes a doing with an embedded elaboration signalling the equivalence or rewording of the doing construed in the non-embedded part of the clause. The presence of the conjunctive element signals a paratactic link to the following clause which construes a mental activity; the projection of a 'hope'. The projection is linked paratactically by the conjunctive element to a relational process which is also linked by the same conjunction to a fourth clause. Thus, the lexicogrammar projects four clauses which could have stood alone as being connected and of being of equal status. Intonationally we might therefore expect a speaker to signal the relationship between the paratactic clauses through the selection of rises projecting that the proposition contained within the clause is not to be considered in isolation from what is to follow. However, as previously noted, all of the paratactic clauses are far too long to be articulated within a single tone unit and, thus, we would expect the paratactic clauses to be spoken in a manner which signals the flow of information within each independent clause. Thus, the heads of the clauses should tend to be marked as more informationally significant and be projected by falls. As example (6) illustrates more than one systemic option would appear to be available to the speaker at certain points within the text.

(6) I am just going to make a short statement to you on the terrible events
          Fall   **Fall/rise/fall-rise**
=[[that have happened in London earlier today]],
            Rise

+2 α and I hope
    Fall
  ʻxβ you understand
     Fall
xʻγ that at the present time we are still trying to establish
           Fall

x[[exactly γ1 what has happened,]]
  Fall-Rise   **Rise**
+3 and there is a limit =[[to what information I can give you]],
      Fall   **Fall**   **Rise**
  +4 1 and I will simply try and tell you the information as best
             Fall
  x[[I can at the moment]].
    Rise

In clause 1 we would expect a speaker to produce a falling tone to correspond with the head of the clause.[7] The circumstantial element, which modifies what the statement will be about, can be projected in speech as a piece of major information equal to the statement through the choice of a fall. A rise conversely would project that the circumstantial element limits content of the statement while a fall-rise would project an implication shared by speaker and audience. As the embedded clause is downgraded informationally we would expect it to be articulated with a rise. In the second clause a speaker would be expected to produce a sequence of falls on the projecting clause signalling the speaker's action and on the head of the projected clause. The embedded clause is expected to be articulated with a rise. Similarly in clauses 3 and 4 we would expect the speaker to project the downgraded informational status of the embedded clauses with a rise.

Table 5.8 shows the tone choices and the number of paratones each speaker selected when articulating clause complex 1. The first thing to note is that Blair was one of only two readers whose intonation projects clause complex 1 as a single unified semantic unit. He, however, projected the clause complex as comprising two parts while the other reader projected it as comprising three parts. The other readers did not in their readings project the clause complex as a single semantic unit – three of them CB1, ME5 and CG7 projected the clause complex as being part of a larger semantic unit while the remaining readers projected the clause complex as being divisible into smaller semantic units, for example SB2 who subdivided the clause complex into three paratones. Three other readers divided the clause complex into two semantic units. The symbol + indicates that the particular paratone/minor paratone included material from a following clause complex.

Table 5.8 Number of tones and paratones in clause complex 1.

	\	/	–	\/	/\	Total	Paratones	Minor paratones
Blair	7	4	2	3	0	16	1	2
CB1	9	2	1	2	1	15	0	2
SB2	8	1	0	3	0	12	3	4
CD3	9	0	1	2	0	13	1+	3
MD4	9	2	0	2	0	13	2+	3
ME5	6	2	1	3	0	12	0	3
CG6	8	1	1	4	1	15	0	1+
TJ7	11	1	0	0	0	12	2	3
HM8	9	3	0	1	0	13	1	3
FR9	6	1	1	4	0	12	2	3
NS10	11	2	2	0	0	15	1+	3+
RT11	8	0	2	2	0	12	2	4

Example 7 presents Blair's articulation of clause complex 1. The numbers in brackets label paratones and minor paratones.

(7) ||{1.1} i am just going to MAKE a –SHORT|| \STATEment|| to you on the
                Major/incomplete   Major
   \/TERRible events || that have /HAPPened|| in \LONdon||EARlier /↓TOday||
   Major/implication   Minor   Major   Minor
   || {1.2} and i HOPE you under\/STAND|| that at the ↑PREsent \TIME|| we are
                    Theme highlighting   Major/complete
   || STILL TRYing to e\/STABlish exactly ||what has \HAPpened||
              Major implication   Major
   || and theres a /LIMit|| to WHAT inforMAtion||i can ↑/GIVE you ||
       Major/incomplete   Major   Minor
   || and i'll simply TRY and \TELL you || the in–FORMation as || as ... BEST i
       Major   Major/incomplete
  \↓CAN at the moment ||
    Major/complete

If we look at Blair's reading we can see that the four clauses are predictably examples of marked tonality. In Blair's reading the minor paratone boundary at the end of clause 1 projects that it is partially segmented off from the remainder of the clause complex. He packages the flow of information as follows: the heart of the clause, the actor, and process are presented in two information units with the first indicating incomplete major information and the second major information. The following circumstance is presented as an implication. By so doing Blair communicates an unspoken implication about the terrible events to his audience, which they and they alone are projected as being able to infer. The embedded clause is broken down into a series of three tone units with the circumstantial adjunct incongruently presented as major information. This results in the foregrounding of the location of the bombing.

The effect of this reading is to create a flow of information markedly different to that projected by the lexicogrammar. Rather than simply being the first clause (with an embedded clause) in a paratactic sequence Blair packages the information flow of his message as containing four pieces of major information and two pieces of minor information. The presence of the fall-rise in the middle of the sequence is of interest in that it invites the hearer to infer that something does not need to be said about the terrible events.

Only three of the speakers, CB1, CG6 and TJ7 did not articulate a reading which separated the initial clause, which functioned as the abstract of the text, from the remainder of the clause complex. This suggests that the speakers' decisions about how to package the information flow were more influenced by the organization of the text into stages than they were by its formal arrangement into clauses and clause complexes. Blair's articulation of the remaining three clauses, which functioned together as the orientation to the text, was not in full accordance with the predictions set out in example (6). Blair articulated the orientation as predominantly a sequential chain of tone units which were projected as containing major information. Blair articulated two of the embedded clauses with falling tones and consequently he projected them as chunks of major information. The embedded clause in clause 3 was articulated with a rise and projected as limiting the type and amount of information available to the audience.

HM8 is the speaker whose articulation is closest to Blair's. Like Blair he projected the entire clause complex as a single paratone but, unlike Blair, he segmented it into three minor paratones. Like Blair his first minor paratone was coterminous with clause 1 which functioned as the abstract. However, unlike Blair, he placed clauses 2 and 3 into one minor paratone and separated it from clause 4. HM8's articulation is presented in example (8).

(8) || {1.1} i am just ↑GOing to make a SHORT \STATEment || to /YOU || on the
                                           Major   Minor
TERrible e\VENTS || that have \HAPpened in london || EARlier \↓to\DAY ||
    Major   Major   Major
|| {1.2} and i hope you under\↑STAND || that at the PREsent /TIME || we are
                    Major   Major incomplete
still TRYing to e/STABlish || eXACTly what has \HAPpened ||
        Major/incomplete   Major
|| and theres a LImit to what inforMAtion i can \/GIVE you ||
                               Major Implication
||{1.3} will simply ↑TRY and tell you the infor\MAtion || as BEST as i \CAN ||
                               Major   Major
at the \↓MOment ||
Major

The opening clause realized as minor paratone (1.1) contains four pieces of major information. The sole rising tone is used to project the limiting of the audience of the text to the immediate hearers. Clauses 2 and 3 are projected as major information with the information in clause 3 projecting an implication. Clause 4 articulated as minor paratone (1.3) is realized as a sequence of three tone units which project major information. The other readers similarly did not mark the embedded clausal material as informationally less important. All of them selected at least one falling tone coterminous with the embedded elements. They presented the initial clause complex as a sequence of chiefly major chunks of information with the occasional piece of minor information. Fall-rises were used to project contextually bound implications.

The speakers, including Blair, projected a flow of information which was not in accord with the expectations set out in example 6. Within the remaining eight clause nexuses Blair and the other speakers did not explicitly re-enforce syntactic dependence through their tone choices. For instance as examples (9) to (11) show, throughout the remainder of the text the speakers consistently did not project the informational downgrading of embedded elements through the selection of a rise.

(9)   **It is reasonably clear** ^x**[[that there have been a series of terrorist attacks in London]].**
    || it's reaso↑NABly \CLEAR|| that there have been a ... a SEries of ter\RORist attacks|| in \↓LONdon|| *Blair*

|| it's rea↑SONably /CLEAR|| that there have been a SEries of TERrorist at\TACKS|| in \LONdon|| *CB1*
|| at the MOment it's REASonably \CLEAR|| that there have been –A|| a SEries of TERrorist at\TACKS|| in \/↓LONdon|| *SB2*
|| at the moment it's ↑REAsonably \CLEAR|| that there have been a ↑SEries of \TERrorist attacks|| in \/↓LONdon|| *CD3*
|| {2.3} it's ↑REAsonably \CLEAR|| that there have been a ... a SEries of \/ TERrorist attacks || in \LONdon || *MD4*
|| {1.4} it's ↑REAsonably \CLEAR|| that there have been a ... || a SEries of TERrorist\/ATtacks in london|| *ME5*
|| {1.4} it's REAsonably \CLEAR|| that there have been a SEries of \TERrorist attacks|| in \LONdon|| *CG6*
|| it's ↑REAsonably \CLEAR|| that there have been a SEries of \TERrorist attacks || in /↓LONdon|| *TJ7*
|| it's ↑REAsonably \CLEAR|| that there have been a SEries of TERrorist attacks in \LONdon|| *HM8*
|| it's ↑REAsonably \/CLEAR|| that there have been a seri of ... a SEries of TERrorist atTACKS in \↓LONdon|| *FR9*
|| at the /MOment|| its REAsonably \CLEAR|| that there have been a – SEries|| of TERrorist atTACKS in \/LONdon|| *NS10*
|| it's↑REAsonably \/CLEAR|| that there have been a SEries of TERrorist at\TACKS|| in \↓LONdon|| *TR11*

Five speakers including Blair articulated the embedded element as a sequence of two tone units containing falling tones or as two pieces of major information. Other readers, such as CD3, produced a sequence of a falling tone followed by a fall-rise and projected an unspoken implication about the location of the bombing. TJ7 alone projected the location of the bombing as minor information which limited the location and perhaps the effect of the terrorist attack.[8]

(10)   **and the Ministers ˭[[that have been dealing with this,]]**
   || and the minISters that have been \↓DEALing|| with /THIS|| *Blair*
   || ↑ AND the \/MINisters|| that have been DEAling with \↓THIS|| *CB1*
   || and the \MINisters|| that have been DEAling with \↓THIS|| *SB2*
   || and the \MINisters|| that have been \DEALing with this|| *CD3*
   || and the \MINisters|| that have been DEAling with \↓THIS|| *MD4*
   || and the \MINisters|| that have been \/DEAling with this|| *ME5*
   || and the \MINisters|| that have been \DEAling with this|| *CG6*
   || and the MINisters that have been \↓DEAling with this|| *TJ7*
   || and the \MINisters|| that HAVE been DEAling with /THIS|| *HM8*
   || and the \↓MINisters|| that HAVE been \↓DEAling with this || *FR9*
   || and the /MINisters|| that have been \DEALing with this|| *NS10*
   || and the min\ISters|| that have been \/DEALing with this|| *TR11*

In example (10) as in (9) the majority of the speakers projected the informationally downgraded post modifying element as major information through the selection of a falling tone or as major information with an implication through the selection of a fall-rise. The two exceptions are Blair and HM8. Blair projects the elements *with this* as limiting the actions of the ministers while HM8, in congruence with the grammar, projects the rankshifted clause as less significant informationally.

11   **and reach the conclusions ⁼[[which we were going to reach.]]**
|| and REACH the con/<u>CLUS</u>ions|| WHICH we were GOing to \↓<u>REACH</u>||*Blair*
|| and REACH the con\/<u>CLU</u>sions|| which we were GOing to \↓<u>REACH</u>||*CB1*
|| and REACH the con/<u>CLU</u>sions|| that we were ↓GOing to \<u>REACH</u>||*SB2*
|| and↑REACH the con\<u>CLUS</u>ions|| WHICH we were GOing to \↓<u>REACH</u>||*CD3*
|| and REACH the con\<u>CLU</u>sions|| which we were GOing to \/<u>REACH</u>||*MD4*
|| and REACH the con\<u>CLU</u>sions||which we were going to \↓<u>REACH</u>||*ME5*
|| and REACH the con\<u>CLU</u>sions|| which we were GOing to \↓<u>REACH</u>||*CG6*
|| and REACH the con\<u>CLU</u>sions which we were going to reach|| *TJ7*
|| and REACH the con/<u>CLU</u>sions|| which we were GOing to \↓<u>REACH</u>||*HM8*
|| and REACH the con\<u>CLU</u>sions|| which we were \/<u>GO</u>ing to reach || *FR9*
|| and↑REACH the con\<u>CLU</u>sions|| which we were \/<u>GO</u>ing to reach|| *NS10*
|| and REACH the con\<u>CLU</u>sions|| WHICH we were \/<u>GO</u>ing to reach|| *TR11*

In (11) all the speakers bar TJ7 placed the post modifying embedded clause into its own tone unit and projected it either as a piece of major information or as piece of major information to which a contextually bound implication is attached. TJ7 did not place the rank shifted clause into its own tone unit. Rather he chose to project it in post tonic position and, by so doing, projected that the post modified elements were Given and thus, informationally downgraded.

In the text studied the speakers selected tone to project the information status of tone units. They tended to project their messages as a series of chunks of major information interspersed with contextually bound implications projected by fall-rises. Non final rises and level tones projected major though not compete information. Final rises modified or limited the previous information. In short the speakers' tone choices did not appear to be overly influenced by the tactic relations signalled by the lexicogrammar but focused more on managing their hearers' discourse expectations through the signalling of a dependence/independence relation between information units contained within a paratone.

The falling tone was most common tone chosen by all speakers. This may have been because the speakers had no fear of being interrupted and thus, did not need to manage their hearer's contribution to the discourse. Yet, speakers do not construct discourse in isolation. Hearers, through their presence, influence how speakers manage the flow of information within their discourse. With that in mind the following paragraphs examine the role of non-final rises and level tones in Blair's discourse. In example (12) and in all following examples the tone units under discussion are emboldened.

(12) || {1.1} **i am just going to MAKE a –SHORT** ||\STATEment || to you on the \/TERrible events || that have /HAPpened || in \LONdon ||↓EARlier/ Today || {1.2} and i HOPE you under\/STAND || that at the ↑PREsent\TIME || we are STILL TRYing to e\/STABlish exactly || what has \HAPPened || **and theres a /LIMit** || to WHAT in\FORMation || i can ↑/GIVE you || and i'll simply TRY and \TELL you || **the infor–MAtion as** || as ... BEST i\↓CAN at the moment ||

It appears that as well as projecting incomplete major information the level tones signalled processing problems or simulated processing problems – see also the initial tone unit of example (13); Blair was focusing on assembling his message and not projecting it. The level tone appeared not so much to signal non-completeness but more that the speaker was temporarily disengaged from projecting information as complete or incomplete. Had Blair placed a falling and not a rising tone on limit he would have signalled a point of potential syntactic completion – though at a point which could not have matched any informational expectation of the audience. The fact that there is a limit would have been projected as of equal importance as the content of the limit. However, Blair's choice of a rise signalled that the fact of the limit could not be considered in isolation from the following co-text. The content of the limit was projected as being informationally more salient.

In paratone 3 Blair uses non-final rises to signal non-completeness.

(13) || {3.1} there are obvi–↑OUSly ||ca\SUALties || both \/PEOple ||**that have /DIED** || and people SEriously\INJURED ||

Had he articulated *died* with a fall he would have signalled a possible syntactic completion but one which would have been contrary to the expectations created by the co-text. The rise indicated the beginning of a list; there was more to come. Yet, lists do not have to be articulated through as sequence of rises completed by a fall. Example (14) illustrates.

(14) || {3.2}and our ↓THOUGHTS and \PRAYers of course are with || the ↑\ VICtims || and their \FAMilies ||

Blair articulated *victims* with a high fall and by so doing noted the significance of the tonic item to the unfolding of his message. His audience was invited to focus on the fact that there were *victims*. Accordingly, the normal list like nature of the information flow was disrupted.

In paratone 4 Blair's use of a rising tone on *conclusions* mirrored its placement on *limit* in example (12).

(15) || {4} it is the↑WILL of \ALL || the LEADers at the g\EIGHT || how/EVer || that the \MEETing || should ... con–TINue || in my ab\SENCE || that we should continue to disCUSS the is\/SUES || that we were going to dis\CUSS ||and REACH the con/CLUSions || WHICH we were GOing to \↓REACH ||

Had Blair placed a fall on *conclusions* he would have signalled a point of possible syntactic though not informational completion. By articulating the rise he signalled that his hearer was to interpret the significance of *conclusions* in the light of the forthcoming informationally more prominent tone unit.

The rise on *meeting* in paratone 6 similarly signalled to the hearers that they needed to focus on the content of the meeting and not on the fact of the meeting. Had Blair articulated *Africa* with a fall he would have sent a signal that he had reached a point of informational as well as syntactic completion. The hearers would have been encouraged to interpret Blair's claim prior to accessing the information contained in the remainder of the paratone. The level tone on *try* projects non-completeness but also signals that Blair is focusing on carefully selecting his words.

(16) || {6} its par↑TICularly\BARbaric || that this has \HAPpened || on a \DAY when || PEople are /MEETing || to –TRY to ||HELP the PROBlems of POVerty in af/RIca || and the LONG term \PROBems || of CLImate CHANGE in the en\↓VIRonment ||

The remaining non-final rises in Blair's text similarly signalled that the information unit could only be interpreted in the light of following tone units. The salience of the following information units was foregrounded.

(17) || {7.1} just as it is rea↑SONably\CLEAR || that this is a \/TERrorist attack || or a \/SEries of terrorist at\tacks || it is also reaSONably\CLEAR || that it –IS || de\/SIGNed ||and /AIMed || to coin\CIDE || with the \OPENing of the geight || intervening minor paratone {7.2} || {8} its im\↑PORTant however || that THOSE engaged in \TERrorism ||rea/LIZE || that ↑OUR deter\MINation ||to deFEND our /VALues || and OUR \↓WAY of life || ...

In conclusion, non-final rises in Blair's texts were used not only to bind a tone unit closely to following tone units but also to cue the hearers that significant information was to follow. Table 5.9 considers the tone choices the eleven other speakers made at the points in the text where Blair produced a non-final rise.

Table 5.9 Eleven readers' tone choices at points where Blair choose a rising tone.

Textwith rise	CB1	SB2	CD3	MD4	ME5	CG6	TJ7	HM8	FR9	NS10	TR11
And there's a limit	/\	\	\/	none[9]	none	/\	/*	none	\/	\	none
That have died	/*	\	/*	/*	/*	\	/*	–	/*	\	\
Reach the conclusions	\/	/*	\	\	\	\	\	/*	\	\	\
People are meeting	\	\	\	\	\/	none	\	\/	none	/\	\/
Poverty in Africa	\	\	\	\	/*	\	\	\	\	\	\
And aimed	\	/*	/*	\	/*	/*	\	\	none	none	/*
Defend our values	\	\/	\	\/	\/	\	\	\/	\	/*	\

Table 5.9 illustrates that the meaning potential explicated by Blair's tone choices were not the ones which most speakers choose to project. In other words, there is no evidence in this data that written text constrains tone choice, though there was a tendency for the other speakers to employ rises to project that some items were part of a not as yet finished list, for example *died* and *aimed*. In example (12) Blair chose not to project *victims* and their families as being separate elements in a list. For him they were two separate independent pieces of information contained within the same paratone. The majority of the speakers projected the same relationship. Three readers projected the elements as a single piece of information. One reader, ME5, projected *victims* as being the first element of a list through her choice of a rise. For her alone the fact of victimhood could only be considered with reference to the families. In conclusion it appears that speakers have a decree of freedom to project the dependence of tone units and that they use this degree of freedom to project their message.

5.6 Conclusion

This chapter has illustrated how speakers chose intonational options in order to make their text 'text'. We have seen that the each reader unified their text through their projection of an individual paratone structure. Yet, each reader's as well as Blair's paratone structure showed an awareness of both how the text had been initially organized into orthographic paragraphs. All of the speakers produced a paratone structure which demonstrated that they were cognisant of the unfolding of the stages of the text. Yet their projected paragraph structures produced meaning potentials which were not constrained by the formal arrangement of the text. Though we saw that Blair's projected paratone structure differed in a manner which guided the hearers through an 'interpretative' pathway which foregrounded his thesis that disrupting the G8 was the ultimate target of the terrorist attack. We have further seen that the speakers' tone choices were not constrained by the tactic relations signalled by the lexicogrammar. Instead their tone choices focused more on managing their hearers' discourse expectations by signalling the status of a unit information as independent, dependent on a following information unit or limiting a previous information unit.

Notes

1. I would like to thank an anonymous reviewer for valuable suggestions, Tom Bartlett for assistance with the clause structure analysis of the text and various colleagues at CLCR in Cardiff for their thoughtful questions and comments when I presented these ideas to them at a staff research seminar. Thanks also go to my student participants.
2. The initials refer to the identity of the speaker. A key for the intonation conventions is provided in Appendix 1.
3. Following Martin and Rose (2003), genre is defined here as a staged, goal-oriented purposeful activity in which speakers engage as members of a culture.
4. It is unknowable whether or not Blair intended at the time of speaking to return to a more complete discussion of his thesis that the bombing was an attack on the G8. He could have introduced the thesis and 'deferred' discussion of it simply to put the thesis on the table in the hope that his audience would uncritically accept it.
5. Esser's point that only practised readers may make maximum use of the combination of low termination, significant pause and high onset pitch reset is worth reiterating. It may be that the five readers who projected the transition from scene setting realized by the orientation, to the actual telling realized by the incident attempted but failed mark a major paratone boundary. In other words we need to be cautious about ascribing functional differences to major and minor paratones projected by unpractised readers.
6. As a result of rounding up and down the numbers of tones predicted by a chance distribution do not exactly match the number of actual tones found in Blair's articulation of the text.

7. A speaker is, of course, free to place the object *to you* in its own tone unit and select a fall, rise or fall rise on *you*. Similarly example (6) is not to be read as claiming that the speaker does not have freedom to divide the clausal structure prior to the tone into more than a single tone unit. For instance, in clause 1.4 the elements *and I will simply tell you the information as best*, is likely to be articulated as more than a single tone unit and the example simply claims that we would expect a fall to appear somewhere in the unit.
8. An alternate explanation for TJ7's final rise is that the rise projected the communicative function of deferring to the hearer. Rather than telling the audience the location of the bombing he projected the information as something shared between himself and his audience. Such a tone selection functions to develop solidarity as much as it does to project information flow (O'Grady, 2010).
9. MD4 produced the utterance || and theres a LImit to what information i can \/<u>GIVE</u> you ||. Hence *limit* was projected as pre-tonic. ME5, HM8 and TR11 similarly produced *limit* as a pre-tonic element. *Meeting* was produced as a pre-tonic element by CG6 and FR7 and *aimed* was by FR9 and NS10.

References

Blair, T. (2010) *A Journey*. London: Hutchinson.

Brazil, D. (1997) *The Communicative Value of Intonation in English*. Cambridge: Cambridge University Press.

Brown, G., Currie, K. L. and Kenworthy, J. (1980) *Questions of Intonation*. London: Croom Helm.

Coffin, C. and Derewianka, B. (2008) Multimodal layout in school history books: The texturing of historical interpretation. In G. Forey and G. Thompson (eds) *Text Type and Texture* 191–215. London: Equinox.

Cruttenden, A. (1997) *Intonation*, 2nd edn. Cambridge: Cambridge University Press.

Crystal, D. (1969) *Prosodic Systems in English*. Cambridge: Cambridge University Press.

Crystal, D. (1975) *The English Tone of Voice*. London: Edward Arnold.

Eggins, S. (2004) *An Introduction to Systemic Functional Linguistics*, 2nd edn. London: Continuum.

El Menoufy, A. (1969) A study of intonation in the grammar of English. Unpublished PhD dissertation, University College London.

Esser, J. (1988) *Comparing Reading and Speaking Intonation*. Amsterdam: Rodopi.

Goffman, E. (1981) *Forms of Talk*. Oxford: Blackwell.

Halliday, M. A. K. (1967) *Intonation and Grammar in British English*. The Hague: Mouton.

Halliday, M. A. K. (1970) *A Course in Spoken English: Intonation*. London: Oxford University Press.

Halliday, M. A. K. (2005) English intonation as a resource for discourse. In J. Webster (ed.) *Studies in the English Language: Collected Works of M. A. K. Halliday*, vol. 7, 287–92. London: Continuum.

Halliday, M. A. K. and Greaves W. S. (2008) *Intonation in the Grammar of British English*. London: Equinox.

Halliday, M. A. K. and Hasan, R. (1976) *Cohesion in English*. London: Longman.

Halliday, M. A. K. and Matthiessen, C. M. I. M. (2004) *An Introduction to Functional Grammar*, 3rd edn. London: Edward Arnold.

Hood, S. (2009) Texturing interpersonal meanings in academic argument: Pulses and prosodies of value. In G. Forey and G. Thompson (eds) *Text Type and Texture* 216–23. London: Equinox.

Ladd, D. R. (2008) *Intonational Phonology*, 2nd edn. Cambridge: Cambridge University Press.

Martin, J. R. (1992) *English Text: System and Structure*. Amsterdam: John Benjamins.

Martin, J. R. and Rose, D. (2003) *Working with Discourse*. Continuum: London.

Nation, I. S. P. (1984) Understanding paragraphs. *Language Learning and Communication* 3(1): 61–8.

O'Grady, G. (2010) *A Grammar of Spoken English Discourse: The Intonation of Increments*. London: Continuum.

Pierrehumbert, J. and Hirschberg, J. (1990) The meaning of intonation contours in the interpretation of discourse. In P. R. Cohen, J. Morgan and M. E. Pollack (eds) *Intentions in Communication* 271–312. Cambridge, MA: MIT Press.

Smith, B. A. (2008) Intonational systems and register: A multidimensional exploration. Unpublished PhD dissertation, Macquarie University.

Tench, P. (1990) *The Roles of Intonation in English Discourse*. Frankfurt am Main: Peter Lang.

Tench, P. (1996) *The Intonation Systems of English*. London: Cassell.

Tench, P. (1997) The fall and rise of the level tone. *Functions of Language* 4: 1–22.

Wichmann, A. (2000) *Intonation in Text and Discourse: Beginnings, Middles and Ends*. London: Longman.

Appendix 1: Key to intonation notation

‖ = tone unit boundary	\ = Falling tone
CAP = Prominent syllable	/\ = Rise-Falling tone
<u>CAP</u> = Tonic syllable	/ = Rising tone
↑CAP = High onset	\/ = Fall-Rising tone
↑<u>CAP</u> = High tonic	– = Level tone
↓CAP = Low onset	↓<u>CAP</u> = Low tonic

Appendix 2: Text marked up in stages with orthographic paragraph structure with orthographic paragraph notated by capital letters

Abstract

(A) I am just going to make a short statement to you on the terrible events that have happened in London earlier today,

Orientation

and I hope you understand that at the present time we are still trying to establish exactly what has happened, and there is a limit to what information I can give you, and I will simply try and tell you the information as best I can at the moment.

Incident

(B) It is reasonably clear that there have been a series of terrorist attacks in London. There are obviously casualties, both people that have died and people seriously injured, and our thoughts and prayers of course are with the victims and their families.

Repercussions

(C) It is my intention to leave the G8 within the next couple of hours and go down to London and get a report, face-to-face, with the police, and the emergency services and the Ministers that have been dealing with this, and then to return later this evening.

Interpretation

(D) It is the will of all the leaders at the G8 however that the meeting should continue in my absence, that we should continue to discuss the issues that we were going to discuss, and reach the conclusions which we were going to reach.

Orientation

Each of the countries round that table have some experience of the effects of terrorism and all the leaders, as they will indicate a little bit later, share our complete resolution to defeat this terrorism.

Evaluation

(E) It is particularly barbaric that this has happened on a day when people are meeting to try to help the problems of poverty in Africa, and the long term problems of climate change and the environment.

Incident repeat

Just as it is reasonably clear that this is a terrorist attack, or a series of terrorist attacks,

Thesis

it is also reasonably clear that it is designed and aimed to coincide with the opening of the G8.

Deferral

There will be time to talk later about this.

Argument/grounds

(F) It is important however that those engaged in terrorism realise that our determination to defend our values and our way of life is greater than their determination to cause death and destruction to innocent people in a desire to impose extremism on the world.

Argument/conclusion

Whatever they do, it is our determination that they will never succeed in destroying what we hold dear in this country and in other civilised nations throughout the world.

Appendix 3: The clause structure of the statement

1.   1 I am just going to make a short statement to you on the terrible events
    = [[that have happened in London earlier today]],
    +2 α and I hope
        '×β you understand
    ×'γ that at the present time we are still trying to establish ×[[exactly
    ×γ1what has happened,]]
    +3   and there is a limit =[[to what information I can give you]],
    +4   and I will simply try and tell you the information
    as best ×[[I can at the moment]].

2.   1 It is reasonably clear ×[[that there have been a series of terrorist attacks in London]].

3.   1 1   There are obviously casualties, =[[both people =[[that have died]] and people seriously injured]],
    +2 and our thoughts and prayers of course are with the victims and their families.

4.   It is my intention +[[1 to leave the G8 within the next couple of hours
    +2 and go down to London
    +3 and get a report, face-to-face, with the police, and the emergency services and the Ministers =[[that have been dealing with this,]]
    +4 and then to return later this evening.

5. 1 It is the will of all the leaders at the G8 however
    ˣ [[that the meeting should continue in my absence]],
    ⁺2 that we should continue to discuss the issues
    ˣ[[that we were going to discuss,]]
    ⁺3 and reach the conclusions ⁼[[which we were going to reach.]]

6. 1 Each of the countries ⁼[round that table] have some experience of the effects of terrorism
    ⁺2 α and all the leaders,
    ˣβ [[as they will indicate a little bit later,]]
        α share our complete resolution to defeat this terrorism.

7. 1α It is particularly barbaric ˣ[[that this has happened on a day]]
    ˣβ when people are meeting
    ˣβ to try to help the problems of poverty in Africa,
        ⁺γand the long term problems of climate change and the environment.]]
        ]]

8. 1 1α Just as it is reasonably clear
    ˣ [[that this is a terrorist attack, or a series of terrorist attacks,]]
    ⁺2 it is also reasonably clear
    ˣ[[1 that it is designed
        +2 and aimed to coincide with the opening of the G8.]]

9. There will be time to talk later about this.

10. 1 It is important however,
        [[that α those ⁼[[engaged in terrorism realise
    'β that our determinationˣ[[to defend our values and our way of life]]
    is greater than their determination ˣ[[to cause death and destruction to innocent people in a desire to impose extremism on the world]]]].

11. ˣβ Whatever they do,
    α it is our determination
    ˣ[[that they will never succeed in destroying
    ˣ [[what we hold dear in this country
    and in other civilised nations throughout the world.]]]]

Part C

The effects of choice in text-type

6

Choice and domain: A corpus-based study with special reference to the BNC Baby

Inas Mahfouz[a]

6.1 Introduction

The availability of as much information as possible pertaining to the structural and semantic properties of language has always been recognized as the bottleneck of automatic text analysis. This can be attributed to the fact that language depends primarily on a number of choices which contrast with each other to signify different meanings and, unless computers are equipped with such information, not much progress could be achieved. The problem is further complicated by the fact that language users are not always free in their choices due to intra- or extra-linguistic constraints. Transitivity analysis is a prominent example of the impact of these constraints. Intra-linguistic constraints include syntactic and semantic rules governing the syntagmatic and paradigmatic relations among words, whereas extra-linguistic constraints refer to such constraints as the domain of the text, the relationship between participants and the situational context. Consequently,automatic transitivity analysis has always posed a problem to those working on computational linguistics and systemic functional grammar.

This makes the process of automatic word sense disambiguation (WSD) a remote possibility. WSD is one of the central areas of computational linguistics; it is defined as 'the problem of assigning semantical senses to words in an open text' (Mihalcea and Moldovan, 2001: 5). Polysemy is

<hr>

a Inas Youssef Mahfouz is an assistant professor of Computational Linguistics at Ain Shams University, Egypt. She has published several papers on the computational analysis of language, lexicography and systemic functional grammar. The outcomes of these publications include a process type database for transitivity analysis, a database for sentiment analysis and an Arabic ontology of state terrorism.

a widespread phenomenon in English, thus it is important to determine which meaning is manipulated in the text under investigation before determining the process type a polysemous verb realizes. The immediate context and the domain of a text act as constraints on the choice of meaning and consequently on process type, which signals differences in situations. The present study adopts Fairclough's (2003) view that a text cannot be divorced from the context of its production, distribution and reception. The meso-level links the linguistic features of text at the micro-level to wider social, political, economic and cultural contexts. Hence it is important to examine both the immediate context of the verb and the domain of the text in which it occurs in order to determine its meaning and the process type it realizes. Yarowsky (1992) emphasized the importance of WSD and that it is related to other fields such as speech synthesis, information retrieval, machine translation, content analysis, grammatical analysis and text processing. It is an intermediate step that paves the way to more complicated human language technology (Ide and Veronis, 1998). The present study focuses on WSD and transitivity analysis through investigating domain as an extra-linguistic constraint on the choice of meanings and the influence of this on process type.

The advent of computers has provided linguists with a large number of electronic corpora to test the validity of linguistic theories. This study investigates the notion of choice in a large corpus, namely the BNC Baby, through the framework of M. A. K. Halliday's theory of systemic functional grammar (SFG) (1994). It probes into the BNC Baby as an example of an electronic corpus that covers various domains in order to assess the role of domain as an extra-linguistic factor in restricting the sense expressed by a polysemous verb and consequently the process realized by this verb as far as transitivity analysis is concerned.

According to Halliday:

> types of linguistic situation differ from one another ... in three respects: first, as regards what actually is taking place; secondly, as regards what part the language is playing; and thirdly, as regards who is taking part. These three variables ... determine the range within which meanings are selected and the forms which are used for their expression. (Halliday, 1978: 31)

Along with this Hallidayian view, the present chapter attempts to assess the influence of domain on choice in language, that is, how far field (what the text is about) influences users' lexical and syntactic choices. This is done through focusing on polysemous verbs and examining the senses they express in various domains as well as the process type realized by each sense.

6.2   Theoretical background

To achieve its purpose, the study is built on three cornerstones: the BNC Baby, polysemy and SFG. The interaction of these three foundations provides a clear vision of the relation between choice and domain. The BNC Baby v. 1.0 is a collection of corpora that includes four million words extracted from the British National Corpus (BNC). It first appeared in August 2004 with the purpose of demonstrating the full potential of the English language. The BNC Baby was produced at Oxford University Computing Services (OUCS) by Lou Burnard, Martin Wynne and Ylva Berglund. It comprises four major parts, namely academic writing, imaginative writing, newspaper texts and spontaneous conversation. Each part includes approximately one million words. All these texts are taken from the BNC World Edition.

The BNC Baby provides an excellent resource of information on various linguistic phenomena, including polysemous verbs. Polysemous words are quite common in English. 'Given a large lexicon, based on say the OED, one could safely assume that virtually all words are polysemous' (Wilks, 1997: 84). According to Moon (2000), 25 per cent of a total of 49,420 items included in the second edition of *Collins COBUILD English Dictionary* (1995), which was based on 200 million words from the Bank of English, are polysemous. Moon argues that frequency and polysemy are directly related. Polysemous words are more frequent than monosemous ones. Polysemous words require disambiguation, 'clarifying lexical or structural ambiguity ... of linguistic expressions by the linguistic or extralinguistic context' (Bussman, 1996: 130). Consequently, focusing on polysemous verbs in the BNC Baby and ignoring monosemous ones serves the objectives of the chapter and facilitates assessing the role of domain in disambiguation.

Hence, language users are all the time engaged in a process of disambiguation. When a person understands a sentence with an ambiguous word in it, they successfully choose the suitable meaning from a range of possibilities. However, this choice is restricted by intra-linguistic factors such as the immediate context of the word and extra-linguistic factors such as domain. In this study WSD is a preliminary step towards automatic transitivity analysis, which represents the third cornerstone.

According to the ideational metafunction, language is viewed as a tool for building a mental picture of reality. This involves two strands of meaning: the experiential and the logical. The experiential metafunction organizes our experience and understanding of the world, whereas the logical metafunction examines meaning between clauses. The study deals with the experiential strand of meaning only as it aims at exploring how speakers and writers construe their experience of reality through a number of choices. The grammatical system through which this is achieved is that of Transitivity. The unit that acts as the entry condition for the Transitivity choices is the clause. 'Each clause chooses a particular combination of type of process, types of participant and circumstance' (Berry, 1975: 150) The transitivity system construes the world of experience through six process types, where each process type has a special model that construes a specific type of experience. Processes are realized by the verbal group. Hence, the study concentrates on verbs only as they are the clearest token of the process type construed and the involvement of the participants.

6.3   Review of literature

In order to understand how the different components which underpin the theoretical foundations of this study have become interwoven together, it is important to examine their development. The appearance of electronic corpora can be considered as the earliest step in the computational analysis of human language. The first computer corpus was the Brown Corpus which appeared in the early 1960s. The corpus comprises 1,000,000 words of American English compiled so that prospective linguistic studies would be based on a body of data that truly represents the language. This marks the birth of electronic corpora as a methodological basis of linguistic analysis.

Automatic word sense disambiguation (WSD) was related to machine translation in its early stages. In 1947, Weaver pinpointed the possibility of using computers to translate. Weaver's efforts were brought together in his memorandum 'Translation' which appeared in 1949 (Weaver, 1949). Weaver pinpoints several ideas, most of which remain influential not only to Machine Translation but also to WSD. First, he calls for the importance of context in disambiguating words.[1] To Weaver context is the words that accompany an ambiguous word, that is, words that come directly before or after the word under investigation. However, he does not state the exact amount of context – how many words before and after the ambiguous node word; he simply states that it differs according to the topic of the text. He points to the role of domain which has given rise to several micro glossaries which provide words along with their translation with special reference to a certain domain.

The earliest attempt to disambiguate words depending on a corpus was undertaken by Weiss (1973). He depended on a manually sense-tagged corpus to extract disambiguation rules. Kelly and Stone (1975) depended on a corpus of half a million words to extract Keyword in Context (KWIC) concordances of 1800 ambiguous words. Black (1988) used a corpus of 22 million words to disambiguate five words. Similar studies, based on supervised learning from manually sense tagged corpora, include Bruce and Wiebe (1994) and Miller *et al.* (1994).

Several computer systems have used SFG to investigate language. According to Matthiessen (1984), SFG is appropriate for computational analysis and generation of language because it includes two major features. First, SFG treats language as a systems network which comprises a number of choices, and second, it adopts the view that language performs three metafunctions. Such limited choices facilitate computational analysis.

The notion of domain is central in SFG. In 1964, Halliday, McIntosh and Strevens discussed the Field of discourse as part of the context of situation. In the 1970s, Halliday emphasized that the domain in which language is used exerts a clear impact on its structure (Hasan, 2009). Domain is activated by and construes the field. 'By definition a field is a set of activity sequences that are oriented to some global purpose within the institutions of family, community or society' (Martin and Rose, 2003: 252). It should be noted that while participating in a certain activity, participants can make predictions about what to expect. This clarifies how domain helps in disambiguating polysemous verbs once the domain of a text is determined; language users start forming their own expectations which help them in understanding the text.

6.4   Framework of analysis

The macro-context of the 50 most frequent verbs in the BNC Baby is examined in order to answer the question of how far the domain of the text can restrict the choices of language users and be a tool in WSD and transitivity analysis.

6.4.1   Corpus

The BNC Baby is chosen as a starting point for this study due to various reasons:

- Its ample size.
- It comprises a variety of genres to reach a comprehensive understanding of the relationship between domain and choice.
- It represents written and spoken language.
- The equality in the length of its four subcorpora facilitates comparing various domains with each other.

The BNC Baby is delivered in Extensible Markup Language, abbreviated XML, which describes a class of data objects called XML documents and partially describes behaviour of computer programmes which process them. It is a descriptive markup language which 'applies labels to fragments of text without necessarily mandating any particular display or other processing semantics' (Wikipedia, 2006). XML is designed 'to describe data and to focus on what data is … to structure, store and to send information' (w3schools.com, undated). The tagging scheme of the BNC Baby conforms as far as possible to the published recommendations of the Text Encoding Initiative (TEI).[2] On the simplest level, the corpus consists of <w> (word) and <c> (punctuation) elements that are grouped into <s> (sentences); where <w> elements typically correspond with orthographic words, <c> elements with punctuation marks and <s> elements with sentences.

Each written text is documented for the following: the title, edition, size, publication information and the source from which the text is taken. For spoken texts the following information is provided: date of recording, duration of recording, time of day when the recording took place, and the equipment used in recording. The BNC Baby is tagged using the CLAWS4 (Constituent-Likelihood Automatic Word-Tagging System) automatic tagger. This is a tagger developed by Roger Garside 'for assigning to each word in a text an unambiguous indication of the grammatical class to which this word belongs in this context' (Garside, 1987: 30). Each orthographic unit (word) is assigned a tag except compound conjunctions and compound prepositions such as: *as well as, so that,* and *instead of.* In this case the two or more orthographic units may be assigned a single grammatical tag. The percentage of errors is estimated at 1.7 per cent of all words (Burnard, 2003).

6.4.2   Instrumentation

The BNC Baby can be searched via a programme called Xaira. Xaira is an acronym for XML Aware Indexing and Retrieval Architecture. One of the positive qualities about Xaira is that it enables the user to examine only one subcorpus at a time. Figure 6.1 illustrates the drop-down menus through which a user can choose which subcorpus to examine.

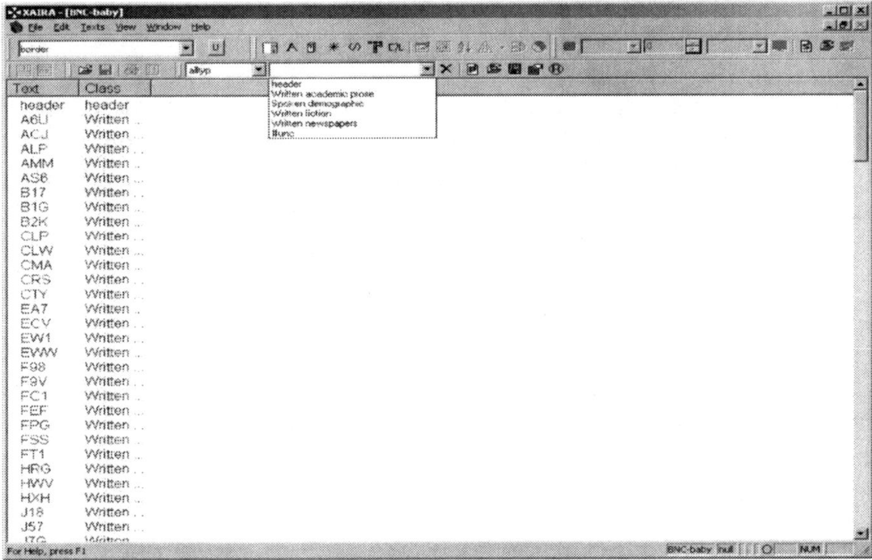

Figure 6.1 The drop-down menu that a user can choose from.

6.4.3   Procedure of analysis

Since the present study aims at examining the influence of domain on WSD of polysemous verbs and the processes they realize, it is necessary to investigate each genre separately. The selection of instances to be tagged is based on the lexical model, where a set of words is chosen and then instances for each of these words are sampled from a certain corpus to be disambiguated (Kilgarriff, 1998). The lexical model is chosen because it is necessary to limit the scope of the study to verbs only because the final objective is to investigate the role of extralinguistic constraints in WSD and automatic transitivity analysis. Verbs are examined in all their grammatical forms, namely:

- VVB – the finite base form of lexical verbs (e.g. *forget, send, live, return,* including the imperative and present subjunctive).
- VVD – the past tense form of lexical verbs (e.g. *forgot, sent, lived, returned*). VVG – the *-ing* form of lexical verbs (e.g. *forgetting, sending, living, returning*).

- VVI – the infinitive form of lexical verbs (e.g. *forget, send, live, return*).
- VVN – the past participle form of lexical verbs (e.g. *forgotten, sent, lived, returned*).
- VVZ – the *-s* form of lexical verbs (e.g. *forgets, sends, lives, returns*).

This study examines the fifty most frequent verbs in the BNC Baby which are roughly equivalent to verbs whose overall frequency is 1000 or more. This figure has been determined on the basis of various pilot studies that proved that instances of less frequent verbs do not give accurate information about their senses. Moreover, these verbs are not as ambiguous as those that are highly frequent. It has been highlighted previously that the more ambiguous words are generally more frequent than less ambiguous ones. Table 6.1 provides the verbs that are tackled in this study. It states their overall frequency as well as their frequency in each subcorpus. It also clarifies that the sample size of tokens per type ranges between 19,031 and 1034 depending upon the frequency of the verb and its level of polysemy. The researcher had to prepare a concordance of the most frequent verbs as such a concordance does not exist.

The steps followed in the practical analysis can be summed up in the following points:

1. Examine each subcorpus on its own.
2. Prepare a concordance for all the forms of the verb.
3. Group together clusters of similar context of a polysemous verb.
4. Manually disambiguate polysemous verbs. Each context is assigned an appropriate sense depending on the *Oxford Advanced Learner's Dictionary* (7th edition, 2006).
5. Estimate the role of the immediate context following the verb.
6. Add notes on usage where necessary.
7. Assign a specific process type to each sense.

It is noteworthy that the paper adopts the Hallidayan approach in dealing with phraseological units and treats them as lexicogrammatical patterns which represent 'an order of mutual expectancy. The words are mutually expectant and mutually prehended' (Firth, 1957: 181). From the point of view of SFG, lexicogrammatical patterns derive their meaning from the dependency relationship between a sign and its habitual context of use which makes their investigation in the framework of this study quite difficult. Also it should be noted that phrasal verbs were excluded because a detailed analysis of them would be beyond the scope of the present chapter.

Table 6.1 The most frequent verbs in the BNC Baby.

	Verb	Academic prose	Fiction	Newspaper	Spontaneous conversation	Total
1	say	830	6855	4898	6448	19,031
2	get	439	3136	1449	12,643	17,667
3	go	606	4128	1829	9046	15,609
4	know	780	3781	824	8084	13,469
5	think	417	2853	689	5616	9575
6	see	1448	3050	1041	3891	9430
7	come	491	3453	1220	2709	7873
8	take	1407	2176	1872	1808	7263
9	make	1663	2099	1855	1487	7104
10	look	461	2611	694	2522	6288
11	want	231	1809	756	3466	6262
12	give	1324	1243	1169	1370	5106
13	mean	441	731	319	3003	4494
14	put	349	865	653	2490	4357
15	tell	211	1696	743	1318	3968
16	find	1124	1232	744	693	3793
17	use	1537	399	534	489	2959
18	like	92	855	227	1468	2642
19	ask	254	1373	438	546	2611
20	need	521	514	483	1083	2601
21	leave	264	970	544	693	2471
22	seem	728	1003	454	254	2439
23	try	252	869	483	726	2330
24	show	1130	350	525	290	2295
25	feel	207	1247	419	411	2284
26	keep	216	789	483	672	2160
27	work	384	527	495	482	1888
28	call	305	620	449	513	1887
29	become	840	388	567	35	1830
30	turn	177	892	349	330	1748
31	hear	51	898	244	480	1673
32	sit	53	804	133	680	1670
33	play	108	219	716	578	1621
34	start	147	443	433	574	1597
35	bring	274	480	426	388	1568
36	write	558	290	330	376	1554
37	hold	414	488	404	212	1518
38	let	178	621	188	477	1464
39	talk	155	604	183	461	1403
40	run	114	518	471	263	1366
41	move	222	573	264	295	1354
42	happen	188	516	268	349	1321
43	help	183	391	483	261	1318
44	pay	118	221	455	518	1312
45	begin	312	585	344	49	1290
46	provide	808	61	370	28	1267
47	follow	511	327	364	61	1263
48	believe	203	400	472	142	1217
49	live	159	373	269	248	1049
50	set	232	246	465	91	1034

6.5 Analysis

6.5.1 Monoreferential verbs

Monoreferential verbs are verbs that signify only one sense and realize only one process type regardless of the domain of the text. The impact of

Table 6.2 Monoreferential verbs and the processes they realize.

Verb	Process Type	Domain	Example
Want	Mental: desiderative process	Spontaneous conversation	No, no, we would have wanted that.
Tell	Verbal process	Written fiction	At the time I met her, Angela told me that she was involved with someone else.
Use	Material process	Academic prose	Hobbes is not using an inductive argument here.
Like	Mental: emotive process	Written fiction	'You don't like your mother, then?' asked Greg.
Ask	Verbal process	Written fiction	'Do you still love me?' she asked anxiously.
Need	Mental: desiderative process	Spontaneous conversation	Ooh I need a couple of them tickets Ju!
Seem	Relational: attributive process	Written fiction	'She seems like a very happy person,' says Sylvia.
Become	Relational: identifying process	Academic prose	Computer power is becoming cheaper, digital data more readily available, and GISs are becoming hybrid systems involving other technologies.
Hear	Mental process: perception	Written fiction	You heard what your lady wife said
Sit	Behavioural process	Written fiction	They sat at a circular wrought iron table shaded by a willow
Talk	Behavioural process	Spontaneous conversation	I talk to some people and they think I'm crackers cos I took my kid out of a state school!
Happen	Material process	Written fiction	Carradine knew that something momentous was happening.
Believe	Mental: cognitive process	Newspapers	Is there anyone who believes in a military victory over the IRA?
Live	Behavioural process	Not related to one domain in particular	'I've been living at Moorlake.'

domain can only be detected in the frequency distribution of these verbs over the four subcorpora of the BNC Baby. These verbs represent 28 per cent of the verbs analysed. Table 6.2 provides information on the default process that each of these verbs permanently performs and the domain where this monoreferential verb has the highest frequency.

6.5.2   Frequency-based disambiguation

The researcher has coined the term 'Frequency disambiguation' to refer to certain polysemous verbs that can be disambiguated according to the frequency of their senses. In some cases, one sense of the verb permanently dominates other senses regardless of the domain. The verbs 'play' and 'help' have two senses that appear in all four domains but sense #1 has higher frequency than sense #2 which makes the former the default sense. 68 per cent of the total occurrences of the verb 'play' and 93 per cent of the total occurrences of the verb 'help' express sense #1.

Table 6.3 Frequency-based WSD.

Verb	Sense	Percentage of this sense in all domains	Process type	Domain
Play	1. To do things for pleasure as children do; to enjoy yourself rather than work	68%	Behavioural	All domains
	2. To perform or act in a play, film, movie, etc.	32%	Material	All domains
Help	1. To make it easier for sb to do sth by doing sth for them or by giving them sth that they need	93%	Material	All domains
	Idiomatic expression	7%		
Begin	1. To start doing sth or to do the first part of sth	98%	Material (sometimes this is not true as the verb following begin affects its process type)	All domains
	Fixed expression	2%		

6.5.2.1 Play

The verb 'play' for instance has two senses and both of them appear in all four subcorpora. Sense #1 is the more dominant one as its frequency (68%) is higher than the other sense (Unless otherwise stated each example represents a subcorpus: spoken conversation, newspaper, fiction and academic prose respectively):

- I gotta let him win else he won't play with me. (Sp)
- He plays more on the left hand side which is not my favourite position, I prefer to play on the right. (News)
- Dougal played with his glass. (Fic)
- She had been worried that he was still playing too much and not learning anything. (AP)

The frequency of sense #2 is 32 per cent of the total occurrences of the verb:

- And then we can play *Tummy Ache* without any interruption. (Sp)
- Well, according to Mr Argyle, money plays a small part but does not have as big an effect as people might think. (News)
- If I were playing an indisputably virtuous character, then cliché dictates that I would at least be spared death, imprisonment or degradation. (Fic)
- You may have seen a film, but wish to talk about who did the cinematography or who played a particular character. (AP)

6.5.2.2 Help

Similarly, the verb 'help' has two senses. Sense #1 is the dominant sense of the verb as its frequency exceeds 93 per cent in all subcorpora.

- You two, sshh, if you two are gonna help me with the biscuits, then we can't have rows about Thomas can we? (Sp)
- It helps him relax. (News)
- Dalgliesh was helping Meg Dennison into her jacket when the telephone rang, sounding unnaturally strident in the quiet room. (Fic)
- While Kahlo's art helped her to deal with the vicissitudes of her life, for most audiences it is her life story which allows access to her art. (AP)

The low frequency of sense #2 is due to the fact that it is an idiom and idioms are commonly considered informal.

6.5.2.3 Begin

This verb is highly frequent in written fiction subcorpus. It is quite similar to the lemma 'help' because it has two senses, the first of which is the most dominant one as the second sense is a fixed expression. Sense #1 is the dominant sense – its frequency exceeds 98 per cent in all subcorpora except in the spoken conversation subcorpus where it represents 77 per cent of the overall occurrences of the lemma in this subcorpus:

- No, I want you sitting down now before we begin. (Sp)
- Michelle Shocked begins a national tour on 16 November. (News)
- The changes since he first began working in the service had been radical, to say the least. (Fic)
- Once the assessment had begun Mrs. Jones soon became disillusioned. (AP)

However, it should not be assumed that domain does not affect WSD because the frequency distribution of the senses of other verbs such as 'write' and 'begin' differs from one domain to another. For example, the significantly high frequency of sense #1 of the verb 'write' in spoken conversation and academic prose subcorpora makes language users more ready to accept this sense as the default one in each of these two domains, which again points to the important role domain plays in WSD and transitivity analysis.

Table 6.4 Frequency-based WSD.

Verb	Sense	Process type	Favourite domain (s)	% in favourite domain
Write	1. To produce sth in written form so that people can read, perform, or use it, etc.	Material	Spoken conversation	73.6%
			Academic prose	75.8%
	2. To write letters or numbers on a surface, especially with a pen or a pencil	Behavioural	Written newspapers	77.3%
			Written fiction	65.2%

6.5.2.4 Write

This verb has two senses, the first of which is the default one which dominates spoken conversation and academic prose subcorpora:

- Write down the next two lines of a pattern of the bottom of the opposite page. (Sp)
- These days, he writes the books intended to help children learn to read. (News)
- I no longer believe that I am just writing a treatment of her life. (Fic)
- Perry (1985) has written an interesting book on emergency planning and evacuation, covering both natural and technological hazards. (AP)

In written newspapers and written fiction subcorpora sense #2 is the dominant one. In the written newspapers subcorpus it is preceded by a comma and usually followed by a proper noun to refer to the writer; it represents 77.3 per cent of the total occurrences of the lemma in this domain. In the written fiction subcorpus sense #2 constitutes 65.2 per cent. This high frequency of sense #2 in these two domains may be attributed to the fact that reporting is quite important in these domains:

- Then I was gonna write about a hotel you know, erm Heartbreak Hotel. Thought no, wouldn't write about that. (Sp)
- 'Ernst & Young will be writing to all depositors within 48 hours advising them of the position', said Jason Elles. (News)
- I wrote, my dear – oh, a week ago. (Fic)
- The writer, on the contrary, may look over what he has already written, pause between each word with no fear of his interlocutor interrupting him. (AP)

6.5.3   Domain-based disambiguation

Domain restricts the processes realized by approximately 89 per cent of the polysemous verbs analysed. The study has focused on the most frequent 50 verbs in the BNC Baby and, of these verbs, 14 are monoreferential, 4 exhibit the same degree of ambiguity in all domains and 32 are highly ambiguous, having senses that differ from one domain to the other. Some senses are quite common in all domains but some of them are restricted to certain domains. Hence the domain of the text affects the disambiguation process. The majority of these verbs are highly polysemous having more than 3 senses. This group comprises most of the verbs analysed in this study. The role of domain in WSD is pinpointed in the appendix, which gives the senses of polysemous verbs that are restricted to certain domains.

6.5.3.1 Get

The most polysemous verb that the researcher has tackled is 'get'. About 27 different senses of this verb could be detected in various domains. It is highly frequent in spontaneous conversation. This subcorpus comprises 71.5 per cent of the instances of the verb 'get' in the BNC Baby. Moreover, it is part of several lexicogrammatical patterns. The following table sums up some of the various senses of the verb 'get' and determines the domains in which each sense is detected.

Table 6.5 The various senses of the verb 'get'.

Verb	Sense	Process type	Micro-context	Macro-context	Example	Notes
Get	1. To receive or obtain sth	Material	Core meaning	All domains	• He gets a free, free ticket! (Sp) • 'I always got a great service from Andy at Wigan.' (News)	* The form *gotten* is used only in this sense and it appeared twice in the spoken conversation subcorpus.
	2. To have or possess sth	Relational	Core meaning. Only with VVN	All domains	• Well he has got a job you • know (Sp) 'I've got enough problems as it is!' he joked. (News)	This sense is common only with *has* or *have*. Informal.
Get	3. To go to a place and bring sb/sth back	Material	The verb is usually preceded by *go and*	Spoken and fiction domains only	• On? Right, I'll go and get a video, okay? Yeah I don't know what's on. (Sp) • So I went back to the car and got my torch. (Fic)	
Get	4. To under-stand sb/sth	Mental: cognitive	The verb is usually followed by *it+* !/?/,/. Or *your meaning/ message/ idea.*	All domains except academic prose sub-corpus	• Have you got it? (Sp) • Inevitably they do not always get it right. (News) • He was getting the idea quickly, guys. (Fic)	Informal; not commonly used in progressive tenses

As the table above clarifies senses #1 and #2 represent the core meaning of the verb and they are common in all four domains. The rest of the senses are restricted to certain domains. Sense #4 is informal and consequently, it is not used in the academic domain which tends to prefer a formal style.

6.5.3.2 Go

This verb has 17 senses. It is highly frequent in the spoken conversation subcorpus which comprises 57.9 per cent of the total occurrences of this verb in the four subcorpora. This verb is least frequent in the academic prose subcorpus. Table 6.6 sums up the different senses of this verb.

Sense #1 represents the core meaning of the verb. It is the most frequent sense that could be detected in all domains:

- I only need my money now before I go.
- If he ever goes anywhere, I'd bet on England.

Sense #2 could not be detected in the academic prose subcorpus. It has the highest frequency in the spoken conversation subcorpus and the least frequency in written newspaper:

- Do you, suggest you go for a meal as well? (Sp)
- Mrs Vowden said Leena was going for a bike ride when the accident happened at 6.10 pm on Wednesday at the junction of Edinburgh Road and Hamilton Road, Newmarket. (News)
- Afterwards, with her foursome, she changed into her swimsuit and went for a bathe before lunch. (Fic)

Table 6.6 The various senses of the verb 'go'.

verb	Sense	Process type	Micro context	Macro-context
Go	1. Move or travel from one place to another	Material	This is the core meaning of the verb. Significant collocates include: *across, ahead, away, back, down, home, in, into, out, past, through, up.*	All domains
Go	2. To leave a place or travel to a place in order to take part in an activity	Material	Followed by: *for + a + noun* *for + pl. noun*	All domains except written academic subcorpus
Go	3. To become different in a particular way	Relational: attributive	Followed by an adjective except *direct, far, near and straight.*	All domains
Go	4. To say	Verbal	Followed by: *Oh, what, yeah*	Spoken conversation subcorpus only

6.6   Domain and process type: A closer look

In this section the most frequent verbs in each of the four subcorpora along with their most frequent sense and process type are highlighted in order to evaluate the impact of domain on WSD and process type determination.

6.6.1   Academic prose

Table 6.7 shows that VVN is the dominant verb form in academic prose. This may be attributed to the fact that passive voice is the usual way of expressing facts, instructions or steps in a process. The most frequent process type in this domain is the Material. Material processes construe an event in which one entity exerts a certain impact on another entity. This again is another feature of academic prose.

Table 6.7 The ten most frequent verbs in academic prose.

Verb	Frequency	Dominant form	Dominant process type
Make	1663	VVN	Material
Use	1537	VVN	Material
See	1448	VVB	Mental
Take	1407	VVN	Material
Give	1324	VVN	Material
Show	1130	VVN	Material
Find	1124	VVN	Material
Become	840	VVD	Relational: attributive
Say	830	VVN	Verbal
Provide	808	VVI	Material

6.6.2   Written fiction

The fact that the most frequent verb in this subcorpus is 'say' reflects its role as a verb commonly used to introduce the direct or indirect utterance of speakers in written fiction. The most frequent form is the VVD and this suits the nature of narrative discourse. Though the most frequent verb is 'say' which typically realizes a Verbal process, the most frequent process type in written fiction is Behavioural as fiction is almost always about people's actions or their feelings and, again, this is reflected in the relatively high frequency of Mental processes which refer to feelings and perception.

Table 6.8 The ten most frequent verbs in the written fiction subcorpus.

Verb	Frequency	Dominant form	Dominant process type
Say	6855	VVD	Verbal
Go	4128	VVG	Behavioural
Know	3781	VVI	Mental
Come	3453	VVD	Behavioural
Get	3136	VVI	Material; relational
See	3050	VVI	Mental
Think	2853	VVD	Mental
Look	2611	VVD	Behavioural
Take	2176	VVD	Material
Make	2099	VVI	Material

6.6.3   Written newspaper

This subcorpus encompasses a wide variety of process types as newspapers discuss different issues related to multifarious domains. The processes in this subcorpus are mainly Material or Mental; in other words, they express either actions or feelings. The most dominant form is the infinitive which represents one of the features of journalese.

Table 6.9 The ten most frequent verbs in the written newspaper subcorpus.

Verb	Frequency	Dominant form	Dominant process type
Say	4898	VVD	Verbal
Take	1872	VVI	Material
Make	1855	VVI	Material
Go	1829	VVG	Behavioural
Get	1449	VVI	Material
Come	1220	VVD	Behavioural
Give	1169	VVN	Material
See	1041	VVI	Mental
Know	824	VVI	Mental
Want	756	VVB	Mental

6.6.4   Spoken conversation

This section represents informal conversation and consequently, there are various instances of incomplete utterances, hesitance and repetition. The most frequent verb form is the VVB because usually the speaker is talking about themselves. The most dominant process type is Mental. This can be interpreted in the framework of the fact that people are always expressing their feelings and ideas in conversation. People talk primarily about their ideas and attitudes. This represents a sharp contrast to academic prose where Material processes dominate the scene.

Table 6.10 The ten most frequent verbs in the spoken conversation subcorpus.

Verb	Frequency	Dominant form	Dominant process type
Get	12,643	VVN	Material; relational
Go	9046	VVI	Behavioural
Know	8084	VVB	Mental
Say	6448	VVD	Verbal
Think	5616	VVB	Mental
See	3891	VVB	Mental
Want	3466	VVB	Mental
Mean	3003	VVB	Mental
Come	2709	VVB	Behavioural
Look	2522	VVB	Behavioural
Put	2490	VVB	Material

6.7   Conclusion

To sum up, the notion of choice is central to any linguistic analysis. The importance of this notion is significantly higher in SFG as it is based on the principle that language is a system of choices for creating meanings. This chapter has examined the role of domain in disambiguating polysemous verbs and its impact on Transtivity analysis. Domain is regarded as an extralinguistic constraint on choice. On disambiguating a polysemous verb, each domain triggers certain senses and disfavours others. An analysis of the 50 most frequent verbs in the BNC Baby has illustrated that polysemous verbs can be categorized into three types:

1.   Monoreferential verbs: verbs that express a single sense and realize a certain process type.
2.   Frequency-based disambiguation: verbs that can be disambiguated through the frequency of their senses in various domains.
3.   Domain-based disambiguation: verbs that can be disambiguated by determining the domain in which they occur.

The study has highlighted domain and how far it is crucial to WSD techniques. Domain, as an extralinguistic constraint on choice, should receive more attention from researchers as certain senses are restricted to certain domains; domain should be regarded as a way of activating certain senses and suppressing others.

This chapter has examined the influence of domain on transitivity analysis and how far the domain of a text can restrict users' choices among process types. This investigation has proved the dominance of certain process types in certain domains:

- The most frequent process type in academic prose is the Material.
- In written fiction, Behavioural and Mental processes dominate the scene as fiction is always describing people's behaviour and feelings.
- In newspapers, the dominant process types are Material and Mental, describing either events or people's attitudes and this is one of the features of journalese.
- Finally, in spoken conversation Mental processes are the most common type.

The benefit of this approach is that once the domain of the text is determined, transitivity analysis becomes easier. However, it is not always easy to determine the domain of the text automatically. Another limitation of the suggested methodology is that it is dependent on prior manual analysis which requires much time and effort. In order to build robust systems that achieve the required accuracy in transitivity analysis, it is important to devise a methodology to determine the domain of the text. Domain solves several problematic cases in WSD and transitivity analysis; consequently, it should gain greater emphasis in future studies.

Notes

1. It is important to note that this approach is different from the one used in this chapter. Weaver depends on the immediate context for disambiguating words, whereas context here is defined as the domain of the text where an ambiguous word is used.
2. A set of comprehensive guidelines for the encoding and interchange of electronic documents amongst researchers.

References

Berry, M. (1975) *An Introduction to Systemic Linguistics: 1. Structures and Systems.* London/Sydney: B. T. Batsford Ltd.

Black, E. (1988) An experiment in computational discrimination of English word senses. *IBM Journal of Research and Development* 32(2): 185–94.

Bruce, R. and Wiebe, J. (1994) Word-sense disambiguation using decomposable models. In *Proceedings of the 32nd Annual Meeting of the Association for*

Computational Linguistics, Las Cruces, New Mexico, 27–30 June 139–145. Stroudsburg, PA: Association for Computational Linguistics.

Burnard, L. (2003). *Reference Guide to BNC-Baby.* BNC Baby CD-Rom. Oxford: Oxford University Press.

Bussman, H. (1996) *Routledge Dictionary of Language and Linguistics.* London/ New York: Routledge.

Fairclough, N. (2003) *Analysing Discourse: Textual Analysis for Social Research.* London: Routledge.

Firth, J. R. (1957) *Papers in Linguistics 1934–1951.* Oxford: Oxford University Press.

Garside, R. (1987) The CLAWS word-tagging system. In R. Garside, G. Leech and G. Sampson (eds) *The Computational Analysis of English: A Corpus-Based Approach* 30–41. London: Longman.

Halliday, M. A. K. (1978) *Language as Social Semiotic.* London: Edward Arnold.

Halliday, M. A. K. (1994) *An Introduction to Functional Grammar*, 2nd edn. London: Edward Arnold.

Halliday, M. A. K., McIntosh, A. and Strevens, P. (1964) *The Linguistic Sciences and Language Teaching.* London: Longman.

Hasan, R. (2009) The place of context in a systemic functional model. In M. A. K. Halliday and J. Webster (eds) *Continuum Companion to Systemic Functional Linguistics* 166–98. London: Continuum.

Ide, N. and Veronis, J. (1998) Sense disambiguation: The state of the art. *Computational Linguistics* 24(1): 1–40.

Kelly, E. F. and Stone, P. J. (1975) *Computer Recognition of English Word Senses.* Amsterdam: North-Holland.

Kilgarriff, A. (1998) Gold standard datasets for evaluating word sense disambiguation programs. *Computer Speech and Language* 12(4): 453–72.

Martin, J. R. and Rose, D. (2003) *Working with Discourse: Meaning Beyond the Clause.* London: Continuum.

Matthiessen, C. (1984) Systemic grammar in computation: The Nigel Case. In *Proceedings of the 1st Conference of the European Chapter of the Association for Computational Linguistics, Pisa, Italy* 155–64. Stroudsburg, PA: Association for Computational Linguistics.

Mihalcea, R. F. and Moldovan, D. I. (2001) A highly accurate bootstrapping algorithm for word sense disambiguation. *International Journal on Artificial Intelligence Tools* 10: 5–21.

Miller, G. A, Chodorow, M., Landes, S., Leacock, C. and Thomas, R. (1994) Using a semantic concordance for sense identification. ARPA Workshop on Human Language Technology, Plainsboro, NJ, March, http://dl.acm.org/citation. cfm?id=1075866 (accessed 9 May 2013).

Moon, R. (2000) Lexicography and disambiguation: the size of the problem. *Computers and the Humanities* 34: 99–102.

w3schools.com (undated) Introduction to XML, www.w3schools.com/xml/ xml_whatis.asp (accessed 17 June 2005).

Weaver, W. (1949) The 'translation' memorandum, http://www.mt-archive.info/ Weaver-1949.pdf (accessed 26 July 2008).

Weiss, S. (1973) Learning to disambiguate. *Information Storage and Retrieval* 9: 33–41.

Wikipedia (2006) Markup language, http://en.wikipedia.org/wiki/Markup_language (accessed 25 October 2006).

Appendix: Domain-based disambiguation

Verb	Sense	Process type	Micro-context	Macro-context	Notes
Get	To stand up after sitting; to wake up	Behavioural	Followed by: *up*. It is restricted to VVB	Spoken conversation subcorpus only	Idiom; informal
Get	To put sth on	Material	Followed by: *On*; this sense has been recorded only with VVN	Spoken conversation subcorpus only	Phrasal verb; this sense appeared only 29 times
Get	To be busy with sth	Behavioural	Followed by: *up to*	Written fiction subcorpus only	Phrasal verb
Get	To annoy sb	Mental: emotive	Followed by: *On* + noun/ pronoun + wick	Spoken conversation subcorpus only	Idiom; informal
Go	To become very angry	Mental: emotive	Followed by: *Banana*(s)	Spoken conversation subcorpus only	This sense could not be recorded except with VVB
Go	To start working on sth; to tackle	Material	Followed by: *about* + noun	Academic prose only	Phrasal verb
Go	To resist or to oppose	Material	Followed by: *against*	Academic prose only	Phrasal verb
Go	To exceed	Relational: attributive	Followed by: *beyond*	Academic prose subcorpus only	Phrasal verb
Go	To look at or examine sth carefully	Material	Followed by: *through*	Academic prose subcorpus only	Phrasal verb
Go	To experience or suffer from	Mental: perceptive	Followed by: *through*	Academic prose subcorpus only	Phrasal verb
Know	Used to criticize sb	Mental: cognitive	Followed by: *as well as I do*	Written fiction subcorpus only	Idiom
Know	To be very aware of a fact	Mental: cognitive	Followed by: *full well*	Written fiction subcorpus only	Idiom
Think	To create sth in your mind	Mental: cognitive	Followed by: *up*	Spoken conversation subcorpus only	Phrasal verb

Verb	Sense	Process type	Micro-context	Macro-context	Notes
See	To assess a certain situation	Mental: cognitive	*As far as* + noun/pronoun + can/could + *see*	Written fiction subcorpus only	This use is restricted to VVI
Come	To start	Behavioural	Followed by: *on*	Spoken conversation subcorpus only	Phrasal verb
Come	To add up to a particular cost or sum	Relational: intensifying	Followed by: *Out* + *at* usually followed by a cardinal number	Written fiction subcorpus only	Phrasal verb
Take	Consider or think about	Mental: cognitive	Followed by: *example; for instance*	Written newspapers subcorpus only	This sense appears only 4 times in the BNCBaby
Take	To include sth within its scope	Material	Followed by: *in*	Written newspapers subcorpus only	Phrasal verb
Take	To become successful or popular	Behavioural	Followed by: *off*	Written newspapers subcorpus only	Phrasal verb; this sense is problematic
Take	To fill or use an amount of space and time	Relational: circumstantial	Followed by: *up*	Academic prose subcorpus only	Phrasal verb
Make	To make a loud angry argument	Behavioural	Followed by: *a scene*	Written fiction subcorpus only	Idiom
Make	To move towards sth; to head	Behavioural	Followed by: *for*	Written fiction only	Phrasal verb
Make	To help to make sth possible	Material	Followed by: *for*	Academic prose subcorpus only	Phrasal verb
Look	To think about or consider sth	Mental: cognitive	Core meaning (in academic subcorpus only)	Academic prose subcorpus only	
Look	To show that you are not ready to buy sth in shops	Behavioural	It takes one form 'be just looking'	Spoken conversation subcorpus only	This sense is restricted to VVG; fixed expression

Verb	Sense	Process type	Micro-context	Macro-context	Notes
Look	To visit or make contact with sb after a long time	Material	Followed by: *up*	Written fiction subcorpus only	Phrasal verb
Look	To admire or respect sb	Mental: emotive	Followed by : *up to* + noun	Written newspapers subcorpus only	Phrasal verb
Give	To show that sth is not true	Material	Followed by: *the lie*	Academic prose subcorpus only	Idiom
Give	To show that you want sth very much	Mental: desiderative	Followed by: *my eye teeth*	Written fiction subcorpus only	Idiom
Give	To cause sth to happen or exist	Material	Followed by: *rise to*	Academic prose subcorpus only	Idiom
Put	To ask sb to stop talking about sth and do it	Material	Put up or shut up	Written newspaper subcorpus only	Fixed expression
Put	To treat sth as more important than sth else	Mental: cognitive	Put + noun + before + noun	Written newspaper subcorpus only	Phrasal verb
Find	To be able to speak or express your opinion	Verbal	Followed by: the words	Written fiction subcorpus only	Fixed expression
Find	In a poor state worse than usual	Mental: emotive	Followed by: *at a low ebb*	Spoken conversation subcorpus only	Idiom
Leave	To say or do nothing more about sth	Material	Followed by: *it at that*	Written fiction subcorpus only	Fixed expression
Feel	In a very good physical condition	Mental: emotive	Followed by: *fit as a fiddle*	Written fiction subcorpus only	Idiom
Feel	To have sympathy for sb	Mental: emotive	Followed by: *for*	Written fiction subcorpus only	Phrasal verb
Keep	Used to ask about sb's health	Behavioural	This sense occurs only with VVG	Spoken conversation subcorpus only	In questions only

Verb	Sense	Process type	Micro-context	Macro-context	Notes
Keep	To prevent sb/sth from coming near sb/sth	Material	Followed by: *off*	Written fiction subcorpus only	Phrasal verb
Keep	To stick to sth	Material	Followed by: *to*	Academic prose subcorpus only	Phrasal verb
Work	To develop in a successful way	Behavioural	Followed by: *out*	Spoken conversation subcorps only	Phrasal verb
Turn	To choose to ignore wrong behaviour	Mental: cognitive	Followed by: *a blind eye*	Spoken conversation subcorpus only	Idiom
Start	Used to tell sb not to complain or be critical	Verbal	This sense is restricted to VVI	Spoken conversation subcorpus only	Fixed expression
Start	To begin to move; to begin to happen	Material	Followed by: *off*	Spoken conversation subcorpus only	Phrasal verb
Hold	To arrange an event, a meeting, etc.	Material	Core meaning in written newspapers	Written newspapers subcorpus only	This sense is very common with VVN
Hold	To own or have sth	Relational: possessive	Followed by: *a cardinal number + sth*	Written newspapers subcorpus only	
Hold	To say nothing although you would like to	Behavioural	Followed by: *your tongue*	Written fiction subcorpus only	Idiom
Hold	To stop yourself from expressing how you feel	Verbal	Followed by: *back*	Written fiction subcorpus only	Phrasal verb
Hold	To remain strong and working effectively	Behavioural	Followed by: *up*	Academic prose subcorpusonly	Phrasal verb
Run	To happen	Material	Core meaning in academic prose subcorpus only	Academic prose subcorpus only	

Verb	Sense	Process type	Micro-context	Macro-context	Notes
Run	To read through or practice sth quickly	Material	Followed by: *over*	Written fiction subcorpus only	Phrasal verb
Run	To pass quickly through sth	Material	Followed by: *through*	Academic prose subcorpus only	Phrasal verb
Move	To make progress in the way mentioned	Material	No clear collocates	Written fiction subcorpus only	
Move	To do everything you can to achieve sth	Material	Followed by: *heaven and earth*	Written fiction subcorpus only	Idiom
Follow	To understand an explanation or meaning of sth	Mental: cognitive	No clear collocates	Written fiction subcorpus only	Usually followed by: *you*
Follow	To be guided by your sense of smell	Material	Followed by: *your nose*	Spoken conversation subcorpus only	Idiom
Set	To leave a place and begin a journey	Material	Followed by: *out*	Academic prose subcorpus only	Phrasal verb

7

Investigating thematic choices in two newspaper genres: A methodological proposal

Julia Lavid[a], Jorge Arús[b] and Lara Moratón[c]

7.1 Introduction

Most current corpus-based work in systemic functional linguistics (SFL) uses an analytical methodology based on the manual extraction of linguistic features from authentic texts, usually on the basis of some pre-established theoretical categories. However, as pointed out by Teich (2007), 'the creation, exploration and sharing of SFL descriptions is impeded because of inadequate tools, lack of accountability and diverging terminology'.

a Julia Lavid is Professor of English Linguistics and Chair of the Department of English Philology I at Universidad Complutense de Madrid (UCM). Her research expertise focuses on the systemic-functional and corpus-based study of English in contrast with Spanish and other European languages, as well its application to educational and computational contexts. She is the author of the book: *Lenguaje y Nuevas Tecnologías: Nuevas perspectivas, métodos y herramientas para el lingüista del siglo XXI* (Madrid, Cátedra, 2005), and co-author with Jorge Arús of the research monograph: *Systemic-Functional Grammar of Spanish: A Contrastive Study with English.*

b Jorge Arús Hita is Assistant Lecturer in English Linguistics at the Department of English Philology I, Universidad Complutense de Madrid (UCM) and member of the UCM research group on Functional Linguistics (English-Spanish) and its Applications, led by Prof. Julia Lavid. He has published on corpus-based contrastive linguistics and EFL teaching and is a co-author with Julia Lavid of the research monograph: *Systemic-Functional Grammar of Spanish: A Contrastive Study with English.*

c Lara Moratón Gutiérrez is a doctoral student in the PhD Doctoral Programme of English Linguistics at Universidad Complutense de Madrid, under the supervision of Professor Julia Lavid. She has both academic and professional experience in the field of language technologies, having worked for the companies Infospeech, Fonetic, Redknee and Appen Butler Hill Inc. and participated as researcher in the CONTRANOT project, financed by the Spanish Ministry of Science and Innovation with Julia Lavid as principal investigator.

Indeed, most SFL corpus analysis work has been produced using inadequate computational tools (e.g. word processors), resulting in formats which are not amenable to computational treatment. The analytical scheme and the procedure are often not included, the terminology used may vary from other research and may not be complete or may be unknown (*ibid.*). The linguistic descriptions resulting from such analysis methodology are often neither accountable nor replicable by other researchers and impede the sharing of resources within the SFL community. While this situation was difficult to overcome in the pre-computing age, this is clearly not the case in the current state of linguistic knowledge, where the need for and the importance of computation for better practice is evident in different areas of linguistic enquiry, from language documentation to language description and theory building. This is even more evident in linguistic work centred around corpora where methodological refinement is essential in data analysis.

In this chapter we investigate the linguistic phenomenon of thematization in two newspaper genres using an empirical methodology which combines a preliminary corpus analysis with a number of corpus annotation tasks, as proposed and developed within the CONTRANOT project.[1] Our final aim in this project, part of which is the work reported in this chapter, is to contribute to the task of creating, exploring and sharing linguistic resources in English and other languages, as currently practised by some members of the SFL community (see Teich, 2008). Our most immediate goal in this chapter is to illustrate the methodology used in our project with a study of the thematic choices which characterize news reports and commentaries, thus advancing and extending previous corpus research on the correlations between thematic choice and genre in English and other languages (Eiler, 1986; Francis, 1989, 1990; Fries and Francis, 1992; Ghadessy, 1995; Nwogu and Bloor, 1991; Lavid, 1998, 2000, 2010; Lavid *et al.* 2012; etc.)

The chapter is structured as follows: §7.2 outlines the methodological steps that we propose for investigating thematic choices in news reports and in commentaries; §7.3 reports on the results of the preliminary corpus analysis performed on the initial training corpus and §7.4 describes the core and the extended tagset of the annotation scheme used in this study. §7.5 explains the annotation procedure used and describes the two agreement studies performed and their results. On the basis of these agreement studies, we describe the procedure for the semi-automatic annotation of the investigated thematic choices in §7.6. Finally, §7.7 provides a summary of the work reported in this chapter and some concluding remarks.

7.2   Methodological proposal

Our methodological proposal consists of a number of tasks, some of which are outlined in this section, while others are explained in detail in §7.3, §7.4 and §7.5. We begin with the first task, the compilation of the training corpus.

7.2.1   Compiling the training corpus

Our first task in this study was to compile an initial corpus of newspaper texts to create what is known as the 'training corpus', that is, the data set on which the annotations would be coded. The training corpus for the current study consisted of a total of 901 clause complexes (895 declaratives, 2 interrogatives and 4 imperatives) belonging to two groups of texts collected from published sources in 2008 and 2009. The first group comprised seventeen newspaper commentaries extracted from the Project Syndicate (www.project-syndicate.org). The second group was made up of sixteen news reports from the news section of *The Times* online (www.timesonline.co.uk). The motivation for compiling this corpus rested mainly on the electronic availability both in English and in other languages of newspaper texts and on our current interest in journalistic discourse, more specifically in newspaper genres. Within newspaper genres, news reports and commentaries offered an interesting contrast in terms of their communicative purposes which made them a good data source for investigating thematic choice. As explained in Lavid *et al.* (2012), the main communicative purpose of news reports is basically informative, while the goal of news commentaries is analytical, evaluative and persuasive.

7.2.2   Instantiating the theory

The next step was the definition and delimitation of the theoretical categories that would be tested in the corpus annotation task. As explained in Hovy and Lavid (2010: 19):

> instantiating the theory encounters the problem that no theory is ever complete, and few if any are developed to an equal degree for all variants of the phenomena they address. Since theories tend to focus on some phenomena over others, uncertainty arises about exactly which categories to define as tags for annotation, how to define them exactly, and what to do with the residue not covered by the theory.

In order to decide which categories would be used for the annotation of our corpus, we first selected four coarse-grained categories from the recent SFL-based model of thematization developed by Lavid *et al.* (2010), and performed a preliminary corpus analysis on the training corpus, adding some realizations of one of the categories (the Thematic Head). This analysis allowed us to generate hypotheses about the behaviour of thematization in the two genres under study, as described in §7.3 below.

7.2.3 Designing the annotation scheme and guidelines

This task involved instantiating all or part of the features of the selected theoretical model and developing a core and an extended tagset to be used in the process of annotating the training corpus. The process is a complex one which requires step-wise refinements and modifications during the whole annotation process. On the basis of the preliminary corpus analysis we selected certain thematic features of the two genres under study and created a simplified annotation scheme which was modified and improved during the annotation process. The annotation scheme is described in §7.4.

7.2.4 Performing agreement studies

In order to test the reliability of the core and the extended tagsets of the annotation scheme, we performed two agreement studies on some fragment of the training corpus and evaluated the results in order to determine the replicability of the annotation schemes. The results of these agreement studies are presented in §7.5.

7.2.5 Annotating a larger corpus using tags from a reliable annotation scheme

Once the annotation scheme was validated through the agreement studies, we proceeded with the semi-automatic annotation of the investigated thematic choices using the UAM corpus tool, a computational coding tool specifically designed to support SFL-based annotation (see O'Donnell, 2008). This final phase is described in §7.6 below.

7.3   Preliminary corpus analysis

As explained in §7.2 above, we performed a preliminary corpus analysis on the training corpus. Although such an analysis is not generally carried out in the NLP community, and it may be considered unnecessary for some computational applications, we think that it is a useful preliminary step for deciding which features to include in the core and the extended tagsets of the annotation scheme and to generate hypotheses about the behaviour of a given linguistic phenomenon in specific contexts of use.

Our analysis focused on four general thematic categories from the Inner and the Outer Thematic Fields of the English clause complex, as defined in Lavid *et al.* (2010). These were, within the Inner Thematic Field (ITF), the Thematic Head (TH) and the PreHead (PH), and within the Outer Thematic Field (OTF), the Interpersonal Theme (IT) and the Textual Theme (TT). The main motivation for using these categories for our analysis was the fact that these have been recently proposed and needed empirical validation. The definitions and realizations of these categories are provided in Appendix 1 at the end of this paper. The Thematic head is the first element with a function in the nuclear experiential configuration of the clause, that is, excluding circumstances, experiential configuration of the clause; it is central to the unfolding of the text by allowing the tracking of the discourse participants.[2] With respect to the Thematic Head, which in English is typically but not obligatorily the Subject, we made two observations: first, it could conflate with different experiential roles in the transitivity structure of the clause (e.g. with Actor, Senser, Phenomenon, etc.). Second, it was usually realized by different types of Nominal Groups (either concrete or abstract) and these groups could be simple or complex. On the basis of these observations we undertook a quantitative analysis on the two newspaper genres, obtaining the following results, for example:

(a) The two newspaper genres choose different types of experiential roles as Thematic Heads in their clause complexes. News reports usually opt for Sayers as Thematic Heads, while commentaries prefer to choose Carriers, as illustrated in examples (1) and (2), respectively. Differences were also observed in the selection of 'There' as Thematic Head (6.15% in reports (3), where it is particularly helpful to introduce new information, versus only 0.52% in commentaries).

(1)   [Thematic Head/Sayer:] <u>Mr Tilmant</u> said the bank had the trust of its customers and had not seen a large outflow of funds. (Report 7)

(2)   [Thematic Head/Carrier:] <u>The main expectations</u> are for a reduction of nuclear armaments. (Commentary 2)

(3)   *Later* [Thematic Head:] <u>there</u> were unconfirmed reports that six people were still alive in the rubble of a building. (Report 10)

(b) News reports and commentaries also seem to differ in the types of nouns selected as Thematic Heads. While news reports typically select concrete nouns, referring to individuals, groups of people or institutions, as illustrated by (4), commentaries prefer abstract nouns, as shown in (5). As we see in (4), although Nominal groups in reports are shorter, they are often clarified through the use of appositions which clearly identify the referent. Conversely, the higher complexity of Nominal groups in commentaries gives an impression of academic, formal discourse and of a more elaborated style than that of news reports.

(4)   [Thematic Head:] <u>Dominique Strauss-Kahn, the French head of the International Monetary Fund</u>, escaped dismissal for a one-night stand with a subordinate today, but was denounced by board members for a 'serious error of judgment'. (Report 1)

(5)   As a result, [Thematic Head:] <u>its ability to maintain services – and the military capacity to respond to any manoeuvre by the Khartoum government aimed against the peace agreement</u> – is seriously compromised. (Commentary 1)

(c) Both newspaper genres show a low frequency of Interpersonal Themes, which points to a preference for the use of linguistic means other than Theme for expressing interpersonal meanings. A cursory analysis reveals the use of alternative resources such as verbal modality and evaluative lexis, as illustrated in (6).

(6)   Reaching out to the SCO would <u>certainly seem</u> to support NATO's stated objectives. (Commentary 5)

(d) As for textual Themes, differences were found pointing to the different textual structures which characterize these two genres. In news reports textual Themes are not frequent, and this genre employs paragraphing for textual organization. Each paragraph reports a finding or a comment by the writer. By contrast, textual Themes are a fundamental tool for writers of commentaries, who systematically rely on textual Themes to scaffold the text's argumentative structure, and to signal logico-semantic relations between complex ideas, as illustrated by (7).

(7)   [Textual Theme:] *Thus, for example,* [PreHead:] <u>at the SCO summit in August,</u> [Thematic Head:] <u>Russia</u> did not get the support of other members regarding the Georgia conflict. (Commentary 5)

As shown by the results described above, the preliminary corpus analysis on the initial sample reveals interesting differences in the thematic choices characterizing these two newspaper genres. These thematic choices served as the theoretical basis for the creation of the core and the extended tagsets of the annotation scheme in the subsequent corpus annotation phase, as explained below.

7.4   Annotation scheme

The thematic features extracted in the corpus analysis phase served as the theoretical basis for the design of a preliminary annotation scheme, which includes both coarse- and more fine-grained annotations of some of the features. The coarse-grained annotations are specified in a core tagset and the more fine-grained ones in an extended tagset. Our preliminary core tagset includes four tags, reflecting the range of possible thematic types which can occur as part of the Thematic Field in English declarative clauses, both in news reports and in commentaries. Definitions and realizations of these tags are provided in Appendix 2 at the end of the chapter. The four tags of the core tagset are the following:

1.   Thematic Head (TH)
2.   PreHead (PH)
3.   Textual Theme (TT)
4.   Interpersonal Theme (IT)

The extended tagset includes more fine-grained subtypes of some of the tags contained in the core tagset. These tags reflect the more fine-grained thematic choices investigated in the preliminary corpus analysis phase, namely, the conflation of the Thematic Head with certain experiential roles (e.g. Actor, Senser, Phenomenon, etc.), the semantic nature (concrete or abstract) and the complexity (simple or complex) of the Nominal Group chosen for its realization. Table 7.1 presents a preliminary extended tagset for Thematic Head realizations, subject to further refinements.

The PreHead category in the core tagset was also specified as a simple Circumstance (PH-Circumstance),[3] realized by Adverbial or Prepositional Groups, as (PH-CCL), when realized by a dependent clause, or as a Finite (PH-Fin), since these are the main choices. Similarly, the Textual Theme was specified with three possible tags: Linker (TT-Link), Binder (TT-Bind) and Correlative (TT-Cor).[4] The Interpersonal Theme was further divided

Table 7.1 Preliminary extended tagset for Thematic Head types.

Participant type as Thematic Head
TH-Actor
TH-Goal
TH-Beneficiary
TH-Senser
TH-Phenomenon
TH-Sayer
TH-Carrier
TH-Token
TH-Value

Semantic nature of NG
TH-Concrete
TH-Abstract

Complexity of NG
TH-Simple
TH-Complex

---

into Vocative (IT-Voc), Comment Adjunct (IT-Com), and Modal Adjunct (IT-Mod) (see Appendix 2).

In §7.5 below we will explain how we tested the reliability of the core and part of the extended tagset presented here, using inter-annotator agreement measures.

7.5 Agreement studies and annotation procedure

Agreement studies (also called reliability studies) are common in the NLP community where the quality of the annotations is essential for the success of an annotation project. As explained in Hovy and Lavid (2010: 23):

> It is taken as axiomatic that any annotation must be performed by at least two, and usually more people acting independently, so that their tagging decisions can be compared; if they do not agree with enough reliability then the whole project is taken to be ill-defined or too difficult ... The underlying premise of annotation is that if people cannot agree enough, then either the theory is wrong (or badly stated or instantiated), or the annotation process itself is flawed. In any case, training of computer algorithms is impossible on inconsistent input.

In the Linguistics community, and within the CONTRANOT project, agreement studies are used to test hypotheses about the behaviour of linguistic categories empirically (Hovy and Lavid, 2010). More specifically, agreement studies are designed to test the reliability of the tags included in the annotation scheme. In the current study we performed two agreement studies on a small fragment of the training corpus consisting of a total of 143 clause complexes. The first study measured inter-annotator agreement on the identification of thematic spans, while the second measured inter-annotator agreement on the type of label chosen by the annotators on the previously selected spans.

We used two types of agreement metrics: the Agreement Metric and Kappa. For the first task – the identification of thematic spans – we used the Agreement Metric (AGR) rather than Kappa because the annotators could be coding different expressions ('markables') in identifying thematic spans. For the second task – the labelling of the thematic types – we used the Kappa (K) coefficient, which measures agreement when two independent coders are analysing the same element. The operation is based on the difference between the actual agreement and the expected agreement by chance. The K value ranges from 0 (the agreement is no other than the expected by chance) to 1 (there is total agreement), as shown in Table 7.2.

Table 7.2 Interpretation of Kappa (from Viera and Garret, 2005: 362).

	Poor	*Slight*	*Fair*	*Moderate*	*Substantial*	*Almost perfect*
Kappa	0.0	0.20	0.40	0.60	0.80	1.0

Kappa	*Agreement*
< 0	Less than chance agreement
0.01–0.20	Slight agreement
0.21– 0.40	Fair agreement
0.41–0.60	Moderate agreement
0.61–0.80	Substantial agreement
0.81–1.00	Almost perfect agreement

The annotation procedure was the following: two annotators (or coders), #1 and #2, were asked to analyse the thematic features of six texts individually, both having studied Lavid *et al.*'s model of thematization in depth and internalized the definitions for the core and the extended tagset contained in the annotation scheme and guidelines.[5] The lead researcher of the project, the first author of this chapter, managed the annotators and organized regular meetings with them. The annotators were given coding sheets with instructions, each corresponding to a different type of task. In each agreement study there were two tasks: in Agreement Study 1 the two tasks focused on the identification of thematic spans; in Agreement Study 2 the two tasks focused on the labelling of the agreed thematic spans.

7.5.1 The agreement studies

Agreement Study 1 consisted of two tasks focused on the identification of markables. The first task was aimed at the identification of the whole set of potential thematic markables. This was carried out by asking the two coders to identify the Thematic Field of each clause complex in each text. The definition and realizations of the Thematic Field are provided in Appendix 1 at the end of this chapter. The second task focused on the identification of spans realizing only specific thematic types from the Thematic Field. Here the two coders were asked to identify in each clause complex the spans realizing the Thematic Head (TH), the PreHead (PH), the IT (Interpersonal Theme), and the Textual Theme (TT). The definitions and realizations of these tags are provided in Appendix 2 at the end of this chapter.

Agreement Study 2 consisted of two tasks focused on the labelling of markables. The first task of this study focused on the labelling of the thematic markables agreed in the previous agreement study. For this task the agreed thematic spans were highlighted in the coding sheet so that coders could carry out the classification task on the same span. We also included some 'red herrings' in this task, that is, we highlighted items which did not correspond to any of the thematic types of the core tagset and asked the coders to classify those as 'none' with the aim of checking their knowledge of the different types. The second task here was the labelling of the Thematic Heads as one of the possible subtypes specified in the extended tagset (i.e., as Actor, Goal, Beneficiary, Senser, Phenomenon, Sayer, Verbiage, Token, Value, Carrier, Attribute, Process, and the 'There' element).

To sum up, the process consisted of two rounds in which the annotators worked individually and agreement results were measured. In the first round coders were asked to identify thematic spans, and in the second, to label specific thematic types, with an intermediate phase in which results were discussed and a consensus was reached with respect to the spans realizing the thematic markables. The results of the two agreement studies are presented in the following sections.

7.5.2 Results of Agreement Study 1

The first agreement study focused on the identification of two types of thematic spans.

In the first task, annotators had to identify the whole Thematic Field in each clause span. The results of the first task are graphically presented in Table 7.3.

Table 7.3 Inter-annotator agreement: Spans expressing Thematic Field.

	Coder1	*Coder 2*	*agr(1||2)*	*agr(1||2)*	*Average*
Text 1	1	2	0.96	0.93	
Text 2	1	2	0.973	1	
Text 3	1	2	0.906	1	
Text 4	1	2	1	1	
Text 5	1	2	1	1	
Text 6	1	2	0.92	1	
Average					0.97408

As shown by the figures in Table 7.3, the agreement between annotator (1) and annotator (2) was very high on average (0.97%).

In the second task the annotators were asked to identify the spans realizing thematic categories of the core tagset in our annotation scheme. The results for each of the thematic categories are collectively presented in Table 7.4.

Table 7.4 Inter-annotator agreement: Spans expressing TH, PH, IT and TT.

	TH	*PH*	*IT*	*TT*
Average (%)	0.9384	0.787	0.375	0.965

As illustrated in Table 7.4, agreement was high in the identification of the span expressing the Thematic Head and the Textual Theme, but lower – although still substantial – in the identification of the PreHead (0.787%). By contrast, agreement was only fair (0.375%) in the identification of the Interpersonal Theme. As shown in Table 7.5, the main reason for the lower agreement in the identification of the Interpersonal Theme was the labelling, by one of the annotators, of some Textual Themes as Interpersonal Themes. It is worth considering, therefore,

Table 7.5 Textual Themes annotated as Interpersonal Themes by Coder 1.

	Text 2: The vanishing bomb		
Clause #	*Text Clause*	*Coder 1*	*Coder 2*
19	For example, although the United Nations mission in Sudan is supposed to monitor implementation of the CPA, Darfur has practically monopolized its attention.	For example	–
	Text 3: The limits of energy innovation		
Clause #	*Text Clause*	*Coder 1*	*Coder 2*
30	For example, if 20% of the world's electricity were to be generated by wind turbines, then, considering their inherently low load factor of about 25% (compared to 75% for thermal stations using steam turbines), we would need to install new capacity of some 1.25 TW in these machines.	For example	–

whether the definitions for TT and IT may need some sort of reformulation or extension so as to make them more clearly distinguishable from each other. Before doing so, however, further tests will have to be conducted to check whether the confusion was simply a performance error, in which case there might be no need for such reformulation, or whether the problem persists.

7.5.3 Results of Agreement Study 2

The second agreement study focused on the labelling of markables. As in the previous study, we designed two tasks.

In the first task, annotators had to label the thematic markables which had been agreed on in the previous agreement study. As mentioned above, coders were requested to classify the highlighted thematic spans on the coding sheet, including those spans which did not correspond to any of the thematic types of the core tagset. The results of this task are graphically presented in Table 7.6. The numbers 1 through 5 correspond to the five labels coders were to choose from: PH, TH, TT, IT and 'none', respectively (note that coder 1 did not mark any span as IT, hence the absence of category 4 in the vertical column). As we can see, the overall Kappa value is quite high, at 0.915, indicating almost perfect agreement.

Table 7.6 Inter-annotator agreement: Labeling of thematic spans.

Contingency table Coder 1 * Coder 2						
		Coder 2				
		1	2	3	4	5	Total
Coder 1	1	18	0	0	0	0	18
	2	1	85	0	0	5	91
	3	0	0	19	1	0	20
	5	0	0	0	0	14	14
Total		19	85	19	1	19	143

	Value	*Asymp. std. error (a)*	*Approx. T (b)*	*Approx. sig.*
Kappa Agreement Measure	0.915	0.031	17.355	0.000
Number of valid cases	143			

Symmetric measures: (a) not assuming the null hypothesis; (b) using the asymptotic standard error assuming the null hypothesis; approx. T: approximate t-test value; asymp. std. error: asymptotic standard error (ASE), calculated in the same way as the standard errors (standard deviation of each parameter); approx. sig: approximate significance – the p-value (the smallest critical value alpha for which we would reject the null hypothesis based on these data).

The second task focused on the labelling of the Thematic Heads in the clause complexes. Annotators had to choose the tags from the extended tagset for Thematic Head types, corresponding to different experiential roles conflating with Thematic Heads, as specified in Table 7.1 above. As shown in Table 7.7, the Kappa value is rather high – at 0.875 – and agreement is therefore considered to be substantial. Disagreement occurred in 15 cases, probably due to the inherent difficulty in disambiguating experiential roles conflating with Thematic Heads. As seen in Table 7.8, which refers to the text with the highest number of disagreements, these often reflected different interpretation of process types for non-clear-cut cases, which automatically involved the assignation of different participant roles. The dividing line between material and metaphorical relational processes proved to be particularly problematic. Within relational processes, the differentiation between attributive and identifying, as well as the directionality of identifying processes, were also important sources of disagreement.

Table 7.7 Inter-annotator agreement: Thematic Head types (Experiential roles).

Contingency table Coder 1 * Coder 2

		1	2	5	6	7	9	10	11	12	13	14	15	*Total*
								Coder 2						
Coder 1	1	39	1	1	0	1	0	4	0	1	0	0	0	47
	2	0	12	0	0	0	0	0	0	0	0	0	0	12
	5	0	0	6	0	0	0	1	0	0	0	0	0	7
	6	0	0	0	1	0	0	0	0	0	0	0	0	1
	7	2	0	0	0	9	0	0	0	0	0	0	0	11
	9	0	0	0	0	0	1	0	0	1	0	0	0	2
	10	1	0	0	0	0	0	8	0	1	0	0	0	10
	11	0	0	0	0	0	0	1	5	0	0	0	0	6
	12	0	0	0	0	0	0	0	0	24	0	0	0	24
	13	0	0	0	0	0	0	0	0	0	6	0	0	6
	14	0	0	0	0	0	0	0	0	0	0	6	0	6
	15	0	0	0	0	0	0	0	0	0	0	0	11	11
Total		42	13	7	1	10	1	14	5	27	6	6	11	143

Symmetric measures	Value	Asymp. Std. Error (a)	Approx. T (b)	Approx. Sig.
Measure of Kappa Agreement	0.875	0.031	26,282	0.000
Number of valid cases	143			

Table 7.8 Disagreement in the assignation of experiential roles to thematic Heads.

Text 1. The bigger issue in Sudan

Clause #	*Clause*	Coder 1	Coder 2
3	<u>What is most needed now</u> is to build an international consensus on a strategy to implement fully the 2005 Comprehensive Peace Agreement (CPA) for Sudan.	Value	Token
6	After all, <u>the oppressive nature of the regime in Khartoum</u> is at the root of the many conflicts that have torn the country apart.	Actor	Token
7	If the government in Khartoum persists in undermining the reform process and derailing the referendum on self-determination promised for the South in January 2011, <u>a return to full-scale civil war, with calamitous consequences for the peoples of Sudan and the entire region,</u> is a real possibility.	Token	Carrier
18	<u>The government of Southern Sudan</u> suffers from serious financial constraints, owing to unrealistic assumptions about its oil revenues.	Receiver	Carrier
28	<u>China, a close ally of the government in Khartoum,</u> is now carefully weighing its oil interests and its strategic concerns in the South.	Actor	Senser

7.6 Steps in the semi-automatic annotation of thematic features

On the basis of the agreement studies described in the previous section, we undertook the final phase of the study, namely, the semi-automatic annotation of the investigated thematic choices.[6] For this purpose we used a well-known tool in the SFL community, the UAM corpus tool (available at www.wagsoft.com/CorpusTool/). This tool is specifically designed to support SFL-based annotation, which makes it very useful for the kind of annotation carried out in our study (see O'Donnell, 2008 for details).

Although annotation with the UAM corpus tool is still done by a human annotator, and not automatically by a computer programme, there is a difference with purely manual annotation: here the programme offers annotators a number of labels from which to choose. These labels are automatically generated by the tool based on the schemes previously created. The procedure for the creation of schemes for thematic annotation and how this enabled the semi-automatic annotation of the texts in our corpus was as follows:

Step 1

The first step involved the creation of a system network which captured the whole set of potential thematic elements in the English clause complex (i.e. the Thematic field). Being SFL-oriented, the UAM Corpus Tool allows the creation of system networks, called *schemes* in this tool, by means of a user-friendly application, where the user adds subsystems to the general network and features to each system. Figure 7.1 shows a screenshot from the application in use, and Figure 7.2 shows the final product – the system network for Thematic Field.

The created annotation scheme is therefore the resource feeding the text-segment annotation template. The features included in the scheme will appear in the template in the same sequence as in the scheme. This can be seen in Figure 7.3, where the highlighted thematic segment has already been annotated: the features in the 'assigned' box – 'thematic-field', 'outer-thematic-field', 'textual-theme', 'linkers', 'no-interpersonal theme', 'inner-thematic-field' and 'no-prehead' – can be traced in the system network in Figure 7.2, from left to right and from top to bottom.

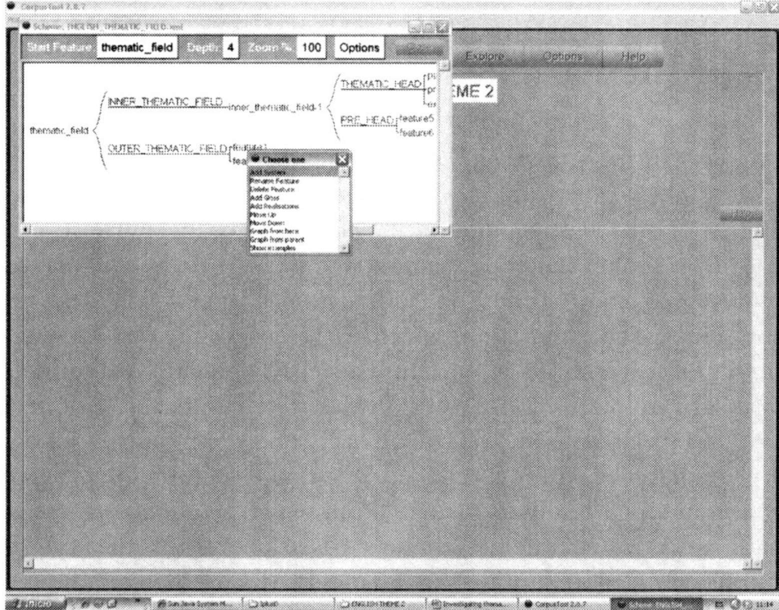

Figure 7.1 Creating a scheme (system network) for Thematic Field.

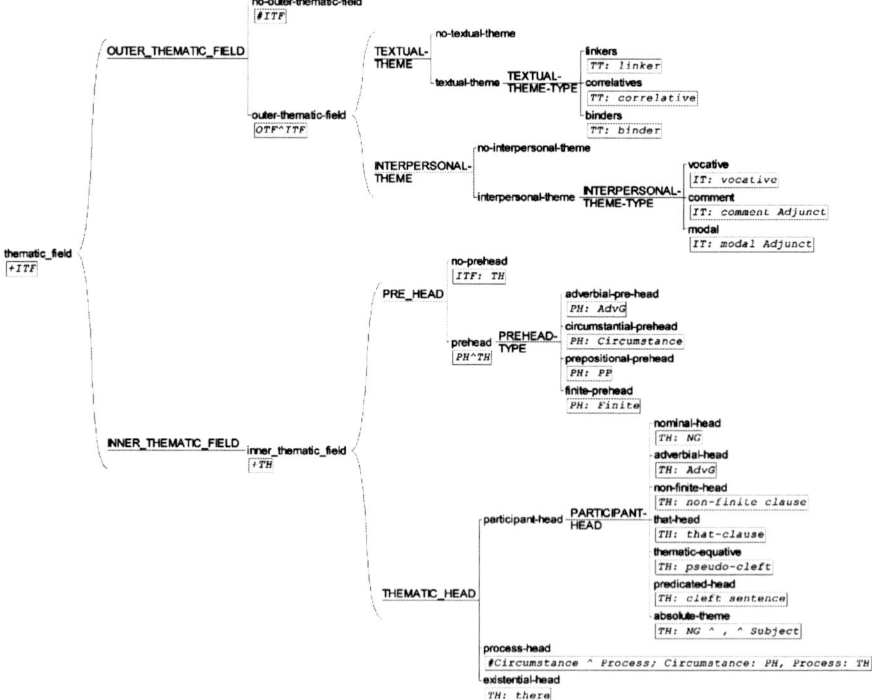

Figure 7.2 System network for Thematic Field based on annotation guidelines.

Step 2

After creating the annotation scheme, the next logical step was to upload our corpus to the tool so as to run some preliminary annotation tests. Given the semi-automatic nature of the annotation, it was important to make sure that annotators would be given the right labels at the right stage. In fact, what the testing revealed was that the scheme in Figure 7.2 was only suitable for the annotation of whole thematic fields, where the annotator specifies the existence or otherwise of an Outer Thematic Field, a PH, etc., as shown in Figure 7.3, where the whole Thematic Field *'Moreover, Sudanese security forces'* has been annotated. The scheme is not suitable, however, for the annotation of the specific components of the Thematic Field (i.e. TT, IT, PH and TH), where, once one of them and its dependant features have been selected, the annotation for that component should end. With annotation based on the scheme in Figure 7.2, if one chooses, for instance, 'textual-theme: linker', the tool will then offer choices for 'interpersonal-theme', for 'prehead' and, finally, for 'thematic-head'. This is shown in Figure 7.4, where the textual Theme *'Moreover'* has already been annotated as such (see the annotation in the 'assigned' box, on the left), and the annotator is still faced with further choices to make, this time for Interpersonal Theme (see the labels in the 'interpersonal Theme' box).

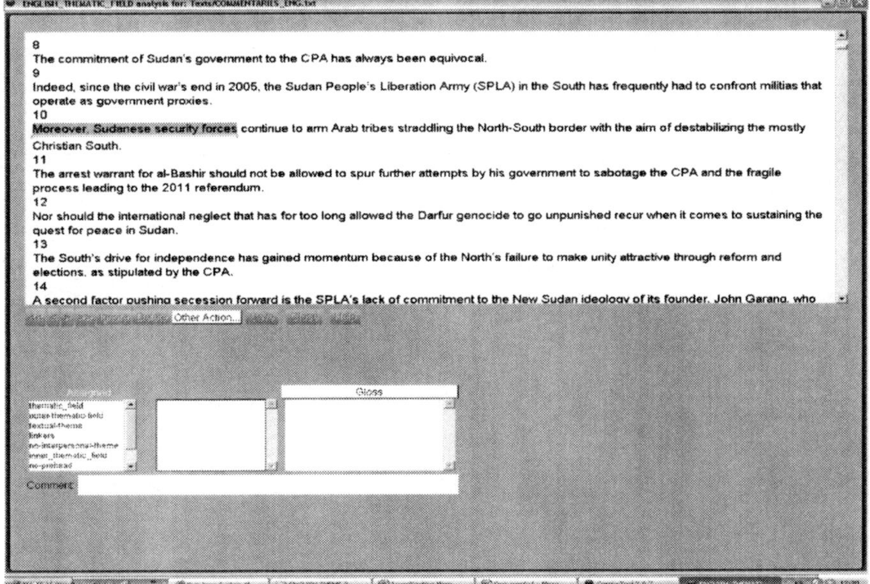

Figure 7.3 Annotating Thematic Field.

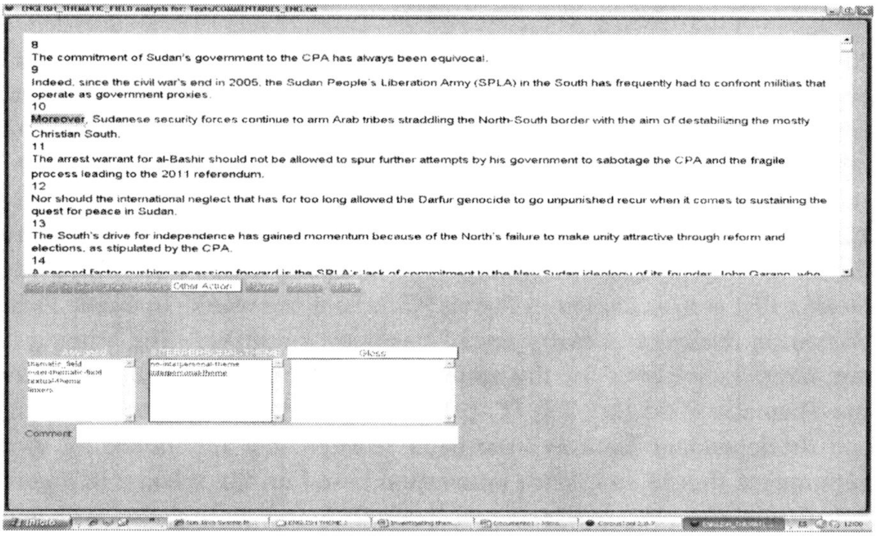

Figure 7.4 Problems in annotation of textual Theme.

Step 3

The scheme shown in Figure 7.2 is therefore valid for the correct description of the systems of English Theme for representational purposes, as well as for the annotation of the whole Thematic Field, with specification of its complexity but without the possibility to segment and tag its internal components. To overcome this annotation problem, it was necessary to create a second annotation layer with a scheme – see Figure 7.5 – where the features TT, IT, PH and TH are presented as alternative rather than parallel. This is reflected by the different kind of brackets used in each system: braces for parallel features, square brackets for alternative ones. The new scheme cannot be used for representational purposes, as the relations within the network are not the real ones, but it now allows the independent annotation of each of the thematic components, as illustrated in Figure 7.6. Here, once the corresponding labels for the annotation of *Moreover* have been selected and duly assigned, no more choices are given to the annotator for that segment, because they are not needed.

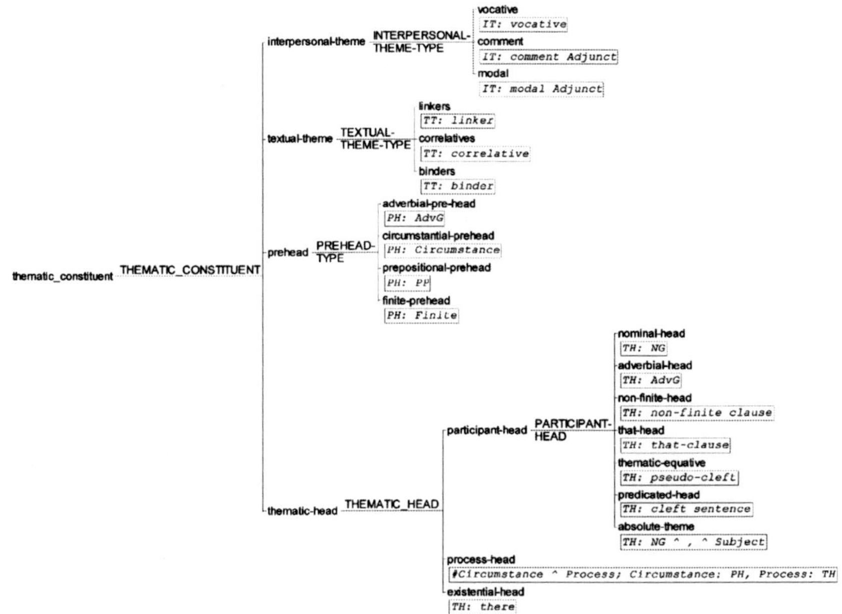

Figure 7.5 Annotation scheme for components of Thematic Field.

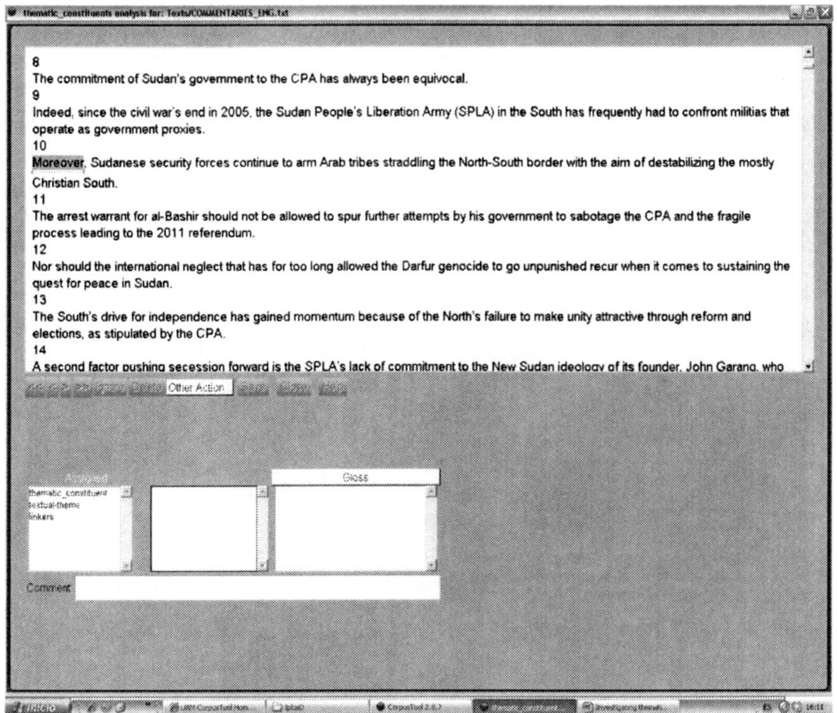

Figure 7.6 Annotating thematic components.

Step 4

Once the annotation layers for Thematic Field and its components were created, the rest of the annotation layers to account for the features in the extended tagset in Table 7.1 (§7.3 above) were created and tested. The result is shown in Figure 7.7, where five different annotation layers can be differentiated – 'English-thematic-field', 'thematic constituents', 'thematic-head-participant', 'semantic-nature-of-NG' and 'complexity-of-NG' – so that it is possible to annotate our corpus for each of those parameters. This is the phase we are in at the present moment: the texts constituting our training corpus are being annotated in the manner specified here. This will be followed by the annotation of a larger number of texts. At any stage in the annotation process, statistics concerning the annotated texts can be obtained (see the 'Statistics' tag in Figure 7.7). This will help us to validate – and, if necessary, adjust – the results obtained in the manual annotation phase given that automatic data mining is a more reliable way of tackling statistical tasks than manual scrutiny, which tends to be not only laborious but also error-prone.[7]

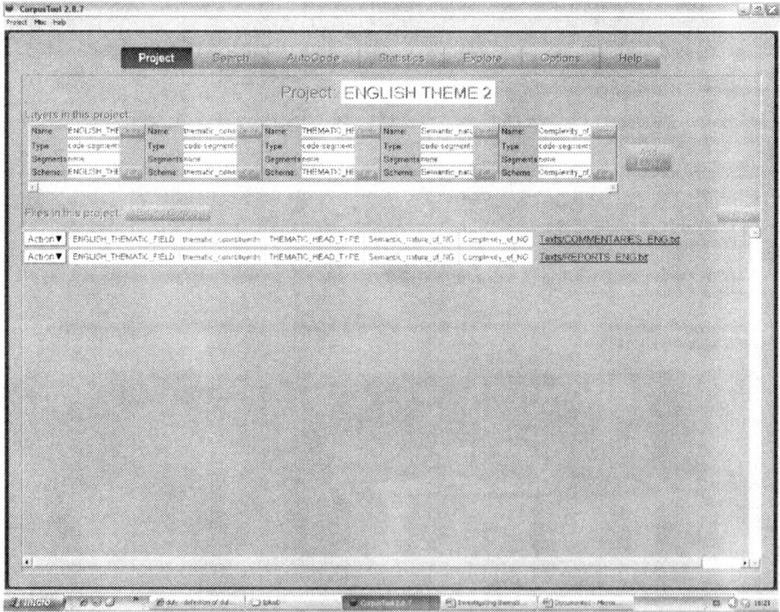

Figure 7.7 Annotation layers for corpus annotation.

7.7 Summary and concluding remarks

In an attempt to contribute to current efforts within the SFL community oriented to the task of creating, exploring and sharing linguistic resources in English and other languages in more comprehensive and effective ways, in this chapter we have presented a methodology for the creation of quality (reliable) data in the area of thematization in English. By quality data we refer to a corpus annotated with thematic features where the annotations have been tested experimentally to ensure their replicability. We have shown how it is possible to create such a corpus following a number of methodological steps which include the compilation of a training corpus, the performance of a preliminary corpus analysis to extract relevant choices to be included as tags of an annotation scheme, and the validation of the annotation scheme through agreement studies. The final phase of the current study has focused on illustrating a procedure for the semi-automatic annotation of the investigated thematic choices. On the basis of such reliable annotations and provided we get enough data, it should be possible to develop machine-learning algorithms for the automatic annotation of a larger corpus with the thematic features investigated in this chapter. We expect that such a corpus would not only be a useful resource for the SFL community, but also of potential interest for NLP tasks in general, such as information extraction and text classification.

Notes

1. The CONTRANOT project is financed by the Spanish Ministry of Science and Innovation under the I+D Research Projects Programme (reference number FFI2008-03384). As team leader (Julia Lavid) and members of the research group (Jorge Arús and Lara Moratón), we gratefully acknowledge the support provided by the Spanish Ministry for the work reported in this chapter.
2. We are aware that Theme in the standard SFL literature ends with clause-initial circumstance, when there is one. Yet, as we are here taking the tracking of participants as a core feature of Theme, we extend the Thematic Field as far as, and including, the first participant function in the clause. We expect further research to allow us to differentiate between circumstances contributing to participant-tracking and therefore exhausting the thematic potential, such as (i) **With that hammer** *he managed to make a big hole,*

and those which, as pointed out by Downing (1991: 127), simply serve to set up a circumstantial framework, such as (ii) ***Until we meet up again, we won't be able to take decision.***

3. See note 2, above.
4. See Appendix 2 for a definition of these textual elements.
5. The two annotators were two members of our research group at UCM, namely Dr M. Juan Rafael Zamorano and Dr Marta Carretero.
6. Although our agreement studies, as seen, proved substantial agreement in general (except for what we have at this point taken to be a performance error concerning the mixing up of some TTs and Its), we are aware that the ideal starting point for the semi-automatic annotation stage would be one of almost absolute inter-annotator agreement.
7. See Counsell *et al.* (2006) on the advantages of automatic over manual data collection. For these authors, although manual data collection can be more accurate than expected, and is sometimes unavoidable, automatic data collection is usually preferable.

References

Counsell, S., Loizou, G. and Najjar, R. (2006) Quality of manual data collection in Java software: An empirical investigation. *Empirical Software Engineering* 12(3): 275–93.

Downing, A. (1991) An alternative approach to theme: A systemic functional perspective. *Word* 42(2): 119–43.

Eiler, M. (1986) Thematic distribution as a heuristic for written discourse function. In B. Couture (ed.) *Functional Approaches to Writing, Research Perspectives* 49–68. Norwood, NJ: Ablex.

Francis, G. (1989) Thematic selection and distribution in written discourse. *Word* 40: 201–22.

Francis, G. (1990) Theme in the daily press. *Occasional Papers in Systemic Linguistics* 4: 51–87.

Fries, P. H. and Francis G. (1992) Exploring Theme: Problems for research. *Occasional Papers in Systemic Linguistics* 6: 45–59.

Ghadessy, M. (1995) Thematic development and its relationship to register and genres. In M. Ghadessy (ed.) *Thematic Development in English Text* 129–46. London: Pinter.

Halliday, M., and Matthiessen, C. (2004) *An Introduction to Functional Grammar*, 3rd edn. London: Arnold.

Hovy, E. and Lavid, J. (2010) Towards a science of corpus annotation: A new methodological challenge for Corpus Linguistics. *International Journal of Translation* 22(1): 13–36.

Lavid, J. (1998) The relevance of corpus-based research for contrastive linguistics and computational studies: Thematisation as an example. In M. T. Turell and E. Vallduví (eds) *IV i V Jornades de corpus lingüistics (1996–1997): els corpus en la recerca semàntica i pragmàtica* 117–40. Barcelona: Publicaciones del Instituto Universitario de Lingüística Aplicada, Universidad Pompeu Fabra.

Lavid, J. (2000) Contextual constraints on thematisation in written discourse: An empirical study. In P. Bonzon, M. Cavalcanti and R. Nossum (eds) *Formal Aspects of Context* 37–47. Dordrecht/Boston/London: Kluwer Academic Publishers.

Lavid, J. (2010) Contrasting choices in clause-initial position in English and Spanish: A corpus based analysis. In E. Swain (ed.) *Thresholds and Potentialities of Systemic Functional Linguistics: Multilingual, Multimodal and Other Specialised Discourses* 49–68. Trieste: EUT.

Lavid, J., Arús, J. and Moratón, L. (2012) Genre realized in Theme: The case of news reports and commentaries. *Discours* 10, http://discours.revues.org/8623.

Lavid J., Arús J. and Zamorano J. R. (2010) *Systemic-functional Grammar of Spanish: A Contrastive Study with English.* London: Continuum.

Martin, J. R., Matthiessen, C. and Painter, C. (1997) *Working with Functional Grammar: A Workbook.* London: Arnold.

Nwogu K. and Bloor T. (1991) Thematic progression in professional and popular medical texts. In E. Ventola (ed.) *Functional and Systemic Linguistics: Approaches and Uses* 369–84. Berlin/New York: Mouton de Gruyter.

O'Donnell, M. (2008) Demonstration of the UAM Corpus Tool for text and image annotation. *Proceedings of the ACL-08: HLT Demo Session (Companion Volume), Columbus, Ohio, June 2008*, 13–16. Stroudsburg, PA: Association for Computational Linguistics. www.aclweb.org/anthology-new/P/P08/P08-4004.pdf (accessed 15 December 2011).

Teich, E. (2007) SFL and linguistic computing: An analysis and some recommendations. Plenary talk at the *34th International Systemic Functional Congress*, Odense, Denmark.

Teich, E. (2008) IRSFL: An initiative for a repository of SFL resources. Presentation at the *35th International Systemic Functional Congress*, 21–25 July, 2008, Sydney, Australia.

Viera, A. J. and Garret, J. M. (2005). Understanding interobserver agreement: The Kappa statistic. *Family Medicine* 37(5): 360–63.

Appendix 1: Definition of Thematic Field

Thematic Field: Initiating clause span of varying length up to and including the first nuclear constituent [FNC] in main clause (in bold in the examples), or one of the following:

- Predicated Theme construction [PT].
- 'There' in Existential clauses.

Examples of Thematic Field (in bold) ending in [FNC]:

(1)   **[FNC:] The cat** is on the mat.
(2)   **[FNC:] Eating** is vital.
(3)   **[FNC:] That he refused to do it** worried me.
(4)   **[FNC:] Of unequal relevance** is ...
(5)   **On the table [FNC:] stood** a lamp.
(6)   **But, surprisingly, before the meeting [FNC:] everybody** was glad to hear the news.
(7)   **[FNC:] What I want** is you.
(8)   **In my opinion, [FNC:] Real Madrid,** their players have been holding up a banner.

Examples of Predicated Theme Construction [PT] and 'There' in Existential clauses:

(9)   **In fact [PT:] it is love** that makes the world go round.
(10) **When I arrived, [THERE:] there** were three people waiting for the bus.

Appendix 2: English core tagset for Theme categories (declarative clauses)

1. Thematic Head (TH)

The **Thematic Head** is defined as the first nuclear constituent (not circumstantial) element in the clause. This can be a *participant,* a *process, an absolute Theme,* a *thematic equative, a Predicated Theme* or the 'There' element in existential clauses. When the Thematic Head is a *participant,* it can be realized as:

- a nominal group. (e.g. **The cat** is on the mat; **Peter** is at home; **She** saw him yesterday);
- an adverbial group (e.g. **Tomorrow** is a holiday);

- a non-finite clause (e.g. **Eating** is vital; **To live** is to die);
- a nominal That-clause (e.g. **That he refused to do it** worried me);
- an absolute Theme (e.g. **Real Madrid, their players** have been holding up a banner);
- a thematic equative (e.g. **What you need** is love);
- a predicated Theme (e.g. **It is you** who are to blame).

When the Thematic Head is a *process*, it is realized as a verbal form, preceded by a Pre-Head element, such as, for example, a circumstance (e.g. *On the table stood a lamp*) or an auxiliary. When the clause is existential, the Thematic Head is realized by the 'There' element (e.g. *There were three people waiting for the bus*).

2. Pre-Head (PH)

The **Pre-Head** element is any circumstantial and/or finite element preceding the Thematic Head. This includes the following realizations (in bold):

- adverbial groups (e.g. [PH-Circ:] **Afterwards** there will be another meeting);
- prepositional phrases (e.g. [PH-Circ:] **On your right** you can see the Royal Palace);
- circumstantial clauses (e.g. [PH-CCL:] **After dropping her off,** he continued his trip);
- finite verbal forms, i.e. auxiliaries, preceding the lexical verb (e.g. [PH-Finite:] **Should** you decide to leave the country, please let me know. **Had** I known you were so near, I would have flown to meet you).

3. Textual Theme (TT)

Elements which are instrumental in the creation of the logical connections in the text, such as linkers, binders or correlatives. These include:

- linkers (paratactic nexus) (e.g. [TT-Link:] **And** don't tell me you didn't know; **but** let's change the topic);
- binders (hypotactic nexus) (e.g. [TT-Bind:] **However**, the situation now is different; **now** we needed to promote the event, **secondly,** you should go to a doctor);

- correlatives: (not only … but; either … or) (e.g. [TT-Cor:] **Not only** didn't he call but also forgot completely about us; **either** you're with us **or** you're against us).

4. Interpersonal Theme (IT)

These are elements which express the attitude and the evaluation of the speaker with respect to his/her message. These include:

- vocatives, i.e., any item used to address (e.g. [IT- Voc:] **Tom!** This is a nice surprise; **Sir,** could you follow me, please?)
- comment adjuncts (e.g. [IT- Com:] **Surprisingly** he didn't mention anything; **understandably,** he kept a low profile)
- modal adjuncts (e.g. [IT- Mod:] **Probably** that's the only lesson we learned; **Surely** you didn't do that!)

Appendix 3: Extended tagset (Thematic Head types)

The definitions for Participant types are based on Halliday and Matthiessen (2004) *IFG* and Martin *et al.* (1997) *Working with Functional Grammar.* All examples include the defined participant in thematic position.

1. TH-Actor – the participant doing the deed in a material processes, as in: [TH-Actor:] Peter went home; [TH-Actor:] Mary received the letter; [TH-Actor:] John gave Mary a kiss.
2. TH-Goal – the participant impacted by a doing in a material process, as in: [TH-Goal:] Mary was kissed by Peter; [TH-Goal:] the letter was put in the mail; or [Goal:] the bathrooms are cleaned hourly.
3. TH-Beneficiary – the participant benefiting (positively or negatively) from the doing in a material process, as in: [TH-Beneficiary:] Mary was given a letter; [TH-Beneficiary:] he was granted a scholarship; or [TH-Beneficiary:] they were inflicted a crushing defeat.
4. TH-Range (or Scope) – the participant that construes the domain over which the process takes place, as in: [TH-Range:] that mountain is climbed mostly on its northern side; or the participant that construes the process itself, either in general or in specific terms, as in: [TH-Range:] showers should be taken in the morning.

5. TH-Senser – the participant sensing in a mental process, as in: [TH-Senser:] she likes ice-cream; [TH-Senser:] I can't see the light; [Senser:] she knows a lot of stories; [TH-Senser:] they prefer to stay.

6. TH-Phenomenon – the participant being sensed in a mental process, as in: [TH-Phenomenon:] he is hated everywhere; [TH-Phenomenon:] deer can be seen crossing the fields; [TH-Phenomenon:] that's well known by everybody; or [TH-Phenomenon:] that ring is very much coveted.

7. TH-Sayer – the participant saying, telling, stating, informing, asking, threatening, suggesting, and so on, in a verbal process, as in: [TH-Sayer:] she never tells the truth; [TH-Sayer:] they ordered me to leave; or [TH-Sayer:] she threatened to kill herself.

8. TH-Verbiage – the content of saying in a verbal clause, when expressed as a nominal group, as in: [TH-Verbiage:] that story has been told many times; [TH-Verbiage:] questions will be asked; or [TH-Verbiage:] that word was never uttered by me.

9. TH-Receiver – the addressee of a speech interaction in a verbal process, as in: [TH-Receiver:] I was told to leave at once; [TH-Receiver:] the kids were told a story; or [TH-Receiver:] she was asked her name.

10. TH-Token – the participant representing the expression, symbol, form, name, function, position or actor in an identifying relational process. Identifying relational processes are reversible and the Token tends to appear in the first position with respect to the Value, as in: [TH-Token:] Mary is the best; [TH-Token:] green means 'go'; or [TH-Token:] She played the leading role. The Token is also the participant that tends to go first in possessive and circumstantial identifying relational processes, as in, respectively: [TH-Token:] they own the house; or [TH-Token:] tomorrow is January the 1st.

11. TH-Value – the participant representing the content, symbolized thing, meaning, referent, filler, holder of position or role in an identifying relational process. Identifying relational processes are reversible and the Value appears in initial position when the process is reversed, as in: [TH-Value:] the best one is Mary; [TH-Value:] 'go' is symbolized by green; or [TH-Value:] the leading role was played by her. The Value is also the participant that goes first in possessive and circumstantial identifying relational processes when these are reversed, as in, respectively: [TH-Value:] the house is owned by them; or [TH-Value:] January the 1st is tomorrow.

12. TH-Carrier – the participant to which an Attribute is assigned in an attributive relational process, whether intensive, possessive or circumstantial. These relational processes are not easily reversed. Examples: [TH-Carrier:] she is quite wise in general, [TH-Carrier:] I have a guitar; or [TH-Carrier:] the movie is about a multimillionaire.

13. TH-Attribute – what is assigned to the Carrier in an attributive relational process, whether intensive, possessive or circumstantial. As attributive processes are not easily reversed, Attributes are not found in thematic position except in exclamations such as: How [TH-Attribute:] clever she is!

14. 'There' – The starting element in an existential process. It is not a participant. Examples: There is a hair in my soup; there are many people here.

15. TH-Process – a whole process, whether material, mental, verbal, relational or existential.

8

A probabilistic approach to choice: The impact of contextual factors on the tactic system in research article abstracts

Akila Sellami-Baklouti[a]

8.1 Introduction

This study argues for the suitability of a conditional probabilistic approach to Choice, which constitutes a defining concept in systemic functional theory, where structure is to be interpreted as 'the outward form taken by systemic choices' (Halliday and Matthiessen, 2004: 23). As a text is an 'instantiation' of the system (*ibid.*; Eggins, 2004), the quantification of structural choices in a text can give insights into the probability of choices in the system. In a text, however, probabilities are rather local, 'particular to one subsystem or text type, or even to one body of text' (Halliday and Webster, 2009: 252). These local probabilities are conditioned by the context, which 'exerts pressure' (Hasan, 2009: 170) on the speaker's choice of meaning and, consequently, on the structural realization of this meaning. This study seeks to show how contextual factors condition the probabilities of choice of clause structure. To this end, the tactic system is studied in a corpus of 100 research article abstracts (henceforth, RAA), representing two academic research disciplines, namely Linguistics and Medical Science. The first part of this study justifies the need for a probabilistic approach by outlining some major assumptions of systemic functional linguistics (henceforth, SFL) and the interaction between

---

a   Akila Sellami-Baklouti received her PhD in Linguistics from the University of Metz (France) and is currently Associate Professor at the Faculty of Arts and Humanities of Sfax (Tunisia). Her research interests include systemic functional linguistics, quantitative and computational approaches to language, and the syntax–semantics–discourse interface with a special focus on academic writing.

them. The second part anchors the notions of probability and conditioning variables in their mathematical background. In the third part, the frequency of clause structure choices in the corpus, first between the clause simplex and clause complex (§8.4.2), then between parataxis and hypotaxis (§8.4.3), is used as a basis to estimate the probabilities of these systemic choices. These probabilities are explained by contextual factors relevant to the RAA genre of the corpus and the discipline of research.

8.2   Motivation for a probabilistic approach: Text, context and choice in SFL

This part will develop the argument that a probabilistic approach follows from the interaction between elements of grammatical analysis in SFL. In fact, contrary to a formal approach, where the subject of study is competence, this functional theory assumes that the text is the major source of information about the grammatical system (§8.2.1). This assumption has led to a corpus-based approach (§8.2.2), which resulted in the need for computational and quantitative methods in order to handle large-size data (§8.2.3). The picture is made more complex by the importance assigned to context in SFL (§8.2.4): as texts are not uniform, they display some variation in systemic choices, with elements having varying frequencies because of contextual factors, hence the need for a probabilistic framework (§8.2.5).

8.2.1   Text as a 'window' on the system

A text may be defined as language in use, spoken or written. In this sense, text can be equated with discourse, though the 'term *discourse* has more sociocultural connotations while text is rather viewed as a process of language' (Halliday and Webster, 2009: 247). The text, as such, has been approached differently in various theories of grammar, namely the formal versus functional paradigm, reflecting a difference of objectives, focus and method of work.

On the one hand, a 'syntactocentric' perspective, as Van Valin and LaPolla (1997: 8) call it, perceives syntax as the central aspect of language. A pioneering example of this formal perspective is generative theory, which has the study of linguistic competence as its major objective. This approach has led to the exclusion of any external criteria in sentence structure and the neglect of the communicative function of language. Within this framework, explanation is theory-internal and structural phenomena have been explained by a set of principles which the theory tried to make universal. Despite the interesting insights into the structure of language offered by generative theory, some of its approaches have been largely criticized as 'increasingly failing because its hypotheses are disconnected from verifiable linguistic data'. (Manning, 2003: 296). In fact, a major shortcoming of such an approach is that explanations and representations work very well with fabricated decontextualized examples provided in textbooks, but are not very helpful if ever one tries to apply them to some authentic data. The neglect of text or language use in authentic contexts is, therefore, a major reason why this approach has been criticized.

An alternative approach to grammar is what Van Valin and LaPolla (1997: 11) call the 'communication-and-cognition perspective', in which syntax is not the central aspect of language structure. In this approach, although language is an abstract system, it can only be studied as a part of human communication and cognition as it cannot exist outside these two spheres. In fact, as communication occurs between language users in social settings, the meanings conveyed by language utterances may be interpreted only in relation to the social context in which the act of communication takes place. Consequently, the issue of interest is rather how syntax interacts with semantics and pragmatics in the act of communication through language. SFL adopts this approach and assigns an important role to language use, broadly referred to as Text.

Being defined as '*any* instance of language, in *any* medium' (Halliday and Hasan, 1976; cited in Halliday and Matthiessen, 2004: 3; [emphasis added]), a text need not be an elaborate piece of language in order to be considered informative about the system; it also does not need to be written in order to be worth studying, as has long been the case in grammar studies. In fact, both 'a trivial service encounter, like ordering coffee', and 'a momentous event in human history, like Nelson Mandela's inaugural speech' may be equally considered 'as instances of an underlying System' (Halliday and Matthiessen, 2004: 26). Because the text is the 'instantiation' of the system, SFL conceptual framework is based on the assumption that 'description of grammar is based on text' (*ibid.*: 33). As Halliday (1994: xxii) claims, '[i]t is of little use having an elegant theory of the system if it cannot account for how the system engenders text; equally, it adds little to expatiate on a text if one cannot relate it to the system that lies behind it'. So, for a theory of grammar to be comprehensive and to deal with language in its entirety, the text and the system should be equally important and worth investigating. This conception of the text as 'window on the system' (Halliday and Matthiessen, 2004: 3) has engendered a major methodological implication, making the corpus 'fundamental to the enterprise of theorizing language' (*ibid.*: 34).

8.2.2   A corpus-based approach

The importance assigned to text in SFL has engendered the adoption of corpora as a basis for grammatical investigation. A corpus can be defined as 'an extensive body of text assembled for use in linguistic research' (Halliday and Webster, 2009: 249). Being a window on the system, texts should be representative enough of speakers' use of language, hence the importance of the corpus size. The corpus makes it possible to investigate 'real' text rather than 'virtual' text consisting of 'examples made up by grammarians inside their heads to illustrate the categories of the description' (Halliday and Matthiessen, 2004: 33). The reliance on corpora has been made possible by computers which may store and process large amounts of spoken and written data to be used for investigation. This corpus-based approach allows the linguist to have access to authentic texts, spoken and written, elaborate and spontaneous, offering, thus, the opportunity to have better insights into the system. This reliance on corpora provides the theory with a scientific basis as it constitutes the domain of observation necessary for theorizing (*ibid.*). In addition, corpora allow for a quantitative analysis of systemic choices in texts.

8.2.3   Quantification of systemic choice in the text

The quantitative approach to text and system is also enhanced by the notion of choice, a fundamental concept in the systemic theory of language. As far as the system is concerned, 'systemic theory is a theory of meaning as choice, by which a language, or any other semiotic system, is interpreted as networks of interlocking options' (Halliday, 1994: xiv), and grammar is based on the choice of a given alternative; in other words, it tries to explain 'patterns in what *could go instead* of what' (Halliday and Matthiessen, 2004: 22; original emphasis). This emphasis on alternation, which represents the paradigmatic ordering of language, stresses the importance of systemic choice in the interpretation of a text, as each choice is meaningful to the analyst only if contrasted with other choices available at that entry of the system.

This idea of alternation makes of each system 'a candidate for quantitative analysis' (Halliday, 2005: 95), with entries in the system having different probabilities of occurrence; for example, the indicative mood has a higher probability in the system than the interrogative mood. A methodological issue that needs to be raised at this point concerns the way probabilities in the system are estimated. The role of the text is of paramount importance in dealing with this issue.

As the text is the instantiation of the system, systemic choice is realized in the text by a structural form, for example the wh-interrogative mood is realized in English by a wh-movement putting the wh-element in the thematic position and engendering the necessary subject auxiliary inversion. Rather than occupying a central position, as is the case in formal approaches, structure in SFL is relegated to a secondary position because it is regarded as 'the outward form taken by systemic choices' (Halliday and Matthiessen, 2004: 22), which are considered more basic. Structure is, therefore, determined by choice to the extent that 'structural operations – inserting elements, ordering elements and so on – are explained as realizing systemic choices' (*ibid.*: 24). It follows that the analysis of a text consists in showing the functional organization of its structure and showing what meaningful choices have been made (*ibid.*). In this process of analysis, the quantification of choices through their outward structural manifestations gains importance because part of the interpretation of a given option is the frequency of this choice in the text.

These frequencies are important for the interpretation of the text, as well as for the estimation of probabilities in the system. In fact, given the dialectical relation between text and system, frequencies in the text reflect probabilities in the system, which are in turn instantiated by frequencies in the text (Halliday, 2005: 82). The text is therefore important not only to determine which options are available in the system, but also to estimate the probabilities of these options, hence the need for a quantitative probabilistic approach to both text and system. The quantitative study of the text, in this perspective, provides the empirical basis for the study of the system; as Plum (2004: 4–5), argues, 'an empirical study of text is of necessity in some sense concerned with the quantification of choice.'

So far, it has been argued that a quantitative probabilistic approach is a methodological need following from fundamental notions in SFL; namely, system, text and choice and the relations they entertain. The text, however, is not a homogeneous concept because language use is, to a large extent, affected by genre, which is considered as a major contextual factor determining frequencies of choices in the text. The following section will elaborate on the position of context in the SFL model and argue that this position enhances the need for a conditional probabilistic framework that makes it possible to estimate probabilities from varying frequencies in the text.

8.2.4 The impact of context on systemic choice

A major cause of criticism addressed to formal approaches is the decontextualization of language. Because structure is at the focus of analysis and because explanation is theory-internal, little attention has been paid in formal approaches to the semantic, pragmatic or communicative dimensions of language. This focus on *langue* as the sole concern of 'linguistics proper' (Hasan, 2009: 168) has led formalists to ignore 'as far as possible the study of context where it interferes with the study of competence' (Leech, 1974: 80; cited in Hasan, 2009: 168).

For a theory like SFL, which relies on text to study the system, the consideration of context as a dimension of analysis becomes a methodological necessity, as a text cannot exist outside context. Similar to text, the context occupies an important position for SFL theorists who 'claim quite confidently that there can be no comprehensive scientific linguistics without parole, and no study of parole without context: a viable linguistics needs to incorporate both' (Hasan, 2009: 168). This leads to two major points which need to be clarified while dealing with context: the first is theoretical and concerns what to be considered as context and the second is methodological and concerns the measurement of contextual manifestations in the text.

Broadly speaking, context can be defined as 'the extra-linguistic environment in which language operates, as spoken or written discourse' (Halliday and Webster, 2009: 240). A more precise definition is provided by Hasan (2009: 176), who argues that the three vectors of Field, Mode and Tenor 'are relevant by virtue of the fact that they would always leave a 'trace' in the text: what is relevant in the context of situation would be illuminated by the language of the text'. Hasan defines these terms as follows: Field concerns the nature of social action, undertaken with some goal or purpose and involving the use of language; Tenor is concerned with social relation, lending itself to descriptions of role; and Mode concerns contact, involving both channel (i.e. aural in the case of spoken and visual in the case of written language) and medium, referring to 'what language was doing'. The variation in these three vectors will cause a variation in text type or registers, defined as a functional variety of language (Halliday, 1978; cited in Halliday and Matthiessen, 2004: 27).

From a textual-oriented perspective, the concept of functional variety may be used to refer to what genre theorists call *genre* with communicative purposes (Johns, 1997; Swales, 2004) and formal text features/conventions (Johns, 1997) as characteristic features. In fact, communicative purposes are such an 'important consideration' to the extent that 'genres are often categorized according to the particular jobs they are said to accomplish' (*ibid.*: 24). The empirical part of this study will illustrate how the probability of choices in text can be mapped (in the mathematical sense) from the genre features of the text.

The concept of functional variety is, however, more general than genre as it may also be used to include disciplinary variation in the case of academic writing. According to Hyland (2004: 3), texts 'produce' what 'goes on in the disciplines'. In this sense, the discipline of research may also be considered as a contextual factor that determines the probability of choices in a text. This position is also adopted by Charles (2006: 493), who claims that 'there are fundamental differences between disciplines, both in what constitutes knowledge and in the way in which it is constructed'. Based on this assumption, the empirical part of this study will compare the choice of taxis in a corpus of 100 research article abstracts representing two academic disciplines, namely Linguistics and Medical Science. The objective of this comparison is to show how the probability of choice may vary with respect to the discipline of research.

Assuming that genre and disciplinary variation affect the probability of systemic choices in a text, some methodological issues need to be considered, that is, how is context manifested in the text, and how can its traces be measured?

SFL theory assumes that context leaves traces in text by virtue of being 'modelled as a stratum in the linguistic hierarchy, "above" (i.e. realized by) the stratum of semantics' (Halliday and Webster, 2009: 240). This high position in the hierarchy makes it possible for context to affect lower strata. Hasan (2009: 170) speaks about an 'activation-construal dialectic'. The relationship is dialectical because it works in both directions: going downwards, the context 'activates' semantic choices, which in turn activate lexicogrammatical choices; going upwards, lexicogrammatical choices 'construe' semantic choices, which in turn construe contextual ones (*ibid.*: 170). Figure 8.1 may help visualize this relationship.

This schematization entails some methodological implications for both the relationship between text and system and the probabilistic approach to this relationship. On the one hand, quantifying structural choices in the text helps construe meanings, which in turn construe context. On the other hand, the context, as an activation force, helps explain the

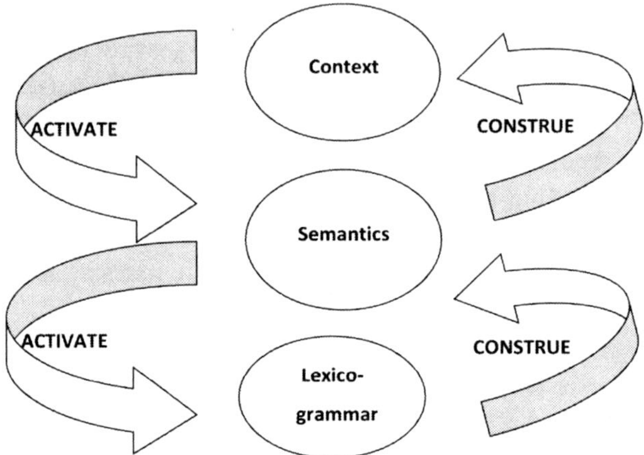

Figure 8.1 Relations between context, text and lexicogrammar.

motivation behind such semantic and structural choices. This approach gains significance because of the importance of explanation in any grammatical theory. In fact, translating a given text into frequencies of structural options is of little significance unless explanation is provided for such frequencies and this explanation can be provided only through mapping those choices to the contextual factors that have activated them.

The empirical part of this study will investigate two moments of choice in order to illustrate how this works: in a first illustration, the probability of clause structure (simplex vs. complex) is computed, relying on the frequency of choice in texts representing Linguistics and Medical Science. Varying probabilities are then explained in terms of contextual variation – the belonging of the disciplines to the hard–soft continuum (Hyland, 2004). The second example will show how the probability of the hypotactic structure (vs. the paratactic one) at the level of the clause complex in RAA can be explained by the characteristics of the genre. The argument in this section – and the empirical study – is based on the assumption that probabilities are not absolute, but rather variable, and that this variation follows from functional variation, hence the distinction between global and local probabilities.

8.2.5　Global vs. local probabilities

SFL assumes that probability varies in different functional contexts (Halliday and Matthiessen, 2004). Based on the relationship between system and text, varying probabilities are displayed by varying frequencies of structural options in the text. These are local probabilities which are 'particular to one subsystem or text type, or even one body of text' (Halliday and Webster, 2009: 252). These local probabilities are opposed to global probabilities 'pertaining to the language as a whole, in all contexts and registers' (*ibid.*). Halliday (2005: 48) argues that local probabilities may be conditioned by two types of factors: on the one hand, intrastratal conditioning concerns probabilities conditioned by factors which are internal to the system. He illustrates this type with a study carried out by Nesbitt and Plum (1988; cited in Halliday, 2005: 48), who investigated how the probabilities of taxis in the clause complex are determined by logico-semantic relationships. On the other hand, interstratal conditioning is concerned with one stratum affecting probabilities in another; for example probabilities of verbal deixis in the finite clause being conditioned by social class, as investigated by Plum and Cowling (1987; cited in Halliday, 2005: 48). The analysis of the corpus in the present study investigates both types of conditioning at work. Although the main argument is that lexicogrammatical probabilities in given text types (local) are conditioned by context (factors pertaining to a different stratum), the quantitative analysis will show that some of these probabilities are conditioned by factors internal to the system (tactic interdependency conditioned by logico-semantic relationships).

8.2.6 Synthesis: The need for a probabilistic approach

This part of the study has tried to argue that the probabilistic approach is not an ornament but rather a methodological need required by the systemic functional approach to language and linguistic study. Contrary to a syntactocentric approach, which excludes external criteria in the study of sentence structure, entailing the neglect of text, hence of corpus-based studies and assuming that 'the notion "probability of a sentence" is an entirely useless one, under any known interpretation of this term' (Chomsky, 1969: 57; also 1956, 1957, etc.; cited in Manning, 2003: 289), SFL theory puts the text at the heart of linguistic investigation. This position of the text has called for a corpus-based approach and recognized context as a full status stratum in linguistic investigation which affects the lexicogrammatical stratum. Consequently, a quantitative (more specifically, a probabilistic) approach is a necessary methodological framework that may handle all these elements of grammatical analysis. It is, therefore, the objective of the following section to review some mathematical notions that may be useful for such a probabilistic approach.

8.3 Mathematical background: Some notions on probability and their applicability to systemic choice

Although the study of probability in mathematics is a fully independent branch with complex notions and theorems, its application in other fields of study is based on the most basic notions in probabilistic calculus. Two such notions relevant to this study are presented in this section together with their applicability to the functional linguistic background outlined in the first part of this chapter.

8.3.1 Random variables and samples spaces

Grinstead and Snell (1997: 18) introduce probability as a framework to study experiments. Their definition of probability can be summarized as follows.

Suppose we have an experiment whose outcome depends on chance:

- Let the outcome (X) = random variable.
- Let the sample space of the experiment W be the set of all possible outcomes.
- The elements of a sample space = outcomes $0 \leq p \leq 1$.

To illustrate this definition, Grinstead and Snell (1997: 19) provide the following example:

(1) Example: A die is rolled once. We let X denote the outcome of this experiment. Then the sample space for this experiment is the 6-element set:

$$\Omega = \{1, 2, 3, 4, 5, 6\}$$
$$E: p = 1/6 = 0.16$$

As all the elements in the set have equal chances of occurring, this distribution may be called *uniform distribution*. It is a function m defined by:

$$m(\omega) = \frac{1}{n}$$

The following example illustrates the applicability of this formula to grammatical analysis:

(2)   A linguistic example: We express a logical meaning/logical content in a text, for example a causal link between two propositions, linguistically realized by two clauses. We let X denote the outcome of this experiment; X here denotes the structural form that the causal relation may take, as Figure 8.2 shows:

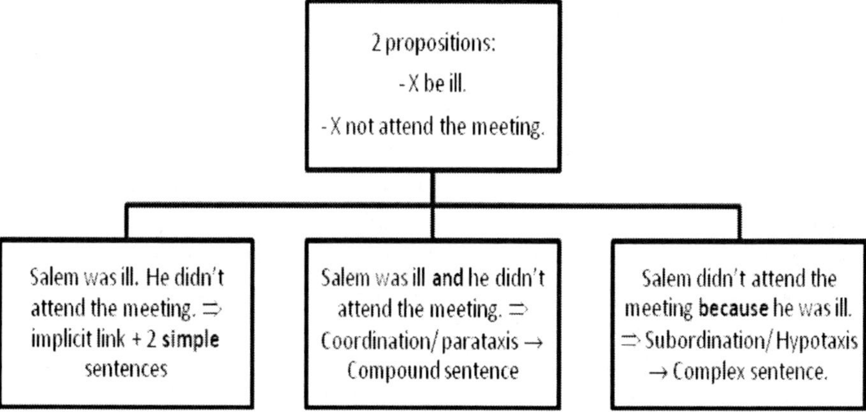

Figure 8.2 Structural form of a logical relation.

In this example, the sample space contains the three possible structures which have equal probabilities of occurrence:

$$\Omega = \{\text{simple, compound, complex}\}$$
$$P\ (E) = 1/3\ 0.33$$

It is, however, not always the case that experiments result in a uniform distribution. The probability of occurrence of a given random variable X may be conditioned by external factors.

8.3.2   Conditional probability

Grinstead and Snell (1997: 133) define conditional probability in the following terms: 'Suppose we assign a distribution function to a sample space and then learn that an event E has occurred. How should we change the probabilities of the remaining events? We shall call the new probability for an event F the conditional probability of F given E and denote it by P(F|E).' Conditional probability is, therefore, the probability of an event E while bearing in mind some other interfering factor(s). To illustrate this conditional probability, the authors give the following example:

> **Example 4.1** An experiment consists of rolling a die once. Let X be the outcome. Let F be the event {X = 6}, and let E be the event {X > 4}. We assign the distribution function m(ω) = 1/6 for ω = 1, 2, ... 6. Thus, P(F) = 1/6. Now suppose that the die is rolled and we are told that the event E has occurred. This leaves only two possible outcomes: 5 and 6. In the absence of any other information, we would still regard these outcomes to be equally likely, so the probability of F becomes 1/2, making P(F|E) = 1/2. (Grinstead and Snell, 1997: 133)

This notion of conditional probability seems suitable to handle linguistic phenomena where the context may affect meanings which, in turn affect structural forms. This framework has been adopted in some formal probabilistic theories of syntax, where the objective of the linguist working with a probabilistic framework is 'to learn the probability distribution P (meaning | utterance, context) – a mapping from form to meaning conditioned by context' (Manning, 2003: 291).

Conditional probabilities seem also suitable to handle the systemic functional relations between context, semantics and lexicogrammar (§8.2.4) and the relation between text and system. While global probabilities (§8.2.5) can be considered as uniform distributions, local probabilities are conditioned by contextual factors which affect semantic choices, which in turn affect structural choices. Assuming that the text is the instantiation of the system, global probabilities (in the system) would be a joint distribution of local probabilities (in different texts). It is, therefore, clear that the probabilistic framework constitutes a suitable analytic tool for the SFL model of grammar. The following section will try to illustrate how this works for a corpus of texts.

8.4 The probabilistic model at work: Contextual factors and clause structure

This part of the study seeks to estimate the probability of structural choices– first, between clause simplex and clause complex, then at the level of clause complex between parataxis and hypotaxis. This estimation is based on the frequency of these structural forms in a corpus of RAA representing two academic disciplines.

8.4.1   Corpus description and methodology

The corpus under study consists of 100 RAA randomly downloaded from two online academic journals representing two academic disciplines, namely Linguistics and Medical Science. The following table displays the titles of the journals and the number of words in each set of abstracts after unnecessary data has been removed (names of authors, key words, etc.).

Table 8.1 Corpus description.

Discipline	Journal title	Number of abstracts	Number of words
Linguistics	*Journal of English Linguistics*	50	7521
Medical Science	*American Journal of Hospice and Palliative Medicine*	50	7463
Total		100	14,984

The choice of the RAA is motivated by the hypothesis that the probability of options (i.e. parataxis and hypotaxis) is conditioned by the RAA genre as a contextual factor. In fact, a major generic characteristic of this genre is its compactness, as the length of an abstract is limited by the journal's guidelines. Along with this compactness, however, the abstract is to represent the macro-propositions of the accompanying article. For this reason, Mulvaney and Jolliffe (2005: 125) argue that 'an effective abstract works hard to re-create the arguments of the text and to make every sentence count'. These two features led Punch (2000: 69) to consider abstract writing as the 'skill of saying as much as possible in as a few words as possible'. In addition to that, the abstract of the research article plays an important role in attracting the attention of the reader, because it is the abstract that the reader reads first in order to decide 'whether, why and how to read' (Yudkin, 2006: 45). The implications of such studies can be seen in research methodology writings which instruct researchers to carefully write their abstracts in order to fulfil the function of persuading the reader to read the whole article; in Day's (1993: 31) words: 'If you cannot attract the interest of the reviewer in your abstract, your cause may be lost'. Considering abstract writing as action undertaken with the goal of persuading readers to read the whole accompanying article (i.e. the Field vector (§8.2.4), one would expect this contextual vector to 'leave its traces' in the text by activating some lexicogrammatical choices.

The second contextual factor whose traces are to be investigated in the corpus under study is Tenor. In the case of RAA, it is a researcher–researcher interaction. In fact, an RAA is addressed to other researchers, most of the time belonging to the same discipline of research, with the goal of finding out the latest developments in the field. As different disciplines have different research paradigms and methodologies, this disciplinary variation is expected to be reflected in the writing. In fact, according to Hyland (2004: 3), texts 'produce' what 'goes on in the disciplines'. In this process of production, the form of writing is stressed as a variable that distinguishes disciplines to the extent that writing can be defining of disciplines. In this scope, Hyland (*ibid.*: 3) states 'it is *how* they write rather than simply *what* they write that makes the crucial difference between them [disciplines]' (original emphasis). Therefore, the choice of a corpus representing two disciplines is driven by the objective of investigating whether different disciplines leave different traces in lexicogrammar. This study focuses on lexicogrammatical choices as to clause structure, first between clause simplex and clause complex and then, at the level of the clause complex, between parataxis and hypotaxis. It will first estimate the local probability of these choices based on their respective frequencies in the corpus and then explain how these choices have been activated by contextual factors relevant to the RAA genre. Table 8.2 (adapted from Hasan, 2009: 180) summarizes RAA characteristics in terms of the three vectors: Field, Tenor and Mode.

Table 8.2 Contextual variables in RAA.

Variables	*RAA values of the variables*
Field	Present/summarize a research article $\Rightarrow$ persuade the research community of its value $\rightarrow$ expected outcome: read the whole article.
Tenor	Researcher–researcher interaction $\Rightarrow$ shared knowledge + shared conventions (way of presenting knowledge $\rightarrow$ language).
Mode	Written to be read $\rightarrow$ visual.
	Constraint of space (number of words limited) $\Rightarrow$ compactness.

The corpus was annotated using the UAM CorpusTool, version 2.8.3. A scheme of text annotation was designed taking into account structural options available at each moment of choice. Figure 8.3 displays the scheme created for the corpus under study.

Once the scheme was designed, all the clauses were annotated and the database was ready for the quantification of frequencies necessary to estimate probabilities.

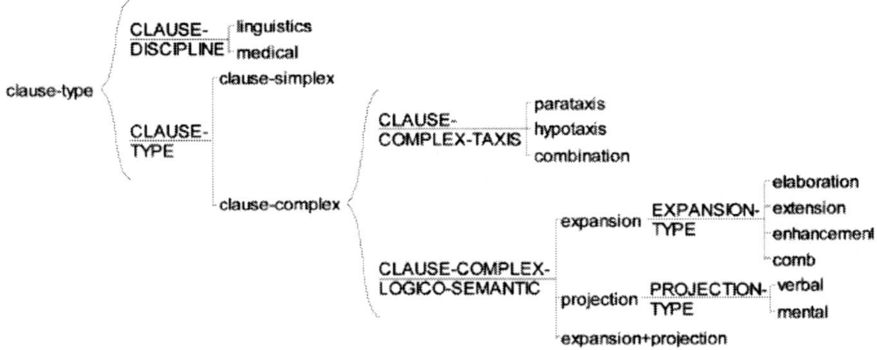

Figure 8.3 CorpusTool scheme of corpus annotation.

8.4.2 Probability of clause structure: Simplex versus complex

Table 8.3 displays the distribution of the clause simplex versus complex according to the discipline of the abstract.

Table 8.3 Distribution of clauses in the corpus.

	Clause simplex	*Clause complex*	*Total*
Medical Science	227	132	359
Linguistics	123	147	270

It is noticeable that the total number of clauses in the Medical sub-corpus (359) significantly exceeds that in the Linguistics sub-corpus (270), despite the fact that the two sub-corpora have nearly equal numbers of words (7463 words in the Medical sub-corpus and 7521 words in the Linguistics sub-corpus). This means that the average length of the clause is 20.78 words in the Medical abstracts and 27.85 words in the Linguistics abstracts. The length of the clause in each sub-corpus is related to the distribution of clause types, as clause complexes represent 36 per cent of the total number of clauses in the Medical corpus, whereas in the Linguistics sub-corpus, they represent 54 per cent. This discrepancy in the distribution of clause types in the two disciplines is evidenced by Yule's correlation coefficient:

$$Q = \frac{A - B}{A + B} = \frac{(227 \times 147) - (132 \times 123)}{(227 \times 147) + (132 \times 123)} = \frac{17133}{49605} = 0.35$$

With a Yule's coefficient equal to 0.35, which is outside the rejection interval, a correlation is proved to be significant between, on the one hand, clause simplexes and Medical RAAs, and, on the other hand, between clause complexes and Linguistics RAAs. Based on the assumption that 'frequency in the corpus is the instantiation (note, not realization) of probability in the grammar' (Halliday, 2005: 82), these frequencies can be translated into probabilities. It can therefore, be deduced that the discipline of research is a conditioning factor of the structural choice between clause simplex and clause complex. Based on the formula of conditional probability presented in §8.3.2, the following probability estimation can be given for Medical RAAs:

(3)   *P (clause simplex/logical link, Medical Science abstracts) = 0.64*

Formula (3) reads as *the probability of choosing a clause simplex structure when expressing a logical link between two propositions, taking into consideration the Medical Science abstract is estimated at 0.64.* As for Linguistics RAA, the following formula can be given:

(4)   *P (clause complex/logical link, Linguistics abstracts) = 0.56*

Formula (4) reads as *the probability of choosing a clause complex structure when expressing a logical link between two propositions, taking into consideration the Linguistics abstract is estimated at 0.56.*

Following Halliday and Matthiessen's (2004: 365) argument, the higher probability of clause simplexes in the abstracts of Medical Science articles shows that the authors opt for 'looser integration in meaning', whereas 'the effect of combining clauses into a clause complex is one of tighter *integration in meaning*'. As I argue (Sellami-Baklouti, 2011: 505), the 'tight integration in grammar and meaning may correspond to different degrees of explicitness'. In fact, despite the existence of the logical relation independently of the linguistic representation, the clause complex is more explicit because this logical link is linguistically expressed, leaving, therefore, little room for speculation by the reader.

The variation in probabilities of clause types in the corpus may be explained by two types of contextual factors. The first is a general one and concerns the belonging of the two disciplines to different research paradigms, and the second is more specific and concerns research methodologies relevant to each discipline. As far as the first type of factors is concerned, the probabilities of clause structure in the corpus under study are consistent with the findings reported in my earlier study (*ibid.:* 514), where I studied clause structure in a corpus of abstracts belonging to six academic disciplines representing the hard–soft distinction and found out that 'hard disciplines abstracts not only display a higher probability of clause simplexes, but also a higher probability of absence of overt conjunctive adjuncts at this level'. This has been explained by the difference between the two research paradigm methodologies. On the one hand, findings in hard disciplines are the outcome of laboratory experiments where the variables are fully controlled. This methodological rigour of hard sciences makes the logico-semantic relations uncontroversial; so, the authors do not need to make these relations explicit through the use of grammatical devices and linguistic techniques. On the other hand, soft sciences are implied to have less rigour, as some variables in experimentation cannot be fully controlled. Authors therefore resort to 'tighter integration in meaning' by making logico-semantic relations more explicit through the grammatical device of clause complexing. These findings are supported by the corpus under study, where the focus is put on the two disciplines which displayed the highest degree of discrepancy 'with Medical Science having the highest probability of clause simplexes in the hard sciences group and Linguistics having the highest probability of clause complexes in the soft disciplines group' (Sellami-Baklouti, 2011: 516). Explanations for these varying probabilities are sought in the corpus of the present study.

A first contextual factor relevant to the research discipline that may have conditioned the probabilities of clause structure in the corpus is the format of the abstract. In fact, the Medical sub-corpus contains structured abstracts, where the moves are presented under headings, which increases the probability of clause simplexes. The following example illustrates this point:

(5)　Medical-Abs. 23
　　　Background: The time before dying can be extremely challenging and stressful.

In example (5), the background to the study is presented by a clause simplex introduced by a sub-title. On the contrary, in the Linguistics sub-corpus, which contains no structured abstracts, the same move is realized by a clause complex where a main clause projects the findings of previous studies, as shown in the following example[1]:

(6)　Linguistics-Abs. 41
　　　α → The political border between England and Scotland has been claimed
　　　'β → to coincide with the most tightly packed bundle of isoglosses in the English-speaking world.[1]

While moves such as Background, Result or Conclusion are introduced by headings in the Medical RAAs, the use of projecting clauses in the Linguistics RAAs to introduce these moves increases the frequency of clause complexes in this sub-corpus and results in the difference observed between the two sub-corpora in clause structure.

A second possible reason for the different probability rates is the way the findings of the paper are presented. In fact, it is noticed that while presenting the results of the paper and their discussion, the writers of abstracts in the two disciplines may resort to different linguistic techniques, as the following two examples from results sections show:

(7)   Medical-Abs. 10
       S → In widows older than 65 years, perception of bad health, negative outlook for the future, and insufficient support seemed to increase the risk of more sedatives and sleeping pills.
       S → Negative outlook for the future also tended to lead to a heightened risk for increased intake of alcohol.

(8)   Linguistics-Abs. 5
       α → Our findings indicate
       'β → a → that Appalachian migrants negotiate their sociolinguistic identities
       xβ → by drawing on the norms both of their family members and of their adopted homes.

In example (7) the results of the study are presented in the form of clause simplexes whereas, in example (8), the clause presenting the results is projected by a main clause where the voice of the authors is signalled through the possessive determiner 'our'. This linguistic difference illustrated by these examples is recurrent in the corpus, increasing thus the probability of clause simplexes in the Medical sub-corpus and clause complexes in the Linguistics one. This difference may be explained by the way knowledge is perceived and represented in the two disciplines. In fact, the way results are presented in the Medical sub-corpus reflects the rhetorical structure of this writing, as the first move in the Results section is 'Indicating Consistent Observation' (Nwogu, 1997: 131). This move 'contains information concerned with stating the overall observation made in the study. It also reports on all other significant observations' (*ibid.*). The presentation of these observations need not be mediated by the voice of the researcher as they are mere descriptions of facts presented as the logical outcome of the application of laboratory experimentation. These observations are linguistically presented in the form of clause simplexes, introduced by a subtitle, if the abstract is a structured one, as is shown by example (9):

(9)   Medical-Abs. 8
       Results:
       S → 62 patients were enrolled.

> S → Fifty completed 7 days of MP with a median age of 69 (range 30–90) years.
> S → Thirty-five received MP 10 mg/day.
> S → Most (96%) had improvement in depression and/or fatigue.
> S → Among the 62 patients, new symptom prevalence throughout the study was agitation (16%), insomnia (16%), dry mouth (15%), nausea (10%), tremors (6%), anorexia (5%), headache (3%), palpitations (2%), and vomiting (2%).
> S → Patients could have more than 1 symptom simultaneously.
> S → Seven (11%) withdrew due to MP S/E.
> S → Some symptoms present before MP showed significant improvement during MP therapy.

In contrast, the use of the reporting verb 'indicate' (to be a sign of) means that findings of the study presented are the outcome of the researchers' interpretation rather than of direct observation. This can be linked to the nature of results presented in the Linguistics abstracts – as the 'negotiation of sociolinguistic identity' in example (8) cannot be directly observed but is rather inferred from methodological tools that the researchers have adopted in their study. Such a pattern, findings projected by discourse act verbs, is frequent in the Linguistics abstracts, thus increasing the probability of clause complexes in this sub-corpus. The following examples further support this argument:

(10) Linguistics-Abs. 30
α → The authors **conclude** that
'β → the relative autonomy of the community, its endocentric versus exocentric orientation, the primary public service constituency of the leader, the different social affiliations and divisions within the community, the speaker's personal background and history, and the socialized demands and expectations for public presentation are all factors in understanding the leaders' use of local vernacular and mainstream standard variants.

(11) Linguistics-Abs. 34
α → a → The study's results, <<β>> **suggest** that
= β → described in detail in relation to the biological category of speaker sex and cultural notions of gender,
'β → the feminine grammar hypothesis is valid.

It may be concluded from these examples that the presentation of findings in the Medical sub-corpus in the form of a sequence of clause simplexes reflects a conception of knowledge in this discipline as 'accomplished by the correct application of prescribed procedures' (Hyland, 2004: 33). This conception leads to the representation of phenomena as 'a reality independent of the observer' (*ibid.*), which, therefore, does not need to be mediated by the author's voice as is the case in the Linguistics abstracts, where the projecting verb can help the researchers express their stance.

A third contextual factor relevant to disciplinary variation that may have led to varying probabilities of clause type in the two sub-corpora concerns the methodological tools employed. In fact, Linguistics may be argued to have less rigour than Medical Science because, as in other soft disciplines, variables are 'more varied and causal connections more tenuous' (Hyland, 1999: 81). This lack of control over the variables leads the authors to try to make as explicit as possible their methodological tools and justify their use and appropriateness. This can be seen in the following example:

(12) Linguistics-Abs. 7
  xβ → Taking a corpus-based approach,
  α → a → the data were analysed not only as a whole, but also with regard to synchronic variation,
  xβ → α → by carrying out concordance analyses of keywords which occurred within tabloid and broad-sheet newspapers, and diachronic change,
  xβ → albeit mainly approached from an unusual angle,
  xγ → by investigating consistent collocates and frequencies of specific terms over time.

Example (12) contains four hypotactic clauses, which express the logico-semantic relation of means. Starting with the major methodological approach (corpus-based) in a thematic position, the writer goes on to explain the techniques followed in this approach, namely concordance analyses and quantifying frequencies and collocations, with each technique introduced by a new hypotactic clause. Through this explicitness about the research methods, the author tries to persuade readers of the methodological rigour of his/her analytical tools, giving, hence, validity to the research findings.

This section has tried to explain the observed varying probabilities of clause simplexes and clause complexes in the two sub-corpora by factors related to disciplinary variation. The next section will investigate whether this variation also plays a role in conditioning the probabilities of choice at the level of clause complex between parataxis and hypotaxis.

8.4.3 Probability of interdependency in the clause complex: Parataxis versus hypotaxis

The second step of analysis consists in exploring the probabilities of the types of interdependency at the level of the clause complex. This investigation is motivated by the hypothesis that the genre of abstracts affects the probability of tactic choices. Table 8.4 displays the frequencies of hypotactic and paratactic nexuses in the two sub-corpora, along with their percentages.

Table 8.4 Distribution of tactic interdependency in the corpus.

	Parataxis		*Hypotaxis*		
	Nb.	*%*	*Nb.*	*%*	*Total*
Linguistics	38	23	125	77	163
Medical	54	37	92	63	146
Total	92	30	217	70	309

Two findings emerge from Table 8.4. The first is an overall higher frequency of hypotactic nexuses as they represent 70 per cent against 30 per cent of paratactic nexuses, and the second is that this probability is higher in the Linguistics sub-corpus than in the Medical one (77% versus 63%, respectively).

Though the overall result is different from Plum's (2004: 386) finding concerning spoken language 'that the choice of parataxis is more frequent than the choice of hypotaxis', it conforms with the findings reported by Matthiessen's (2002: 20) about the probability of hypotaxis in hard news (65%), in scientific reports (60%) and topographic procedures (60%). This finding is also close to my finding (Sellami-Baklouti, 2011: 517) about abstracts representing six academic disciplines, where the probability of hypotaxis was 68 per cent. This implies that the genre of abstract conditions – more specifically, raises – the probability of hypotactic interdependency, so the following formula can be stated:

(13)   *P (hypotaxis/logico-semantic relationship, abstract genre) = 0.70*

Formula (13) reads as *the probability of choosing hypotactic structure when expressing a logico-semantic relationship at the level of the clause complex, taken into consideration the RAA genre is estimated at 0.70.*

The overall high probability of hypotaxis may be explained by the resources of this type of structural interdependency which meet the requirements of the abstract genre in terms of compactness and persuasive goals. I have previously outlined some of these features of hypotaxis (Sellami-Baklouti, 2011), which make it a preferable choice by abstract writers, and the corpus under study confirms my findings. One such factor is the possibility of internal bracketing/nesting, where the modifier clause is itself modified by another clause dependent on it, as can be seen in example (12) above, where the clause complex contains four hypotactic nexuses, enhancing the main clause. This internal bracketing allows the authors to condense information in the least possible number of words and sentences. Hypotaxis is, therefore, one of the devices which 'enable integration' by 'packing information into an idea unit' (Chovanec, 2003: 51), thus achieving a degree of compactness required by the RAA genre.

Another contextual factor that may have conditioned the high probability of hypotaxis in the corpus is the persuasive purpose of RAA (see Table 8.2). In fact, an abstract needs to be carefully written in order to fulfil the function of persuading the reader to read the whole article. Hypotaxis is a suitable structural device to achieve this purpose because it allows authors to elaborate on their claims and persuade readers of their validity, as can be seen in the following example:

(14)   Medical-Abs. 31
       α → Symptoms are important patient-reported outcomes (PRO),
       =β → which help to evaluate the impact of diseases and treatments and assess quality of care.

In the main clause of example (14), the author attributes to symptoms the status of being 'important patient-reported outcomes' and supports this claim by the hypotactic clause which elaborates on the role of the symptoms in helping to 'evaluate the impact of diseases and treatments and assess quality of care'. By doing so, the author anticipates the reader's possible reaction of doubting the claim presented in the main clause and presents a justification for this claim, trying thus to persuade the reader of its validity.

Hypotactic elaboration may also be used to highlight the importance of an area of research. Example (15) illustrates this point:

(15)   Linguistics-Abs. 24
       α → The study of phraseology, <<=β>> has now come into its own and is an increasingly popular and diversified field, with many different approaches and foci of interest.
       =β → which not long ago was often dismissed as a linguistic activity of only minor interest,

In example (15), which is the opening sentence of an abstract, the author sets the background to his/her study by trying to highlight the importance of the study of phraseology by showing the rising interest in this field. The elaborative hypotactic clause sets a contrast between a near past 'not long ago' and present 'now'. This contrast highlights this rising interest in the field, trying to persuade the reader of its importance, thus valorizing the subject of study and invoking the reader's curiosity to read the article.

In addition to elaboration, hypotactic enhancing clauses help abstract authors persuade their readers of the validity of their claims. This is achieved through a variety of enhancing relations such as temporal, manner and causal conditional. The following example shows how some of these relations are used to achieve authors' purposes:

(16)   Linguistics-Abs. 16
   $x\beta \rightarrow$ While the Atlas analyses mostly spontaneous speech data from thirty-three speakers covering a broad social range,
   $\alpha \rightarrow \alpha \rightarrow$ the present study analyses word list data from a larger number of speakers (eighty-six) drawn from a narrower social range,
   $=\beta \rightarrow$ comprising young, university-educated speakers of Standard Canadian English from all across the country.

In example (16), the first hypotactic clause contrasts the number of speakers size of the population used in previous studies (33 speakers) with the larger number of speakers size of the population used in the article (86). This contrast is used by the author to highlight the size of his/her data, thus giving more validity to the outcome of the study.

Authors may also resort to hypotaxis to justify their methods of analysis by stating the purpose of their use, as can be seen in the following example:

(17)   Medical-Abs. 6
   $\alpha \rightarrow$ Logistic regression analyses were performed
   $x\beta \rightarrow$ to determine predictors of staff stress.

The pattern illustrated by example (17) is frequent in the methodology section and indicates some methodological rigour requiring the researcher to justify the methods used and to show the rationale behind their use. Being explicit about this issue helps authors strengthen the validity of their findings which follows from the appropriateness of the methods used.

The analysis of these examples shows, therefore, that hypotaxis is a structural resource that helps authors of abstracts achieve the communicative purposes of the genre through elaboration and enhancement. Although these two logico-semantic relations can be realized by the paratactic structural pattern, hypotaxis offers more verbal economy through the possibility of non-finite structures, which 'by dispensing with finite verb forms ... make the text or utterance more compact' (Chovanec, 2003: 52).

It must be noted, here, that the logico-semantic relationship can also be considered an important factor in determining the structural pattern. While in elaboration and enhancement hypotactic nexuses largely outnumber paratactic ones, with extension it is the opposite, as Table 8.5 shows.

Table 8.5 Distribution of tactic interdependency in the corpus according to logico-semantic relations.

| | Parataxis | | Hypotaxis | |
	Medical	Linguistics	Medical	Linguistics
Elaboration	1	3	12	31
Extension	34	15	2	0
Enhancement	2	4	41	50
	37	22	55	81

Table 8.5 shows that in case of extension, parataxis is more frequent, which goes against the general pattern found in the corpus. This illustrates intrastratal conditioning (Halliday, 2005: 48), where system-internal factors may play a role in conditioning the probabilities of structural choices (§8.2.5). In fact, rather than being conditioned by contextual factors, the probability of interdependency type in this case is conditioned by the logico-semantic choice, which is another entry in the system.

The high probability of parataxis in case of extension conforms with Nesbitt and Plum's (1988; reported in Halliday, 2005: 54) finding that 'If you choose "extending", then there is virtually no choice of taxis; we can treat this as "all extending are paratactic".' This can be explained by its correspondence to the traditional category of coordination. What is worth noting, however, is that the frequency of extension in the Medical sub-corpus is more than twice as high as that in the Linguistics sub-corpus. This leads the discussion to the second point that emerges from Table 8.4 above – that the Linguistics sub-corpus displays a higher probability of hypotaxis than the Medical sub-corpus.

The higher probability of parataxis in the Medical sub-corpus may be explained by the way results and discussions are presented in this discipline. Consider, for example:

(18) Medical-Abs. 43
    Conclusion:
        1 → (1) Intermittent pain is a major problem in patients with cancer,
        +2 → (2) NBP is a common but under-recognized form of cancer pain,
        +3 → (3) NBP is less defined and controlled than BP,
        +4 → (4) incident NBP accounts for 40% of all incident cancer pain,
        +5 → and (5) variable IP definitions and classifications make comparisons between studies difficult.

The enumeration of the results and conclusions in a paratactic clause complex, as illustrated by example (18), is a common pattern in the

Medical sub-corpus, where the abstract presents the results of the experiments and 'reports on all other significant observations' (Nwogu, 1997: 131). However, this enumeration in the form of a clause complex with paratactic nexuses, as illustrated by example (18), is not really different from example (19), the only difference being punctuation and the use of the conjunction 'and':

(19)   Medical-Abs. 22
       Conclusions:
       S → (1) Treatment with MP (10–20 mg/d) in advanced cancer is well tolerated.
       S → (2) S/E symptoms with MP appeared to improve spontaneously despite continued MP therapy.
       S → (3) Depression and fatigue improved at doses lower than those recommended in other clinical conditions.
       S → (4) MP improved depression and fatigue, and some secondary symptoms associated with them.
       S → (5) Methylphenidate (MP) appears safe when used in the treatment of depression and fatigue in advanced cancer.

Although grammatical integration exists in example (18), through the use of parataxis, it cannot be considered as tight as it is in the case of hypotaxis. Following Matthiessen's (2002: 44) 'cline of integration' ranging from 'a single event construed within a circumstantially expanded clause to completely distinct events construed within grammatically separate clauses, where the relationship between them has to be inferred: clause – hypotactic nexus – paratactic nexus – cohesive sequence: conjunctively marked – cohesive sequence: conjunctively not marked' (*ibid.*: 35), the higher frequency of paratactic nexuses in the Medical sub-corpus indicates a looser integration at the level of the clause complex than in the Linguistics sub-corpus. This is in conformity with the findings of §8.4.2 about clause simplexes being more frequent in the Medical sub-corpus.

Accordingly, although the Medical sub-corpus on the whole, displays a high frequency of hypotaxis determined by the abstract genre as a contextual factor, this probability is less important than in the Linguistics sub-corpus because of the interference of another contextual factor, that is discipline of research. This leads to the conclusion that the frequencies of structural choices in a text are the product of a number of contextual factors and that local probabilities can be estimated only if the interaction of these factors is taken into consideration.

8.5 Conclusion

This study has argued that contextual factors, namely the discipline of research and the RAA genre, affect the probabilities of choice of clause structure in the corpus. First, a significant correlation has been found between the discipline of research and clause structure (simplex versus complex), with the Medical sub-corpus displaying a higher probability of clause simplexes than the Linguistics sub-corpus. These varying probabilities have been explained by the differences between the two disciplines in their research methods and the reporting of their findings. Second, it has been shown that hypotaxis is more frequent in the corpus than parataxis and this high probability has been explained by the suitability of this type of interdependency to the characteristic features and communicative purposes of the RAA genre. The analysis has also revealed that, although the corpus as a whole shows a preference for hypotaxis, the two disciplines display varying probabilities, with the Medical sub-corpus having a higher frequency of parataxis than the Linguistics one. This has been explained by the looser grammatical integration which is displayed by the Medical abstracts and supported by the higher probability of clauses simplexes in that sub-corpus.

The findings of this study have a number of theoretical and methodological implications. At the theoretical level, this study provides further support to the claim that the System cannot be studied without reference to Text and Context; and that Text cannot be studied without reference to System on the one hand and Context on the other. This theoretical claim justifies the need for a conditional probabilistic approach as an appropriate methodological framework to approach – and get better insights into – both Text and System. In addition, the study of corpora representing two research disciplines has shown that the comparison of different registers may be a useful methodological tool to estimate local probabilities relevant to each register.

This study focused on the RAA genre and disciplinary variation as examples of contextual factors and the tactic system as an example of systemic choice, but future studies may be based on other academic genres (e.g. research articles, dissertations, review genres) to interpret the meaning of systemic choices instantiated in these texts. Such studies can provide further evidence to the conclusion of this study that a comparative conditional probabilistic approach is a methodological necessity for investigating the interaction between System, Text and Context.

Note

1. The notation used in the examples is based on Halliday and Matthiessen's (2004) system, that is Arabic numerals (1, 2, ...) for parataxis, Greek letters (α, β, ...) for hypotaxis, '=' for elaboration, '+' for extension, 'x' for enhancement, " for projection of a locution and ' for projection of an idea.

References

Charles, M. (2006) The construction of stance in reporting clauses: A cross-disciplinary study of theses. *Applied Linguistics* 27(3): 492–518.

Chovanec, J. (2003) The mixing modes as a means of resolving the tension between involvement and detachment in news headlines. *Brno Studies in English* 29: 51–66.

Day, R. (1993) *How to Write and Publish a Scientific Paper.* Cambridge: Cambridge University Press.

Eggins, S. (2004) *An Introduction to Systemic Functional Linguistics*, 2nd edn. London: Continuum.

Grinstead, C. M. and Snell, J. L. (1997) *Introduction to Probability.* Providence, RI: American Mathematical Society. Available at: www.dartmouth.edu/~chance/teaching_aids/books_articles/probability_book/book.html.

Halliday, M. A. K. (1994) *An Introduction to Functional Grammar.* London: Edward Arnold.

Halliday, M. A. K. (2005) *Computational and Quantitative Studies.* London/New York: Continuum.

Halliday, M. A. K. and Hasan, R. (1976) *Cohesion in English.* London: Longman.

Halliday, M. A. K. and Matthiessen, C. M. I. M. (2004) *An Introduction to Functional Grammar*, 3rd edn. London: Edward Arnold.

Halliday, M. A. K. and Webster, J. J. (2009) *Continuum Companion to Systemic Functional Linguistics.* London/ New York: Continuum.

Hasan, R. (2009) The place of context in a systemic functional model. In M. A. K. Halliday and J. J. Webster (eds) *Continuum Companion to Systemic Functional Linguistics* 166–189. London/New York: Continuum.

Hyland, K. (1999) Persuasion in academic articles. *Perspectives* 11(2): 73–103.

Hyland, K. (2004) *Disciplinary Discourses: Social Interactions in Academic Writing.* Ann Arbor, MI: University of Michigan.

Johns, A. M. (1997) *Text, Role and Context. Developing Academic Literacies.* New York: Cambridge University Press.

Manning, C. D. (2003) Probabilistic syntax. In B. Rens, J. Hay and S. Jannedy (eds) *Probabilistic Linguistics* 289–342. Cambridge, MA: MIT Press.

Matthiessen, C. M. I. M. (2002) Combining clauses into clause complexes: A multi-faceted view. In J. Bybee and M. Noonan (eds) *Complex Sentences in Grammar and Discourse: Essays in Honor of Sandra A. Thompson* 237–322. Amsterdam: John Benjamins.

Mulvaney, M. K. and Jolliffe, D. A. (2005) *Academic Writing: Genres, Samples and Resources*. New York: Longman.

Nwogu, K. N. (1997) The medical research paper: Structure and functions. *English for Specific Purposes* 16(2): 119–38.

Plum, G. A. (1998) *Text and Contextual Conditioning in Spoken English: A Genre-based Approach*, Monographs in Systemic Linguistics 10. Nottingham: Dept of English Studies, University of Nottingham. Available at http://functionaledit.com (accessed June 2009).

Punch, K. F. (2000) *Developing Effective Research Proposals*. London: Sage.

Sellami-Baklouti, A. (2011) The impact of genre and disciplinary differences on structural choice: Taxis in research article abstracts. *Text & Talk* 31(5): 503–23.

Swales, J. M. (2004) *Research Genres: Exploration and Applications*. Cambridge: Cambridge University Press.

Van Valin, R. D. and LaPolla, R. J. (1997) *Syntax: Structure, Meaning and Function*. Cambridge: Cambridge University Press.

Yudkin, B. (2006) *Critical Reading: Making Sense of Research Papers in Life Sciences and Medicine*. New York: Routledge.

9 Contentful and contentlight subject themes in informal spoken English and formal written English

Margaret Berry[a]

9.1 Preliminaries

9.1.1 Introduction

This chapter will report on part of a long term study which hopes to provide information which will be helpful to teachers of English.[1] The general purpose of the study is to gain a greater understanding of the differences between the informal spoken English that children grow up with and the formal English they will need to learn to write if they are to succeed in various careers.[2]

The study draws on the systemic functional linguistic (henceforth SFL) notion of Choice in language. I hope to discover which linguistic choices most distinguish between informal spoken English and formal written English, and which most make the difference between success and failure in each of these varieties.

The present focus of the study is on the Themes of clauses in these two varieties. What thematic options seem to lead to success in informal spoken English? What thematic options seem to lead to success in formal written English? Are the same thematic options valued in the two varieties? Or do the varieties have very different thematic needs? I will say more below about the precise form of thematic analysis I am using.[3]

---

a Margaret Berry, now retired, was Reader in English Language at the University of Nottingham, UK. She has published introductory books on systemic linguistics and articles on exchange structure, Theme and Rheme, register variation, and the application of systemic functional linguistics to the teaching of English. She has lectured in China, Australia and Canada, as well as in European countries.

9.1.2 The story so far

The investigation began with a study of children's writing (Berry, 1995). Since the research is eventually intended to be applied to children's writing, it seemed sensible to begin with an attempt to see what young children, or at least some children, found difficult in this variety. The texts studied were entries in a Grantham Schools' Writing Competition.[4] The groups of teachers with whom I discussed some of the entries thought that the child they judged to be the least successful of the ones discussed was writing as she would speak. I wanted to see if the Themes of her passage were contributing to this impression. Certainly her Themes were noticeably different from the Themes of the children whom the teachers judged to be more successful. So the next question was whether her Themes really were more like the Themes normally to be found in spoken English, while the Themes of the other children were more like the Themes normally to be found in written English. Since the children were writing about a place, Grantham, and its history, I first turned to texts in which adults were writing about places and their history and to texts in which adults were speaking about places and their history. The children were asked to write a passage suitable for inclusion in a guidebook to be published by a major motoring organization. Soon afterwards the RAC did in fact publish a guidebook which covered the Grantham area (Westacott, 1982), so this seemed a good place to start for the written part of the study. For the spoken part of the study, I turned to a book about the history of Wiveliscombe, the little town in Somerset where I grew up (Farrington *et al.*, 2005). As well as lots of writing about the town and its history, this book includes transcripts of interviews in which people volunteered to talk about the town and its history. My initial hypotheses were formulated on the basis of these early studies. I am now moving on to test my hypotheses in relation to other spoken registers and other written registers. I have also been considering radio news and sports bulletins. If spoken English and written English really do differ in their Themes, one might expect there to be problems when language is written but to be spoken, when there might well be a clash between the needs of the writing and the needs of the eventual hearers.

The rest of this chapter will mainly be about the RAC guide and Wiveliscombe history stage of the investigation, though it will be necessary briefly to revisit the Grantham children's writing to show how my thinking developed. I shall also say a little about more recent investigations and their early findings.

9.1.3 A brief note on aspects of the theoretical background to the work

Full discussion of the theoretical background to the work can be found in Berry (forthcoming). Briefly, the study is concerned with choices at two levels: semantic choices and contextual choices; semantic choices because meaning is something that teachers can relate to and also because I share the general SFL view that meaning is central to language, contextual choices because if language users are to choose appropriately from the semantic options available, they need to make decisions about the nature of the situations in which they find themselves.

Although not a central concern of the study, linguistic form plays a part in two ways. Meanings have to be realized by forms. And syntactic structure can provide a kind of map showing the locations of the meaning choices, that is showing **where** the meaning options become available.

I will first discuss some of the contextual choices that are relevant to my study and then move on to a few of the meaning choices that have emerged.

9.2 Some contextual choices

Halliday (e.g. 1978: 142–5) recognizes three main aspects of the context of situation: Field, Tenor and Mode. Hasan (1999: 232) provides discussion and recent glosses for these terms: Field is 'the nature of social activity' relevant to the language; Tenor is 'the nature of social relation' relevant to the language; Mode is 'the nature of contact for the conduct' of the language. In this chapter the focus will be on Mode. What relevance does the nature of the contact have to the success or otherwise of certain semantic options? In subsequent research, where formal written English is being compared with informal written English, Tenor distinctions, such as that between maximum social distance and minimum social distance, are clearly relevant.

9.2.1 Basic Mode choices

From Hasan's comparative tables (e.g. 1999: 244), it seems that the most basic Mode choices include the choice between spoken medium and written medium and the choice between phonic channel and graphic channel. At first I could not see the point of including both the medium choice and the channel choice, as they seemed to be dealing with the same aspect of context. However Hasan says (1999: 229–30) 'intended addressees will come in contact with the text through writing (what I have referred to technically as the *graphic channel*' (original emphasis). Does this mean that channel is from the point of view of the receiver of the text while medium is from the point of view of the producer? If so the distinction could be a useful one.

For most of the varieties of English included in my long-term study the context is *either* spoken medium from the point view of the producer and phonic channel from the point of view of the receiver *or* written medium from the point of view of the producer and graphic channel from the point of view of the receiver. In other words, not surprisingly, spoken medium usually goes with phonic channel and written medium usually goes with graphic channel. Certainly the context for the RAC guide is written medium and graphic channel, while the context for the interviews transcribed in the Wiveliscombe book was spoken medium and phonic channel.

However, the radio news and sports bulletins are written to be spoken. This means that from the point of view of the producer the medium is written, but from the point of view of the eventual receivers, the listeners, the channel is phonic. Analysing the context in this way, with this unusual combination of options, points up the difference between perspective of receivers and perspective of producer and suggests, as indicated above, that there may be a clash between the needs of the writing and the needs of the listening, this leading to problems. I shall in fact be discussing below one particular problem under this heading.[5]

9.2.2   A more active Mode choice

In Berry (forthcoming, §2.8) I suggested that speakers and writers had to make two kinds of choice in relation to the context: choices which had to do with recognizing the features of the context of situation in which they found themselves, choices, in other words, to do with how they construed the context of situation; and choices which had to do with whether they were going to go along with the situation as they had construed it or whether they were going to try to change the situation.

The choices between spoken and written medium and between phonic and graphic channel would seem to come under the first of these headings. Normally all that speakers and writers would have to do would be to recognize these features, and the construal choices they made would be so automatic that they would be likely to be completely subconscious. However, writers in a written medium + phonic channel situation, such as writers of radio news and sports bulletins, would need to make a further, more active – and so probably more conscious – choice: between simply writing as they would normally write, and adjusting their style to take account of possible difficulties of listeners. In effect their choice would be between: consider needs of hearers and ignore needs of hearers. How these options might be realized through the meaning options selected will be discussed below.

9.2.3   Unsuccessful choosing

The fact that these choices exist does not necessarily mean that people will always make the choices successfully.

The child whom teachers thought was writing as she would speak had presumably not yet acquired the choices between spoken medium and written medium and between phonic channel and graphic channel, or at least she had not yet acquired them sufficiently to enable her to implement them in her choices of meanings.

Many writers of radio news and sports bulletins seem totally unaware that they could adjust their styles to help their listeners. That broadcasters do not sufficiently consider the problems of listeners can be seen from the many complaints in articles and letters in *The Radio Times* (e.g. 3–9 July 2010, page 9; 17–23 July 2010, page 149; 26 Feb–4 March 2011, pages 142–3, to name but a few). Sometimes contributors to other publications join in. For instance a contributor to the *Sunday Telegraph*'s *Seven* magazine (6 March 2011, page 70) complains that she cannot make out what presenters are saying. She adds that she would have thought the point of speaking, especially for a presenter, was to make oneself understood.

9.2.4   A mini-network for Mode

If one hopes one's work will be useful in the classroom, it is important to keep one's networks as simple as possible.[6] Although I am well aware that other Mode distinctions may well become relevant as I continue with my work, I am for the moment restricting myself to the three systems I have discussed so far, as shown in Figure 9.1.

I assume that the MEDIUM system and the CHANNEL system are simultaneous, as either term from one system can be combined with either term from the other. As well as language written to be spoken, one can have language spoken to be written, as for instance when someone dictates letters into a dictaphone, although I am not at present investigating the latter variety.

The HEARERS system is dependent on the choice of written medium and phonic channel.

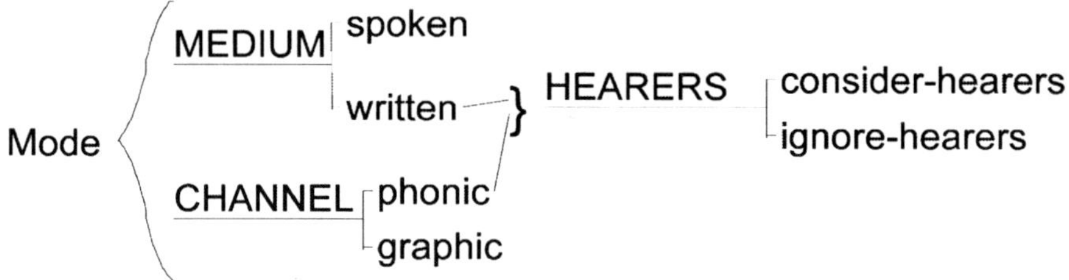

Figure 9.1 A mini-network for Mode.

9.3   Some meaning choices

This is where we come to the Thematic analysis. For the purposes of this study, I am assuming that the Theme of a clause is everything up to the main verb of the clause. (See Berry, 1996, especially pages 29–31, for discussion of other possible views of the extent of the Theme.)

There is room in this chapter only to discuss in detail one part of the Theme, the Syntactic Subject, what I called in my 1995 paper Basic Theme and what Fawcett (e.g. 2008: 182) calls Subject Theme. I will here use Fawcett's term. There is room here only to discuss in detail the Subject Themes of independent clauses, though brief mention will be made of the Subject Themes of other clauses (§9.3.6).

I said in §9.1.3 above that syntactic structure could provide the locations for meaning choices, so that one would know **where** the meaning options became available. This is the importance of the Syntactic Subject aka Subject Theme for my present discussion. It provides the location for the meaning choices I wish to discuss. I am assuming then that the Subject Theme represents a place in the surface syntactic structure, but I am going to discuss Subject Themes from the point of view of the meaning choices they make available. I am going to be particularly concerned with meanings in the sense of what the Subject Themes refer to.

I hope to work my way towards a distinction between contentful Subject Themes and contentlight Subject Themes, and to set up hypotheses about the likelihood of each occurring in spoken medium + phonic channel and written medium + graphic channel contexts respectively. I hope also to shed some light on the problems that occur when contentful Subject Themes are used in written medium + phonic channel contexts, in language written to be spoken.

It is important to emphasise that I shall be discussing content weight in terms of meanings, in terms of what the Subject Themes refer to. Halliday (1985) discusses lexical density, Biber *et al.* (1999) discuss informational density, which they associate, for instance, with a combination of nouns (*ibid.*: 590) and a combination of premodifiers (*ibid.*: 600–1), and Perera (1984: e.g. 292–3 and 315) writes of the difficulty children may have with syntactically complex Subjects. While these approaches are clearly relevant to what I am doing, the type of analysis I am proposing is in principle independent of these other forms of analysis.

9.3.1   The Subject Themes of the Grantham children's writing

I will here set out the Subject Themes of just two of the Grantham children. Child A was the child whose writing was judged by the teachers to be the least successful of the texts discussed at providing a passage suitable for inclusion in a guidebook. This was the child who was said to be writing as she would speak. Child C was one of the children judged by the teachers to be more successful at writing in a suitable style. The children's passages are printed in full and discussed more fully in Berry (1995).

Just a glance at Table 9.1 shows how much the texts of the two children differ in their Subject Themes. Perhaps the two most obvious differences are: (1) that Child A refers to herself – *I* – three times and to her readers – *you* – four times, while Child C does not use *I* or *you* at all; (2) that Child C refers to aspects of the discourse topic – Grantham itself and places and people associated with Grantham – in nine of her Subject Themes, while Child A does so only in two. Child A's such references are right at the end of her passage, while Child C's are evenly spaced throughout.

In the 1995 paper I termed Themes which referred to writer and reader (i.e. to interactants in the discourse) *Interactional Themes*. Themes which referred to aspects of the topic I termed *Informational Themes*.

This is already encouraging for the view that Child A is writing as she would speak, while Child C is more advanced in understanding the conventions of written language. Brown and Yule (1983) suggest that different varieties of English make use of thematic position in different ways. Conversational speech, they say, tends to thematize *I* and *you*, thus marking 'the interactional aspect' and giving 'a clear indication of the speaker's view of what he is using language to do' (*ibid.*: 143). This description seems to fit Child A's text. Certain types of written English, however, make use of the thematic position to identify 'the

Table 9.1 Subject Theme profiles of the children's writing.

Child A	Child C
I	Grantham
I	It
there	The parish church
There	[ell]
they	There
I	Dysart Park
there	it
There	There
You	Wyndham Park
They	It
there	Belvoir Castle and Belton House
You	The Angel Hotel
You	There
They	There
there	The Prime-Minister Margart Thatcher
they	[ell]
there	Grantham
He	a market
He	[ell]
The Prime Minister of Britan	There
she	
You	
Wyndham Park	
There	

[ell] indicates that a Subject Theme has been ellipted.
Spellings are as in the children's own writings.

writer's topic area' and 'the organisation of the paragraph' (*ibid.*: 141). Fries (1981) also recognizes the importance of thematic position for showing how a piece of writing is organized with respect to its topic. Child C has a clear method of development, as Fries calls it, using her Subject Themes to show how she is moving through the various aspects of her topic, Grantham.

What of the children's other Subject Themes, those that do not refer either to an interactant in the discourse or to an aspect of the topic? In the 1995 paper I simply termed all such Themes *neithers* and suggested that they represented a kind of pass option, where the writers had chosen not to use the thematic position to foreground any particular kind of meaning, either interpersonal or experiential. Sinclair and Coulthard (1975: 16) recommend that when setting up a descriptive framework one should include a 'ragbag' category. The *neithers* were in effect my ragbag category.

However, Sinclair and Coulthard make clear that this is only to be a temporary measure. If one finds oneself assigning a large proportion of one's texts to the ragbag, or if one feels 'uneasy about putting certain items together in the ragbag', then one's descriptive framework needs to be revised. As I proceeded with my analysis, this is precisely what happened. I was assigning far too many of the Subject Themes to the ragbag and I became aware that the *neithers* differed in kind.

The differences are in fact already observable in Child A's text. Most noticeable among the *neithers* are the existential *there*s, or as Downing (1990) prefers to call them the presentative *there*s. My teachers' groups criticized both Child A and Child C for overuse of *there*. Biber *et al.* (1999: 953) say that existential *there* is most common in conversation. They add that the number of *there*s in conversation 'is sometimes quite extreme'. This would seem to be one way in which neither child has yet moved from spoken mode to written mode. Perera (1984: 251) regards thematic variety as an indication of mature writing. Repetitive use of *there* would certainly not qualify.

Child A's Subject Themes also include those which, although vaguely to do with the topic, do not have any very precise referent. Two of her four *they*s are of this kind. In *They have a Belton golf corse and deer in it* and *they are building a sport centre beside it*, the *they*s have no precise antecedents. It is possible to guess more or less what is meant, but the meaning is imprecise.

A third type of *neither* is perhaps more problematic with regard to Child A's text. Do her *you*s really refer to her readers? Or do they have more general, and so again imprecise, reference? My teachers' groups were divided on this. Many of them thought that they did refer to the readers. Myself, I suspect that her *you*s are generic, especially when I compare Child A's *You can buy sweets lollys and ice cream* with the *you* of another of the Grantham children who wrote *For the keen golfers among you our town provides the Belton golf course*. The *you* of this other child seems clearly to refer to the readers. For the moment I will reserve judgement on Child A's *you*s, but generic uses of *you* may well be worth looking out for in the subsequent texts to be analysed.

One further type of distinction is relevant. I referred above to Child C's nine Subject Themes which referred to aspects of her topic and to Child A's two such Subject Themes. Strictly speaking Child C has three further Subject Themes which refer to aspects of her topic and Child A has five. But Child C's *its* and Child A's *hes*, *she* and *they*s (the two of her four *they*s that do have antecedents) are clearly different from the Subject Themes discussed earlier. They do not introduce *new* aspects of the topic into the discourse and so do not contribute to the displaying of a method of development.

Dik (1997) distinguishes between New Topic (NewTop), the first introduction of an aspect of a topic, Given Topic (GivTop), reference to an aspect of the topic that has already been introduced, and Resumed Topic (ResTop), reference to a topic that has already been introduced but some time ago so that it needs to be reactivated. Child C's *Belvoir Castle and Belton House* and *The Prime-Minister Margart Thatcher*, for instance, presumably refer to NewTops. Child C's three *its*, referring respectively to Grantham, Dysart Park and Wyndham Park, are presumably referring to GivTops. The second of Child C's Subject Themes to refer to Grantham as a whole, nearly at the end of her passage, is presumably referring to a ResTop.

In my 1995 paper I drew on Brown and Yule's (1983: 173) three-way distinction between New (= NewTop?), Current (=GivTop?) and Displaced (=ResTop?). Dik's terms are more transparent, at first sight at least, and have led to further work in Functional Grammar. However it should be said that I am here using a very much simplified version of Dik's approach. For full discussion of the work of Dik and his successors, see Butler (2003: 61–101). For the purposes of this chapter, I shall assume that any Subject Theme which consists of a third person pronoun and has an antecedent is referring to a GivTop. I shall assume that any Subject Theme which consists of a noun/nominal group and is referring to an aspect of the discourse topic which has been mentioned before is referring to a ResTop. Any other Subject Theme that refers to an aspect of the discourse topic I shall assume is referring to a NewTop.

So far then the options that Subject Themes offer for referential meanings are:

1. no reference – the presentative *there*s;
2. imprecise reference – the *they*s without antecedents and the generic *you*s;
3. interactional reference – reference to interactants in the discourse;
4. informational reference – reference to aspects of the discourse topic.

The fourth category can be subdivided into:

a. reference to a GivTop;
b. reference to a ResTop;
c. reference to a NewTop.

The options that mainly characterize Child A's text are (1), (2), (3) and (4a). The options that mainly characterize Child C's text are (1) and (4), particularly (4c).

A system network for these options is shown in Figure 9.2. I am currently trying to draw my networks for meaning options in such a way that in each system the option that I hypothesize will be more successful in spoken English is placed above the option that I hypothesize will be more successful in written English. (See Berry, forthcoming, §3.5 for discussion.)

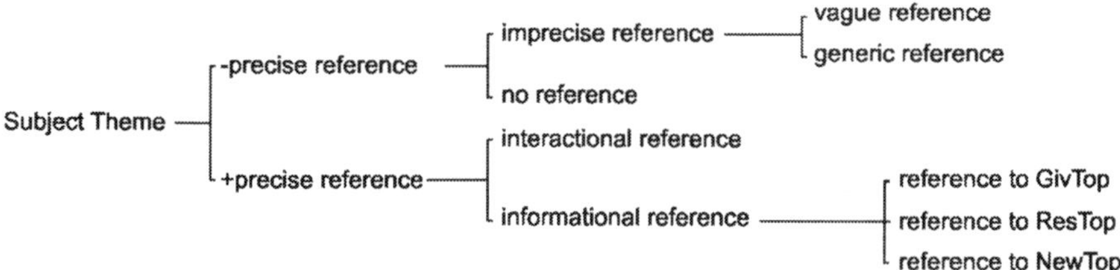

Figure 9.2 A network showing referential meaning options for Subject Themes.

9.3.2 The Subject Themes of the interview transcripts

The texts here are taken from S.M. Farrington and the Wiveliscombe Book Group (2005) *Wiveliscombe: A History of a Somerset Market Town.* Sue Farrington, the lead author and researcher, talked with long-term residents of the town, recorded the conversations, and transcribed the bits she found interesting for inclusion in the book. Some of the transcribed passages are very short. I have chosen four of the longer passages to analyse. Another factor that influenced my choice was the topic – I chose passages whose topics I had some knowledge of in case there should be problems of interpretation.

These profiles resemble that of Child A's passage in that they offer only slight clues to the subject matter and even slighter clues to the way in which the subject matter is organized. Speaker 1's *most of the cloth* is a faint indication of the fact that she is describing her work as a mender at Fox's Woollen factory in the early 1950s. Speaker 2 makes it clear that he is speaking about his apprenticeship and the first three Subject Themes show a form of organization, but one could not guess that his apprenticeship was as a grocer at Ellerton Stores or that he moves from general discussion to a detailed account of what he had to do to a side of bacon.[7] Speaker 3's *Freddy Berry* would be a clue to elderly and

Table 9.2 Subject Theme profiles of the interview transcripts.

Speaker 1	Speaker 2	Speaker 3	Speaker 4
I	My first years apprenticeship	You [g]	We
most of the cloth	the second year	you [g]	There
you [g]	the third	you [g]	there
You [g]	I	There	they [v]
you [g]	I	You [g]	their gun
you [g]	[ell]	Freddy Berry	he
I	You [g]	he	We
	you [g]	You [g]	it
	you [g]	That	the bullets
	you [g]		
	you [g]		
	they [v]		
	You [g]		
	you [g]		
	you [g]		
	They [v]		
	It		
	everybody		

[ell] indicates that a Subject Theme has been ellipted.
[v] stands for vague and indicates that a *they* has no precise antecedent.
[g] indicates a generic use of *you*.

middle-aged Wiveliscombe people that he is talking about tailors. The connection is such that when I go back to Wiveliscombe and people hear that my name is Berry I am still often asked if I am any relation to the tailors who used to be in the middle of Church Street. (Freddy Berry was in fact my uncle.) Speaker 4's *their gun* and *the bullets* are clues to the fact that this is an account of a gun battle during World War II. Wiveliscombe was under the flight path of bombers on their way to South Wales and on one occasion a local searchlight crew engaged one of the bombers. (I actually witnessed this event. Aged 3. I'm told I said 'Look at the pretty lights Mummy.')

The most noticeable thing about these profiles is the large number of *you*s – 17 out of a total number of 43 Subject Themes. And all of them are generic uses of *you*, or something resembling a generic use. This time there is no ambiguity – the *you*s cannot be referring to the addressee, the interviewer, as she was not around in Wiveliscombe at the time being described. When Speaker 1 says *You had to look at the material over a* *bar and see the flaw, then you would mark it with a piece of white chalk* etc., she doesn't mean that her addressee had to do these things, or even that people in general had to do these things. She means that she and her fellow eleven menders at Fox's Woollen Factory had to do these things, but she is giving her remarks a universal application. Scheibman (2002: 79) also found generic uses of *you* as Subject in her study of spoken American English.

Biber *et al.* (1999: 331) comment that when *you* is used with reference to people in general it still tends to 'retain a tinge' of its basic meaning. It is almost as if Speaker 1 is inviting her addressee to imagine herself back into the past in Speaker 1's own situation, so that the *you*s can refer to her. Thus the *you*s retain some of their interactional meaning even though they cannot literally refer to the addressee. The same would apply to Speakers 2 and 3, who also use generic *you*s.

Biber (2010: 188) reports on a study (Reppen, 1994) of elementary student written registers. Among the features that commonly occurred were second person pronouns. From the example that Biber gives it looks as if these had generic reference: *If you wanted to watch TV a lot you would not get very much done.* If Child A's *you*s really were generic *you*s, it would appear that she is not alone in importing this feature into her school written work.

What of the other Subject Themes in the Wiveliscombe interview transcripts? There are three examples of presentative *there*, perhaps rather fewer than might have been expected from the remarks of Biber *et al.* quoted above, and three examples of *they* without a precise antecedent. Speaker 2 has an indefinite pronoun *everybody* which I would also want to regard as having imprecise reference. (Speaker 2 does not literally mean 'everybody'.) Speaker 1's passage and Speaker 2's passage each have two *I*s referring to the speaker, while Speaker 4 has two *we*s referring to the speaker and her family. This means that 30 of the 43 Subject Themes realize the options that I originally classed as *interactional* or *neithers*.

Of the others, five refer to GivTops and there is one example of ellipsis which implies a GivTop. This leaves only seven of the 43 to be candidates for the status of referring to NewTops: *most of the cloth, My first years apprenticeship, the second year, the third, Freddy Berry, their gun, the bullets.* As I have shown, these do give a faint indication of the subject matter of their respective texts, but none contribute to indicating a clear sustained method of development.

Hopefully what I mean by contentful and contentlight is beginning to emerge, though I shall not be attempting precise definitions of these terms until after I have discussed the guidebook texts.

9.3.3   The Subject Themes of the guidebook texts

Table 9.3 Subject Theme profiles of the guide book texts.

Writer 1 Grantham	Writer 1 Lincoln	Writer 2 Gloucester	Writer 2 Worcester
Grantham	Lincoln	The ancient cathedral city, with many splendours	The county town of the merged shires of Hereford and Worcester
it	the Romans	The cathedral, of monastic origins	it
Much of its peace	It	the whole complex of buildings	The pedestrianized High Street
it	the old Roman city	William the Conqueror	The cathedral
The church of St Wulfram	much of the Roman work	Bishop Hooper's Lodging	Timber frame shops, an art gallery and museum
It	One of the towers, known as Cobb Hall	Beatrix Potter's *Tailor of Gloucester*	The canal
the best parts	[ell]	The docks	The lovely river front
There	The iron rings to which the prisoners were chained	Bits of Roman and Medieval Gloucester	the view of the cathedral
It	executions	the A417	Lady Huntingdon Chapel
There	other features	The Cotswold Way Walk	There
The Grantham Museum, St Peter's Hill	Work	the Severn	A good place to walk around, it
	a fire in 1141	Telford's bridge	Spetchley Park, 3 miles east on the A422
	further work		The race course
	it [p.t.]		Lower Broadheath
	The glories of this edifice		west on the B4204
	One [g]		There
	Others, notably		
	Simon of Thirsk		
	his particular masterpiece, the Angel Choir		
	It		
	[ell]		
	The City and County Museum, Broadgate		
	The Usher Art Gallery, Lindum Hill		
	The Royal Lincolnshire Regimental Museum, Sobraon Barracks, Burton Road		

[ell] indicates that a Subject Theme has been ellipted.
[g] indicates a generic pronoun.
[p.t.] indicates a predicated theme.

The Grantham passage and the Lincoln passage have been taken from Hugh Westacott (1982) *Going Places: East Midlands*, an RAC publication. This book seemed an obvious choice in view of the instruction given to the children (see §9.1.2 above). Since I did not wish to be dependent on the style of just one author for my observations, however, I have also taken passages from a companion volume: Kenneth Lindley (1982) *Going Places: Central England*, also an RAC publication. Many of the places discussed warrant only short entries. I have chosen two of the longer entries to analyse, those for Gloucester and Worcester.

The first thing to note about the Subject Themes of these passages is that, in contrast with the Subject Themes of the spoken passages, they include no references to writer or readers, no vague *they*s without antecedents, no generic *you*s (though the Lincoln passage includes one instance of the generic pronoun *one*). The Grantham passage and the Worcester passage each have two instances of presentative *there*. This means that only five (if we include the generic pronoun *one*) out of a total of 61 Subject Themes are realizing options which I originally termed interactional or neithers. This compares with the 30 out of 43 Subject Themes that realized interactional or neither options in the spoken texts.

Although alike in that the vast majority of their Subject Themes refer to aspects of their topics, the two writers differ in other ways. Writer 1's Subject Themes include more references to GivTops – four out of 11 in the Grantham passage, and four (if one includes the two ellipses which imply GivTops) out of 23 in the Lincoln passage. (The other *it* in the Lincoln passage is the anticipatory *it* of a predicated theme.) Writer 2's Subject Themes have no references to GivTops in the Gloucester passage and only two out of 15 in the Worcester passage. Even here the second of Writer 2's *it*s is preceded by an appositional phrase *A good place to walk around*, so that new material is being introduced in the Subject Theme even though the headword refers to a GivTop.

Writer 2 seems to share Child C's view that the general pattern should be to use the Subject Themes to introduce new or resumed aspects of the discourse topic and then to use the rest of the clauses to say something about these aspects. This means that, like Child C, Writer 2 in both his passages has clear methods of development.[8]

Writer 1, in the Grantham passage, gives little more clue to his method of development than Child A. (He differs from Child A in that his Subject Themes include no references to interactants in the discourse, no vague *they*s without antecedents, no generic *you*s). In the Lincoln passage his early Subject Themes make clear that he is discussing Roman aspects of the city and his last three Subject Themes follow the pattern of introducing new aspects of the topic which are to be commented on in the rest of their clauses. But, in between, the method of development is much less clear. Although the Subject Themes refer to aspects of the topic, a number of them are rather vague – for example, *other features, Work, further work.* In general, in the middle section of the Lincoln passage, Writer 1 seems to prefer to introduce new aspects of the topic, particularly important aspects of the topic, after the verb. Probably the most important new aspects of the topic to be introduced in this middle section are the castle and the cathedral. These are introduced as follows: *much of the Roman work was plundered by the Normans to build the castle* and *other features fade into insignificance beside Lincoln Cathedral.*

There seems to be some room for variation in guidebook writing then, particularly over the matter of whether important NewTops are to be introduced in the Subject Theme or after the verb. Writer 2 prefers to introduce them in the Subject Theme. Writer 1 sometimes follows this pattern, as at the beginning and end of the Lincoln passage, but on other occasions prefers to introduce them after the verb.

However, the main purpose of this chapter is to compare formal written English with informal spoken English, so it is worth repeating what the Subject Themes of the two writers have in common, which distinguishes them from the Subject Themes of the spoken passages. The Subject Themes of the independent clauses of the written passages include no references to interactants, no vague third person pronouns without antecedents, no instances of generic *you*. Overwhelmingly, the Subject Themes of the written passages refer to aspects of the discourse topic and, except in the Grantham passage, the vast majority of these refer to NewTops or to ResTops rather than to GivTops.[9]

9.3.4   Contentful versus contentlight Subject Themes

It may eventually be possible to establish a cline of contentweight for Subject Themes. However for the moment I shall assume that a Subject Theme is contentful if it refers to a NewTop or a ResTop, but contentlight if it does not so refer. NewTops clearly advance the subject matter of their texts by introducing new material. ResTops do not introduce new material, but give indications of a new attention to old material. NewTops and ResTops can combine to indicate methods of development.

The hypotheses are:

1. that a majority of Subject Themes will be contentful in formal written texts;
2. that a majority of Subject Themes will be contentlight in informal spoken texts.

As we have seen, Hypothesis 2 is supported by all four of the spoken texts analysed. Hypothesis 1 is supported by three out of the four adult written texts. Clearly further research is necessary to see to what extent the guidebook Grantham passage is typical or untypical of formal written English in general.

Even allowing for this exception, there still seems to be a strong association between contentful Subject Themes and formal written English and between contentlight Subject Themes and informal spoken English. The overall figures for the Subject Themes of the independent clauses of the eight adult texts are: written texts – 45 contentful to 16 contentlight Subject Themes; spoken texts – 7 contentful to 36 contentlight Subject Themes.

It is perhaps worth pausing to consider *why* contentful Subject Themes seem to be particularly suitable for formal written English, while contentlight Subject Themes seem to be particularly suitable for informal spoken English.

Biber *et al.* (1999: 597), attempting to explain why premodifiers are 'most common in written expository registers' but 'relatively rare in conversation', say that the use of premodifiers is 'certainly very efficient, packing dense informational content into as few words as possible'. Maybe a similar motivation can be ascribed to the use of contentful Subject Themes in formal written English. There certainly seems to be a general view that written English should be as economical as possible in its use of words. Maybe contentlight Subject Themes in written English could be regarded as wasting words; every part of a clause should be used to convey the maximum amount of content, the part before the verb as well as the part after it.

Why then does the same not apply in informal spoken English? Why do contentlight Subject Themes seem to be preferable? It should be remembered that, by my definition, interactional Subject Themes, the neithers and now the GivTops, all count as contentlight Subject Themes. It is easy to see why interactional Subject Themes should be valued in informal spoken English. As shown in the earlier quotation from Brown and Yule (1983: 143), this is what conversationalists think spoken language is all about – themselves, their interlocutors and the interaction between them. But do the interactionals have anything in common with the neithers and the GivTops?

Biber *et al.* (1999: 792) also say 'This dense packing of information into noun phrases and prepositional phrases is not possible with the real-time production constraints of conversation, nor would these lengthy prepositional phrases be easy for hearers to process'. Biber *et al.* are concerned with the processing of syntactically complex constructions. I am concerned with different types of referring expression. It is perhaps self-evident that references to NewTops would take more processing than references to GivTops. GivTops can be assumed to be already in the hearer's mind as they have just been mentioned in the text. (More so than ResTops which have to be retrieved from longer ago.) References to interactants are here similar to references to GivTops – the interactants in a discourse can also be assumed to be present in each others' minds, certainly in conversation.[10] Presentative *there*s are easy to process for a different reason – they don't refer to anything. When it comes to *they*s with no antecedents, it is perhaps necessary to distinguish between processing by analysts and processing by ordinary language users. In Speaker 4's text it took me a long time to work out that *they* and the *their* of *their gun* referred to the operators of the searchlight. But it wasn't until I started to analyse the text that I tried to work this out. When I first read the transcript as an ordinary reader of the book, I just assumed that these were the usual vague references of spoken English and simply read over them. Vague *they*, in particular, seems to function like presentative *there* – it fills a grammatical slot, but its importance from the point of view of meaning is simply to signal that something more important is following. And I don't suppose that conversationalists really care whether a *you* is generic or refers to an addressee.

If, then, the Subject Themes of spoken English are contentlight, this gives the conversationalists regular rests which enables them to recoup their energies ready for the more challenging references likely to occur after the verbs. This is not necessary in written English. Subject Themes, however contentful, stay still on the page so that readers can take as long as they need to assimilate their references.

9.3.5 Contentful Subject Themes in radio news and sports bulletins

If there is this difference between what usually happens in written English and what usually happens in spoken English, what about contexts in which language is written to be spoken, contexts characterized in §9.2.1 as written medium from the point of view of the producer, but phonic channel from the point of view of the listeners? Is there a clash between the two perspectives?

In fact Subject Themes in radio news and sports bulletins are often difficult to hear. If the Subject Themes are contentlight, as usual in spoken language, this doesn't matter in the slightest. But if the writer writes contentful Subject Themes, as usual in written language, it matters very much. Should the writer continue to write normal written English? Or adjust in the direction of spoken English to take account of listeners' difficulties?

I recently failed to hear the Subject Themes in the following:

(1)   *? wants to return to women's tennis*
(2)   *? have been killed in a helicopter crash in Afghanistan*
(3)   *? has just arrived in Iraq*

Each left me wondering: who?

In a paper to the European International Systemic Functional Congress in Cardiff in July 2009, I presented eight such examples. In fact they occur practically every time I turn on the radio.

Discussions with friends suggest that I am not alone in having this problem. Also, a complaint was recently read out on the UK's Radio 5 Live breakfast programme. The complaint was about the travel news. As I understood it, the complainer said that the places where there were traffic problems were mentioned first and not repeated. The complainer failed to hear them and so was left knowing that there were traffic problems but not knowing where the problems were. It does seem to be difficult to hear the beginnings of clauses in radio bulletins. (The Subject Themes in travel news bulletins often seem to be names of roads – the M1, the M25, etc.)

The problem seems to be that newsreaders use the unmarked intonation pattern for a clause. For Halliday, in the unmarked case, a clause coincides with a tone-group and the unmarked pattern for a tone-group is for there to be a tonic prominence preceded by a stretch which is intonationally not very prominent. Sometimes for newsreaders this intonationally not very prominent stretch is so lacking in intonational prominence that it disappears altogether. Halliday associates the tonic prominence with new information and the not so prominent stretch with given information. However it is important to recognize that for Halliday given information is information which is *presented* as given and new information is information which is *presented* as new by the intonation as just described.

This is different from the GivTops and NewTops of Dik which I have been discussing, these being *actually* given or new, according to whether or not they have already been mentioned in the text. (For detailed discussion of Halliday's views, see Halliday and Matthiessen, 2004: 87–92.)

If the unmarked intonation pattern is used for a clause with a contentlight Subject Theme, this is fine. The intonation is presenting as given something which is actually given or, for some other reason, is easy to process or doesn't really matter at all, as described in §9.3.4. However if the unmarked intonation pattern is used for a clause with a contentful Subject Theme, then the intonation is presenting as given something which is not actually given and something which does matter because it is something the listeners need to hear.

Complainers tend to blame the newsreaders. A number of the complaints mentioned in §9.2.3 seem to be about inappropriate use of intonation, together with accusations that newsreaders don't seem to understand what they are reading. I wonder, however, if news*writers* could do more to help their newsreaders and, through them, their listeners.

One possibility might be to make their Subject Themes more like the Subject Themes of spoken English. For instance, the news item of (2) above appeared in a later bulletin in the form:

(2b) *there has been a helicopter crash in Afghanistan in which ten American soldiers have been killed*

Here, the presentative *there* Subject Theme allowed all the important information to occur later where it could be heard. The missing information from (1) was provided later in a trailer in the form:

(1b) *we'll hear from Kim Clijsters on her return to the sport*

with an interactional Subject Theme again allowing the important information to occur later.

I had to wait until the next day's papers to find out that the missing information from (3) was Hillary Clinton.

(1b) and (2b) decrease the amount of content in the Subject Theme. Another possibility might be to go in the opposite direction and increase the content of the Subject Theme as longer Subject Themes tend to attract separate tone-groups.[11] This was the case in:

(5) *Hollywood actress Elizabeth Taylor has died ...*

where the separate tone-group meant that the Subject Theme was perfectly audible. This structure would have worked well in the Hillary Clinton example also.

There is indeed a clash then between the practices of written English and the needs of the listener, but the problems could be resolved if writers were more aware of what the clash involved.

9.3.6 Are the options under discussion special to the Subject Theme?

Fries (2008: 9) warns against considering the Theme in isolation from other parts of the clause, as there is a risk that one will assume something is particularly characteristic of the Theme when the characteristic is in fact shared with other parts of the clause. This chapter is mainly about the Subject Themes of independent clauses, but in this section I will briefly consider, from the point of view of the options I have been discussing, dependent clauses and parts of clauses other than the Subject Theme.

Two questions seem particularly relevant: Are any of the options I have been discussing exclusive to the Subject Theme? If not exclusive, is it the case that any of the options are more frequently chosen in the Subject Theme than anywhere else?

The presentative *there* option would seem to be exclusively an option offered by the Subject Theme. One cannot imagine a presentative *there* occurring anywhere else but in the Subject slot.[12]

In the texts discussed here, vague *they* without antecedent also seems exclusive to the Subject Theme. Speaker 2 has one vague *they* outside the Subject Themes of the independent clauses, but that vague *they* occurs as the Subject Theme of a dependent clause. I have not found in these texts any instance of a third person pronoun without antecedent that is not occurring as a Subject Theme.

First and second person personal pronouns in these texts are very nearly exclusive to the Subject Theme. All Child A's first and second person pronouns occur as Subject Themes. Child C does not have any first or second person pronouns in the Subject Themes of her independent clauses, but she does have two *yous*, ambiguous between reference to readers and generic reference, which occur as Subject Themes of dependent clauses. All but one of the first and second person personal pronouns in the spoken texts occur as Subject Themes. In addition to those which are the Subject Themes of independent clauses, there are two *yous* and an *I* which occur as Subject Themes of dependent clauses. The one exception is that Speaker 2 has an *us* which occurs outside the Subject Theme. The guidebook texts do not have any first or second person personal pronouns in the Subject Themes of their independent clauses, but the Gloucester passage has a *you* and the Lincoln passage has a *we*, both probably generic, both of which occur as the Subject Themes of dependent clauses.

The position with regard to the first and second person personal pronouns is as I have just described. However it should be noted that the spoken passages include one possessive pronoun *mine*, two instances of the possessive adjective *my*, and one instance of the possessive adjective *our*. These are outside the Subject Themes of their clauses. However, even if one adds to these the one *us*, it still means that by far the largest number of first and second person pronouns in the spoken passages occur as Subject Themes, 26 occurring as Subject Themes, only 5 not doing so. There are no instances of first or second person possessives in the written texts.

It cannot be claimed of course that the choice between NewTop, ResTop and GivTop is exclusive to the Subject Theme, but it does seem to be in the Subject Theme that there is the greatest difference between spoken texts and written texts from this point of view (the guidebook Grantham passage being the exception here). NewTops frequently appear as the referents of Subject Themes in the written texts, but only rarely in the spoken texts. There is no such contrast in other parts of the clause. After the verb NewTops appear as the referents of nominal groups equally happily in spoken texts and written texts. (Even though Writer 2 has so many NewTops occurring as Subject Themes, he also has plenty of NewTops introduced after his verbs.)

9.4   Conclusions

From the evidence of the texts discussed here, there does seem to be a difference between informal spoken English and formal written English with regard to the referential meaning options chosen in their Subject Themes. The difference is not clear-cut, but there does seem to be a strong tendency for the Subject Themes of informal spoken English to realize contentlight options and for the Subject Themes of formal written English to realize contentful options.

The difference seems to be related to the differing thematic needs of the two varieties. This comes out particularly clearly in the radio bulletins, language written to be spoken, where there seems to be a clash between the needs of the writing and the needs of the hearing. The writers need to write compactly in order to compress as much information as possible into a short space. But the listeners need the information to be presented in such a way that they can hear it and understand it.

I have said that my general purpose is to gain a greater understanding of the differences between the informal spoken English children grow up with and the formal English they will need to learn to write if they are to succeed in various careers. If the texts discussed here turn out to be representative, it seems that children learning to write formal English will need to learn to suppress what seems to be the most natural way of communicating – foregrounding themselves and their readers in their texts. They will also need to learn to avoid vague references and to moderate their use of presentative *there*. Instead they will have to learn to make use of their Subject Themes in a more contentful manner.

However, the texts discussed here amount to only a very small amount of data. I am now moving on to look at other spoken texts, in particular examples of mother–child discourse and child–child discourse, and other written texts, in particular examples of business writing, news writing and academic prose. So far the texts analysed support even more strongly than the texts discussed here the hypotheses (1) that a majority of Subject Themes will be contentful in formal written English and (2) that a majority of Subject Themes will be contentlight in informal spoken English. For instance, in the mother–child discourse I have analysed so far, I have found only one Subject Theme referring to a ResTop and none at all referring to a NewTop.

In spite of the new work it remains the case that I have looked at only a small amount of data. The research must continue.

Notes

1.   I am grateful to Chris Butler, Ben Clarke, Ruqaiya Hasan, Hilary Hillier and the editors of this volume for discussing with me relevant issues even before the chapter reached first draft stage. I am also grateful to those who read the first draft and provided helpful comments: Chris Butler again, Geoff Thompson, Peter Fries. Of course I alone am responsible for any errors or misrepresentations.
2.   For discussion of the importance of including in education the kinds of writing that would enable children to enter the workforce, see Martin (1985).
3.   Biber and his colleagues have provided a great deal of information on the differences between these varieties (e.g. Biber 1988, 2010; Biber *et al.* 1999) and I shall be referring to these in what follows. But as far as I am aware they have not investigated the thematic differences. The term *Theme* does not

    appear in the index of Biber *et al.* (1999). They do discuss 'fronting' (*ibid.*: 900–911), but only briefly, and not in the way in which I shall be discussing Theme.

4. I was persuaded to be one of the judges for this competition by being told that afterwards I could have the entries for teaching and research. I am grateful to the children and to the competition organizers, also to Ron Carter for putting me in touch with the teachers' groups with whom I discussed the passages and to the members of those groups.

5. Gregory (1967) recognized language written to be spoken as an important Mode option.

6. For discussion of system networks and the notation used in them, see Halliday (forthcoming, especially Figures 2, 3, 4, and 5 and the discussion surrounding them. Or, for an introductory account, see Berry (1975, chapters 8 and 9). Also see Berry (forthcoming, §3.5). For assistance in drawing system networks by computer, I am grateful to Chris Butler and to Mick O'Donnell's UAM CorpusTool.

7. Speaker 2 does indicate that he is moving to talk about the bacon, but he does so by means of a preposed theme aka left dislocation, not by a Subject Theme. A number of other passages transcribed in the Wiveliscombe book also make use of this feature, though not the other three analysed here.

8. Many of Writer 2's Subject Themes are more ornate than those of Child C, containing more premodification and postmodification. Such Subject Themes could be regarded as lexically dense, informationally dense and syntactically complex as well as contentful. See the introduction to §9.3.

9. A look at other entries in the East Midlands guide suggests that the Grantham passage may be untypical of Writer 1's work. Although his Subject Themes do not refer to NewTops or ResTops as consistently as Writer 2's, there is usually a higher proportion of NewTops and ResTops to GivTops than in the Grantham passage. For instance, the entry for Belvoir Castle has seven NewTops and three GivTops, the entry for Buxton has five NewTops, two ResTops and two GivTops, the entry for Derby has five NewTops, two ResTops and four GivTops.

10. See Butler (2003: 82) for discussion of this point.

11. I am grateful to Chris Butler for drawing my attention to this point.

12. Biber *et al.* do regard presentative *there* as the grammatical Subject, though they use the term 'notional subject' (Biber *et al.*, 1999: 946) for the phrase after the verb that is introduced by the *there*.

The sources of the texts analysed

Farrington, S. M. and the Wiveliscombe Book Group (2005) *Wiveliscombe: A History of a Somerset Market Town.* Wiveliscombe: Colden Publications.

Lindley, Kenneth (1982) *Going Places: Central England*. London: RAC.
Westacott, Hugh (1982) *Going Places: East Midlands*. London: RAC.

References

Berry, M. (1975) *An Introduction to Systemic Linguistics: I. Structures and Systems*. London: Batsford.

Berry, M. (1995) Thematic options and success in writing. In M. Ghadessy (ed.) *Thematic Development in English Texts* 55–84. London: Pinter.

Berry, M. (1996) What is Theme? A(nother) personal view. In M. Berry, C. S. Butler, R. P. Fawcett and Guowen Huang (eds) *Meaning and Form: Systemic Functional Interpretations. Meaning and Choice in Language: Studies for Michael Halliday*, Advances in Discourse Processes, Vol. LVII 1-64. Norwood, NJ: Ablex Publishing Corporation.

Berry, M. (forthcoming) Towards a study of the differences between formal written English and informal spoken English. In L. Fontaine, T. Bartlett and G. O'Grady (eds) *Systemic Functional Linguistics: Exploring Choice*. Cambridge: Cambridge University Press.

Biber, D. (1988) *Variation across Speech and Writing*. Cambridge: Cambridge University Press.

Biber, D. (2010) Corpus-based and corpus-driven analyses of language variation and use. In B. Heine and H. Narrog (eds) *The Oxford Handbook of Linguistic Analysis* 159–91. Oxford: Oxford University Press.

Biber, D., Johansson, S., Leech, G., Conrad, S. and Finnegan, E. (1999) *The Longman Grammar of Spoken and Written English*. London: Longman.

Brown, G. and Yule, G. (1983) *Discourse Analysis*. Cambridge: Cambridge University Press.

Butler, C. S. (2003). *Structure and Function: A Guide to Three Major Structural-Functional Theories. Part II: From Clause to Discourse and Beyond*, Studies in Language Companion Series, vol. 64. Amsterdam/Philadelphia, PA: John Benjamins.

Dik, S. C. (1997) *The Theory of Functional Grammar. Part I: The Structure of the Clause*, 2nd edn, K. Hengeveld (ed.). Berlin/New York: Mouton de Gruyter.

Downing, A. (1990) The discourse function of presentative *there* in existential structures in Middle English and present-day English: A systemic functional perspective. *Occasional Papers in Systemic Linguistics* 4: 103–25.

Fawcett, R. P. (2008) *Invitation to Systemic Functional Linguistics Through the Cardiff Grammar: An Extension and Simplification of Halliday's Systemic Functional Grammar*, 3rd edn. London: Equinox.

Fries, P. H. (1981) On the status of theme in English: Arguments from discourse. *Forum Linguisticum* 6: 1–38. Reprinted 1983, in revised form, in J. S. Petöfi and E. Sözer (eds) *Micro and Macro Connexity of Texts* 116–52. Hamburg: Helmut Buske.

Fries, P. H. (2008) The textual metafunction as a site for a discussion of the goals of linguistics and techniques of linguistic analysis. In G. Forey and G. Thompson (eds) *Text Type and Texture: In Honour of Flo Davies* 8–44. London: Equinox.

Gregory, M. J. (1967) Aspects of varieties differentiation. *Journal of Linguistics* 3: 177–98.

Halliday, M. A. K. (1978) *Language as Social Semiotic: The Social Interpretation of Language and Meaning.* London: Edward Arnold.

Halliday, M. A. K. (1985) *Spoken and Written Language.* Victoria: Deakin University Press. Reprinted Oxford University Press 1989.

Halliday, M. A. K. (forthcoming) Meaning as choice. In L. Fontaine, T. Bartlett and G. O'Grady (eds) *Systemic Functional Linguistics: Exploring Choice.* Cambridge: Cambridge University Press.

Halliday, M. A. K. and Matthiessen, C. M. I. M. (2004) *An Introduction to Functional Grammar,* 3rd edn. London: Edward Arnold.

Hasan, R. (1999) Speaking with reference to context. In M. Ghadessy (ed.) *Text and Context in Functional Linguistics,* Current Issues in Linguistic Theory 169, 219–328. Amsterdam/Philadelphia, PA: John Benjamins.

Martin, J. R. (1985) *Factual Writing: Exploring and Challenging Social Reality.* Victoria: Deakin University Press. Reprinted Oxford University Press 1989.

Perera, K. (1984) *Children's Writing and Reading.* Oxford: Blackwell.

Reppen, R. (1994) Variation in elementary student writing. PhD dissertation, Department of English, Northern Arizona University.

Scheibman, J. (2002). *Point of View and Grammar: Structural Patterns of Subjectivity in American English Conversation,* Studies in Discourse and Grammar, vol. 11. Amsterdam/Philadelphia: John Benjamins.

Sinclair, J. M. and Coulthard, R. M. (1975) *Towards an Analysis of Discourse: The English Used by Teachers and Pupils.* London: Oxford University Press.

□ 10

The differential patterned occurrence of ellipsis in texts varied for contextual mode: Some support for the 'mode of discourse-textual metafunction' hook-up?

Ben Clarke[a]

10.1 Introduction

One of the principal concerns for truly functional approaches to language study, that which largely sets them apart from more formal-oriented traditions, must be due consideration of some wider social context within which language is not incidentally couched. Some have commented that the 1960s marked a turning point in the discipline of linguistics in the European tradition, away from the formal approaches, questions and methodologies and towards functional ones (McGregor, 2009). Putting any claims of the demise of formal linguistics on ice, certainly a plethora of work from functional perspectives has been conducted in the last four decades of linguistics research. The influence of the ethnomethodological tradition on linguistic methodology, the predominance of text and discourse as the unit of analysis and the data, methods and even philosophical opportunities afforded by the field of computerized corpus linguistics are just a few notable trends in linguistics over this period.[1]

a   Ben Clarke is a Teaching Fellow in English Language at the University of Leeds, UK. In 2012, he completed his PhD at Cardiff University, subjecting SFL's long assumed 'context-metafunction hook-up' hypothesis to its first large-scale quantitative exploration based on naturally occurring data. His primary research interests are: the relationship between language and context, functional approaches to grammar, reduced/contracted clausal structures, descriptions of language as patterned social behaviour, and the interaction of the language modality with embodied semiotic systems.

Yet for all this interest in relating language to social context, there exists little in the way of agreement regarding the territory involved and no over-arching theoretical or descriptive framework to assist the exploration. What, for example, do we take to be the relevant contextual phenomena, given our primary interest is in language? What theoretical abstractions do we need to make sense of these contextual phenomena and, particularly, their relation to language phenomena? Some scholars may well take issue with the formalism this implies. For example, corpus-driven corpus linguists like Sinclair (1991) and Tognini-Bonelli (2001) argue in favour of resisting the temptation to invoke abstractions for linguistic description unless they are irrefutably necessary given the demands of the language data at hand. Yet systemic functional linguists would not be among those against the aforementioned formalism, seeing several starting theoretical premises as elucidating in the practice of linguistic description. The need for a theory of context incorporated explicitly within the linguistic theory is shared ground for systemic functional linguists. What is largely lacking, however, is the analytical work to test the descriptive adequacy of the initial descriptions of context which have been proposed in systemic functional linguistics.

What follows here is a report of the present author's attempts to test the relationship between language and context as it is theorized in systemic functional linguistics. After §10.2 offers a few more detailed remarks regarding the nature of context and its relation to language in the systemic functional approach, §10.3 explains the detail of the analytical project conducted with a particular focus on methodological matters. §10.4 presents the results of the analysis of the same project foregrounding the most prominent of these in the context of the present discussion. §10.5 summarizes the significance of the results discussed in the previous section and contextualizes them in a critical reflection on both the specific project under discussion here and, more generally, in respect of the present state of understanding regarding the relationship between language and context.

10.2 Providing the context: The relationship between language and context in systemic functional linguistics

The goal of the present section is to detail in a very brief way the approach taken in systemic functional linguistics to account for the relationship between language and context. To do so comprehensively would require a discussion of the practice of linguistic description in systemic functional linguistics *per se*, as well as each of the theoretical abstractions involved. Such theoretical discussions are not the primary goal of this chapter and consequently space does not allow for such an approach. Context itself is considered a semiotic, not material, construct in systemic functional linguistics. That is, the contextual phenomena relevant to a theory of language are those implicated in the enactment of linguistic meanings. Contextual phenomena constitute a higher order of abstraction than even the most abstract linguistic phenomena.

Systemic functional linguists hold a hypothesis regarding the relationship between context and language. The hypothesis under discussion is the consequence of combining two theoretical abstractions which systemic functional linguists take to be fundamental in the process of linguistic description. These are 'metafunction' and 'realization'. The former is based on Halliday's (1967–8) theorizing that, when language is modelled with paradigmatic primacy formalized in the system, three clusters of systems are apparent: experiential, interpersonal and textual. That is, systemic distinctions within any one cluster are highly interdependent; yet systemic distinctions between any two clusters are highly independent. Realization is implied by the fellow theoretical abstraction of 'stratification'. Phenomena at different levels of abstraction are said to largely mirror each other. The existence of such a relationship between two explicit linguistic levels has now long been established. For example, one system of choices at the semantic level tends to be realized by a particular system of choices at the lexicogrammatical level. According to systemic functional scholars, such a relationship is also, more controversially, said to pertain between the level of semiotic context and those linguistic levels which are said to be metafunctionally-diversified: the semantic and lexicogrammatical levels. Specifically, systemic functional linguists make a predictive claim of the relationship between context semiotically-perceived and linguistic meanings and structures. Some systemic functional linguists (e.g. Hasan, 1995; Thompson, 1999) have labelled this prediction the 'context-metafunction hook-up hypothesis' (henceforth CMHH). The CMHH reads as follows:

Three parameters of semiotic context bear a direct relationship to three metafunctions such that:

1. the occurrence of experiential meanings and structures explains and is to be explained by the social action of the text – the 'field of discourse' contextual parameter;

2. the occurrence of interpersonal meanings and structures explains and is to be explained by the relationships pertaining between inter-locutors involved in the text – the 'tenor of discourse' contextual parameter;
3. the occurrence of textual meanings and structures explains and is to be explained by the symbolic form the text takes – the 'mode of discourse' contextual parameter.

Different systemic functional scholars commit to a stricter or weaker interpretation of the CMHH (Thompson, 1999: 106). This is a matter of one's view of the exclusivity of these three specific predictions of the CMHH. Is it the case that interpersonal meanings might also explain and be explained by contextual considerations at the 'field of discourse' and 'mode of discourse' parameters, for example? Those subscribing to a strict deterministic reading would argue not, whereas those taking a probabilistic reading would say that other contextual considerations in addition to those at the tenor parameter are required to fully explain the occurrence of interpersonal meanings. This point shall be returned to briefly in the final section of this chapter.

10.3 Data, method, analytical project: Patterns of ellipsis in text

This section outlines the methodology of the wider analytical project (Clarke, 2012) on which the present chapter reports. As should now be clear, the remit of the analytical project is to test the validity of systemic functional linguistics' theorizing of the relationship between language and context as formalized in the predictions of the CMHH. How is such a vast hypothesis to be tested within the confines of the project in question? One fairly evident, data-driven approach which makes it possible to operationalize and test the CMHH's claims is to take some linguistic phenomenon which operates at one of those metafunctionally diversified strata – i.e. the lexicogrammar and the semantics – and study its occurrence in datasets of text which satisfy the following criteria:

1. different datasets are principally varied in the contextual parameter correlating to the linguistic phenomenon under study as predicted by the CMHH (see points 1–3 of the CMHH, above);

2. each individual dataset is consistent in the same contextual parameter;
3. all datasets are consistent in the remaining two contextual parameters.

Ellipsis, for example, is said to be a textual phenomenon in metafunctional terms (Halliday and Hasan, 1976: 29; Halliday, 1977: 202; Halliday, 1985a: 35–6; Matthiessen, 1995: 158). The CMHH would predict, therefore, that it is those contextual matters at the 'mode of discourse' parameter – the role which language is playing in the text's context (Halliday, 1985b: 12) – which will explain ellipsis's occurrence. Indeed, this was precisely the approach taken and the phenomenon adopted in Clarke (2012). A null and alternative hypothesis can, therefore, be stated thus:

Null hypothesis: the occurrence of ellipsis in different datasets is neither significantly different nor patterned, but purely chance; there is no support for the CMHH;

Alternative hypothesis: the occurrence of ellipsis in different datasets is either significantly different or patterned or both; there is support for the CMHH.

But how, more specifically, should datasets be designed to reflect variation within the 'mode' parameter of context? Given that it is the systemic functional description of mode which is to be tested, the blueprint for the dataset design should be its description in the theory in question. Here problems are encountered, for, firstly, descriptions at the context stratum are in their infancy in systemic functional work and, secondly, the few descriptions which do exist attest differences in their detail. Again, space here prohibits any detailed discussion of issues which are covered at length in Clarke (2012). Briefly, though, as the two most detailed published systemic functional descriptions of matters at the mode parameter of context, there is a significant degree of correlation between Hasan's (1985) and Martin's (1992) accounts. Most importantly, both claim that matters at the mode parameter are derivable from broadly the same two fundamental considerations:

1. the relationship and therefore semiotic distance between the language of the text and the social action of the communicative event; and
2. the spatio-physical contact, both in quantitative and qualitative terms, possible between addressee(s) and addresser(s) of the text.

As well as sharing a significant amount, their mode descriptions do disagree in some of the finer details and, seemingly, Hasan's position on contextual mode has since changed (Hasan, 1999, 2009). For this reason among others, Martin's (1992) systemic description of mode was adopted to inform the dataset – and so methodological – design of the project.

Figure 10.1 displays Martin's (1992: 520) description of mode:[2]

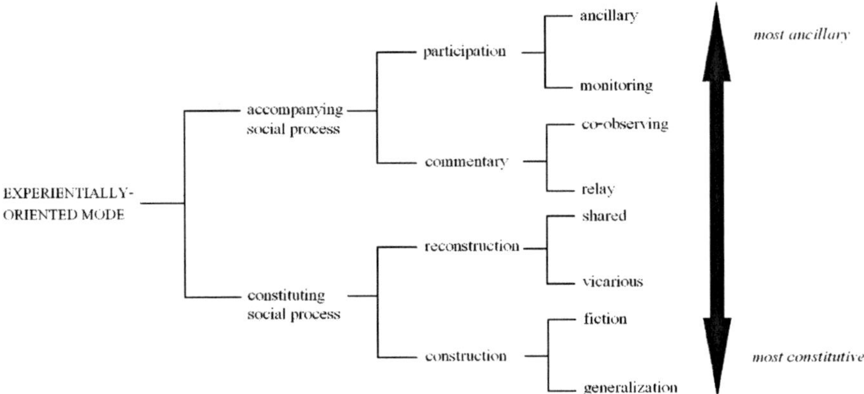

Figure 10.1 Martin's experientially-oriented mode system as the blueprint for dataset design in the current project.

With a map of the territory involved, finalizing the methodology becomes a matter of finding natural language data that satisfy the aforementioned design criteria. That task has both qualitative and quantitative demands and in many respects the two are in competition. The qualitative requirements boil down to the fundamental matter of how accurately the data collected represents the characteristics it is intended to; in this project, contextual attributes stated in systemic functional terms. This important aspect of corpus representivity will be reserved until the discussion section for reasons which will there become obvious. In quantitative terms, a compromise had to be struck between providing enough data for any dataset representing any particular mode value such that it would lead to statistically valid analytical observations and representing a range of different modes as different datasets such that some semblance of a continuum of modes was constituted by the entire dataset. Four datasets to represent four different modes following Martin (1992: 520) – see Figure 10.1 again – were compiled with the benefit of comparably convenient access to the data. Table 10.1 summarizes the selection of data for datasets standing for principally varied modes but consistent fields and tenors.

Table 10.1 The contextual design attributes of the dataset.

	Corpus	Field	Tenor	Mode
	TV football commentary	Oral transmission:[3] specialized: recreational	Status: unequal; Contact: distant; Affect: unmarked	Accompanying: commentary: co-observing
	Radio football commentary	Oral transmission: specialized: recreational	Status: unequal; Contact: distant; Affect: unmarked	Accompanying: commentary: relay
	Guardian 'joy of six' editorial	Oral transmission: specialized: recreational	Status: unequal; Contact: distant; Affect: unmarked	Constituting: reconstruction: shared
	Football newspaper reports	Oral transmission: specialized: recreational	Status: unequal; Contact: distant; Affect: unmarked	Constituting: reconstruction: vicarious

The leftmost column is labelled, vertically: ancillary ←-------→ constitutive

In summary of this section and the methodology it promotes to enable the analytical project under discussion, then, the research question under discussion is:

Do patterns of ellipsis observed in datasets of text which are varied along the contextual parameter of 'mode of discourse', but are otherwise in contextual identity, support the predictions of the 'context-metafunction hook-up' hypothesis?

10.4 Patterns of ellipsis across contextual mode varied datasets

The next three sub-sections report the results of the central analytical work of the wider project and therefore constitute the mainstay of the present chapter. Table 10.2 gives the size, in word count, of each of the datasets as described in the last section.

Table 10.2 Size of sub-corpora in words.

Corpus	Edited size in words
Newspaper reports	50,220
Joy of six	50,918
Radio commentary	12,102
TV commentary	10,081

10.4.1 The occurrence of ellipsis *per se*

In this section, the most general result with respect to the research question is considered. That is, how many cases of ellipsis occur in each of the four datasets? It is a calculation which treats ellipsis as one homogenous phenomenon and does not, therefore, acknowledge ellipsis types or any of the typological variables relevant to ellipsis. A simple raw figures frequency calculation of this result does not appear particularly revealing with respect to the differential occurrence of ellipsis in the four corpora (see Table 10.3).

Table 10.3 Total number of instances of ellipsis by corpus.

Corpus	*Instances of ellipsis*
Newspaper reports	244
Joy of six	227
Radio commentary	269
TV commentary	304

Ellipsis occurs most often in the two commentary corpora and least often in the 'joy of six' corpus. Yet this initial interpretation of the analysis, a raw figure calculation, is largely short-sighted. As stated above (Table 10.2), there is much less data in the 'radio commentary' and 'TV commentary' corpora than in the other two corpora. The reason for this is that these two commentary datasets were collections of spoken language and the analysis of such data is usually far more labour intensive than the analysis of its written equivalent. This means that to render a result which allows for comparison, the figures need to be normalized. The figures for 'instances of ellipsis' in the 'newspaper reports', 'joy of six' and 'radio commentary' corpora are therefore normalized downwards for comparison with the ten-thousand word 'TV commentary' corpus. Table 10.4 shows the results for 'instances of ellipsis' by corpus.

Table 10.4 Total number of instances of ellipsis by corpus based on the analysis of 10,000 words of each dataset.

Corpus	*Instances of ellipsis*
Newspaper reports	49
Joy of six	45
Radio commentary	222
TV commentary	302

Note: All figures are rounded up/down to a whole number.

Now the figures are comparable, a trend certainly does seem to be apparent. Its significance to the research question is fairly evident. It suggests some degree of support for the predictive strength of the 'mode of discourse – textual metafunction' strand of the CMHH following Martin's (1992) systemic description of mode, as a visual representation of this normalized result in bar graph form further emphasises (see Figure 10.2).

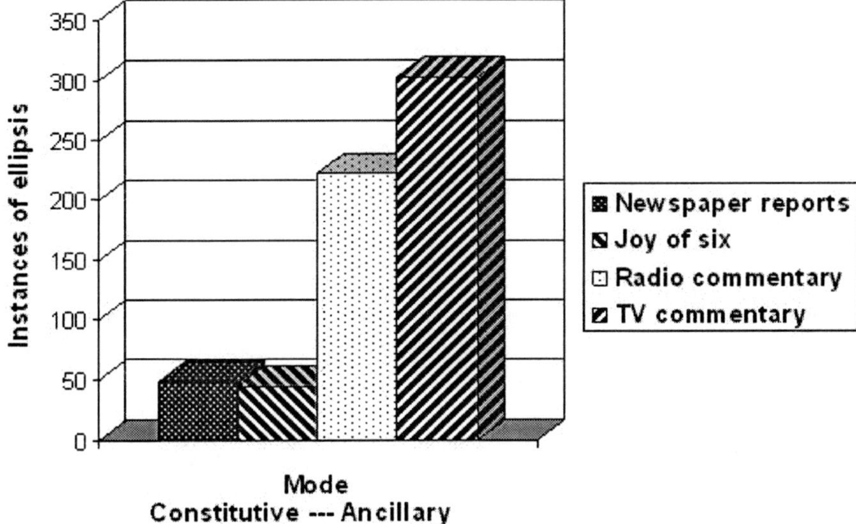

Figure 10.2 Instances of ellipsis by corpus based on the analysis of 10,000 words of each dataset.

Specifically, Figure 10.2 suggests the following trend: the more ancillary a text's context, the more cases of ellipsis it attests. Conversely, the more constitutive a text's context, the fewer cases of ellipsis it attests. There is, of course, one exception to this and it is that the 'joy of six' corpus attests fewer cases of ellipsis than the 'newspaper reports' corpus despite the present method's claim that the former represents a more ancillary contextual mode than the latter (see Table 10.1). This anomaly aside, the occurrence of ellipsis appears to be responsive to those aspects of contextual mode under study.

There is, however, reason to compute a further, third calculation on these results. While the two previous calculations are absolute figure calculations, this third one is actually a calculation of frequency. The two previous calculations differ from a true frequency calculation which requires the assumption of truly comparable environments. It might at first be thought that this was precisely the purpose of normalizing the datasets in terms of size by word count. But this step is not sufficient to claim comparable environments between the different datasets when exactly what is being counted in the analysis of the present analytical project is taken into consideration.

Table 10.5 presents the average word length of clauses in each dataset.

Table 10.5 Average length of clause for each corpus.

Corpus	Average length of clauses in words
Newspaper reports	10.61
Joy of six	17.83
Radio commentary	7.52
TV commentary	7.54

Note: All figures are rounded up/down to two decimal places.

The ellipsis of, say, a clause's Subject can only happen in any given corpus as many times as there are clauses; not as many times as there are X amount of words. That is, if there are one hundred clauses in a corpus, Subject-only ellipsis can only occur a maximum of one hundred times. If two datasets contain a vastly different number of clauses – even if they are the same size in their total number of words – then the one with more clauses is, other things being equal, likely to attest more cases of ellipsis. In sum, ellipsis is a matter of the clause, not of some arbitrary number of words. A frequency calculation of ellipsis, therefore, should be made by calculating ellipsis's occurrence per X number of clauses in any dataset. Doing so rules out potentially confounding variables which contribute to the average clause length in some dataset. Table 10.6 below calculates the 'instances of ellipsis' per one-hundred clauses for each dataset and therefore indicates ellipsis's frequency in the aforementioned corpora.

Table 10.6 Frequency of ellipsis by corpus, calculated per one hundred clauses.

Corpus	Instances of ellipsis per 100 clauses
Newspaper reports	5.16
Joy of six	7.95
Radio commentary	16.71
TV commentary	22.74

Note: All figures are rounded up/down to two decimal places.

As before, this can also be represented visually in bar graph form as Figure 10.3 shows.

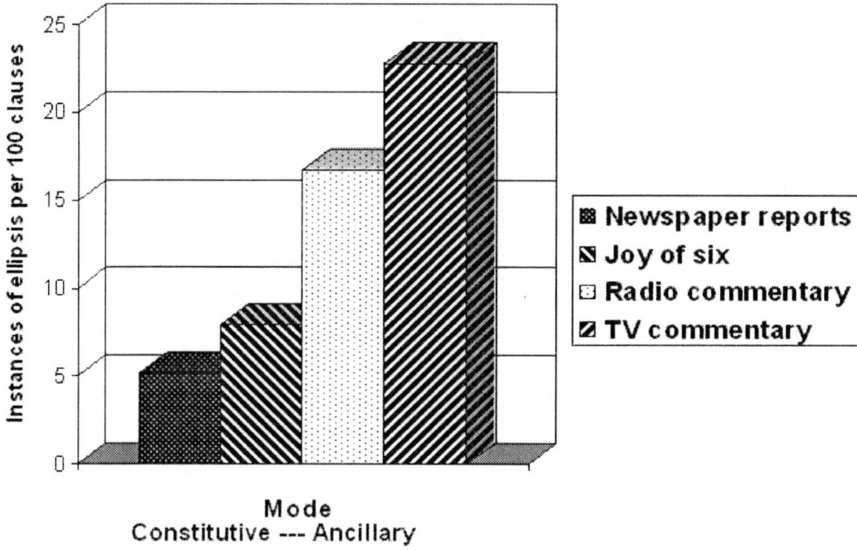

Figure 10.3 Frequency of ellipsis by corpus calculated per one hundred clauses.

The results of this reinterpreted, 'frequency' calculation of 'instances of ellipsis by corpus' are important. They offer even greater support for the CMHH following Martin's (1992) systemic description of 'mode' than the earlier Table 10.4 and Figure 10.2 do. The linearity of the trend of 'instances of ellipsis' which the CMHH would predict is now abided by in its entirety; that is, without the 'joy of six' anomaly revealed in Figure 10.2. It is important to make one further observation. Calculating 'instances of ellipsis' on the basis of analysed corpora normalized by word count (Table 10.4 and Figure 10.2) shows an evident difference in the occurrence of ellipsis between, on the one hand, the 'newspaper reports' and 'joy of six' corpora and, on the other, the 'radio commentary' and 'TV commentary' corpora. But those calculations suggest little difference between the partner datasets of each of the aforementioned pairs. One conclusion which might be drawn from such a result is that there is a difference between the two pairs of corpora which is a variable of importance in the occurrence of ellipsis far outweighing any apparent differences between the partners of either of the pairs of datasets. One such powerful explanatory variable might be, for example, the distinction between spoken and written language. This is indeed a difference in evidence between the two commentary corpora and the 'newspaper reports' and 'joy of six' corpora. Moreover, it has long been assumed that the 'spoken–written' distinction is an overriding factor in the occurrence of ellipsis (Biber *et al.*, 1999; Quirk *et al.*, 1985). Thompson (1999; personal communication) has even suggested the aforementioned distinction largely engenders the possibility of ellipsis in the first place. However, the reinterpretation of the results as a matter of frequency, calculated per one hundred clauses, casts doubt on such arguments. The re-interpretation validates semiotic distinctions, the basis of Martin's (1992) 'mode' description and therefore the blueprint of the dataset design here. Such semiotic distinctions are then seen as equally relevant to material ones, such as 'spoken versus written', in the occurrence of ellipsis. That is, when ellipsis is considered a matter of frequency, the differences between each of the four datasets are reasonably uniform along the implied 'ancillary-constitutive' continuum. This aspect of the above result suggests Martin's (*ibid.*) 'ancillary-constitutive' continuum has some basis for theorizing the relationship between language and context, at least where the textual metafunctional phenomenon of ellipsis is concerned.

The most 'general' result as discussed in this section suggests important support for the predictive strength of the CMHH following Martin's (*ibid.*) systemic description of 'mode'. But what about the results of the analysis of more specific types of ellipsis? Do they corroborate the support for the CMHH which the results of this section appear to offer? Or do they offer no such support and, under such a scenario, should we consequently reinterpret the 'significance' of the present section's results?

10.4.2 Patterns in the occurrence of functional-structural types of ellipsis

In this section, the analysis of 'functional-structural' types of ellipsis is under discussion. What is meant by 'functional-structural type of ellipsis' is the functional-structural elements – Subject, Operator, Main Verb, etc. – which have been omitted through the processes common to ellipsis in any instance of the phenomenon. A functional-structural type of ellipsis might be the predictable omission of a single element or the omission of a combination of more than one such element. The combination of more than one functional-structural element omitted through a process of ellipsis should be recognized as one complex functional-structural type of ellipsis, not simultaneously one instance of several single element functional-structural types. Below are examples to illustrate some of these functional-structural types of ellipsis. These are drawn from the data presently under discussion. The emboldened clause is the one attesting the instance of ellipsis in question. Ellipted elements are re-inserted in curved parentheses and therein the element's functional structural role indicated in squared parentheses.

Subject-only ellipsis:
- *... but Jo lost his footing **and (he [S]) shot tamely at Jussi Jaaskelanien ...;***
- *Matt Busby was a particular fan, **and (he [S]) would often take his Manchester United side up north to play in hotly contested friendlies***

Subject+Operator ellipsis:
- *He was neat and tidy **and (he [S] was [O]) determined to get forward at every chance;***
- *He would stroll up **and, with his body leaning back like a broken Subbuteo player, (he [S] would [O]) simply caress the ball with the instep ...;***

Operator+Main Verb ellipsis:
- *How would United respond? **And (how [A]**[4] **would [O]) Rooney (respond [M]) for that matter;***
- *he's gone past one **and the striker (has [O] gone [M]) by another***

Main Verb-only ellipsis:
- *Some things came off, **some didn't (come off [M]);***
- *...if you come at the king, you best not miss. **Zico certainly didn't (miss [M])***

Table 10.7 presents the number of instances of each functional-structural type of ellipsis by the corpus in which they appear.

Table 10.7 Instances of all functional-structural ellipsis types classified by corpus.

Functional-structural type of ellipsis	*Newspaper reports*	*Joy of six*	*Radio commentary*	*TV commentary*
S-only	159	118	109	130
S+O	19	12	23	22
S+O/M	23	39	59	58
S+O+M	5	7	9	10
S+O/M+C	2	3	6	9
S+O+M+C	4	3	10	16
S+O+M+C+C	–	3	3	2
S+M	5	6	8	9
S+M+C	4	4	9	12
S+M+C+C	–	2	2	1
S+C	–	1	–	–
O-only	–	2	–	1
O/M	11	3	12	16
O+M	1	–	3	2
O/M+C	–	1	–	1
O+M+C	–	1	–	–
M-only	6	7	8	6
M+C	1	8	3	2
C-only	4	7	5	7

Many of these functional-structural types of ellipsis will receive only incidental further comment owing mostly to their infrequent occurrence in the data, which consequently restricts the validity of any conclusions which may be drawn from them. The following two results comprise the main focus of this section:

1. the occurrence of 'Subject-only' and 'Main Verb-only' ellipsis types; and
2. the occurrence of potentially clausal functional-structural types of ellipsis such as 'Subject + Operator/Main Verb' and 'Subject + Main Verb' types.

Drawing conclusions on the basis of raw figure data such as that given in Table 10.7 is not particularly useful for the reasons detailed in the last section. The occurrence of ellipsis *per se* was measured on the basis of a frequency 'per one hundred clauses' statistical measure so as to rule out likely confounding cross-corpora differences – such as the size of corpus and the average clause length – and consequently offer comparable calculations. The present section's consideration of functional-structural types of ellipsis is likewise calculated on the basis of comparable calculations by measuring the occurrence of functional-structural types in a particular corpus as a percentage of all instances of ellipsis in that corpus. This statistical selection may cloud analytical trends which would be revealed by other calculations. However, the statistical calculation by proportional occurrence per corpus highlights several particularly pertinent results relative to the present research question.

'Subject-only' ellipsis, by far the most frequent functional-structural type of ellipsis in all four corpora (see Table 10.7), accounts for the proportions of all cases of ellipsis in each of the four corpora shown in Table 10.8.

Table 10.8 The proportional occurrence of Subject-only ellipsis by corpus calculated as a percentage.

Corpus	*The proportion of S-only ellipsis as a % of all functional-structural types by corpus*
Newspaper reports	65.12
Joy of six	51.97
Radio commentary	40.51
TV commentary	42.75

Note: All figures are rounded up/down to two decimal places.

There is an apparent trend here, namely: the more constitutive a text's context, the greater the proportion of its instances of ellipsis that are of the 'Subject-only' type, with the exception that the 'TV commentary' corpus has a higher proportion of 'Subject-only' ellipsis than the 'radio commentary' corpus. Note that this trend is in the reverse direction to that observed in the last section for the occurrence of ellipsis *per se*. Arguably, the same trend is in evidence when we consider the proportional occurrence of 'Main Verb-only' functional-structural ellipsis across the four corpora (see Table 10.9).

Table 10.9 The proportional occurrence of Main Verb-only ellipsis by corpus calculated as a percentage

Corpus	*The proportion of M-only ellipsis as a % of all functional-structural types by corpus*
Newspaper reports	2.46
Joy of six	3.08
Radio commentary	2.97
TV commentary	1.97

Note: All figures are rounded up/down to two decimal places.

The proportional occurrence of 'Main Verb-only' ellipsis reveals a trend in line with the 'constitutive-ancillary' continuum of mode such that the more constitutive a text's context, the more cases of 'Main Verb-only' ellipsis. However, the calculated proportional occurrence of 'Main Verb-only' ellipsis in the 'newspaper reports' corpus leaves a question mark against the reality of this trend, as do the small numbers of instances of Main Verb-only' ellipsis observed in the dataset (see Table 10.7 above), upon which the figures of Table 10.9 are calculated.

It is more difficult to know just what importance and conclusion to draw from such a functional-structural ellipsis type trend than it was to do the equivalent in respect of the frequency of occurrence of ellipsis *per se*. For one thing, why the observed direction in the trend for 'Subject-only' and 'Main Verb-only' types? Why not the reverse direction which would have been in keeping with the trend of the occurrence of ellipsis *per se* by corpus? Certainly, as proportional percentage calculations, some types must be more frequent with corpora whose texts have a more constitutive context. But why these specific types, particularly given the large raw figure instantial numbers of the former which validates the observed trend in statistical terms? Is, perhaps, the trend currently under discussion actually a consequence of some other more primary result;

for example, the fact that more ancillary texts attest a greater range of different functional-structural types of ellipsis (cf. Table 10.7 above)? What seems to be clear is that there is a trend roughly reflecting the linearity of the 'constitutive-ancillary' continuum of 'mode', even if the reasons for why this is so appear initially difficult to determine.

Let us turn to the second result under discussion in this section. If a certain subset of functional-structural types of ellipsis is recognized, a further trend in line with the 'constitutive-ancillary' continuum of 'mode' can be observed. The following functional-structural types can be grouped together as being, potentially, examples of 'clausal ellipsis' (Halliday and Hasan, 1976: 196–225; Halliday, 1994: 318–21):

> 'Subject + Operator / Main Verb'
> 'Subject + Operator + Main Verb'
> 'Subject + Operator / Main Verb + Complement'
> 'Subject + Operator + Main Verb + Complement'
> 'Subject + Operator + Main Verb + Complement + Complement$_2$'
> 'Subject + Main Verb'
> 'Subject + Main Verb + Complement'
> 'Subject + Main Verb + Complement + Complement$_2$'

By 'clausal ellipsis' (*ibid.*) it is meant that the elliptical structure – that which has been omitted through the processes common to ellipsis – is the entirety of clause elements, adjuncts (grammatical optional elements) aside. Such adjuncts are things like markers of polarity, modality and circumstance. Examples like the emboldened turns of the following invented exchanges would, therefore, be classed as cases of 'clausal ellipsis':

- [A] *Are you going out tonight!?*
  [B] **Probably**;

- [A] *When are you travelling to Cardiff?*
  [B] **Tomorrow**
  [A] *Are you sure?*
  [B] **Yes!**

The proportional occurrence of the aforementioned functional-structural types, potentially instances of clausal ellipsis, are given in Table 10.10. Again, the proportional figures are given as percentages by corpus. The table lists these calculations for each individual functional-structural type. The final 'total' row calculates all occurrences of all potential 'clausal ellipsis' types as a proportion of all cases of ellipsis in that corpus.

Table 10.10 The proportional occurrence of 'clausal ellipsis'.

Functional-structural type of ellipsis	Newspaper reports	Joy of six	Radio commentary	TV commentary
S+O/M	9.42	17.18	21.93	19.08
S+O+M	2.05	3.08	3.35	3.29
S+O/M+C	0.82	1.32	2.23	2.96
S+O+M+C	1.64	1.32	3.72	5.26
S+O+M+C+C	–	1.32	1.12	0.66
S+M	2.05	2.64	2.97	2.96
S+M+C	1.64	1.76	3.35	3.95
S+M+C+C	–	0.88	0.74	0.33
Total	**17.63**	**29.5**	**39.41**	**38.49**

Table 10.10 appears to indicate a trend such that the more ancillary a text's context, the more likely the occurrence of clausal ellipsis. The evidence of this trend corresponds fairly closely to the linearity of the 'constitutive-ancillary' continuum and suggests that clausal ellipsis, therefore, is responsive to the role of language in text. There is, however, a caveat to give in considering this trend. Some examples of some of the types included as **potential** types of clausal ellipsis might not actually have an elliptical structure which is a clause.The emboldened co-ordinated clause of the following invented case of 'Subject + Operator + Main Verb' ellipsis, for example, is not a case of clausal ellipsis as it does not attest the intransitive sense of 'live'.

- *I've lived abroad **and (I [S] have [O] lived [M]) in Britain***

That is, it has a realized obligatory functional-structural element – its Complement.

Of all these 'potentially clausal ellipsis' functional-structural types, the 'Subject + Operator/Main Verb' type is by far the most frequent in the present data. Table 10.11 shows its proportional occurrence in each of the four corpora.

Table 10.11 The proportional occurrence of Subject + Operator / Main Verb ellipsis by corpus, calculated as a percentage.

Corpus	The proportion of S+O/M ellipsis as a % of all functional-structural types in each corpus
Newspaper reports	9.42
Joy of six	17.18
Radio commentary	21.93
TV commentary	19.08

Note: All figures are rounded up/down to two decimal places.

In the case of 'Subject + Operator / Main Verb' ellipsis, there is one exception to the 'the more ancillary the text's context, the more cases of the potentially clausal ellipsis type' trend. That is, the proportional occurrence of 'Subject + Operator / Main Verb' ellipsis in the 'TV commentary' corpus is less frequent than it is in the 'radio commentary' corpus. Absolute evidence of the aforementioned trend would require the opposite to be the case.

This trend is one in reverse of that noted with respect to 'Subject-only' and 'Main Verb-only' types (Tables 10.8 and 10.9). As noted above in considering the proportional occurrence of 'Subject-only' ellipsis by corpus, so too here it is not easy to find a reason in explanation of the trend. Bringing both trends together, is there really something about 'Subject-only' and 'Main Verb-only' types which mean they are more likely to occur in constitutive contexts? Are either or both the facts that these types are (a) single element functional-structural types, and (b) frequent functional-structural types relevant in explaining this trend? Likewise, is there anything about 'clausal ellipsis' functional-structural types like 'Subject + Operator / Main Verb' ellipsis which would explain why they tend in the opposite direction of being more frequent in ancillary contexts? Are these results just chance? The 'chance' explanation is certainly less plausible for functional-structural types which appear in a roughly linear trend, as is the case with 'Subject-only' (Table 10.8) and 'Subject + Operator / Main Verb' (Table 10.11), than those which evidence no such pattern with respect to the 'constitutive-ancillary' continuum, for example 'Subject + Operator' ellipsis (Table 10.7). Similarly, the fact that there are more examples of results of the former type and less of the latter type is yet further refutation of a 'chance' explanation. It appears, therefore, that as well as ellipsis per se being responsive to the mode parameter of context, there is evidence to suggest that at least some functional-structural types of ellipsis behave likewise. Bringing this in relation to the research question and so also the validity or otherwise of the CMHH, the evidence with respect to functional-structural types of ellipsis is partial and so not conclusive in a way comparable with the trend observed in the last section where the frequency of ellipsis per se was shown to increase as the text's context became more ancillary.

10.4.3 Patterns in the occurrence of recoverability types of ellipsis

In this section, a second typological classification of ellipsis is the focus. The division of ellipsis types in this section is based on the environment, or 'context', from which the omitted form is to be recovered in the process of ellipsis. Ellipsis may be defined as a reduced form of some syntactic unit in that fundamental elements are omitted but predictably so, such that what has been omitted is recoverable from some context (Quirk *et al.*, 1985; Crystal, 1988; Leech, 1992). The two types therefore involved in the classification of recoverability types of ellipsis, the focus of this section, are 'textual ellipsis' and 'situational ellipsis'. In the first of these, the omitted form is to be recovered from either the prior ('anaphoric textual ellipsis') or subsequent ('cataphoric textual ellipsis') co-text, a strictly linguistic environment. In contrast, the structure which is omitted in a case of 'situational ellipsis' is to be recovered from the extra-linguistic context, a non-linguistic environment.

Considering the logic of the CMHH and its predictions, a trend would be anticipated such that the more ancillary a text's context, the more likely it is that situational ellipsis occurs and the more constitutive a text's context, the more likely it is to include cases of textual ellipsis. The basis for this expectation is that, in ancillary contexts, non-linguistic semiotic modalities play a prominent role in the production of meaning (Hasan, 1980: 108; Martin, 1992: 516–17). Gesture, proximity, facial expression, and so forth – all modalities capable of conveying the ellipted form – play potentially focal roles in engendering the meaning in such texts. Conversely, texts with truly constitutive contexts are reliant solely on the linguistic semiotic for the production of meaning and situational ellipsis becomes an impossible communicative resource.

Table 10.12 reinterprets the earlier 'raw figure instances of ellipsis by corpus' table (10.3), dividing these instantial figures of occurrence into 'situationally-recoverable' and 'textually-recoverable' types, presented again as raw numbers.

Table 10.12 Instances of recoverability types of ellipsis by corpus.

Corpus	*Instances of ...*		
	Situational ellipsis	*Textual ellipsis*	*Total*
Newspaper reports	49	195	244
Joy of six	73	154	227
Radio comm.	100	169	269
TV comm.	158	146	304
Total	380	664	

A few observations are initially apparent. First, and most obviously, textual ellipsis is by far the more frequent type when the data is considered as a whole, ignoring corpus divisions. Once corpus divisions are taken into account, there is one corpus which offers an exception to this pattern: the 'TV commentary' corpus which is the only corpus to attest more cases of situational ellipsis than textual ellipsis rather than vice versa. Second, the between-corpora differences are far greater in the situational type, both in terms of raw figures generally and more emphatically in proportional terms. Conversely, 'textual' ellipsis is comparatively stable in its occurrence across corpora. Third, the figures of Table 10.12 appear to suggest two trends as follows:

1.   the more ancillary a text's context, the more cases of situational ellipsis; and
2.   the more constitutive a text's context, the more cases of textual ellipsis.

Given that these observations are drawn on the basis of raw figures, it should be stressed that these are two trends, albeit related ones, not one. Neither trend entails the other. Indeed, (1) is absolute in its linearity whereas (2) attests one exception: textual ellipsis is less frequent in the 'joy of six' corpus than it is in the 'radio commentary' corpus.

This last observation is the most important with regard to the research question, suggesting two trends of linearity corresponding to the CMHH's predictions. Again, raw figure calculations do not neutralize potentially confounding differences between corpora and so it is important to calculate the occurrence of recoverability types proportionally per corpus. Reinterpreting Table 10.12 as percentages gives us the figures shown in Table 10.13.

Table 10.13 The proportional occurrence of recoverability-types of ellipsis in each corpus as a percentage.

Corpus	*% of each type in each corpus*	
	Situational ellipsis	*Textual ellipsis*
Newspaper reports	20	80
Joy of six	32	68
Radio commentary	37	63
TV commentary	52	48

Note: All figures are rounded up/down to a whole number.

Table 10.13 offers much increased confidence in the existence of the two aforementioned trends in line with what the CMHH would predict. Representing this visually as a cumulative bar graph, as in Figure 10.4, or as a two line graph, as in Figure 10.5, renders this trend yet more evident and more visible.

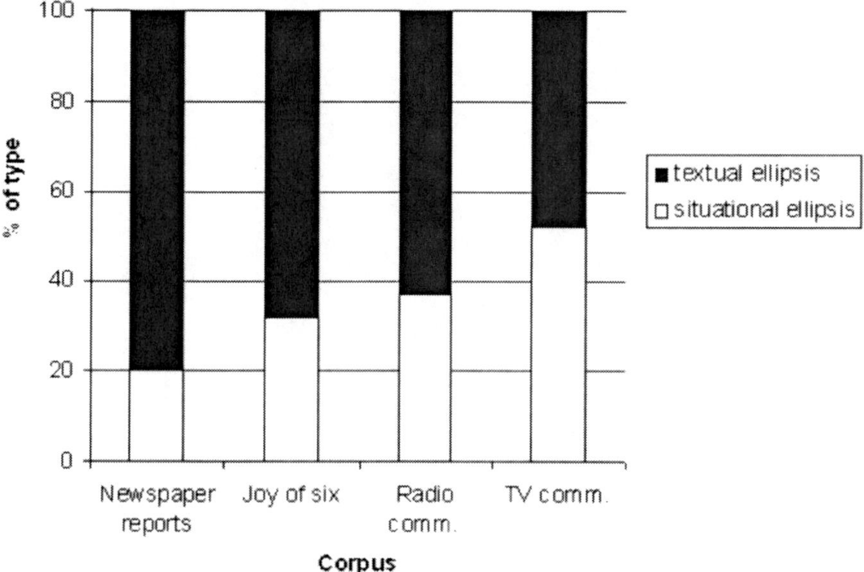

Figure 10.4 The proportional occurrence of recoverability-types of ellipsis in each corpus as a cumulative bar graph.

These graphs reveal further details and subsequent importance relative to the trends under discussion. First, the 'the more constitutive a text's context, the more cases of textual ellipsis' trend appeared partial given calculations based on the instantial, raw figure data (Table 10.12). However, with recoverability types calculated proportionally so as to rule out the influence of the dataset, this trend – as also the 'the more ancillary a text's context, the more cases of situational ellipsis' trend – appears absolute. Second, Figures 10.4 and 10.5, particularly, reveal that the proportional difference of these trends is fairly uniform between all neighbouring corpora as they are organized along Martin's (1992) 'constitutive-ancillary' continuum of mode. The relative straightness of the lines in Figure 10.5, despite there being four integers, signifies this most clearly. Third, moving between corpora along the 'constitutive-ancillary' continuum they are intended to represent sees a movement from recoverability types being very different in their occurrence with textual ellipsis overwhelmingly dominant (at the 'constitutive' end of the continuum) to recoverability types being extremely similar (at the 'ancillary' end of the continuum). Quirk *et al.* (1985: 888–9) suggest that textually recoverable ellipsis is the most prototypical ellipsis, with situational ellipsis much more peripheral. Acknowledging the assumptions inherent in the methodological design of this project, the results here weigh in favour of Quirk *et al.'s* observation (*ibid.*).

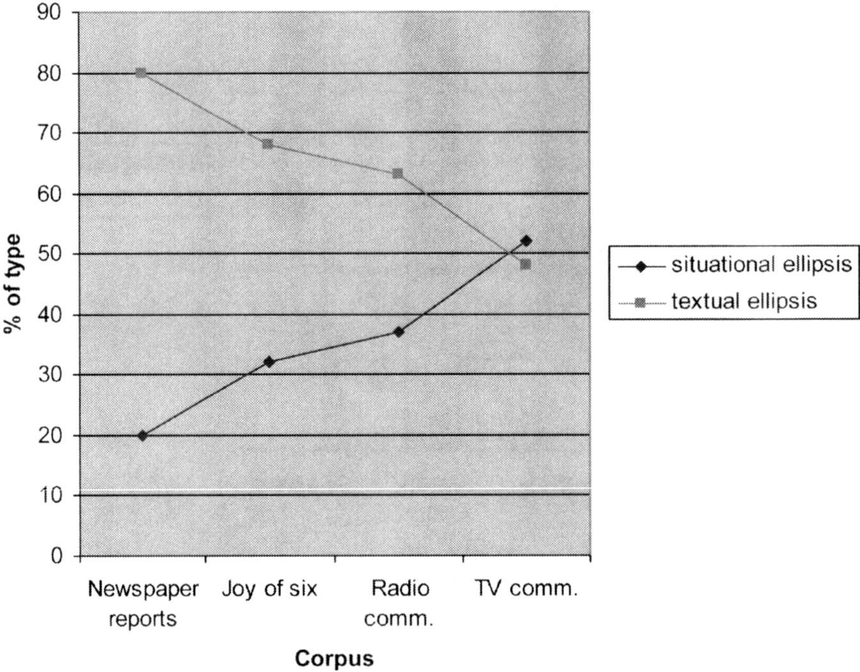

Figure 10.5 The proportional occurrence of recoverability-types of ellipsis in each corpus as a line-by-type graph.

10.5 Conclusions and discussion

What do the results presented in §10.4 tell us in respect of the research question identified at the end of §10.3? Several very important and convincing trends have been observed which weigh in favour of the CMMH's predictions. First, the more ancillary a text's context, the more frequently ellipsis occurs *per se* (see Table 10.6 and Figure 10.3 in §10.4.1). The linearity of this trend in the data here is not only absolute in respect of the 'constitutive-ancillary' mode continuum implied in the dataset design, but the points along it comprised by the individual corpora themselves are also extremely uniform (again, see Figure 10.3). Second, the more constitutive a text's context, the greater the proportion of its occasions of ellipsis that are of the 'textually-recoverable' type and, therefore, the more ancillary a text's context, the greater the proportion of its occasions of ellipsis that are of the 'situationally-recoverable' type (see Table 10.13 and Figures 10.4 and 10.5 in §10.4.3). These trends again follow the linearity of the 'constitutive-ancillary' continuum of mode implied in the present project's dataset design and do so in a uniform manner between sub-corpora. Third, the more constitutive a text's context, the more proportionally frequent the 'Subject-only' functional-structural type of ellipsis as a percentage of all cases of ellipsis (see Table 10.8 in §10.4.2). Fourth, the more ancillary a text's context, the more proportionally frequent the 'Subject + Operator / Main Verb' functional-structural type of ellipsis as a percentage of all cases of ellipsis (Table 10.11 in §10.4.2). Both these last two trends each show one exception from absolute linearity of the 'constitutive-ancillary' continuum of mode implied in the present project's dataset design. This is the same exception in both cases: the relative ordering of the two commentary corpora. These trends also fail to display uniformity in the way observed with the two aforementioned trends. There have also been many results which appear to attest no such trend in support of the CMHH following Martin's (1992) systemic description of mode and the occurrence of the textual metafunctional phenomena of ellipsis. Indeed, the great number of the functional-structural types considered in §10.4.2 fall into this category. These results could be deemed indicative of the 'null-hypothesis' in that they show no support for the predictions of the CMHH relative to the present project. Evidently, such 'null-hypothesis' results would challenge the validity of the CMHH following Martin (*ibid.*). However, such insignificant results might be explained by the small number of observed occurrences of such types. True support for the 'null hypothesis', just like the equivalent for the 'alternative hypothesis', requires sufficient data. In this regard, the 'alternative hypothesis' appears at least more plausible in that types for which sufficient examples are provided in the data tend to corroborate the predictions of the CMHH, as explained just above.

It would be a remarkably rare result if the aforementioned trends in support of the CMHH were purely owing to chance. The fact there are several results in very clear agreement with the CMHH's predictions suggests reasons to assume there is at least some validity to the CMHH following Martin's (1992) systemic description of mode and the occurrence of the textual metafunctional phenomena of ellipsis. However, a balanced but cautious summary of the analytical results must still state that the

CMHH following Martin's systemic description of mode and the occurrence of the textual metafunctional phenomena of ellipsis is inconclusive. Only a great deal of subsequent analytical research similar to that conducted here – though, ideally, bigger in size and scope – can provide an answer with greater confidence than is currently being expressed. Perhaps such evidence as that presented here, partial though it may be, should inform subsequent description and theorizing of semiotic context at the mode parameter in systemic functional linguistics, while the results of further relevant analytical research are awaited with interest.

As a means of bringing the chapter towards a close, two topics of discussion, each situating the aforementioned results in a broader context, are offered. The first was flagged in §10.3 but intentionally withheld until now. This is the matter of corpus representivity, the challenge to ensure that the data used in the project has the design characteristics the methodology requires of it if the results that follow are to stand as a fair answer to the research question. Biber (1993), Williams (2002) and others claim that rigorous corpus design requires both external and internal representivity. The internal criteria are the linguistic properties of the texts. Given that corpus linguistics methods are usually employed by functionally-oriented linguists, 'external criteria' are usually some contextual or situational properties of the texts. In the case of the methodology of the present project, the focus first and foremost is on the external criteria. Recall again the design characteristics for the dataset given as points 1–3 in §10.3. Different datasets were intended to reflect systematic difference at the mode parameter of context and identity at the field and tenor contextual parameters. Yet according to the systemic functional practice of linguistic description, validation for some text having particular contextual values is statement with reference to the linguistic characteristics of that text (Halliday, 1979, 1996).[5] Martin (1992: 514) concedes that his systemic description of the mode parameter (Figure 10.1) is a tentative work-in-progress. Specifically, Martin says: 'The description [of mode systems], like all those to be developed in this chapter, is a very indelicate one. Research **substantiating** the oppositions suggested has in most cases only just begun' (*ibid.,* my emphasis).

Although the systemic functional description of context in general is in its infancy, it is the realizational consequences of contextual options into language systems which are particularly under-developed (Hasan, 2009: 179–82). These, as Hasan says, are the systemic functional linguist's 'checkable criteria' in his or her practice of linguistic and contextual description (*ibid.*). The consequence for the current project is that validating the adherence of data to the contextual properties it was intended to represent is extremely difficult. Benson and Greaves (1981, 1992) have proposed that the collocational profiling of datasets is a diagnostic test for determining a text's context at the 'field' parameter. Similarly, Halliday (1985c) has claimed the merits of lexical density as a diagnostic measure of a text's context at the 'mode' parameter. Assuming the validity of Benson and Greaves (1981, 1992) and Halliday (1985c) on the aforementioned language-context relations, the data here has some degree of support in characteristics (1), (2) and the 'field' strand of characteristic (3) (cf. points 1–3 in §10.3), although space precludes any discussion of this wealth of corpus-building analysis. Again, in the context of the present project, the point to make is as follows. Although some linguistic evidence to support the contextual properties intended for the datasets is in evidence, the diagnostic tests for determining this is the case are few and far between. This takes us back to one of the points with which we started the chapter: there is little in the way of an agreed contextual framework in functional linguistics generally or any sub-school of functional thought specifically. Consequently, external criteria alone are undesirably prominent here in determining what constitutes whether the data collected fulfil the contextual criteria required of them to make the project a 'fair test'. As Biber (1993), Williams (2002) and, in a different way, Hasan (2009) warn, this is not a comfortable position. It is a yardstick little more rigorous than intuition. With this critical reflection on our present state of understanding in functional linguistics acknowledged, it is only in proceeding in spite of such problems that such gaps in knowledge will be filled.

Where the issue of the aforementioned discussion is consequent from the present state of knowledge in the discipline, the second is consequent from methodological decisions in Clarke (2012) on which this chapter reports. §10.3's brief outline of the methodology did not explain that it was in the form of whole texts that natural language data was assigned to datasets. The methodology of any future attempt to build on the present research would do well to account for the observation that texts can adjust contextually within the course of their, as Matthiessen (2002) puts it, logogenetic history. That is, data is not best treated indelicately as whole texts in the act of compiling a corpus with the characteristics listed as 1–3 in §10.3. Indeed, there are consequences in doing so. Examples which illustrate the general point are not infrequent in the data. For example, the emboldened portion of the following extract, drawn from a text assigned to the 'TV commentary' corpus, does not appear to have the values at the 'tenor' parameter which the dataset design claims it should do (cf. Table 10.1):[6]

[A]   the odd man out in this Spain eleven in that he doesn't play for Barcelona or Real Madrid

[B]   **(.) or that he's not very good**

[A]   **(2.0) you can say that**
[B]   **(.) just did**

It would appear that there is a redefinition of the tenor values here such that the emboldened text appears to select for 'AFFECT: marked' and, more debatably, 'CONTACT: involved' even though it is included in a corpus intended to represent 'AFFECT: unmarked' and 'CONTACT: distant'. Similarly, the extract below is drawn from another text assigned to the 'TV commentary' corpus. It should, therefore, represent an 'accompanying: commentary: co-observing' mode. The emboldened part, however, appears to shift mode values to 'accompanying: commentary: relay':

[A]   it doesn't look like happening and time's running out for them now (.) **and though you can't see it immediately below us the managers are disagreeing with one another er about something (.) they're at each others' throats** (.) but (.) the ball's played long again

Consequently, the claims for external representivity, in Biber's (1993) and Williams's (2002) terms, are damaged, at least to a small degree. In this regard, a preferable alternative is to acknowledge the dynamic nature of context (Hasan, 1980; O'Donnell, 1999) and recognize that the methodology could only benefit if data is assigned to sub-corpora in a more incremental fashion. To do so would be tantamount to adjusting the methodology away from one in keeping with the text linguistics tradition, where texts are honoured as wholes, and towards one more aligned with the corpus linguistics tradition, where the interest in the text is incidental to a primary interest in repeated and patterned events (Tognini-Bonelli, 2001: 3–4).

In concluding, one final point should be made which returns to comments given at the end of §10.2. The results of the analytical project discussed here provide evidence in support of the probabilistic reading of the CMHH. First, consider again the first of the two data examples presented in this section. This shift in mode is, in the first instance, an adjustment at the contextual parameter of 'tenor'. That is, there is a redefinition of the categories 'addressee(s)' and 'addresser(s)'. But they have a consequence at the 'mode' parameter of context. They perturb those matters of mode that Hasan (1985) labels 'process sharing' considerations which are largely equal to Martin's (1992) 'interpersonal oriented mode'. It is important to stress that such examples as the above are not rare in the present data. Indeed, texts in the two commentary sub-corpora frequently change from something expressly constructed for a radio or television audience to talk among the commentators themselves. Second and more broadly, the inconclusive nature of the results presented in §10.4, particularly those of §10.4.2, suggests that contextual factors at other parameters may be at play in explaining the occurrence of ellipsis and ellipsis types. Of course, the indefiniteness of the latter observation may originate in our present state of knowledge rather than the nature of the relationship between language and context as it is theorized in systemic functional linguistics. As per Hasan's (2009: 182) sober realization, one thing on which we can surely all agree is that more comprehensive answers to all these questions will require the lifetime's work of some, if not many, scholars.

Notes

1. I should like to thank the Arts and Humanities Research Council for funding my doctoral studies, the research upon which the work presented here is based. Without this funding, the research – and therefore this chapter – would simply not have taken place.

    Additionally, I would like to thank Dr Gerard O'Grady and Dr Tom Bartlett for very useful comments on an earlier version of this chapter.
2. It should be stressed that the 'ancillary – constitutive' continuum that is implied by the two-headed arrow on the right side of Figure 10.1a is a generalization across the distinctions embodied in the network. The continuum is a convenience for talking about the complex range of phenomena involved here. Indeed, its convenience will be taken advantage of throughout the discussions of this chapter. A systemic description is inherently a description of contrastive distinctions, however subtle they may be, and so the continuum is not a reality in the theory.
3. It is necessary to clarify the terminology here, which is faithful to Martin (1992). The use of 'oral' and 'written' in Martin's 'oral transmission' and 'written transmission' labels for field of discourse is <u>not</u> intended to imply the distinction is one of linguistic substance – i.e. phonic or graphic – in which the text gets realized. Rather, following Martin (*ibid.*) on field, these labels reflect that at one end of the field continuum there are those fields which do not <u>require</u>, or rely on for their existence, codification in written genres. Conversely, at the other end of the continuum, there are fields which precisely rely on codification in written genres to exist as things to be 'languaged about.'

4. Ellipsis of adjuncts was considered outside the scope of this project, for reasons discussed later in §10.4.2. Given this stance, the present example is still a case of Operator + Main Verb ellipsis.
5. There is a potential impasse here. In anticipation of it, Halliday (1996: 24–5) concedes that description following trinocular principles is a matter of comprise between the 'from above', 'from below' and 'from roundabout' perspectives and the evidence each yields.
6. Transcriptional notation follows standard conversation analysis conventions.

References

Benson, J. D. and Greaves, W. S. (1981) Field of discourse: Theory and application. *Applied Linguistics* 2: 45–55.

Benson, J. D. and Greaves, W. S. (1992) Collocation and field of discourse. In W. C. Mann and S.A. Thompson (eds) *Discourse Description: Diverse Analyses of a Fund Raising Text* 397–410. Amsterdam: John Benjamins.

Biber, D. (1993) Representativeness in corpus design. *Literary and Linguistic Computing* 8(4): 243–57.

Biber, D., Johansson, S., Leech, G. N., Conrad, S. and Finnegan, E. (1999) *Longman Grammar of Spoken and Written English*. London: Longman.

Clarke, B. P. (2012) Do patterns of ellipsis in text support systemic functional linguistics' 'context-metafunction hook-up' hypothesis? A corpus-based approach. PhD thesis, Cardiff University, Cardiff.

Crystal, D. (1988) *Rediscover Grammar*. London: Longman.

Halliday, M. A. K. (1967/8) Notes on transitivity and theme in English, Parts 1–3. *Journal of Linguistics* 3(1): 37–81; 3(2): 199–244; 4(2): 179–215.

Halliday, M. A. K. (1977) Text as semantic choice in social contexts. In T. van Dijk and J. Petofi (eds.) *Grammars and Descriptions* 176–225. Berlin: Walter de Gruyter.

Halliday, M. A. K. (1979) Modes of meaning and modes of expression: Types of grammatical structure, and their determination by different semantic functions. In D. J. Allerton, E. Carney and D. Holdcroft (eds) *Function and Context in Linguistic Analysis: Essays Offered to William Haas* 57–79. London: Cambridge University Press.

Halliday, M. A. K. (1985a) Register variation. In M. A. K. Halliday and R. Hasan *Language, Context and Text: Aspects of Language in a Social Semiotic Perspective* 29–49. Oxford: Oxford University Press.

Halliday, M. A. K. (1985b) Context of situation. In M. A. K. Halliday and R. Hasan *Language, Context and Text: Aspects of Language in a Social Semiotic Perspective* 3–14. Oxford: Oxford University Press.

Halliday, M. A. K. (1985c) *Spoken and Written Language*. Victoria, Australia: Deakin University Press.

Halliday, M. A. K. (1994) *Introduction to Functional Grammar*, 2nd edn. London: Edward Arnold.

Halliday, M. A. K. (1996) On grammar and grammatics. In R. Hasan, C. Cloran and D. G. Butt (eds) *Functional Descriptions* 1–38. *Theory in Practice*. Amsterdam: John Benjamins.

Halliday, M. A. K. and Hasan, R. (1976) *Cohesion in English*. London: Longman.

Hasan, R. (1980) What's going on: A dynamic view of context. In J. E. Copeland and P. W. Davis (eds) *The Seventh LACUS Forum* 106–21. Columbia, SC: Hornbeam Press.

Hasan, R. (1985) The structure of text. In M. A. K. Halliday and R. Hasan *Language, Context and Text: Aspects of Language in a Social Semiotic Perspective* 52–69. Oxford: Oxford University Press.

Hasan, R. (1995) The conception of context in text. In P. H. Fries and M. Gregory (eds) *Discourse in Society: Systemic Functional Perspectives* 183–283. London: Edward Arnold.

Hasan, R. (1999) Speaking with reference to context. In M. Ghadessy (ed.) *Text and Context in Functional Linguistics* 219–328. Amsterdam: John Benjamins.

Hasan, R. (2009) The place of context in a systemic functional model. In M. A. K. Halliday and J. Webster (eds) *Continuum Companion to Systemic Functional Linguistics* 166–189. London: Continuum.

Leech, G. N. (1992) *Introducing English Grammar*. London: Penguin.

Martin, J. R. (1992) *English Text: System and Structure*. Amsterdam: John Benjamins.

Matthiessen, C. (1995) *Lexicogrammatical Cartography: English Systems*. Tokyo: International Language Sciences Publishers.

Matthiessen, C. M. I. M. (2002) Lexicogrammar in discourse development: Logogenetic patterns of wording. In H. Guowen and Z. Wang (eds) *Discourse and Language Functions* 2–25.Shanghai: Foreign Language Teaching and Research Press.

McGregor, W. B. (2009) *An Outline of the History of Linguistics*. London: Continuum.

O'Donnell, M. (1999) Context in dynamic modelling. In M. Ghadessy (ed.) *Text and Context in Functional Linguistics* 63–99. Amsterdam: John Benjamins.

Quirk, R., Greenbaum, S., Leech, G. and Svartvik, J. (1985) *A Comprehensive Grammar of the English Language*. Harlow: Longman.

Sinclair, J. M. (1991) *Corpus, Concordance, Collocation*. Oxford: Oxford University Press.

Thompson, G. (1999) Acting the part: lexico-grammatical choices and contextual factors. In M. Ghadessy (ed.) *Text and Context in Functional Linguistics* 101–24. Amsterdam: John Benjamins.

Tognini-Bonelli, E. (2001) *Corpus Linguistics at Work*. Amsterdam: John Benjamins.

Williams, G. (2002) In search of representativity in specialised corpora: Categorisation through collocation. *International Journal of Corpus Linguistics* 7(1): 43–64.

Part D

The interplay of choice across different modalities

<table><tr><td>11</td><td></td></tr></table>

Textual and compositional choices in hotel brochures

Arsenio Jesús Moya Guijarro[a]

11.1 Aims and scope of the study

Advertisements, in formats such as television commercials and tourist and other brochures, invade our everyday life through newspapers, magazines and, of course, radio, television and the internet. Through their use of striking and catchy language, they appeal to our needs and emotions as members of a continually more consumerist society (Dyer, 1982: 139–41; Hopearuoho and Ventola, 2009: 183). The main communicative purpose of advertisements is to attract, at least momentarily, the viewer's attention through a range of meaning-making devices (O'Halloran and Lim Fei, 2009: 144; Starc, 2010: 152) and influence the sale of products that appeal to the customer. Adverts may also amuse, worry or warn people about specific aspects and, of course, entertain and inform (Cook, 2001: 9). As a genre, adverts have persuasive illocutionary force and, in turn, they also fulfil an informative function. Promoting and informing are precisely the two functions that the selected texts for this analysis fulfil. On top of informing about the services and installations that the hotels of the company The Leading Hotels of the World Ltd. offer, the texts try to awaken the high class client's desire to stay in one of the superior hotels presented in the hotel guide of 2009, either to develop their professional activities, or to enjoy a well-earned vacation.

Verbal and visual components, together with sound, gestures, and so on, are integrated to achieve the aim of companies and their advertisers

---

a A. Jesús Moya Guijarro is a lecturer of Language and Linguistics at the University of Castilla-La Mancha, Spain. His does research in discourse and text analysis and has published several articles on information, thematicity and multimodality in international journals such as *Atlantis, Word, Text, Functions of Language, Journal of Pragmatics* and *Text and Talk*. He is co-editor of *The World Told and The World Shown: Multisemiotic Issues*. He is also co-editor of *The Teaching and Learning of Foreign Languages within the European Framework*.

(Crystal, 2011: 201; Bateman, 2008: 1–2). Whether static or dynamic, printed on paper or taken from television or the internet, adverts are composite wholes. As semiotic products or events created within a specific social and cultural context, their character consists of a synthesis of different modes: moving images, static images, words, sounds, and so on. For this reason, their full significance can only be obtained if both verbal and non-verbal modalities are read in combination and as inter-dependent components of the same multimodal ensemble.

Due to the multimodal nature of adverts, a systemic-functional social semiotic approach, born of the combination of Halliday's systemic functional linguistics theory (2004) and Kress and van Leeuwen's visual social semiotics (2001, 2006), seems to be appropriate for the analysis of the verbal and visual strategies available to advertisers to create meaning. Halliday's SFL is useful for analysing the specific textual choices made by advertisers to promote their products and make them appealing to customers. In addition, Kress and van Leeuwen's (2006) visual social semiotics, extrapolated from the SFL account, provides an appropriate framework to identify the choices available to advertisers to organize their productions visually as coherent communicative artefacts. The exploration of the verbal and visual choices made by the advertiser to create textual meaning will enable us to identify the strategies used in the brochures to attract the attention of those who perceive themselves to be 'high class' and looking for a luxurious hotel destination such as those promoted in *The Leading Hotels of the World* guide (2009). Both Halliday's SFG and Kress and van Leeuwen's visual social semiotics are concerned with the concept of choice as they both aim to explore the options actually taken by the users of the language to convey representational, interactive and textual meanings in a specific social and cultural context.

Within the frameworks of Halliday's SFL and Kress and van Leeuwen's visual social semiotics, in this chapter I specifically attempt to analyse how the verbal and visual modes are co-deployed to construct textual and compositional meanings in a sample of ten hotel brochures.[1] This chapter also aims to investigate the extent to which the ideologies of luxury and exclusivity (Thurlow and Jaworski, 2006) underlying the marketing philosophy of the Leading Hotels of the World brand may influence the semiotic choices made by marketers at textual and compositional levels to promote the recommended hotel destinations globally (Hopearuoho and Ventola, 2009). Thurlow and Jaworski (2006: 100) argue that discourse is ideological because 'it establishes and maintains structures of inequality and privilege'. Following a similar argument, O'Halloran and Lim Fei (2009: 141) state that 'print advertisements unfold as a genre with associated views and ideologies about the world'. In line with this idea, this study follows the hypothesis that the ideologies of a company are reflected in the semiotic organization and marketing of the products it advertises. As the hotels included in *The Leading Hotels of the World* are primarily intended for those who perceive themselves as belonging to the upper echelons of society, their appeal is probably achieved through the creation of an illusion of distinction and social status (Thurlow and Jaworski, 2006; Lemke, 2009).

This chapter is structured as follows: first, after specifying the aims and scope of this study, the main features of SFL (Halliday, 2004) and Kress and van Leeuwen's visual social semiotics (2006) are briefly outlined in §11.2, directing attention to the textual metafunction. §11.3 then deals with the textual and compositional analyses of the verbal and non-verbal meaning-making devices available to the writer and photographer of the guide to promote the Leading Hotels of the World brand. Aspects related to the thematic progression of the texts and the visual composition of the brochures as a whole, including features related to information value, framing and salience, are investigated. Finally, the results are interpreted in functional terms, and a reflection is made on the meaning potential that is born of the intersemiosis of words and images in hotel brochures.

11.2 SFL and visual social semiotics

Halliday (1978, 2004) develops a SF-grammar in relation to verbal language and establishes a comprehensive description of grammatical systems. These grammatical systems employ three metafunctional meanings, which are present in all instances of communication, independently of their verbal or visual nature: ideational, interpersonal and textual. Ideational meaning constructs our experience of the world and is concerned with the clause as representation of reality. In turn, interpersonal meaning deals with enacting social relationships between the speaker/writer and the listener/reader. Finally, textual meaning is concerned with the clause as a coherent message.

Although SFL focuses essentially on verbal language, Halliday (1978, 2004) assumes that all texts, whether verbal or visual, independently or in combination with other semiotic modalities, simultaneously entail ideational, interpersonal and textual meanings. This idea has led Kress and van Leeuwen (2001, 2006) to develop a social semiotic multimodal approach to describe the meaning-making resources of images. They propose that images are capable of simultaneously realizing three types of meaning:

1. representational, which is related to Halliday's ideational metafunction;
2. interactive, which corresponds to Halliday's interpersonal metafunction;
3. compositional meaning, the focal point of this study, which is associated with Halliday's textual metafunction.

Textuality in texts is equivalent to composition in images. Textuality focuses on the aspects related to thematicity and information which may shed light on the organization of texts as coherent communicative artefacts (Halliday, 2004). In turn, compositional meaning is concerned with the organization of the represented participants within an image and involves features such as the distribution of information, framing and salience (Kress and van Leeuwen, 2006). The textual/compositional metafunction deals with the distribution of information either through text or image and the prominence given to some verbal or visual elements within a stretch of discourse. The challenge is to see how the textual and the compositional meanings work together in communicative artefacts using different modes of realization.

The textual metafunction makes reference to the resources verbal language has for creating coherent texts with relevance to the contexts in which they are produced and understood (Halliday 1978, 2004; Halliday and Hasan, 1985; Martin 1992, 2002; O'Toole, 1994; Kress, 2010). Within these, thematic structure gives the clause its character as a message or a communicative event, analysed as a two-part structure with thematic and rhematic elements. Halliday (1994: 56–7; 2004: 64–5) assumes that all the clauses in a text have a thematic constituent located in an initial position and that the theme of a clause extends from its beginning up to the first element that fulfils a function in transitivity. When speaking of multiple themes, Halliday (1994, 2004) states that only ideational themes are, in principle, referential and can be assigned a topical status. In contrast, textual and interpersonal components, structural elements (*and, but, that, when* ...), conjunctives (*anyway, besides* ...), continuatives (*oh, well* ...), modal adjuncts (*probably, frankly* ...), vocatives, and finite operators, which are typically located before ideational elements, do not exhaust the thematic potential of the clause and do not fulfil a topical function.

The theme/rheme structure does not only operate within the domain of the clause, it transcends the limits of clausal structure in order to contribute decisively to the global articulation of the text (Ghadessy, 1995;

Moya and Pinar, 2008; Moya and Ávila, 2009). In this sense, Daneš (1974) distinguishes three basic patterns of thematic progression (henceforth TP). The first is simple linear TP or TP with linear thematization of rhemes. In this, the rheme of a clause becomes the thematic constituent of the following clause, lending the text a dynamic character. The second basic pattern is TP with a continuous (constant) theme. In this model the same theme is shared by a series of clauses, each of which adds new information to it. The third pattern is derived theme TP. This is a broad spectrum theme, which Daneš calls a hypertheme, and which gives rise to the themes of the clauses which follow to form a chain of subthemes deriving from the general theme. Although texts do not often conform to these models strictly, Daneš's thematic progression theory was and continues to be a necessary point of reference for many posterior studies on textual organization. I shall, therefore, keep it in mind when analysing the choices made by advertisers regarding the structural organization of the hotel brochures.

However, language is just one of the many semiotic modes along with images, sound, music, and so on, that can be used to create meaning (Halliday and Hasan, 1985: 4; Unsworth, 2006: 71; Moya 2011). As Kress (2010: 84) points out: 'Language which had been seen as a full means of expression; as the foundation of rationality; sufficient for all that could be spoken or written, thought, felt and dreamt (Eco, 1979), is now seen as a partial means of doing these' (Kress, 2010: 84). The visual component of the hotel brochures also plays a key role in their overall organization and determines the extent to which some elements within an image or photograph are given more informative value and relative salience than others (Kress and van Leeuwen, 2006). In order to analyse how images are organized and structured, Kress and van Leeuwen (*ibid.*: 177) distinguish between three types of meanings within composition, all of which are concerned with the arrangements of elements on a semiotic space: information value, salience and framing.

Information value refers to the placement of elements in relation to one another and in different locations (left or right, top or bottom and at the centre or margin) within a visual composition. Adopting Halliday's notion of information focus, Kress and van Leeuwen (*ibid.*) distinguish between given and new information in images. In language, 'given' is associated with information that is known or familiar to the reader and tends to be placed at the beginning of the clause and mapped onto the theme. New information, however, tends to be located at the end of the clause, in rhematic position, and embodies the part of the message that is unknown to the reader (Martin, 1992: 452; Halliday, 2004: 89). Similarly,

Kress and van Leeuwen (2006: 179) argue that in Western cultures given information is located on the left of a visual composition while new information is placed on the right. Thus, the information placed on the left is ideologically interpreted as the domain of the given whereas the right tends to be ideologically constructed as belonging to the domain of the new. To this distinction (given/new), Kress and van Leeuwen (*ibid.*) add further descriptions of information patterns which are only applicable to visual language. Here they differentiate between the real and the ideal, which represent the second type of polarization of visual space. Van Leeuwen (2005) and Kress and van Leeuwen (2006) assume that the visual space of a multimodal text has to be approached from two axes: the horizontal and the vertical. In Western cultures the upper half of a composition is associated with the ontological space of the ideal while the bottom part represents the real. While the real embodies specific and concrete information, the ideal usually includes more imaginary, abstract and generalized information.

Salience is the second type of compositional meaning distinguished by Kress and van Leeuwen (2006) and refers to the ability of an element to capture the viewer's attention. Salience can make some elements more important than others from an informative perspective, since salient elements catch the viewer's attention first and determine the reading path of an image. The nucleus of information is usually at the centre of the composition while other, less relevant, subordinate elements tend to be placed in the margins (Kress and van Leeuwen, 1996: 206). Salience is determined by different factors such as:

1. size (the larger the represented participant (RP), the greater its salience);
2. sharpness of focus (RPs have less salience when they are out of focus);
3. tonal contrast (areas of high tonal contrast have greater salience);
4. the placement of an object in the foreground or background of a composition (an RP in the foreground has greater salience than an RP in the background);
5. colour contrast (strongly saturated colours have greater salience than soft colours).

However, none of these criteria alone are sufficient to measure visual relevance, which is always dependent on the complex interaction between all the elements referred to above (Kress and van Leeuwen, 2006). Colour modulation plays a key role in salience but also in visual modality (*ibid.*: 154). In fact, colour functions as an open system in the sense that, unlike other discourse systems, it is capable of realizing more than one metafunction simultaneously (O'Halloran and Lim Fei, 2009: 145; LimFei, 2004: 223).

The informative relevance of an element can also be influenced by framing, the third feature of composition, which is a visual device used to connect or disconnect elements (Kress and van Leeuwen, 2006). While framing emphasizes the individuality of a visual element, a lack of framing represents the element as part of a group. The fact that a visual composition is unframed (e.g. a photograph that covers the whole area of a page) constitutes an invitation to view its elements from within. Elements can be grouped together by continuity of colour and shape and by connecting vectors. A lack of frame lines and empty spaces between the RPs may also join elements together. These sets of choices stress group identity, involvement and absence of social distance between the RPs and the viewer.

11.3 The analysis: Textual/compositional meaning

In this section the textual and compositional choices made by hotel advertisers will be analysed to determine how the combination of verbal and visual modalities create a coherent whole that achieves the presumed aim of promoting luxury and exclusivity in hotel brochures. As stated in the introduction, the sample texts have been taken from *The Leading Hotels of the World* 2009. A total of ten hotel brochures taken from this guide and their twenty photographs will be studied. However, for reasons of space, not all the visual material has been inserted in the present contribution. The four photographs that have been included are shown in Figure 11.1. The results make evident the communicative potential that is born of the interaction between text and image in hotel brochures. For the purposes of this chapter it has been assumed that all major clauses, whether dependent or independent, have a thematic constituent located in the initial position. Although Halliday (2004) admits the possibility of a clause complex as theme in a compound clause, for the purposes of this chapter I have assigned a theme to each of the clauses that form a compound sentence. As Halliday (*ibid.*: 394) states, in the case of compound sentences, 'the point to bear in mind is that there will be two thematic domains – that of the clause nexus and that of the clause'. Thus, a theme-rheme structure can be allocated to the hypotactically related clauses of a clause complex. In a clause such as 'Located in London's Belgravia, close to Knightsbridge and Mayfair, the hotel has become the benchmark for contemporary hotels around the world' (The Halkin, *The Leading Hotels of the World*, p. 293), 'located' and 'the hotel' have been analysed as the topical themes of the corresponding dependent and independent clauses. With regard to embedded clauses, these are not considered full constituents in the clause complex structure as they function either as part of a group element, usually as post-modifiers in a group complex, or as constituents or nominal elements in their own right (Martin and Rose, 2003: 173). Thus, as they do not have the same function as independent or dependent clauses because of their down-ranked status, their thematic contribution to the discourse is minimal and can, for practical reasons, be ignored (Halliday, 2004: 100). This is the case of the embedded clause 'that features red brickwork and beautiful arch detailing,' in the clause complex 'The Landmark London is a classic of Victorian Gothic architecture that features red brickwork and beautiful arch detailing' (The Landmark London, *The Leading Hotels of the World*, p. 294).

11.3.1 Textual analysis of the hotel brochures

Let us start now with a linguistic analysis of the hotel brochures, specifically the typology of themes that predominate in the verbiage, to see how they are structurally organized. As shown in Table 11.1, both simple and multiple structures have been identified, but the simple type occurs more frequently (91.8% of the cases counted).

Table 11.1 Simple and multiple themes.

	Absolute value	*Value (%)*
Simple theme	112	91.8%
Multiple theme	10	8.2%
Total	122	100%

Evidence of this fact is shown in excerpt (1), where the thematic slots of the clauses tend to be realized by sole ideational elements that make reference to Langtry's Restaurant in the Cadogan Hotel through a nominal group, pronominalization and ellipsis. The rhematic parts of these inform the reader about the excellent cuisine and dining experience that the hotel offers. There are also ten instances of multiple themes (8.2% of the token identified), formed by textual (*and, when, while*) and experiential components, which also make reference to the facilities and services provided by the hotel, essentially their restaurants. An example of an ideational component (*The Halkin*) preceded by a textual theme (*when*) is shown in excerpt (2). In the thematic structure no interpersonal elements have been found as there are no vocatives and there are no modal adjuncts expressing either modality or attitudinal comments. In addition, there are no finite operators or wh-interrogatives since most of the clauses identified in the ten hotel brochures are declarative in mood.

(1) ... **Langtry's restaurant** offers a new dining experience in Knightsbridge. **It** combines an intriguing relaxed atmosphere with excellent cuisine and offers British menus with unique and inventive flavor combinations[2] (Cadogan Hotel, *The Leading Hotels of the World*, p. 291)

(2) **When The Halkin** first opened in 1991, **its aim** was to offer uncompromising standards of service and style (The Halkin, *The Leading Hotels of the World*, p. 293)

Regarding the marked or unmarked typology of themes (see Table 11.2), most themes (94.3%) are unmarked or prototypical realizations, as they tend to be realized by clause constituents that fulfil the syntactic function of subject in a declarative mood structure (see excerpts (1) and (2)). However, 5.7 per cent of the cases counted are marked themes and they are realized by ideational components that fulfil a syntactic function other than subject, such as adjuncts of time, place or manner. These marked themes typically fulfil two different functions in discourse. They either mark the temporal frame in which a facility in the hotel has been renovated or newly built (excerpt (3)) or give information about the prime locations or unparalleled services of the hotels included in the book, which are signs of their exclusivity and high standards (excerpts (4) and (5)).

Table 11.2 Unmarked and marked themes.

	Absolute value	Value (%)
Unmarked theme	115	94.3%
Marked theme	7	5.7%
Total	122	100%

(3) **In early 2009** an exciting new bar and restaurant will open to replace the Cellars Bar, featuring casual dining and relaxing spaces to meet and drink (The Landmark London, *The Leading Hotels of the World*, p. 294)

(4) **Just steps from fashionable Bond Street**, Brown's Hotel is the ideal luxury retreat in the heart of London (Brown's Hotel, *The Leading Hotels of the World*, p. 290)

(5) **Luxuriously** appointed guest rooms will evoke a residential feel, and guests will be indulged with natural service and finesse, always anticipating, but never overbearing (The Langham, London, *The Leading Hotels of the World*, p. 295)

Added to these thematic features is the notable coincidence throughout the texts of the grammatical function of subject, the textual function of theme, and the pragmatic-discourse function of topic[3] carried out by the hotel themselves or by their different facilities or services. In fact, theme and topic overlap in 87.7 per cent of the cases counted (see Table 11.3).

Table 11.3 Overlapping theme and topic.

	Absolute value	*Value (%)*
Theme and topic overlap	107	87.7%
Theme and topic do not overlap	15	12.3%
Total	122	100%

As is shown in excerpt (6), by following this strategy, the entities about which information is given are activated from the beginning of the clause, usually in subject position. All this corresponds to the idea of focusing the reader's attention on the hotels and the exclusive services and facilities they might provide to the prospective customer. The analysis verifies that the correlation between theme and the hotels or their facilities is notable: The Landmark London > The centrepiece of this hotel > Its style. By placing the facilities and services of the hotels described in thematic position, the writer highlights the main areas of interest that are being described and attracts the reader's attention to the 'product' that is being promoted. Following this pattern, s/he makes identifying the topic easy and highlights the hotel destinations, their exclusive areas and efficient services.

(6)　　**The Landmark London** is a classic of Victorian Gothic architecture that features red brickwork and beautiful arch detailing. **The centerpiece of this luxury hotel** is an eight-story glass atrium that can be viewed from all internal facing guest rooms. **The style of the hotel** is classic British with a hint of Eastern influences. (The Landmark London, *The Leading Hotels of the World*, p. 294)

Theme and topic were not realized by the same clause constituent in only 12.3 per cent of the cases counted. This lack of correlation usually happens when the theme is realized by adjuncts of place, time and manner that introduce spatial, temporal and circumstantial information linked to the facilities built inside a hotel (excerpts (3), (4) and (5)). In addition, as shown in Excerpt (7), theme and topic do not overlap when the theme is realized by a historic character who visited the hotel in the past, giving it the prestige associated with high-class society and royalty. By placing the experiential elements that carry out a topical function in the final slot of the clause, the writer creates expectations and attracts the reader's attention to the topical entities in a unique way. On some occasions the persuasive function of the hotel brochure leads the writer to use linguistic strategies by which s/he moves the new topical entities away from the thematic slot of the clause. This way the activation of the main topic is postponed and the reader's attention is directed to the hotel or the facilities offered.

(7)   King Edward VII frequently visited **the Cadogan** to see his mistress and Oscar Wilde was arrested **in the hotel** (Cadogan Hotel, *The Leading Hotels of the World*, p. 291)

The analysis of the thematic structure of the brochures would be incomplete without the study of the thematic progression of their clauses and how these are thematically organized to achieve coherence. An overall view of the thematic progression of the hotel brochures shows that the derived progression is the most predominant thematic choice of all types (40.2%).

Table 11.4 Patterns of thematic progression.

Thematic progression	*Absolute value*	*Value (%)*
Constant TP	22	19.6%
Linear TP	5	4.5%
Derived TP	45	40.2%
No TP	40	35.7%
Total	112	100%

As evidenced in excerpt (8), the pattern of derived thematic progression may require inferences and associations from the reader who has to establish a connection between the Baglioni Hotel and its different features or facilities: décor, suites, bathrooms, rejuvenation spa, and so on. This pattern is very effective and appropriate for advertising texts since, through the subthemes deriving from the hyperthemes (the hotels themselves), the writer highlights the main facilities included in each hotel and draws the potential customer's attention to the exclusive resorts that are being advertised. In turn, the high rate of subthemes contributes to the topical continuity of the brochures and to their specific thematic and global organization. The ten brochures are essentially centred on a sole topical chain, defined on the basis of the association that is made between the main topic – the different hotels – and their subthemes, realized by the entities that refer to their luxurious installations and the services they offer. Subthemes fulfil a function in topical continuity due to their dependence on the main entities that activate them. Subthemes signal the beginning of a discourse segment which is clearly subordinate to the preceding one, or which is at least at the same level of subordination (Moya, 2006a).

For this reason, the writer of the hotel brochures generally introduces a sole topical sequence, with the purpose of focusing the attention of the reader on the 'product' that is being promoted and highlighting its exclusive properties.

(8)   **Situated** in the heart of Kensington with views of Kensington Palace overlooking Hyde Park, **the hotel** is a stone's throw from the city's cultural highlights ... **The hotel's décor** is both baroque and contemporary ... **Some of the suites** have walls lined up in gold leaf representing the Italian Sun. **A water feature in the hotel entrance** pays homage to the fountains found in Italy's piazzas ... **Bathrooms** have dark wood floors, mirrored walls and hand-made copper basins from Morocco ... LEISURE. **The Rejuvenation Spa** offers prescriptions facials, purifying cleansing rituals, meditation yoga ... (Baglioni London, *The Leading Hotels of the World*, p. 289)

Although the derived thematic scheme is the most predominant pattern, this is not the only type. Throughout the hotel brochures, at different intervals, the writer also produces sequences of constant and linear thematic progression. 19.6 per cent of the clauses counted follow a constant theme pattern (Daneš, 1974), realized by the repetition of same theme in a sequence of clauses. In excerpt (9), for example, The Cadogan Hotel is kept in thematic position in two subsequent sentences. In the first clause it is realized by a proper noun; in the second the thematic element is realized by a definite expression. Proper nouns, as Downing and Locke (1992: 432) state, 'denote unique entities and so are definite in themselves without needing the article the' or, as Givón (1993) affirms, allude to currently inactive entities which have a high degree of topical persistence. In fact, Givón (*ibid.*) defines proper nouns as a subcategory of defining nouns which are used to introduce referents that are currently inactive in the discourse, but which have overall topical importance. In turn, definite expressions, that is noun phrases which are preceded by definite articles, are usually used in English to select or identify a referent as a known element or to make it stand out from a group of entities. For this reason, they are a prototypical resource of topical continuity in hotel brochures (Moya, 2006a). The constant thematic progression is also a very appropriate choice for advertising texts. With this tactic, given information is reiterated and either the hotels or their facilities and services are placed in thematic position in a sequence of several clauses. This way the writer draws the reader's attention to the specific information he wishes to highlight, in this case the exclusivity and luxury of the hotels promoted in the guide.

(9)   **The Cadogan** is an elegant townhouse hotel at the midpoint of two opulent worlds, between Knightsbridge and Sloane Square, *that* weaves contem-porary styling with classic Edwardian decadence. **The hotel** is central to

> fashionable shops such as Gucci, Tiffany, Harrods and Harvey Nichols. Built in 1887, it was once home of famous actress Lillie Langtry (Cadogan Hotel, *The Leading Hotels of the World*, p. 291)

Although its frequency is low, five cases of linear thematic progression have been identified in the sample texts (4.5% of the cases counted). In excerpt (10), the themes of the second and third clauses, *it/which*, come from the rhemes of the preceding clauses: *The Ritz Club/The Ritz Salon*, respectively. These chains give the texts a sense of dynamism as they allow the writer to place key informative features in alternative thematic positions. The commas in excerpt (10) show that the relative clause, 'which has been served in the Drawing Room for over 120 years' is non-defining, and so is hypotactically related with the relative pronoun as topical theme.

> (10) **Guests** may enjoy *The Ritz Club*, an exclusive members club that is situated in the hotel's former ballroom. **It** offers a bar, fine dining, a casino, and The Ritz Salon, **which** is home to the ultimate in relaxation, offering health and beauty treatments and hairdressing for ladies and gentlemen (The Ritz London, *The Leading Hotels of the World*, p. 298)

The derived, constant and linear thematic progressions identified are sometimes altered throughout the brochures by the presence of circumstances of time, place or manner in thematic position, already exemplified in excerpts (3), (4) and (5) and by the location of places of interest, such as Hyde Park, The London Eye, and so on, rather than the hotels themselves or their facilities in thematic position (see excerpt (11)). The fact that Hyde Park is near The Milestone Hotel emphasizes the hotel's convenient location in central London. Therefore, although some fragments that follow clear, derived or constant progressions are found, in their totality the hotel texts do not always follow a defined thematic pattern. Despite this, the analysis reveals that there are sections in the sample texts that respond to the derived thematic progression scheme. Overall, through the activation of constant themes and subthemes the writer of hotel brochures places those entities that make reference to the hotels in initial position. Once located in the thematic slot, the writer introduces information about the luxurious facilities and efficient services offered in rhematic position, drawing the reader's attention to the most exclusive features of the hotels included in the guide.

> (11) **Hyde Park, opposite the hotel,** is ideal for jogging (The Milestone Hotel, *The Leading Hotels of the World*, p. 296).
>
> **The London Eye, The National Gallery and Tate Modern** are nearby (One Aldwych, *The Leading Hotels of the World*, p. 297)

11.3.2 Compositional features

Having analysed the textual patterns of the hotel brochures, I will now focus attention on their compositional characteristics in the visual mode. As stated in §11.2, compositional meaning is concerned with the organization of the RPs within an image and involves features such as the distribution of information, framing and salience (Kress and van Leewen, 2006).

With regard to the distribution of information, I will first comment on some aspects related to the semiotic organization of the hotel brochures that form the sample texts. Later, features related to the given/new and ideal/real organization of the brochures will be dealt with.

As evidenced on the right-hand side of Figure 11.1 (The Cadogan Hotel), the city and the country that the hotel belongs to appear at the top of the page; the name of the hotel is in black in capital letters and the name of the company publishing the information is highlighted in blue letters. In the upper half of the left-hand side, a landscape format photo of the interior of a room is shown and to the right of the photo the name of the hotel appears once again, in cursive font, with its logo, followed by the address, telephone number, fax number, webpage and the number of rooms and suites that are available, as well as the distance in minutes from one of the international airports in the city where it is located.

The lower half of the page follows a similar structure, but this time the visual part is displayed in a portrait format on the right-hand side. The text that is placed beside the photograph plays a determining role in the promotion of the hotel: first, a general overview is given, followed by information about dining, leisure activities and additional features. At the foot of the page, the name of the company and its web address is repeated in lower case, inviting the reader to obtain more information online about the specific hotel that he or she is consulting. When the verbal and visual information is on a left-hand page (Brown's Hotel), the layout is basically the same though with minor differences. The landscape photograph is placed in the upper right section of the page and the rectangular one in the lower left area. The name of the company publishing the information is presented at the foot of the right-hand side, preceded in capital letters by a reference to pages 558–9 of the hotel guide for making reservations. This organization guarantees that the different hotels are presented as interconnected, since the visual mode reinforces the framework within which their locations and the information referring to dining, leisure activities and other additional features are inserted.

In terms of compositional meaning, adverts do not necessarily have a left–right compositional pattern of information, so there is no need

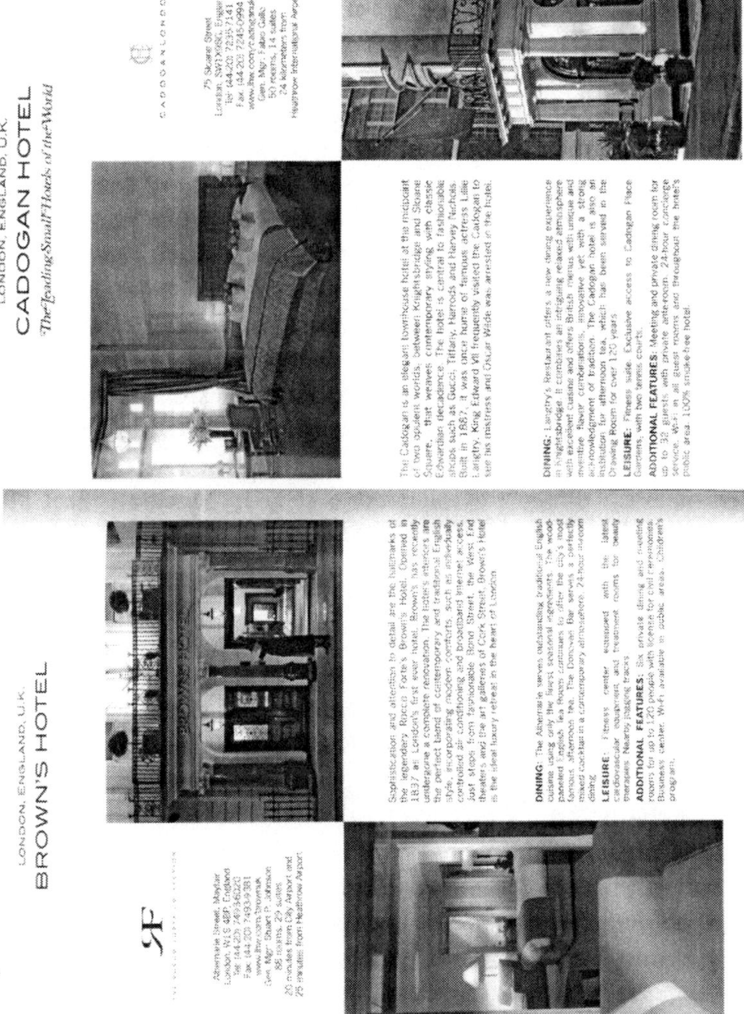

Figure 11.1 Pages for Brown's Hotel and Cadogan Hotel from *The Leading Hotels of the World*. Reproduced by permission of The Leading Hotels of the World Ltd.

to limit given and new information to the left or right positions of the visual composition in a print advert (Cheong, 2004: 194). In fact, the printed pages of the ten London hotel brochures analysed do not follow the specific information distribution given plus new. The left and right hand sides of the pages contain both verbal and visual components which introduce the exclusive features of the different hotels included in the guide. Some hotel brochures adapt more easily to the real and ideal patterns of information. In Kress and van Leeuwen's approach and in its application to print adverts, the ideal often embodies the promise of the product or company, which is based on the consumer's desires. The real, however, is 'the solid foundation of the edifice of the promise' (Kress and van Leeuwen, 1996: 193). In the ten brochures sampled, the top half is essentially occupied by visual information which clearly shows the interiors of the hotels, part of their rooms or their façades. The more specific information: location, dining and leisure activities and additional equipment features, is placed between the centre and the bottom half of the page. Thus, the verbiage tends to be located toward the centre and bottom of the page and corresponds to the sphere of the real. However, the visual component also seems to have weight in the lower part of the page, which makes it difficult to establish a clear information ideal plus real pattern where the ideal would be displayed at the top of the page and the real at the bottom.

Regarding salience, the photos lack a unique element that is given prominent informative status or that is placed in the centre of the composition to attract the viewer's attention in a special way. As the photographer tries to create a feeling of comfort and exclusivity, there is usually more than one visual element displayed in the visual composition. To a certain extent, this responds to the advertiser's intention to offer an overall view of the luxurious interior parts of the hotels promoted. The printed page is organized in such a way that the visual part draws the reader's attention towards the information that is given in the verbiage. The range of colours (yellow, green, orange, lilac) which create a warm and friendly atmosphere, the good quality of the photographs and the texture of the paper (which is thick and glossy throughout the book) are factors that draw the reader's attention towards the information featured in the verbal part: the location of the hotels, leisure activities, restaurants and other additional aspects. The photos, therefore, provide the frame within which the verbal part is placed.

Framing is another aspect of the compositional metafunction. In the ten hotel brochures there are frames, which, according to Kress and van Leeuwen (2006), are an indication of the social distance between the RPs and the viewer. The hotels are offered to the viewer as objects of desire which are solely accessible to their clientele. Sometimes the objects are reflected metonymically (Forceville, 2009), or as a part for the whole (part of a bed, a sofa, a façade, etc.). This trope fulfils a persuasive discourse function. By showing only part of the rooms, the advertiser highlights the spaciousness of the rooms, creating a sensation of luxury which is typically associated with five-star hotels. It is implied that the rooms are so large that they cannot be included within a single shot of a photographic camera. Only part of their full dimensions can be displayed in the two photographs shown on every page dedicated to a specific hotel. Besides, the frames around the visual elements create detachment between the visual and verbal modes, which do not mesh with one another.

11.4 Conclusion: The interplay of images and words

Following the theoretical frameworks of SFL and visual social semiotics, my aim was to identify the verbal and visual choices made by the advertiser of the ten London hotel brochures included in *The Leading Hotels of the World* to convey textual and compositional meanings. This last section of this chapter summarizes the main findings of the analysis carried out in §11.3 and shows how the verbiage and the visual component complement each other to make a coherent whole. Aspects related to information value and salience will be commented on in this final part as key features of the intersemiosis that is created between verbal and visual modalities to express textual and compositional meaning.

The persuasive function of the hotel brochure leads the writer to use certain linguistic devices through which he or she tries to have an influence on the reader's behaviour in order to obtain a positive response. The names of the hotels and their facilities and exclusive areas tend to be located in the thematic slot of the clause in an unmarked position. This way, the writer facilitates the identification of the entities about which information is given in the different clauses of the text. Once the name of a specific hotel is activated within the scope of the theme, information about its main areas and features is introduced in rhematic position to highlight the exclusive facilities and efficient services it offers. In addition, the close relationship that is established between the topical themes (usually realized by the names of the hotels included in the guide) and the subthemes (realized by the facilities and areas included in each hotel) determines the global thematic organization of the hotel brochures, which is normally characterized by a sole topical sequence. Almost all the information included in the verbiage centres around the specific hotel that is being advertised or its exclusive facilities and efficient services. The activation of other secondary topical sequences that may distract the attention of the reader from the promoted hotel is kept to a minimum.

This thematic pattern through which given information tends to be located in the initial position of the clause does not seem to have a correspondence in the visual mode. Due to space restrictions, the photographs on the printed page do not follow the prototypical distribution of information by which given elements tend to be placed on the left-hand side of the page and new elements on the right-hand side. The photographic material is located both on the right and left-hand sides without establishing a clear relationship between their placement and the given/new character of their content. In addition, as has been demonstrated in §11.3, the photographs do not respond entirely to the information pattern of ideal and real. Although the visual component seems to have heavier weight at the top of the page, the presence of the visual mode is also relevant at the bottom of the page, the domain prototypically reserved for the real in Kress and van Leeuwen's account (2006).

In the bottom part of each double spread there is the web address of the company that has published the material, which invites the reader to open a new reading path. The information scheme of the printed page differs from that of the web page. The internet expands the options that are made available to the reader on the printed page to explore and find the appropriate hotel for his or her vacation or professional stay. Unlike on the printed page, the information on the webpage follows the prototypical schema of distribution described by Kress and van Leuwen (2006) and Kress (2010). The information that is introduced as known is found towards the left side of the web page while the right side is reserved for information considered to be new about a hotel, be it verbal or visual. Thus, the left side of the page is reserved for sections regarding reservations and destinations, which are expected items on a web page intended to advertise hotels. On the right side of the web page, however, less expected information for a web page is shown: the offers of the hotel during the period chosen by the reader and the option to join a leaders club and earn rewards. In reference to the informative pattern ideal/real, the visual information is usually found between the middle and the top part of the page, where a display of photos that show the interior and exterior of the hotels can be found. On the contrary, the verbal part offers concrete information about the hotel (dining, recreation, health and other features) and tends to be included towards the bottom of the page. These prototypical informative patterns as distinguished by Kress and van Leeuwen (2006) cannot be found on the printed page, since there is not enough space available to organize the information in order from the familiar to the most unknown, or from the more abstract to the more concrete.

This apparent lack of prototypical information patterns in the visual component does not imply that the printed page does not contain a clear and well-structured layout. The colouring of the photos, their good quality and the sheen of the paper on which the attractive photos of the interior and exterior of the hotels are printed are all factors that attract the reader's attention, inviting him/her to explore the verbal part in some way. Both the landscape photos and the two portrait photos, in full colour, lead the visual reader to a world of luxury and efficiency, described essentially by the verbal component. The use of a catchy vocabulary, a simple and attracting syntax and subjective epithets in the verbiage generate a positive attitude toward the hotels. Meanwhile the photographs show the exclusivity of the areas shown on each page of the book, serving as proof of the warm and elite atmosphere created in each specific hotel. Sometimes the photos display specific aspects of the hotels promoted in a metonymic way, suggesting that their rooms are so spacious that they cannot be included in a single shot. Thus, the visual component acts as a spider's web that captures the gaze of the viewer and guides it towards the information described in the verbal component. The co-deployment of images and words creates a reading path from the visual to the verbal, leading the viewer even deeper into a world of luxury and exclusivity. Text and image are united as a single whole whose main function is to convince the potential client about the convenience of booking a stay in a hotel from *The Leading Hotels of the World*. Both words and images are essential components of the final multimodal product and reinforce each other to promote the hotels as unique destinations. Bortuluzzi (2010: 174) states that 'the world construed by adverts appeals to one of the main needs of human nature: the desire to improve living conditions moving from a problematic situation to a world of ideal progress'. In the case of hotel brochures, there is no previous problem, but they appeal to the desire to escape from the ordinariness of everyday life into luxury. Through the interaction of images and words the hotel brochures analysed in this chapter sell not just a service, but a high-class lifestyle and an ideology of exclusivity.

Writers, artists and web designers are trained in such a way that they know how to choose the appropriate verbal and visual strategies available within a specific language to design adverts which are semiotically sensitive and compositionally appealing to their intended customers (Hopearuoho and Ventola, 2009). Awareness of the tools of multisemiotics helps us to understand how adverts are construed by advertisers to make particular meanings and how they may be critically interpreted by the verbal or visual reader. In turn, readers of adverts should develop a critical multisemiotic awareness in order to understand the complex strategies behind multisemiotic products and resist the manipulation often present in everyday adverts. Only if readers are familiar with the meaning potential of multisemiotic tools in the process of making meaning will they be able to unravel the persuasion strategies of hotel adverts and, as a result, make rational choices and decisions about the products they truly need.

Notes

1. The hotels, included in *The Leading Hotels of the World* (2009) on pages 289–98, are: Baglioni London, Brown's Hotel, Cadogan Hotel, Dukes, The Halkin, The Landmark London, The Langham, The Milestone Hotel, One Aldwych and The Ritz London.
2. 0 is used to signal an ellipsed theme.
3. In line with Cornish's (2004) views, in this chapter the topic is defined as a contextual, salient and referential entity about which information is given at the clause level. The clausal topic is a constituent that is at the forefront of the interlocutor's consciousness at the time of speech and which, after its first activation, is maintained through the continuous references that are made to it throughout the text (Givón, 1983, 1995). The topic is thus a discursive and contextual function which goes beyond the rigid syntactic order of the English clause. The subject, however, is basically identified syntactically by its position in declarative and interrogative structures and does not always carry out a topical function as it does not necessarily express what the clause is about. In turn, as has been previously pointed out, the theme, the first ideational constituent of the clause, is primarily a structural concept, fundamentally defined as the point of departure of the clause as message (Halliday, 2004). For further information about the differences between the pragmatic function of topic and the grammatical function of subject, as well as their correlation with the structural category of theme, see Moya (2006a, 2006b).

References

Bateman, J. A. (2008) *Multimodality and Genre: A Foundation for the Systematic Analysis of Multimodal Documents.* London: Palgrave.

Bortuluzzi, M. (2010) Energy and its double: A case-study in critical multimodal discourse analysis. In E. Swain (ed.) *Thresholds and Potentialities of Systemic Functional Linguistics: Multilingual, Multimodal and Other Specialised Discourses* 158–181. Trieste: EUT Edizioni Università di Trieste.

Cheong, Y. Y. (2004) The construal of ideational meaning in print advertisements. In K. O'Halloran (ed.) *Multimodal Discourse Analysis* 163–95. London: Continuum.

Cook, G. (2001) *The Discourse of Advertising.* London: Routledge.

Cornish, F. (2004) Focus of attention in discourse. In J. Lachlan Mackenzie and María Gómez (eds) *A New Architecture for Functional Grammar* 117–150. Berlin: Mouton de Gruyter.

Crystal, D. (2011) *Internet Linguistics.* London: Routledge.

Daneš, F. (1974) Functional sentence perspective and the organization of the text. In F. Daneš (ed.) *Papers on Functional Sentence Perspective* 106–28. Prague: Academic.

Downing, A. and Locke, P. (1992) *A University Course in English Grammar.* New York: Prentice Hall.

Dyer, G. (1982) *Advertising as Communication.* London: Routledge.

Forceville, C. (2009) Metonymy in visual and audiovisual discourse. In E. Ventola and A. J. Moya Guijarro (eds) *The World Told and the World Shown: Multisemiotic Issues* 56–74. London: Palgrave Macmillan.

Ghadessy, M. (ed.) (1995) *Thematic Development in English Texts.* London: Pinter.

Givón, T. (1983) *Topic Continuity in Discourse: A Quantitative Cross-language Study.* Amsterdam: John Benjamins.

Givón, T. (1993). *English Grammar. A Functional-based Introduction II.* Amsterdam: John Benjamins.

Givón, T. (1995) *Functionalism and Grammar.* Amsterdam: John Benjamins.

Halliday, M. A. K. (1978) *Language as Social Semiotic: The Social Interpretation of Language and Meaning.* London: Edward Arnold.

Halliday, M. A. K. (1994) *An Introduction to Functional Grammar,* 2nd edn. London: Edward Arnold.

Halliday, M. A. K. (2004) *An Introduction to Functional Grammar,* 3rd edn, revised by C. M. I. M. Matthiessen. London: Edward Arnold.

Halliday, M. A. K and Hasan, R. (1985) *Language, Context and Text: Aspects of Language in a Social-Semiotic Perspective.* Oxford: Oxford University Press.

Hopearuoho, A. and Ventola, E. (2009) Multisemiotic marketing and advertising: Globalization versus localization and the media. In E. Ventola and A. J. Moya Guijarro (eds) *The World Told and the World Shown: Multisemiotic Issues* 183–204. London: Palgrave Macmillan.

Kress, G. (2010) *Multimodality: A Social Semiotic Approach to Contemporary Communication.* London/New York: Routledge.

Kress, G. and van Leeuwen, T. (1996) *Reading Images: The Grammar of Visual Design*. London: Routledge.

Kress, G. and van Leeuwen, T. (2001) *Multimodal Discourse: The Modes and Media of Contemporary Communication*. London: Edward Arnold.

Kress, G. and van Leeuwen, T. (2006) *Reading Images: The Grammar of Visual Design*, 2nd edn. London: Routledge.

Lemke, J. (2009) Multimodality and reading: The construction of meaning through image–text interaction. In C. Jewitt (ed.) *The Routledge Handbook of Multimodal Analysis* 140–50. London: Routledge.

Lim, Fei, V. (2004) Developing an integrative multisemiotic model. In K. L. O'Halloran (ed.) *Multimodal Discourse Analysis* 220–46. London: Continuum.

Martin, J. R. (1992) *English Text: System and Structure*. Amsterdam: John Benjamins.

Martin, J. R. (2002) Fair trade: Negotiating meaning in multimodal texts. In P. Coppock (ed.) *The Semiotics of Writing: Transdisciplinary Perspectives on the Technology of Writing* 311–38. Begijnhof: Brepols and Indiana University Press.

Martin, J. R. and Rose, D. (2003) *Working with Discourse: Meaning Beyond the Clause*. London: Continuum.

Moya, A. J. (2006a) The continuity of topics in journal and travel texts: A discourse functional perspective. *Functions of Language* 13(1): 37–76.

Moya, A. J. (2006b) On pragmatic functions and their correlations with syntactic functions: A functionalist perspective. *Atlantis* 28(1): 9–28.

Moya, A. J. (2011) Engaging readers through language and pictures: A case study. *Journal of Pragmatics* 43(12): 2982–91.

Moya, A. J. and Ávila, J. A. (2009) Thematic progression of children's stories as related to different stages of cognitive development. *Text and Talk* 29(6): 755–74.

Moya, A. J. and Pinar, M. J. (2008) Compositional, interpersonal and representational meanings in a children's narrative: A multimodal discourse analysis. *Journal of Pragmatics* 40(9): 1601–19.

O'Halloran, K. and Lim Fei, V. (2009) Sequential visual discourse frames. In E. Ventola and A. J. Moya (eds) *The World Told and the World Shown: Multisemiotic Issues* 139–56. London: Palgrave Macmillan.

O'Toole, M. (1994) *The Language of Displayed Art*. London: Leicester University Press.

Starc, S. (2010) Textual patterning and information flow (theme/rheme) in the generic evolution of 19th century Slovene newspaper advertisements. In E. Swain (ed.) *Thresholds and Potentialities of Systemic Functional Linguistics: Multilingual, Multimodal and Other Specialised Discourses* 133–57. Trieste: EUT Edizioni Università di Trieste.

Thurlow, C. and Jaworski, A. (2006) The alchemy of the upwardly mobile: Symbolic capital and the stylization of elites in frequent-flyer programmes. *Discourse and Society* 17(1): 99–135.

Unsworth, L. (2006) Towards a metalanguage for multiliteracies education: Describing the meaning-making resources of language–image interaction. *English Teaching: Practice and Critique* 5(1): 55–76.

Van Leeuwen, T. (2005) *Introducing Social Semiotics*. London: Routledge.

12 | A multimodal perspective on the front cover choices of Halliday's *Introduction to Functional Grammar*

Ann Montemayor-Borsinger[a], Eija Ventola[b] and Célia M. Magalhães[c]

12.1 Introduction

In systemic functional linguistics (SFL), the core concept is choice. This notion covers not only the choices in meaning-making in texts, but also the choices in visuals, for example on book cover designs. This chapter illustrates this point by discussing the choices 'of' and 'on' the front covers in the successive editions of Michael Halliday's *Introduction to Functional Grammar* (IFG).

We all buy books that are readily 'packaged' for us – they have front and back covers. Sometimes books as a packaged artefact are sealed, and we can only see their front and back covers at the time of making a purchase decision, but frequently we can also see the inside flaps and

---

a   Ann Montemayor-Borsinger is Professor of Linguistics at Río Negro and Cuyo National Universities, Patagonia, Argentina, and Invited Professor on postgraduate programmes at the University of Buenos Aires. Her research interests focus on functional grammar, discourse analysis, and translation studies. She has published widely, drawing on systemic functional linguistics to investigate different types of discourse in English, Spanish and French.

b   Eija Ventola is an established linguist who has previously held professorial posts in several countries. She has published and edited widely on functional linguistics, discourse analysis, genre studies, multimodality, literary stylistics, on translation issues. She has recently taken a position as Professor of International Business Communication at Aalto University, in Helsinki, Finland.

c   Célia M. Magalhães is a Full Professor in Linguistics and Applied Linguistics at Universidade Federal de Minas Gerais, Brazil. Her research interests lie in the areas of corpus-based translation studies and their recent focus on the style of translations and audiodescription in relation with multimodality.

flick through the content of the books (or at least get some examples of the content, e.g. when the books are sold on the web). Within marketing, some research suggests that the subject matter of the book together with the author's reputation and especially the inside flaps and the back cover texts are the most important influences on the buying decisions of the readers (see www.authorinsider.com/insightfulstatistics.php and www.authorinsider.com/article.php?subaction=showfull&id=1154356384&archive=&start_from=&ucat=10&). In magazine sales, the designs of the covers also seem to have an influence on the appeal of the product and the sales (see e.g. Iedema and Eggins, 1997; Held, 2005). In the book publishing industry, if the books are bestsellers following editions appear in 'new packages' with freshly designed front covers.

However, to our knowledge little is known about the 'histories' of the book design selections and what they are intended to 'do'. This chapter precisely reflects on the histories and the significance of the changes on the front covers of the three editions of Halliday's *IFG*. It takes on board variations in context, research on multimodality and the grammar of visual design with its new developments on colour and typography to discuss the highly distinctive representations on the covers: the image of a sculpture, oriented towards language-as-function in the 1985 edition, a colour wheel oriented towards language-as-representation in the 1994 edition, and conceptual blocks oriented towards language-as-system in the 2004 edition. The black and white versions of the actual covers are reproduced in Figures 12.1, 12.2 and 12.3, by kind permission of the Henry Moore Foundation and Hodder Education for the first edition, and Hodder Education for the second and third editions.

Front covers are considered here as a particular genre. This concept of genre is crucial both in functional discourse analysis (cf. Martin and Rose, 2003 and 2008 for recent discussions) and also in multimodal analysis (cf. Bateman, 2008; O'Halloran, 2005; Thomas, 2009). We have initially tended towards following a typical Hallidayan tri-partite analysis, without forgetting that Bateman (2008: 246) has asked seminal questions about the relevance of a tripartite metafunctional view to multimodal analysis, discussing for instance how music genres are more textual and interpersonal than ideational. Furthermore, O'Halloran (2009: 231) has provided an interesting multimodal discussion on the prominence that acquires certain metafunctions over others, taking as an example mathematics in text books, where the textual and the experiential metafunctions are given prominence over the interpersonal.

When examining some front covers of textbook genres in linguistics, more specifically textbooks in systemic functional linguistics of the 1980s

Figure 12.1 *IFG* front cover, first edition, 1985.

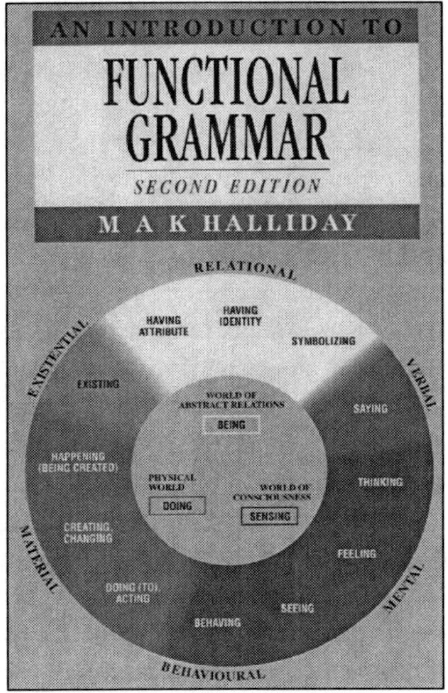

Figure 12.2 *IFG* front cover, second edition, 1994.

Figure 12.3 *IFG* front cover, third edition, 2004.

and 1990s, they appear to follow the more established practice for academic books of marketing themselves as serious and important works with sober monochromatic covers or discretely texturized ones, rather than adopting more aggressive marketing strategies of appealing to prospective buyers. If colours are given prominence, they are typically confined to a sober palette of orange, red or green, such as in the classic Oxford University Press textbooks edited by Frances Christie, or the Cambridge Textbooks in Linguistics. Another example is Benjamins, which opts for a uniform pale pink for its hard covers of Current Issues in Linguistic Theory. If images are chosen, such as in the case of the covers of the first and second editions of various SFL textbook classics (e.g. Eggins, 1994, 2004; Butt *et al.*, [1995] 2001; or Thompson [1996] 2004), they function as conventionally textured background settings for the title of the book. Moreover, for the first and second editions these background textures stay virtually the same with slight changes in hue, except for Eggins, but in this latter case the context of situation (different publishers) explains the change.

In this chapter we argue that in clear contrast with the established academic practice of monochromatic or discretely texturized, non-representational backgrounds, the *IFG* covers represent aspects of *IFG* theory.

We show that whereas textbook front covers traditionally seek to appeal interpersonally to prospective readers with the compositional (textual) also being given prominence, the *IFG* covers focus on realizing the ideational function. Each *IFG* cover clearly invites the readers to make the ideational link between the cover and the theory presented in the book, and this link is established multimodally by the image chosen for the cover. Furthermore, the readers are guided to consider the link between the multimodal differences across the three cover images and the theoretical changes in the three volumes.

The chapter is organized as follows. §12.2 discusses in detail the context of situation of the three covers and what the authors say about the decisions that were actually made when choosing them. §12.3 refers to the method of analysis used for the *IFG* covers, that is the system networks which represent the meaning potential of visual language as choice (Kress and van Leeuwen, 2006), which are hypothesized here as making it possible for 'knowledgeable' readers to make two types of link, first between the *IFG* covers and the theory in the book, and second across the three covers and the theory. §12.4 presents a detailed account of the analysis. Finally, §12.5 concludes that the *IFG* covers stand out as multimodal artefacts that strongly draw on choices in the ideational metafunction: the choice of an external representation of SFL theory for the first edition that displays a different paradigm from Chomskyan linguistics, and different choices of internal representations that reflect the evolution of SFL theory in the second and third editions.

12.2 Author perspectives: Choice and context of situation

At times authors have no say in designing the front covers (as is often the case with textbook covers or book series covers, see §12.1). However, we have a different context of situation in the case of the *IFG* covers, where the authors were consulted by the publisher and took an active part in their design. To find out the 'author perspectives' for the three *IFG* designs, Michael Halliday, and in the case of the third edition also Christian Matthiessen, were interviewed (by Ventola, 16 February and 17 July 2009), and were specifically asked how the covers came about and what they saw as important choices for the meaning-making on the individual covers.

Halliday worked on the first edition (hereafter *IFG 85*) for many years (many of his students at the University of Sydney fondly remember his lectures and handouts, and the previous compilations of the *IFG*). When the edition was about ready, the editor for Edward Arnold, Leslie Riddle, approached Halliday. As he had no immediate proposal for a cover, she made a suggestion of a representation of modern artwork as the cover. Both simultaneously thought about Kandinsky. Kandinsky's 'middle period' (before Bauhaus) paintings had always particularly appealed to Halliday. He could no longer remember which specific painting the editor and he had thought about, but showed in the interview a similar painting by Kandinsky and explained:

> you have to look at it [the painting with geometric forms and lines] with different depths of focus, so you got to look at it from the distance and you also got to look at it close up, and you see very different things, and that of course was a very good metaphor for what I think about language ... you know, you've got to look at it from close up but you've also got to look at it from the distance. (Halliday, 16.2.2009)

Having promptly agreed on a Kandinsky painting as a cover, they soon had to cancel the plan: the Kandinsky foundation demanded such a high fee for the use of the painting that it threatened to triple the cost of the book. The search for a cover image continued and eventually they settled for Henry Moore's sculpture *Three Points*. The decision was easy because, as Halliday commented, the significance of the image to the content in the book is so obvious: 'the three prongs representing the three metafunctions of language' (Halliday, 16.2.2009). The use of the image was free and kept the price of the *IFG 85* reasonable. Once the choice was agreed upon, the actual detailed design and the colours of the cover were left to the publisher and were not discussed further with Halliday.

This history of the *IFG 85* front cover shows how financial factors may have a very strong influence on the choice of the visual representations of covers. However, from the author's perspective, although the original idea was not realized (the Kandinsky painting), the final choice successfully represents another fundamental metaphor for what he thought about language. This is the view of language as a tri-functional meaning potential – the idea that Halliday strongly put forward in the book and which is also discussed in the analysis of the cover in §12.3.

When the second edition (hereafter *IFG 94*) was prepared, the question of the cover was raised again. Having learnt about the possible high fees connected with the use of artwork, Halliday rejected the publisher's suggestion of another artwork and proposed that one of his own diagrams, 'colour circle', should be used for the cover (see Figure 12.2). In the interview, he did not comment on the origins of the wheel, but pointed out how he, when teaching grammar, always had used colours (coloured chalk) to help his students visualize the different process types in the transitivity analysis. Putting the figure representing the various transitivity process types on the *IFG 94* cover in colour gave Halliday an opportunity to express the importance of learning to code the differences between the processes through colours. Colours on book pages at that time were still very rare (the same 'colour wheel' appears in the *IFG 94* on page 108 as a black and white figure, Fig. 5-0): 'what I wanted to do in designing the diagram in the first place was to show the continuities all around so that the colour chart is the continuity in the sense of the primary colours and the mixtures in between … so you've got the red … orange, yellow, green, blue, violet' (Halliday, 16.2.2009). The first version of the colour circle which the publisher showed to Halliday had very clear distinctions between the colours. Halliday, however, wanted to add a further meaning to the display of the front cover figure: the boundaries between the colours had to be fuzzy at the edges so that the colours actually merged into one another. Halliday's motivation for this was: 'I wanted to say that they are not clear-cut categories; they are like all other linguistic categories; they are fuzzy' (16.2.2009). The publisher's graphic artist did merge the colours, and the final result successfully represented the meanings that the author wanted to bring out in the figure and which we will also show in §12.4 to be prominent in the analyses:

> I was in fact very pleased with this because … the other was not very colourful [the *IFG 85*], this one brought in the colour but in a very motivated way and also I hope … gave a sense … of the general approach and a part of the descriptive framework [transitivity] that you find in the book that you read. (Halliday, 16.2.2009)

The third edition of the book (hereafter *IFG 04*) was produced in close co-operation with Christian Matthiessen. Halliday recounts Matthiessen having done 'most of the work of the revision. We shared it up but I would say that the main burden of it fell on him' (Halliday, 16.2.2009; Matthiessen was interviewed by Ventola 17.7.2009). The issue of how to show the authors on the cover was settled by saying that the *IFG 04* 'was revised' by Matthiessen. The *IFG 04* front cover is in Halliday's description 'a rather nice colourful cover, in this case based on the three … more or less primary colours: blue, red and yellow' (Halliday, 16.2.2009). The cover issue for the *IFG 04* was settled by choosing a figure that would represent something essential to systemic functional linguistic theory and description, something that once again could be highlighted by colour. The authors' unanimous decision for the cover was Matthiessen's important figure which represents the stratification and the instantiation aspects of language. Matthiessen explained the choice as follows:

> so we used the diagram ... that was around in a few different versions but I constructed a diagram with the colours of the metafunctions and so on ... and it was intended as a sort of global overview with the metafunctions and this stratal organization and the cline of instantiation so they did have sort of a map and a way to zoom in and show where the grammar was located in the overall ... model of language in context ... and so I drew that and we thought that that was alright and then we sent it to the publisher and I think they also asked professional graphic artists and he or she improved it using one of these very high-powered illustration programmes and they gave it more of a 3-D look ... so that was the result of the collaboration ... so that was quite nice to see what the professional graphic artists would do with it and how they'd improve it ... I think it suggests how sharp the designer was ... she or he picked up on what the figure was intended to do ... and then improved on that ... so it was an interesting example of ... the designer who is very good at seeing the possibilities of forms of whatever is in the original design. (Matthiessen, 17.7.2009)

Halliday was very satisfied with the representation and described Matthiessen as 'a genius for producing diagrams of all kinds, graphic representations of everything in language' (Halliday, 16.2.2009). When describing the representative function of the diagram, Halliday referred to the primary dimension of the figure on the cover as bringing out the 'instantiation' and praised it for recapitulating his original idea with Kandinsky and the message of his paintings and its application to looking at language:

> it shows you ... the different depths of focus with which you have to look at ... language as a system and instance ... so this [the figure] does just that; it sets it up as a relation from the potential, the system, to the instance here [pointing to the figure] and then ... within that framework it separates out two other dimensions – the scales from the old scale and category terminology ... so you've got the strata down here ... and ... the rank scale down in this corner for the grammar ... so this one is entirely thanks to Christian and again I think they made a very good job in reproducing it. (Halliday, 16.2.2009)

Matthiessen described the colour choices, this time for the metafunctions and not just for transitivity, in the figure as follows:

> it was sort of standard colours – blue for the experience – ideational – experience of the sky and the sea ... red for this interpersonal – interactive – and then yellow – the highlighting colour for the textual ... so those were the colours we chose ... and then we had a little bit of shading into phonology to show that they sort of permeate a little bit into phonology for the tone group but not further into phonetics because they are essentially the modes of meaning ... erm elsewhere I've played around ... with using a real spectrum to represent the metafunctions so you get a sense of how they overlap or shade into one another but here [in the cover figure] they're, you know, more clearly differentiated. (Matthiessen, 17.7.2009)

Matthiessen explained that the cover figure of the *IFG 04* actually represents the graphic rewriting of the first couple of chapters in the book and reflects on the changes that had taken place in the systemic theory and linguistics during the period between the first and the third editions, 1985–2004, changes that will be discussed in the analyses of the three covers in Section 12.4. Both Halliday and Matthiessen were keen to show on the *IFG 04* cover a 'map' that captured the developments since 1985, particularly in the descriptive and analytical work on areas other than lexicogrammar. Both also felt the urge 'to make sure that people were not focussed only on the grammar but could see it ... from an ecological perspective of the grammar ... [having] a ... sense of what else there is' (Matthiessen, 17.7.2009). Matthiessen in particular emphasised the fact that too frequently other linguists take 'systemic functional linguistics as synonymous with systemic functional grammar ... SFL equals SFG ... and that's possibly understandable but it's unfortunate ... you should be able to see that the grammar is one region but that there's all this whole rest of the world of semiosis' (Matthiessen, 17.7.2009). Indeed, systemic functional linguistics is somewhat unique in its aims of describing the role of language in the whole multisemiotic meaning-making process in social contexts.

12.3 Method of analysis: Choice and visual language

Having discussed the context of situation of the *IFG* covers, they will now be analysed on the basis of the system networks which represent the meaning potential of visual language (Kress and van Leeuwen, 2006). Following the Hallidayan metafunctions, Kress and van Leeuwen claim that visual communication also aims at making three different and simultaneous meanings: representational, interactive and compositional meaning. Each is represented as a system network where, given an entry point, the desired meaning can be made through a choice which is then realized through alternative or simultaneous systems/system features.

Based on the concept of *tilting* as the creation of 'oblique lines and a sense of vectoriality' (*ibid.*: 57), Kress and van Leeuwen claim that when representational meaning is constructed in visual communication there are two kinds of different choices to be made. On the one hand, there are *narrative structures* which 'serve to present unfolding actions and events, processes of change, transitory spatial arrangements' (*ibid.*: 59), that is they 'design ... social action' (*ibid.*: 45), and, on the other, there are *conceptual structures* which represent 'participants in terms of their class, structure, or meaning ..., in terms of their more generalized and more or less stable and timeless essence' (*ibid.*: 59), that is these structures 'design ... social constructs' (*ibid.*: 79).

Kress and van Leeuwen also claim that 'visual communication ... has resources for constituting and maintaining ... interaction between the producer and the viewer of the image' (*ibid.*: 114). Thus there are 'two kinds of participants, *represented participants* ... and *interactive participants* ... and three kinds of relations' (*ibid.*: 114), the ones between represented participants, the ones between interactive and represented participants and the ones between the interactive participants. Based on this claim, they provide a system network for interactive meanings with systems/features for contact, social distance, and attitude (*ibid.*: 149, Fig. 4.23).

Moreover these authors suggest that patterns of representational and interactive meanings 'do not exhaust the relations set up by ... image[s]' (*ibid.*: 176) in visual communication. Thus they add a compositional meaning which 'relates the representational and interactive meaning ... to each other through three interrelated systems' (*ibid.*: 177), which are informational value, salience, and framing (*ibid.*: 210, Fig. 6.21).

Finally, Kress and van Leeuwen are also concerned with the 'coding orientations ..., sets of abstract principles which inform the way in which texts are coded by specific social groups, or within specific institutional contexts' (*ibid.*: 165), among them the naturalistic coding orientation, dominant in Western society. In the grammar of visual design, Kress and van Leeuwen study the role of colours as one of the six modality markers (*ibid.*: 160). They point out that colours could be accounted in terms of *saturation, differentiation* and *modulation, scales* or *continua* (for example, colour saturation would be 'a scale running from full colour saturation to the absence of colour' (*ibid.*: 160). They also develop 'a feature approach to the semiotics of colour' with 'a complex and composite meaning potential' integrated by six scales including the previous three, *value, saturation, purity, modulation, differentiation,* and *hue* (Kress and van Leeuwen, 2002: 354–7).

These features in the system networks for representational, interactive and compositional meaning, together with the meaning potential of the semiotics of colour, will now be used in the analysis of the three *IFG* covers.

12.4 Analysis and discussion of the *IFG* front cover choices

This section brings together the three meanings of the different images on the front covers, with a focus on the different choices in representational and compositional meanings. There is comparatively less to say regarding choices in interactive meanings, which are going to be covered briefly first.

12.4.1 Interactive meanings

Choices in interactive meanings are interesting in that they are related in the three covers, with a similar use of perspective in image representation in the three covers. *IFG 85* presents a photo of Henry Moore's three-dimensional sculpture *Three Points*, an image reminiscent of knowledge-oriented objectivity in the system of Attitude. The *IFG 94* wheel with foregrounding and backgrounding, and the *IFG 04* three-dimensional plane of design are also reminiscent of knowledge-oriented objectivity in the system of Attitude. The sign producers seem to be explicitly inviting observers to new developments in the theory in each edition.

12.4.2 Representational meanings

There are two possible, complementary ways of analysing the *IFG 85* front cover representing *Three Points* (see Figure 12.1). The first involves analysing the sculpture as a single represented participant. The left and right points seem to be growing as the natural endings of a line from the sculpture base; the third point grows from the middle of the line in order to meet the first two, bending points. The points in the sculpture come together at the top, justifying the interpretation as a narrative structure, but as a non-transactional one, without an explicit goal. It is the 'coming together' that justifies the association of the three functions: ideational, interpersonal and textual. *Three Points* can also be interpreted as a symbolic process of the suggestive type. The idea is of a single carrier with the detailed points de-emphasized in favour of an atmosphere created by the sculpture as a whole with its meaning deriving from its strength. Whichever analysis is taken, it points towards the three metafunctions and their working together. We thus can understand the choice of the sculpture for the cover of *IFG 85* as a realization of the language-as-functional-oriented hypothesis and of its simultaneous tripartite realization.

In the next, *IFG 94*, edition, the cover shows a colour chart, as it is commonly named by colour theorists such as Chevreul and Hayet (Gage, 1999: 206). Kress and van Leeuwen (2002: 348) recognize that colours often have ideational meaning. The *IFG 94* cover explores this by using, first of all, the ideational meaning of colours in clauses and its realization at the level of lexicogrammar as the transitivity structure. Secondly, the colour circle uses three out of the five primary colours of early colour systems, black, white, yellow, red and blue, as elementary. Yellow, red and blue represent relational, material and mental processes respectively as elementary choices of the processes in the transitivity system. The representational link is established by setting the label next to the colour.

However, *IFG 94* also uses other colours, the result of mixing the three primaries in different ways. Clockwise in the circle, green, as a mixture of blue and yellow, represents verbal processes; violet, as a mixture of blue and red, represents behavioural processes, and orange, as mixture of red and yellow, represents existential processes.

The circle is a represented participant on the cover and, in turn, the colours can also be taken as the cover's represented participants. They could be interpreted simultaneously as compounded, conjoined, and/or fused participants. Each colour, be it primary or mixed, is distinct from the others due to the marked lines between the sections, as with compounded participants. At the same time, the space where these colours mix at the edges of the marked lines can be taken as a process that connects them, so the colours would thus also be conjoined participants. This space also seems to be there to remind us of the status of mixed colours: there is no longer any separate identity of the primary colours that have been mixed to produce a third one. This should be the locus of fused participants.

The cover thus simultaneously takes two different approaches to *colour*, a system based on *hue* and *value* (Kress and van Leeuwen, 2002: 351). It represents both basic colour units and their consonant combinations and also a system of colour complementarity (*ibid.*: 352), in which the primary colours are said to harmonize with mixtures of, for example, the other two primaries. Complementarity of colours[1] could be taken as a representation of complementarity of processes in the transitivity system.

In the same fashion, pure colours such as yellow, red and blue may become hybrid, bearing some resemblance with processes when their main feature is blurred, as we get in-between locus of choice. This would explain the choice of representing the chart as a circle – an ideal representation of complementarity and its more complex meanings in terms of colour hues, values and modulation.

In the latest *IFG 04* edition, there seems to be a predominant conceptual representation of social constructs, which leads observers to the essence of the geometrical figures, more specifically to an analytical structure. Potential, sub-potential and instance are possessive attributes of a carrier, the language in context being represented not visually but verbally.

Going right into levels of delicacy, this would be a structured analytical construct and the type of process an exhaustive one: from potential to instance – the horizontal layers of content and expression, the vertical layers of the semantic components, and, finally, the horizontal layers of clause, phrase/group/word and morpheme – and back again. Notice that the numbering of different levels reinforces the idea of exhaustiveness in a structured process. Going further right, the geometrical figures are conjoined participants, connected both through the repeated colours and the soft, modulated blue lines associating them at the top and bottom. Going further right again, there would thus be 'plus conductivity' between geometrical figures. But geometrical figures are in themselves also compounded participants – subdivided into the vertical semantic layers and the horizontal stratal layers by demarcated lines. This feature would be one of 'minus conductivity'. After all, even though the language strata and the semantic components as metafunctional cannot be separated in language instances, in the terrain of language potential they must be separated if we are to be oriented towards abstract, theoretical knowledge.

In the system of *accuracy* the choice is one of topographical dimension, that is the carrier and possessive attributes are drawn to scale. In the system of *abstraction*, the geometrical figures can be taken as more concrete than abstract, even though they symbolically represent aspects of *IFG*. Notice that as they are obliquely drawn they give a sense not only of length and height but also of width, their third dimension, which is reinforced by the softer, blurred colour line below the three flat, saturated colourful layers.

Interestingly, context is not an exhaustive analytical structure on this cover. The observer might assume that context is associated to the potential/typology/instance cline. As typology is here for the first time explicitly included as a level of the language system, it could be inferred that context in *IFG* will be restricted to language typology, text types and register. The wider, cultural level of context would thus be either suppressed or backgrounded (in the terms of Kress and van Leeuwen, 1996), suppressed for those who encounter the *IFG* for the first time and backgrounded for those who already know the theory from its very beginning. Either way, the choice seems to be one of focusing explicitly on the context of situation and leaving the context of culture as a 'blurred' given.

12.4.3 Compositional meanings

With reference to the system of information value, there is no horizontal polarization in the *IFG 85* as the sculpture is presented in the middle of the cover, so an analysis of given and new would not apply.

There is vertical polarization on *IFG 85* with the title at the top and the sculpture at the bottom. A hierarchy is established between what was most important in the first publication of *IFG* – legitimating the theory and its author – and what perhaps was less important, representing the theory through a modernist sculpture by Henry Moore. It is an abstract work of art that has been taken to represent systemic functional linguistic theory to the linguistic community as another ideal choice.

With reference to salience, though the sculpture is not fully represented it acquires maximum salience due to its size and forms on the cover. Part of the title also acquires maximum salience due to the size of the font. Both the grammar and the sculpture are functional, with the sculpture growing to generate the 'three-points-as-metafunctions' that in the end point up and at each other.

Regarding framing, title and sculpture (verbal and visual) are maximally connected through the choice of the colour blue. The blue of the title is flat and fully saturated, and the blue of the sculpture can almost be seen as an effect of the play of light and shade in the bronze which gives it a bluish brightness.

On the grey monochrome background of the *IFG 94* cover there is the colour chart with verbal information on the transitivity system at the bottom and the *IFG* title, edition and author within a two-coloured rectangle at the top. Choice from the information value system could be interpreted as vertical polarization (if there is polarization at all) between simultaneous verbal and visual information on the cover as the ideal and simultaneous visual and verbal information on transitivity as the real.

The chart has maximum salience due to its size and number of colours. Even though there is framing to foreground the wheel and rectangle on the grey cover, they are not maximally disconnected from one another. Yellow and green establish a strong connection between the two figures and what they represent. Yellow is major in the rectangle and perhaps more powerful in the circle because of its position on the top. Green defines the top and bottom lines of the rectangle – *An Introduction To* and *M A K Halliday* respectively, evocative of the author's voice and representing the world of saying and verbal processes in the circle.

The top half of the *IFG 04* cover is a display of colours. The primary colours blue, red and yellow come on the first layer at the very top. Black is the second, largest layer and background for the title, *An Introduction to Functional Grammar*, centred in huge capital letters right below the primaries of transitivity. Right below this layer comes another layer, similar to the transitivity layer in width, in soft, modulated blue, the edition number centred in smaller capital letters of a different font to the one used for the title. The primaries of transitivity, represented visually through the colours, plus the title *An Introduction to Functional Grammar* and *Third Edition*, represented verbally through typographical resources and visually through colour, are the essence of the book.

The first layer of the bottom half of the cover is white with geometrical blocks and charts. Right below this white layer, there is a black layer with the author's and reviser's names centred on it. Blocks and charts as the *IFG* strata/concepts and the author's and reviser's names are practical, real information for the *IFG* readers. The repeated colours are the salient element in the composition. The foregrounded and labelled semantic block is also salient. Layers, blocks and charts are framed but connected both through the repeated colours in the different layers, blocks and charts, and the soft, modulated blue and black lines in between blocks.

Because they are composed of layers, ideal and real seem not to be at stake on *IFG 04*. The layers indicate the theory's strength as building blocks for its development from the foundations onwards – from the first *IFG* edition to the third.

The analysis of composition at the horizontal axis takes as a basis only the white layer of the cover with its blocks and charts. Even though blocks are centred on the layer, the first block to the left – verbally the meaning potential and verbally/visually the semantic stratum – could be said to correspond to the given of *IFG*. Context and language as larger strata are also represented verbally in capital letters as given, with language as system subdivided into content and expression. The layered block to the far right, instance, is the new of *IFG*. The whole figure is a triptych since the far left and the far right blocks are mediated by a middle layered block, instance type/subpotential.

There would thus seem to be a cline between language potential and language instance, from potential to instance and from instance to potential, with language typology as subpotential in the middle. Interestingly enough, it is the language typology as mediator between potential and instance as explicitly displayed and labelled on the cover that seems to be the *IFG* new, at least for the first time explicitly labelled within the theory and displayed on the cover. The new in this composition seems not to be opposed to the given due to double – actually multiple – directed lines heading to the different levels.

12.4.4 Similarities and differences in the visual choices

As we mentioned in the previous sections, analyses based on interactive meanings have little to contribute towards an interpretation of front cover *CHOICES*. Compositional meanings, on the other hand, have helped to support a more detailed interpretation of choices in representational meanings, especially of *IFG 04*. These front cover choices in representational meanings are actually the ones that definitively stand out.

The tripartite metafunctional hypothesis for language seems to be a constant choice on the *IFG* covers. In *IFG 85*, this hypothesis comes out through the organic[2] three-pointed sculpture in strong narrative structure, as the design of the theory as a social action; but also in conceptual structure, as the design of the theory as a social construct. In *IFG 94*, the representation at first seems not to be organic because the choice is a geometrical figure and the meaning is mainly conceptual. But the geometrical figure is a circle, in itself an organic, nature-associated figure. And colours as participants or possessive attributes of the carrier as language transitivity system also lead us into language as organically constructed. The primary colours are the main possessive attributes of the transitivity system, and the mixed colours help to build a sense of complementarity in the system. Material processes were analysed as given, mental processes as new, and relational processes as ideal in the transitivity system, but without the sense of oppositeness between these possessive attributes. Verbal signs in the middle and around the circle associated to the visual for the first time on the *IFG* cover seem to be playing the role of the third in the relation. But as verbal signs are included on *IFG 94*, and the cover is interpreted as mainly conceptual, the focus on metafunctions could be interpreted as foregrounding a science-like theory more than an organic and nature-like theory. Again, an analysis based on representational meanings stands out as particularly strong, with the other two kinds of meanings contributing comparatively little, or supporting representational ones as is the case of compositional analysis.

In *IFG 04* the structure is mainly conceptual with rectangle geometrical figures that seem to wipe out organicity from the general *IFG* constructs. Nevertheless, the dotted line emanating from the semantic component, one of the possessive attributes of the carrier, now explicitly displayed as a cline between meaning potential to typology and on to instance, brings the narrative structure back ('semantic potential is realized through lexico-grammar') and with it the organic nature of the theory. The foregrounded semantic component on the cover also brings back the metafunctional component, and also, in a way, the language-as-metafunctional notion. Verbal signs, mainly lexical items, and a more packed, abstract repre-sentation of theoretical synthesis than the collocations on *IFG 94*, are nevertheless still there together with the other visuals, which again blur or background the notion of organicity. From *IFG 94* to *IFG 04*, and especially at the moment the latter is published, the theory is more in the realm of abstraction (system) than in the realm of language use (instance), though, again, complementarity is at stake. The theory, because it is a language theory, can thus be interpreted as a post-modern, hybrid, scientific and nature-like theory. In addition, in *IFG 04*, the analysis based on the system of representational meanings is prominent, with the system of compositional meaning adding information to support it. The analysis of the three covers confirms the implications of those previously cited multimodal studies that have suggested that a tripartite analysis may not be equally applicable to all instances of multimodal signs.

12.5 Choice, context and text

This chapter first discussed the author's (and editor's) views about how they chose the covers for the different editions of *IFG* and what these were intended to visualize. This provided a context for discussing the choices of the visual potential and the kind of meanings that the choices highlight in the analyses of the covers. It then examined the strongly felt functional prominence that the *IFG* covers seemed to realize multimodally and showed how the covers present in different ways explicit systemic functional representations of language, in particular different ideational representations. The front cover of the first *IFG 85* edition used an artefact external to systemic functional theory – Henry Moore's famous sculpture, *Three Points*, a work of art – to explain the tripartite and dynamic view of language that is highlighted in SFL theory. The second *IFG 94* edition used a representation internal to SFL, the colour chart, to make Halliday's representation of experiential analysis and the transitivity analysis explicit to readers. These choices for the first and second editions are particularly interesting because the second edition is only a slight revision of *IFG 85*, with no dramatic changes in the actual text. However, the covers show completely different SFL representations. The first cover uses an external representation of SFL theory as a strong argument for the tripartite metafunctional view of language, very different from the established cognitive Chomskyan paradigm of the seventies and early eighties which, in its idealization, left out most of what is discussed in systemic functional theory (see Halliday, 1978: 37–8). The second *IFG 94* edition, nine years later, was virtually the same text but the cover had to be changed for marketing reasons and there were copyright problems with works of art. Halliday and the publisher finally decided to use a particularly striking representation that Halliday had made of the experiential metafunction, which was being given prominence in SFL studies of that time. This choice of an internal representation of SFL theory was also consistent with a different context in linguistics, where the Chomskyan paradigm was not as prevailing as in the previous decade.

The third *IFG 04* edition, double the size of the previous editions, was characterized as 'some way between a revision and a new book' (Halliday, 2004: ix), relating to the extensive contributions by Matthiessen. The cover and the text of this third edition focus much more on the system networks upon which Halliday's lexicogrammar is based, and is described as being 'one step in the direction of fleshing out the relationship between grammar and discourse semantics in context (*ibid.*: x). The multimodal analyses of the cover show the complexities involved and how this front cover reflects the shift towards the system made in the book, where the contextually placed 'potential' is foregrounded and leads to the 'instance'. The author interviews indicated that the meaning shifts that were then revealed by the multimodal analyses were actually intended and conscious choices on the part of the authors.

The *IFG* covers stand out as multimodal artefacts that strongly draw on systematic choices from all three Hallidayan metafunctions at once, which make them particularly interesting as representatives of the genre of book covers. As the analyses and the author perspectives have shown, the *IFG* covers help prospective readers to work out and understand what language is and how it functions in context. The covers sell the editions of the *IFGs* as serious academic works by drawing on the multi-semiosis of art and artwork in an unprecedented way for this particular 'packaging' genre. They also function textually as kinds of macroThemes to the information in the book and provide clear multisemiotic representations of language. The covers are pedagogically successful as they can easily be used for teaching purposes in the classroom. Rather than just presenting 'settings' for book titles, the *IFG* cover choices present three MEANINGFUL points of departure for language analysis in language teaching. Such representations are hard to find in other front covers of the same genre, and, surprisingly perhaps, are hard to find in the front covers of other academic works of the same period.

When Matthiessen was asked about the possible fourth edition of *IFG*, he stated that the publisher had contacted the authors and had in fact discussed a possible fourth edition:

> ... so it is interesting to see what we could do for the cover if there is a fourth edition ... I imagine that the fourth edition would be maybe more of a maintenance edition than the third edition was ... in other words, the third edition did have fairly major ... well added materials, rewrites, but ... er, you know, one shouldn't prejudge the fourth [edition] but it depends of course on the publisher ... how much the publisher is willing to let us do but ... er I think a possibility would be to experiment with some other version of the sort ... of global map and see if it is possible to do something that still retains this sort of sense ... of the location of the grammar in the overall system but provides another projection as it were on this ... it's always nice to experiment and if there is another edition it should be represented by another cover, I mean that's now been the principle ... the very very nice first cover of Henry Moore's statue that is brilliant as the way of suggesting the sort

of three metafunctions coming together ... but maybe we should see whether Kandinsky is cheaper now. (Matthiessen, 17.7.2009)

At the time of finishing this chapter, some time after the original interview, the publication of the fourth edition has already been agreed upon, but it does not seem likely that the fourth edition cover will be a suitable Kandinsky painting to represent the choices that Halliday had first wanted to represent. Rather, when contacted, Matthiessen wrote to us saying that the new cover is planned to be something similar to the second and third editions – some 'colourful representation of some key diagram in the book', but that he had not yet finalized the figure representation. But it surely will be something that will show how the theory of making meaningful choices has developed and keeps developing, rather than the 'usual cliché of language as letters', a representation so common on book covers.

Notes

1. On the notion of colour complementarity see also the colour circles by Hayet and Chevreul; the second image was probably a source of inspiration for *IFG 94*.
2. On the notion of organicity, see the words of Henry Moore, quoted by Edouard Roditi: '[a work of art] should always give the impression, whether carved or modeled, of having grown organically, created by pressure from within' (www.artcyclopedia.com/artists/moore_henry.html, accessed December 2009).

References

Bateman, J. (2008) *Multimodality and Genre: A Foundation for the Systematic Analysis of Multimodal Documents.* Basingstoke: Palgrave Macmillan.

Butt, D., Fahey, R., Spinks, S. and Yallop, C. ([1995] 2001) *Using Functional Grammar: An Explorer's Guide.* Sydney: Macquarie: University National Centre for English Language Teaching and Research.

Eggins, S. (1994) *An Introduction to Systemic Functional Linguistics.* London: Pinter.

Eggins, S. (2004) *An Introduction to Systemic Functional Linguistics*, 2nd edn. London: Continuum.

Gage, J. (1999) *Colour and Meaning: Art, Science and Symbolism.* London: Thames & Hudson.

Halliday, M. A. K. (1978) *Language as Social Semiotic.* London: Edward Arnold.

Halliday, M. A. K. (1985) *Introduction to Functional Grammar.* London: Edward Arnold.

Halliday, M. A. K. (1994) *Introduction to Functional Grammar*, 2nd edn. London: Edward Arnold.

Halliday, M. A. K. (2004) *Introduction to Functional Grammar*, 3rd edn. revised by C. M. I. M. Matthiessen. London: Edward Arnold.

Held, G. (2005) Magazine covers: A multimodal pretext-genre. *Folia Linguistica* 39(1–2): 173–96.

Iedema, R. A. and Eggins, S. (1997) Difference without diversity: Semantic orientation and ideology in competing women's magazines. In R. Wodak (ed.) *Gender and Discourse* 165–96. London: Sage.

Kress, G. and Van Leeuwen, T. (1996) *Reading Images – The Grammar of Visual Design.* London: Routledge.

Kress, G. and Van Leeuwen, T. (2002) Colour as a semiotic mode: Notes towards a grammar of colour. *Visual Communication* 1(3): 343–69.

Kress, G. and van Leeuwen, T. (2006) *Reading Images: The Grammar of Visual Design.* London/New York: Routledge.

Martin, J. R. and Rose, D. (2003) *Working with Discourse: Meaning Beyond the Clause.* London/New York: Continuum.

Martin, J. R. and Rose, D. (2008) *Genre Relations: Mapping Culture.* London: Equinox.

O'Halloran, K. L. (2005) *Mathematical Discourse: Language, Symbolism and Visual Images.* London/New York: Continuum.

O'Halloran, K. L. (2009) Inter-semiotic expansion of experiential meaning. In C. Jones and E. Ventola (eds) *From Language to Multimodality: New Developments in the Study of Ideational Meaning* 231–54. London: Equinox.

Thomas, M. (2009) Developing multimodal texture. In E. Ventola and A. J. Moya Guijarro (eds) *The World Told and The World Shown: Multisemiotic Issues.* 39–55. Basingstoke: Palgrave Macmillan.

Thompson, G. ([1996] 2004). *Introducing Functional Grammar.* London: Edward Arnold.

9 781908 049551